101 Projects for Woodworkers

101 Projects for Woodworkers

The Editors of
The Woodworker's Journal

Charles Scribner's Sons
New York

First Charles Scribner's Sons paperback edition published 1985.

Copyright © 1977, 1978, 1979, 1980, 1981
The Madrigal Publishing Co., Inc.

Library of Congress Cataloging in Publication Data

Main entry under title:

101 projects for woodworkers.

1. Woodwork.   1. Woodworker's journal
TT180.A13   684'.08   81-8879
ISBN 0-684-18506-7   AACR2

Published simultaneously in Canada
by Collier Macmillan Canada, Inc.—
Copyright under the Berne Convention.

3 5 7 9 11 13 15 17 19 Q/P 20 18 16 14 12 10 8 6 4

Printed in the United States of America.

Contents

The Projects

Preface

Every successful woodworking project begins with some sort of plan. Depending on the project, this plan may be nothing more than a simple sketch on a piece of scrap wood, or it may be several pages of detailed drawings and a bill of materials.

Some amateur woodworkers have both the time and the ability to design and draw up their own plans, but most prefer to work from published plans. All of the plans contained in this book have appeared in past issues of *The Woodworker's Journal,* and many of the projects have generated letters and photographs from readers who have built the pieces. When reviewing these photographs, the editors have often been intrigued by the different appearance of pieces built by people working from the same set of plans. In many cases, it was quite apparent that the plans merely provided a starting point or springboard from which the individual added his or her own ideas.

The novice is generally inclined to follow instructions to the letter, and this is the best approach until some degree of skill and confidence is achieved. However, the more advanced woodworker should, and probably will, feel free to substitute more sophisticated joinery methods if they are appropriate. The materials, methods of joinery, and finish for each project in this book are not the only possible choices but rather were chosen for their compatibility with the character of the piece and the skill level for which the project was intended.

It was our intention to appeal to as many woodworkers as possible with a great variety of projects that are both attractive and practical. The designs presented here cover a time span of more than three hundred years—from the seventeenth-century Hutch Table to the contemporary Stereo/End Table—and range from the utter simplicity of the Skyhook toy to the challenge of the Rolltop Desk.

No matter what projects you attempt, please keep in mind that working with wood should be a pleasurable experience. Above all, don't rush! The quality of your work and the degree of pleasure you'll derive will be in direct proportion to the degree to which you have a deliberate, relaxed attitude.

The Editors

Acknowledgments

The editors wish to express their thanks to the following people whose contributions and cooperation helped to make this book a reality:

RICHARD WONDERLICH, design and photos of the rolltop desk and inlaid spool chest.

TED PAGELS, record and tape cabinet design.

ROGER SCHROEDER and JOHN SIMONELLI, porch swing design and photo, respectively.

CHARLES LAMB, gossip bench design and photo.

HENRY DIAMOND, pipe cabinet, curio table, and eighteenth-century water bench designs and photos.

THE MASON & SULLIVAN CO., octagonal clock design.

JOHN O'MARA, artwork for Parsons table, contemporary end table, and animal mobile.

CATHY UTTER, artwork for collector's pier cabinet.

. . . and to the readers of *The Woodworker's Journal,* whose specific requests brought many of the designs into being.

The Projects

Walnut Serving Tray

Nothing quite matches the elegance of walnut, and this contemporary serving tray is handsome enough to be displayed on a wall. The project is designed to provide an introduction to the fascinating but often maligned art of veneering. For those who believe that veneer work is a hallmark of inferior furniture, we respectfully submit that the museums of America and Europe are full of the most outstanding examples of the cabinet-maker's art, and a good deal of it is veneered. An eighteenth-century English kneehole desk completely veneered in walnut burls is a thing of unforgettable beauty.

Veneering conserves rare and costly woods by using them in extremely thin sheets rather than thick boards. Also, projects can be enhanced with striking grain effects, easy to achieve with veneers and impossible to duplicate with solid stock. Of no less importance is the fact that proper veneering provides dimensional stability and resistance to warping, a definite advantage in furniture construction.

Most veneers are sold by the square foot and come in three-foot lengths. Widths vary, but generally range from 4″ to 12″. The serving tray consists of a core of ½″ plywood covered on both sides with walnut veneer, a total of about three square feet. Tray handles are fashioned from solid ¾″ walnut, and the rims are thin walnut strips. The catalogs offered by veneer suppliers show color photos of the various grain patterns available, depending on how the walnut log is

sliced (see p. 244 for a list of veneer suppliers). If you have never worked with veneer before, choose a striped and quartered veneer for this project, rather than a burl or crotch which are more difficult to handle.

Begin by cutting ½″ plywood to a rectangle 10½ x 26″. Referring to Figure 1, measure down 2¼″ from opposite corners, and ¾″ from the center. Drive small nails at these points. Next, cut a strip ¼″ thick x 28″ long from the edge of a piece of clear ¾″ pine. Bend this strip around the nails, holding it in place with additional nails driven in on each side of the strip. This should give you a nice fair curve, and by running your pencil along the inside edge, you can scribe one side of the tray. Cut along this line as smoothly as possible with a jig or saber saw. The waste piece can then be used to draw the curve of the opposite side. Save both waste pieces to be used later when clamping the rims to the veneered tray.

Cut 2¼″ from both ends of the plywood, and form the ⁷⁄₃₂ x ¾″ rabbets on the bottom edges of the ends as shown in Detail A. Next, cut 3 x 8″ handles from ¾″ walnut, and cut the grooves to receive the plywood. The finger grips shown in Detail B are cut by lowering the pieces over an 8″ circular saw blade, or they can be cut with a router. Trim the handles to match the curves of the plywood, using a waste piece of plywood previously cut as a template. Trim the handles slightly long to be filed down flush later when they are glued to the tray.

If the veneer sheets you have on hand are not wide enough to cover the plywood core, it will be necessary to joint two together. To do this lay one sheet on top of the other, align the edges, and, using a steel straightedge and veneer saw, cut a new straight edge through both sheets. Veneer saws are inexpensive and will cut a perfectly straight line, whereas a knife has a tendency to wander off with the grain.

After cutting the sheets, align the cut edges and clamp them between two boards so that the cut edges project slightly. Plane these edges flush with the boards using a plane set for a very fine cut. Lay the sheets on a flat surface, with jointed

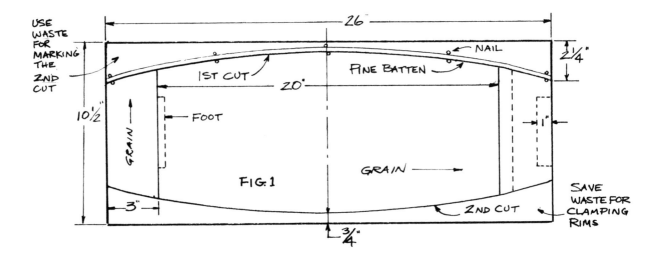

FIG. 1

edges together, and close the joint with veneer pins driven in about 1″ from each side of the joint. Cover the joint with gummed veneer tape applied on the face side, the side that doesn't get glued.

Turn over the assembled veneers to the untaped side, open the joint slightly (the tape acts as a hinge), and run a thin bead of glue along the joint. Brush the glue across the joint and wipe away the excess.

Veneer can be applied with ordinary white glue but this requires careful clamping. The easiest method is to use a contact glue developed especially for veneers and sold by veneer suppliers. This glue eliminates the need for presses, clamps, and other such cumbersome devices.

Before applying glue to the plywood core, fill all dents and other imperfections and sand the surface level. Working in a well-heated room, apply the glue according to the directions on the container, trying for an even coverage on both plywood and veneer. Allow the glue to set for at least 30 minutes. Meanwhile, cut a slip sheet from wax or brown paper, slightly larger all around than the core. When the glue has dried sufficiently so the slip sheet can be moved about without sticking, align the slip sheet about ¼″ down from one rabbeted end. Carefully align the veneer, taped side up, with the plywood, and press down so that the two glued surfaces come in contact just along the ¼″ strip exposed by the slip sheet. Continue slipping the sheet down, allowing the glued surfaces to come together. Use

a wooden veneer roller, applying firm pressure to bond the surfaces together, and being careful to keep from breaking off the delicate overhanging veneer edges.

After the veneer has been bonded, turn the panel over and cut off the overhang with a sharp knife. Repeat the gluing process on the reverse side of the panel. To remove the gummed tape, dampen it with a sponge and gently peel it off with a blunt-edged knife. If it doesn't peel off easily, apply more water, but be careful not to soak the veneer. This is a good time to finish sand the top surface of the tray.

The handles can now be glued in place. When they are dry, file them flush with the ends of the panel, taking care to keep the curves fair. Referring to Detail C, cut a rabbet along the edge of a piece of ¾ x 28″ walnut. Then rip the ¼″-wide rabbeted strip from the board. Bend this strip around the edge of the tray and mark where each handle meets the tray. Trim this portion to a thickness of ³⁄₃₂″, using the table saw to start the cut and finishing up with a chisel.

Gluing, bending, and clamping the rims in place is a fussy procedure, so plan on doing one at a time. Spread glue carefully on the mating surfaces, making certain not to slop any on the face veneer. Nail a stop strip to the work surface and place one of the waste pieces of plywood against it with the curve facing you. Align a rim against this and bring the tray against the rim, forcing it into a curve. Place the second piece of waste against the other edge of the tray and

4

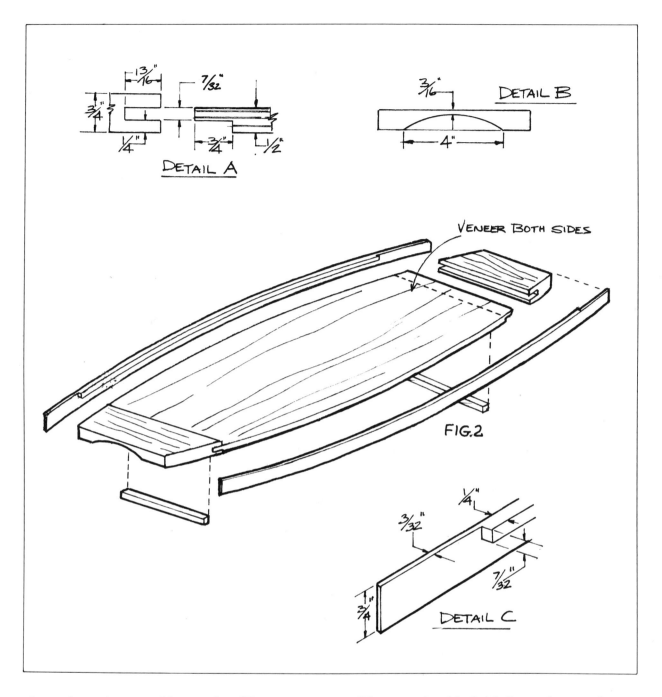

DETAIL A

DETAIL B

VENEER BOTH SIDES

FIG.2

DETAIL C

clamp the entire assembly together. Use as many clamps as possible; or if you lack clamps, nail another strip to the work surface along the other side of the tray and drive wedges in to draw everything together. Allow to dry overnight before removing the clamps and repeating the process with the other rim. Trim off the excess rim ends flush with the handles, and sand the tops of the rims flush with the handles. Finally, glue two ⅜ x ⅜ x 4″ walnut strips to the tray bottom to serve as feet, and slightly round off all sharp edges of rims and handles with sandpaper.

The most durable finish for such a tray is urethane varnish. The open-grain walnut should first be filled with a walnut-tinted filler. Mix a small amount of filler with benzine or turpentine according to the manufacturer's directions, and apply to all surfaces. Allow to dry about 10 minutes and wipe off excess filler with a pad of burlap, wiping across the grain. After 24 hours apply several coats of a clear finish. To avoid a high gloss use low-luster varnish, or rub down with fine steel wool or pumice after the varnish dries.

Rabbit Pull Toy

Small children love to march back and forth with their "pets" in tow. Thus, pull toys have been and probably always will be particular favorites of the preschool group. If the toys bounce or wiggle as they're pulled, so much the better.

This bouncy cottontail is a delight. As it's pulled along, the off-center rear wheels give him a very lifelike bobbing motion. Construction is simple, and if you have a band saw, the parts can be stack-sawed for a number of rabbits.

After enlarging and transferring the pattern, the body is cut from ¾" pine or maple (maple is preferable, for it can be smoothed nicely). Cut two ears and the forelegs from ½" stock.

The wheels are cut using a 2" hole saw, which will leave center holes that should be plugged before sanding. It's best to use ¾" stock for the wheels to provide stability when it's pulled.

Locate off-center holes in the wheels (as shown) and drill ⅜"-deep sockets for a tight fit of the ¼ x 2" dowel axle. It's logical to assume that the greater the offset of the axle, the more motion will be imparted to the toy; but if you drill the hole too near the wheel rim, the wheel will resist turning, especially on a smooth floor.

The 1"-diameter front wheel is cut from ½" stock and is a loose fit on the dowel axle, which is glued into the sockets in the legs.

It is easier to sand the body before gluing and clamping the leg-wheel assembly and the ears in place. Round all edges and try to make the toy as smooth and as pleasant to the touch as possible. Wood is a warm and friendly material and so much better than plastic, but only if it is finished with care.

The eyes and mouth can be added using black enamel. A commercial penetrating-oil finish is quick and easy to apply and will provide all the protective finish needed. The pull cord is inserted into a small hole bored in the head as shown, and secured with a small peg glued in place.

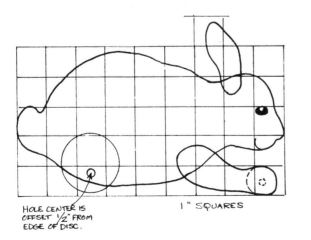

HOLE CENTER IS OFFSET ½" FROM EDGE OF DISC.

1" SQUARES

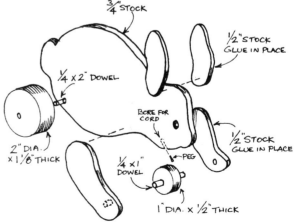

¾" STOCK

½" STOCK GLUE IN PLACE

¼ X 2" DOWEL

BORE FOR CORD

2" DIA. X 1⅛" THICK

¼ X 1" DOWEL

PEG

½" STOCK GLUE IN PLACE

1" DIA. X ½" THICK

Queen Anne Stool

This classic stool with gracefully curved legs is a good example of the Queen Anne period of design. It is typical of the type of sophisticated furniture produced by professional colonial cabinetmakers during the early and mid-eighteenth century. It's a fine project for the woodworker who would like to sharpen his or her skills and produce an authentic reproduction without becoming overwhelmed by a large project. By mastering the construction techniques of shaping and joining compound curved legs and tenoned rails, the woodworker will have a good foundation of experience for building many other pieces in the Queen Anne style, particularly coffee or tea tables and lowboys.

Walnut is the preferred wood, but Honduras mahogany (see page 68) or cherry are also perfectly acceptable and authentic to the period. Rail stock should be dressed to $\frac{13}{16}''$ thickness. The legs are shaped from blocks $2\frac{3}{4}''$ square x $17''$ long.

It's easier to lay out and bore mortises in the leg blocks before they are shaped. Use a $\frac{3}{8}''$ bit and remember that the post section of the leg, where the mortises are located, will be sawed to $1\frac{3}{4}$ x $1\frac{3}{4}''$ when the leg is shaped. Refer to the illustration of the end view of the rails for mortise size and location in relation to the rail tenons and shoulders. After the mortises are bored and chiseled out, you may proceed with the bandsawing of the shaped legs.

Cutting these legs may appear to be a formi-dable task, but it's really quite simple. Begin by making a leg template, transferring the pattern as shown to $\frac{1}{4}''$ plywood or hardboard, and cutting to shape. Now use this template to mark the leg outline on two adjoining sides of a squared block of the required length. Step 1 shows how the shape is transferred to the block. Mark the two sides A and B.

Now turn the block with the A side up as in Step 2, and bandsaw the outline of the leg, but do not complete the cuts. Leave about $\frac{1}{4}''$ of material remaining so that the block can lay flat for the next operations. Step 3 shows the block with the B side up. Cut completely along all marked lines on this side, and remove the waste pieces. The final step, shown in Step 4, consists of completing the cuts on side A.

The leg must then be shaped and smoothed with a spokeshave, cabinet file, and sandpaper.

Next, prepare the four rails, forming tenons $\frac{3}{8}$ x $\frac{7}{8}''$ long on each end. Cut the $\frac{3}{8}$ x $\frac{3}{8}''$ rabbets for the plywood seat, and shave the height of all tenons to $2\frac{1}{8}''$. Check all parts for a good fit before coating the mortise surfaces and tenons with glue and clamping the legs and end rails first. Then add the side rails, turn the assembly upside down, and clamp the side rails, spanning the clamps that hold the end assemblies. Check the assembly for squareness before setting it aside to dry.

When the glued joints are dry, bore $\frac{1}{4}''$ holes to a depth of $1''$ through all mortise and tenon joints. Add glue to the holes and drive in pins cut slightly long for trimming flush later. The four outer corners of the rails must be rounded to a radius of $\frac{13}{16}''$. Set a compass to this radius and from the top center of each leg scribe the outside radius; then, using the same center, scribe an inner radius of $\frac{7}{16}''$. Before rounding the outside corners with a chisel, make a slight saw kerf at the point where the rail joins the knee of the leg. This will allow chiseled waste to fall free. Next, cut the leg tops down to conform with the rail rabbets, following the scribed $\frac{7}{16}''$ radius as shown in the illustration. Remove waste in small

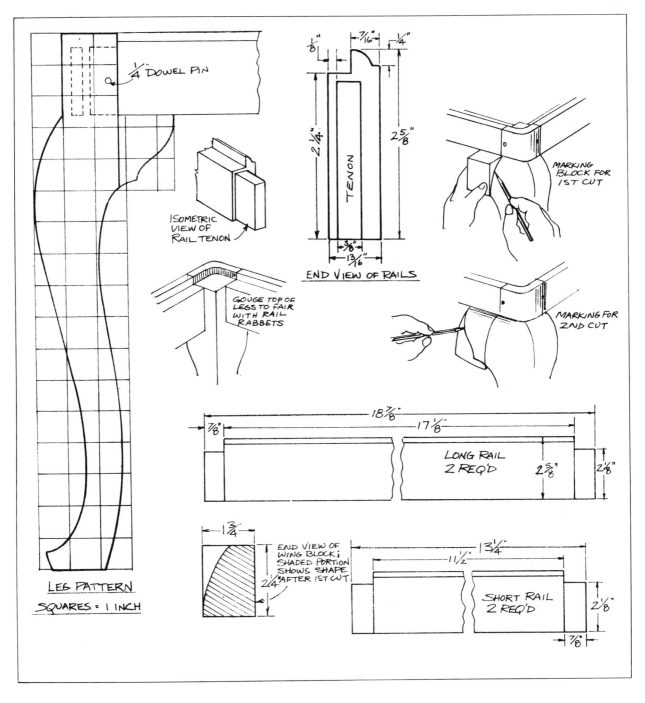

ISOMETRIC VIEW OF RAIL TENON

¼ DOWEL PIN

TENON

END VIEW OF RAILS

GOUGE TOP OF LEGS TO FAIR WITH RAIL RABBETS

MARKING BLOCK FOR 1ST CUT

MARKING FOR 2ND CUT

LEG PATTERN
SQUARES = 1 INCH

LONG RAIL 2 REQ'D

END VIEW OF WING BLOCK; SHADED PORTION SHOWS SHAPE AFTER 1ST CUT

SHORT RAIL 2 REQ'D

bites with a chisel and mallet, keeping the leg firmly clamped to the work surface. Use a gouge to shape the curved inside corner.

Eight wing blocks are cut to 1¾ x 1¾ x 2¼″ with face grain matching that of the legs. Fit each block as shown, holding it squarely against the leg and the rail, and scribe the curve of the leg on the face surface. Number each block and leg as there will be slight variations in the leg curves and each block must be carefully fitted.

Bandsaw the blocks to the scribed line, then hold them in place again and with a pattern mark the curve that continues from the leg. Make the second cut on all eight blocks.

Because of their shape, the blocks are glued in place without clamps, so a hot glue or a quick-setting type is preferred. Apply glue to the block, only on the face that will join the leg. Press the block against the leg and rub it into position. Apply hand pressure for a couple of minutes and

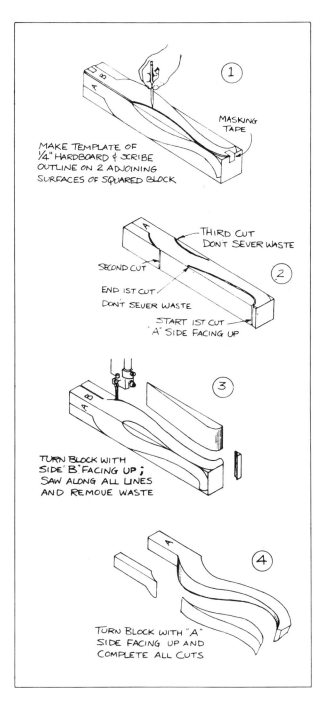

MAKE TEMPLATE OF ¼" HARDBOARD & SCRIBE OUTLINE ON 2 ADJOINING SURFACES OF SQUARED BLOCK

MASKING TAPE

①

THIRD CUT DON'T SEVER WASTE

SECOND CUT

END 1ST CUT DON'T SEVER WASTE

START 1ST CUT "A" SIDE FACING UP

②

TURN BLOCK WITH SIDE "B" FACING UP; SAW ALONG ALL LINES AND REMOVE WASTE

③

TURN BLOCK WITH "A" SIDE FACING UP AND COMPLETE ALL CUTS

④

then release. When all the blocks have been glued on, allow them to dry overnight.

The top edge molding may be formed with a shaper or router, or by running the stool upside down over a circular saw set to a depth of ¼". It will be necessary to clamp a low wooden fence to the table as the knees will not clear a standard fence. Make the cut just the thickness or kerf of the blade, by clamping the wooden fence right against the blade. Pass each rail over the blade,

and while maintaining pressure against the fence, swing the stool around each corner to follow the outside curve. This is not difficult but if you're apprehensive about this operation, you might try it first with a lower blade height.

After the edge has been cut, round off the lip as shown in the end rail view. Smooth the molding with medium and then fine sandpaper (60 and 120 grit). Finish sand all surfaces with 120 paper and follow up with a rub-down using 220 paper. A piece of work as fine as this demands as careful a sanding as you can give it.

Upholstery is attached to a ½" plywood board cut to fit the rail rabbets with a ³⁄₁₆" clearance all around. Round off the upper edges of the board and sand it smooth. Cement 1"-thick foam rubber to the board and bevel the top edge with scissors. Unbleached muslin is stretched over the rubber and tacked to the bottom edge of the board. The covering material is added over this, pleated around the corners, and tacked to the bottom. Cover the bottom of the board with black cambric, folding the edges under and tacking it in place. The upholstered board is fastened to the stool by screwing up through ¾ x ¾ x 2" glue blocks fastened to the rails just below the rabbets. Use one block per rail.

The stool may be finished with stain, filler, sealer, and varnish applied in that sequence. An excellent and authentic treatment is an oil finish that will darken the wood without the need for stain. To apply this finish, mix an equal amount of boiled linseed oil and turpentine. Warm the mixture in a container placed in a pan of hot water; warm oil will soak into the wood more readily. Apply this mixture with a soft cloth or bare hands two or three times during the day, until the wood will absorb no more oil. Sprinkle fine pumice powder over the surfaces and rub vigorously with a burlap pad.

Repeat the application of oil, pumice, and rubbing for several days. Clean off all residue after each rubbing. After three applications of oil and pumice, switch to straight oil without turpentine. The last rubbing should be done with oil and rottenstone, a finer abrasive, which will bring up a higher gloss. Finish off with a thin coat of carnauba wax polish. This type of finish can be renewed every couple of years by rubbing in another coat of oil and rewaxing.

Hobby Horse

A few evenings spent in the workshop will reap big dividends when a small child sees this hobby horse for the first time. Easily obtained white pine of ¾″ stock (1⅛″ thickness) is used for most parts, and can also be resawed for the ½″ slats that form the body of the horse.

It will be necessary to edge join two or more pieces in order to shape the head, and if reinforcing dowels are used, they should be located where they will not be exposed when the head shape is cut out. The legs can be cut out from 1 x 10s.

Duplicate the 1″ grid on a sheet of heavy kraft paper and outline the head by connecting a series of dots made at the proper grid intersections. Cut out the head shape and use it as a template for transferring the shape to the wood. Cut the head with a saber saw and notch it squarely to butt against the leg unit.

Shape the legs and notch them to fit over the rockers. The bottom curve of the rockers can be drawn on ¾ x 6″ stock by bending a thin strip of clear pine to the desired curve, holding it in place with a few box nails, and tracing along its edge with a pencil. This should provide a reasonably fair curve. Shape one rocker and use it to mark the second one.

Lay out the locations of the front and rear leg units, clamp them in place on the rockers, and drill through the legs and into the rockers for ½″ dowels, which are then glue-coated and driven home. Make sure that the legs remain perpendicular to the rockers when fastening. Three-inch carriage bolts can be substituted for dowels if you wish to remove the rockers for easier storage.

Mount the head to the front leg unit with glue and two ½″ dowel pins. Notch the rear leg unit and install the rope tail, which is knotted on the inside end to prevent it from pulling out. Next, cut ten ½ x 2 x 18″ slats and, starting at the top, notch the first two slats around the horse's neck. Rasp flats on the curved surfaces so that the slats make good contact, and fasten with counterbored screws and glue. Plug the screw holes with ⅜″ plugs chiseled flush, and use a rasp to round the outer surfaces of the slats. Add foot pegs, handlebars, and ears cut from triangular scraps of leather. The ears are folded and nailed in place so that they lean slightly forward.

Round off all edges carefully and sand to reduce the possibility of splintering. The horse may be painted, stained, or left natural and sealed with a couple of coats of a synthetic varnish such as Deft. A spotted-pony effect can be achieved by applying a brown stain in irregular shapes on the raw wood. A toy such as this, one that will most likely be around for a long time, should be signed and dated in an inconspicuous place. It's a nice touch that will add to the sentimental value of the piece over the years.

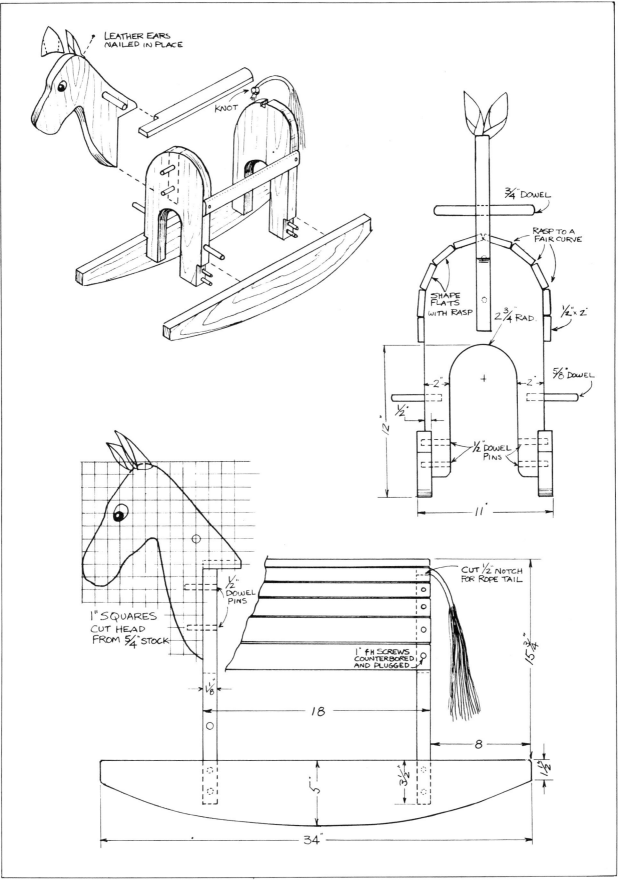

LEATHER EARS
NAILED IN PLACE

KNOT

¾" DOWEL

RASP TO A
FAIR CURVE

SHAPE
FLATS
WITH RASP

2¾" RAD.

½" x 2"

2"

5/8" DOWEL

½"

12"

½" DOWEL
PINS

11"

1" SQUARES
CUT HEAD
FROM 5/4" STOCK

½" DOWEL PINS

1/8"

18

CUT ½" NOTCH
FOR ROPE TAIL

1" FH SCREWS
COUNTERBORED
AND PLUGGED

15¾"

8

1/2"

5"

3½"

34"

Two Boomerangs

There's something almost magical in the flight of a boomerang. It is merely a piece of wood, but yet, when shaped and thrown properly, the boomerang will take off on a straight line, go into a climbing swing to the left, and then drift back to its point of release. Each boomerang has its own unique flight characteristics, and seemingly identical models will perform in different ways.

Although similar types developed separately in Africa, India, and among the Hopi Indians of Arizona, the familiar boomerang is invariably associated with the Australian aborigines, who used them for hunting. Actually, there are quite a few wooden devices that will describe a circular flight and return to the thrower. Of these devices, which we shall refer to collectively as "boomerangs," the Australian model is perhaps the least predictable in its behavior. It is also the most difficult to make, and certainly the most dangerous to use, for it is capable of inflicting serious injury.

Simple cross-stick and pinwheel boomerangs can be carved from thin pine in a matter of minutes, and will outperform the Australian types with respect to accuracy and precision return. Unlike the heavy, fast-moving Australian boomerang, the cross-sticks do not require a vast open space for throwing.

Australian Boomerang

The Australian version must be made of clear, even-grained hardwood, and oak, maple, or ash is suitable. Lay out and cut the shaded portion of the boomerang from ⅞" or 1" stock; then rip the piece lengthwise to get two perfectly identical wings. A band or scroll saw will cut a narrower kerf, leaving two pieces of about ⅜" thickness. Cut a half-lap joint on each piece, leaving the top lap a little thicker than the bottom to allow for the shaping of the top surface. Glue the two wings together using a form with two ¾" blocks to force the wings into a permanent upward deflection of ¼" to ⅜". Sand or plane a bevel on the bottom of each leading edge as indicated by the dotted lines on the drawing. Remove no more than 1/16" of wood for a distance of 5" from the tips.

Now turn the boomerang over, clamp it to the bench, and plane and rasp the top surface from about ⅜" thick at the center to ¼" thick at the wing tips. Round the top surface into a smooth curve with a sharp edge as shown in the cross section. Smooth up with sandpaper.

The curved boomerang is thrown in a vertical position. Hold it at the end of one wing tip, with the curved top side facing you and throw it straight forward at shoulder level, giving it wrist action for a fast spin. An average boomerang will

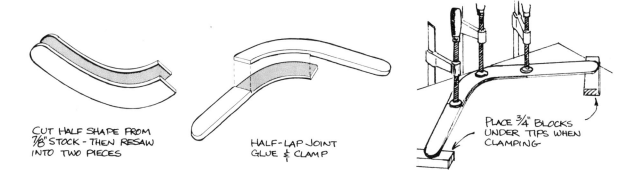

CUT HALF SHAPE FROM ⅞" STOCK - THEN RESAW INTO TWO PIECES

HALF-LAP JOINT GLUE & CLAMP

PLACE ¾" BLOCKS UNDER TIPS WHEN CLAMPING

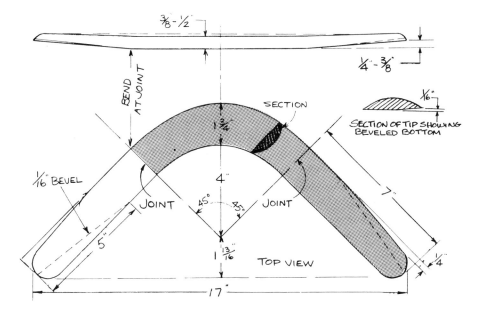

go forward for about 40 yards, then start climbing and swinging to the left before planing back in a wide curve. Failure to return may be caused by too flat a top or not enough bevel on the bottom. A double flight loop indicates too much bevel. Breezy conditions may also cause erratic flight. *Please* do not permit unsupervised children to use this type of boomerang.

Cross-Stick Boomerang

To make a cross-stick boomerang you will need two pieces of clear white pine ⅛″ thick x 1¼″ wide x 18″ long. Round off the ends, place each stick on the edge of a knife blade, and mark the balance points. At a point 1″ from each side of the balance point, shape the upper surface of each stick into a roughly convex form as shown in the cross section. Leave the bottom side flat.

Make a mark on the flat side 6″ in from each end and then hold the stick over a candle flame so that the flame touches the flat undersurface at the 6″ mark. When it is heated, take the stick in both hands and bend one end slightly upward at the 6″ mark, and hold it in this position for a few seconds. The end of the stick should remain permanently bent in an upward deflection of about ¼″. Repeat the process at the other end, and then bend the second stick in the same manner. All that remains is to glue and clamp the sticks together, one on top of the other at their balance points.

Throw the boomerang by holding it near the tip of one wing in a vertical position, with the convex side facing you. Throw the boomerang

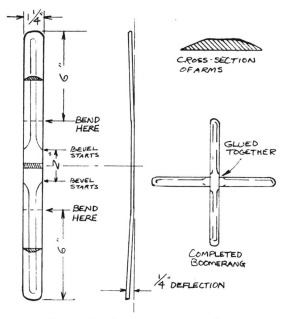

straight forward with a wrist snap downward to give it plenty of spin as it is released. If the boomerang does not return properly, try throwing it at an angle, inclined either toward or away from the head. This type of boomerang requires calm air conditions to perform properly.

13

Quilting Frame

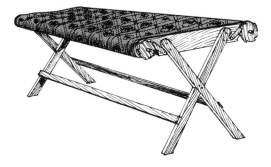

Quilting can be more enjoyable if you have a good frame to support the work at a comfortable height and keep it taut. This frame is easily built and can be partially disassembled for storage. Hardwood should be used for all parts, especially the long quilt bars.

Lay out and cut the upper frame ends first, shaping the rounded ends with a saber or band saw. Locate and drill 1″-diameter holes for the quilt-bar tenons. Lay out the two ratchet wheels on ¾″ stock by scribing first a 2½″-diameter circle, then a concentric 2″ circle. Divide the circles into eight equal parts and use these dividing lines to mark and cut notches as shown in the detail.

The pawls are shaped to fit the rachets as shown.

Rip the leg stock and cut it to rough length, but before notching for the lapped joint, lay a frame end on a flat surface and place the ratchets and pawls in position. Now locate the upper ends of the legs so they just touch the bottom ends of the pawls. There should be enough clearance to allow the pawls to be fully disengaged from the rachets. After the legs have thus been located, mark at the intersection for the lapped joint.

The long quilt bars can either be bored at both ends to take 1″-diameter x 3″ tenons, or the tenons can be rasped to shape from the squares. If the latter method is used, be sure to allow for three inches of additional length when cutting stock.

Glue the ratchets to the tenons and screw the pawls to the frame ends, backing off on the screws enough to permit movement. Assemble the legs and stretchers with countersunk flat-headed screws and give the frame a couple of coats of sealer.

To fasten a quilt to the frame, sew short lengths of bias tape to two edges of the quilt and tie these to the quilt bars.

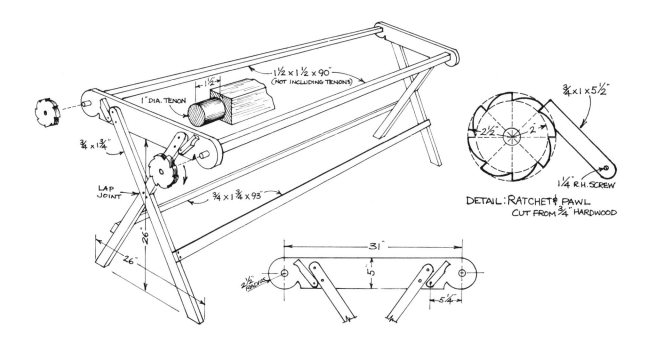

DETAIL: RATCHET & PAWL
CUT FROM ¾″ HARDWOOD

Lap Desk

Made entirely of ¾″ white pine, this is a good project for the novice. Veteran woodworkers can upgrade the piece to heirloom quality by substituting ½″ walnut and dovetailing the case corners. Nevertheless, built as shown, it's a handsome item.

Clear pine is preferred and all parts should be well sanded first. The case back fits flush between the sides and the bottom butts against it. Use 5-penny (2″) box nails and file the heads to a rectangular shape to simulate antique nails.

Glue and nail the sides to the bottom with the grain running as shown. Cut the case back and front for an exact fit and glue and nail it to the sides and bottom; then add the top flush with sides and back.

The lid is made of three parts as shown, glued and clamped together. Rest the lid on the case and mark the front and back edges for bevel. Cut the bevel by planing toward the center from the edges to avoid splintering.

Give the desk a final sanding and stain it for an antique-pine effect. Finish with at least two coats of satin-finish varnish and mount decorative brass hinges similar to those shown.

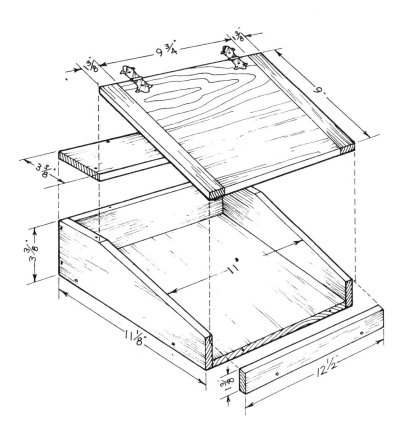

Pipe Cabinet

Although it was originally built for pipe and tobacco storage, this little cabinet can easily be modified to store a wide variety of items and placed in just about any room of the house. Use it for spice or utensil storage in the kitchen, as an additional storage unit in the bathroom, or even as an eight-track tape cabinet near the stereo. It's also a good item for a house-warming or wedding gift and should sell well in gift shops. The well-defined scroll work of the back and sides makes this a most appealing piece for any home.

The original was made of ½″ maple, but pine will fill the bill very nicely. Begin construction by enlarging the pattern for the side scroll on a sheet of cardboard. Using the cardboard as a template, transfer the outline to the ½ x 6 x 20″ sides. Cut the design with a coping or jig saw, and then run ½″ dadoes for the upper and lower shelves. Rabbet the back edges of both sides ¼ x ½″ to take the back panel.

The three shelves are cut from ⅜″ stock that can be resawed from thicker boards. Corresponding stopped dadoes are routed into the sides to hold the pipe stem shelves, which are drilled as shown. The shelf on which the pipe bowls rest has

a piece of beveled trim glued to the front edge.

The back panel is made up of four or five horizontal ½″ boards, which are edge joined and glued. No splines or dowel pins are really necessary here if the joints are well fitted. Again, a pattern is made by enlarging the squares and transferring the design to cardboard, which is then cut to shape.

The cabinet bottom is cut to extend beyond the front and sides by ⅝″, and these three edges are shaped as shown. Sand all parts of the case well and attach the sides to the bottom with ¼″ blind dowel pins and glue. Add the shelves and then brad the back panel in place.

The cabinet doors may be cut from wide ½″ boards or glued up from narrower stock. If they are glued up, care should be taken to make a pleasing grain match. Note that the doors have a rabbeted lip and one door is ¼″ wider than the other. Cleats, which are beveled for a pleasing appearance, are screwed to the back sides of the doors. You may wish to conceal the screw heads under wood plugs. Small brass butt hinges are notched into the case sides and doors.

The drawer sides and backs can be made from ½″ stock, although ⅜″ looks a bit better. The drawer front is rabbeted to receive the sides and is also dadoed for the bottom, while the drawer back and bottom are fastened with small nails. We like to join small drawer sides to the fronts by gluing and clamping, and after the glue has dried, holes are bored for ⅛″ dowel pins. These help to make a very strong and neat joint.

Give all exterior surfaces a final sanding and apply the stain of your choice, followed by several coats of a clear sealer rubbed to a satin finish. The cabinet also looks very attractive if painted with a muted color and given an antique glaze.

Although this little cabinet is shown freestanding, it can of course be hung on the wall by mortising two small hanger plates at the top back edge of each side.

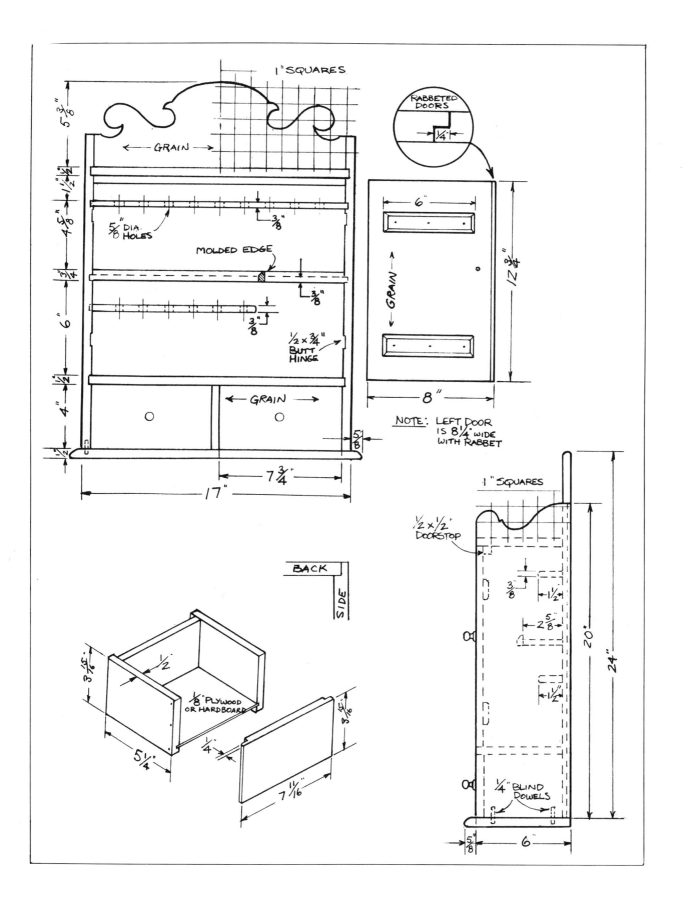

1" SQUARES

5 3/8"

GRAIN

1/2"

1 1/2"

4 5/8"

5/8" DIA. HOLES

3/8"

MOLDED EDGE

3/4"

3/8"

6"

3/8"

1/2 × 3/4" BUTT HINGE

1/2"

4"

GRAIN

5 8"

7 3/4"

17"

RABBETED DOORS

1/4"

6"

GRAIN

17 3/4"

8"

NOTE: LEFT DOOR IS 8 1/4" WIDE WITH RABBET

BACK

SIDE

1/2 × 1/2" DOORSTOP

1" SQUARES

3/8"

1 1/2"

2 5/8"

1 1/2"

20"

24"

3 5/16"

1/2"

1/8" PLYWOOD OR HARDBOARD

5 1/4"

1/4"

3 5/16"

7 11/16"

1/4" BLIND DOWELS

5/8"

6"

Eighteenth-Century Water Bench

In the days before indoor plumbing, water benches, like dry sinks, were used for storage of buckets of water drawn from the well. Buckets were kept in the lower cupboard section while the upper drawers and shelf were handy for various small kitchen implements.

More functional than decorative, many water benches were rather crude home-built affairs, but one occasionally sees particularly well-designed and executed examples. These invariably command a high price on the antique market. The bench offered here—a very nice reproduction of a late eighteenth-century piece —is typical of one that might have been made by a rural cabinetmaker for a customer who had the means to "farm out" such work.

Though it is no longer needed for its original function, the water bench fits in well in the modern home. Use it in the dining room, kitchen, or anywhere an attractive storage unit is needed. Most utilitarian furniture was built of pine or poplar, and either painted or left unfinished. The

present-day use of stain is an attempt to enhance the wood and simulate the coloring of old pine that has been exposed to years of sunlight and use.

Select flat, well-seasoned #2, 1″ pine for this project. Begin construction with the sides, which are glued up from two or more boards, joined with ⅜″ dowel pins and glue. Locate the dowels so you will not be cutting into them when shaping the curves.

Run two dadoes across the inside face of each side, one for the bottom and one for the countertop. Next, lay out and cut the stopped rabbets along the back edges of each side. Note that the upper rabbet, which holds the shaped upper back board, is 7½″ long and ends at the lower drawer frame.

Cut rabbets to hold the lower back flush with the back edges of the bench sides; then run a ¼ x ¼″ stopped rabbet up from the bottom of the rear foot to meet the lower back rabbet. A router will make an easy job of cutting these rabbets. If you lack power equipment, cut the wide rabbets by hand, and nail and glue a ¾ x ¾″ strip of quarter-round molding along the inner faces of the sides and set back ¼″ from the edge. This strip provides a fastening surface for the recessed plywood panel. Next, run the short dadoes to hold the drawer support and top shelf.

It will be necessary to edge join boards to make the bottom and countertop. Note that the countertop is notched around the sides and the exposed edges are well shaped. A plate groove was cut on the original, and you may wish to duplicate this feature or add a small half-round molding for standing plates. The counter butts against the lower back, which is nailed to it. The bottom is given a ¼ x ¼″ rabbet to hold the plywood back panel.

Cut the upper and lower back boards, drawer support, dividers, shelf and back panel and assemble the bench with finishing nails and glue. As you proceed check the assembly constantly with a framing square, and nail diagonal braces across the back if necessary to maintain squareness. Cut the parts for the front-door-frame as-

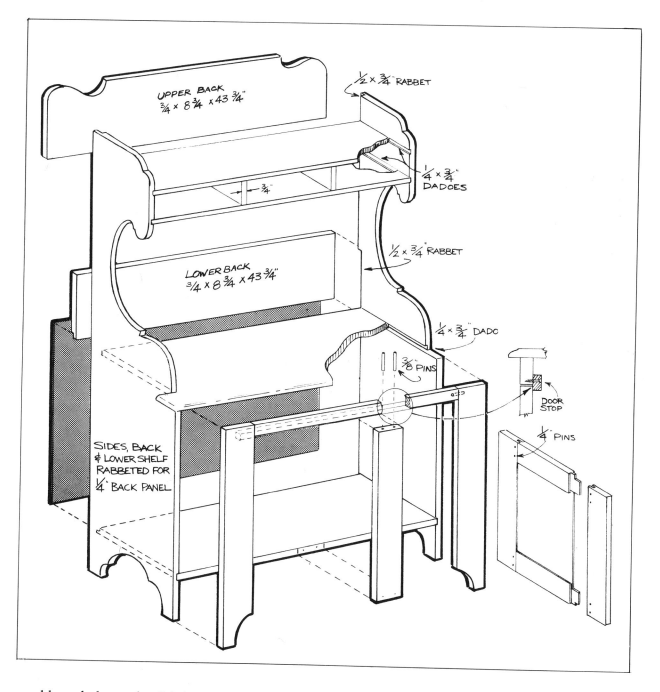

UPPER BACK
¾ × 8¾ × 43¾"

½ × ¾" RABBET

¼ × ¾" DADOES

¾"

½ × ¾" RABBET

LOWER BACK
¾ × 8¾ × 43¾"

¼ × ¾" DADO

⅜ PINS

DOOR STOP

¼ PINS

SIDES, BACK & LOWER SHELF RABBETED FOR ¼" BACK PANEL

sembly and glue and nail it in place. Countersink all finishing nails.

Use wide boards or glued-up stock for the raised-panel doors. On the original the raised panels, which are ¾" thick, were placed without glue in a groove formed by a molding nailed on the front and ¼ x 1″ strips glued to the door backs (Detail A, page 21). This method has the advantages of utilizing easily obtainable ¾" stock for the door panels and making use of a large and rather attractive quarter-round molding, which is mitered at the corners.

Detail B and the exploded view show a method that uses ½″ panel stock riding in grooves in the frame. There's not much room for a prominent molding here, but you can either add a small mitered molding or simply round the edge slightly. Commercially produced doors of this type have moldings that are shaped on the frame edges and coped at the corners. This is done by machine, with matched shapers; the work is rather tricky and time-consuming to do by hand.

Panel frames are mortised and tenoned, the haunched tenons pinned after the glue dries. Do

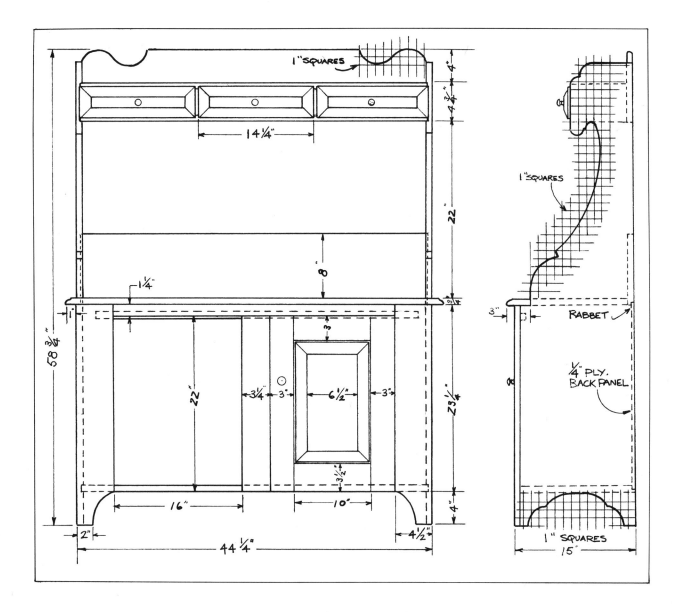

not glue the raised panel in place. It should be left free to expand and contract with changes in humidity. It's not a bad idea to stain the raised panels before gluing the doors together. Later shrinkage may leave a strip of unstained lip showing which will have to be touched up.

The small drawers are made of ⅜″ or ½″ pine with ¼″ lipped drawer fronts of ¾″ stock. Drawer fronts are rabbeted to form a lip around all edges and to receive the sides. Fronts and sides are grooved for ⅛″ plywood bottoms. Fasten the drawer sides to the fronts with glue and ¼″ dowel pins or finishing nails.

The present trend in finishing pine furniture is to use a dark walnut stain, but the original bench has the very attractive dark honey tone of aged pine. Minwax Early American stain duplicates

this fairly well if the pigmented stain is not laid on too heavily. Depending on the type of wood and the smoothness of the surface, we prefer to brush on the stain; let it sit for a few minutes, and then even it off by wiping with a cloth. In this way you can control the depth of tone around knots and accentuate them if they will add to the interest of the piece.

Before staining examine all surfaces for machining marks that you may have missed when sanding the various parts. Fill nail holes with wood putty and sand smooth, or wait until the finishing is done and fill the holes with a color-matched wax. When finish sanding pay particular attention to the rounding off of any sharp edges.

Stain is applied to all exterior surfaces and to

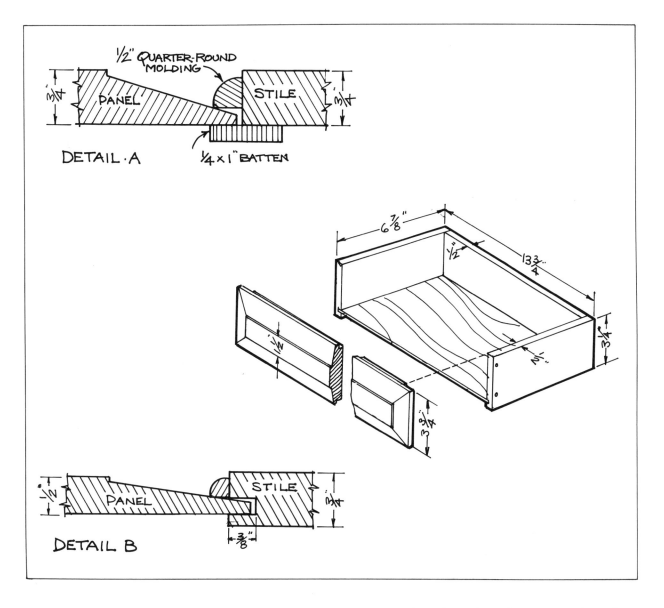

DETAIL·A

½" QUARTER-ROUND MOLDING

PANEL

STILE

¼ x 1" BATTEN

DETAIL B

PANEL

STILE

both sides of the doors. The inside of the cupboard and drawers may be left unstained but should be sealed. Many old cupboards and chests were painted a pale blue or green on the inside. There's a lot of area to finish, so you might choose to use one of the synthetic varnishes which does not require previous sealer coats of thinned shellac. Be sure to use one of the low-luster types, though, and sand or use steel wool on each coat, cleaning with a tack cloth before proceeding with additional coats. For more protection and a fine, soft glow, apply wax and buff with a soft cloth or lamb's-wool buffer. The addition of antique-finish black H hinges and well-turned wooden knobs completes the project.

Octagonal Clock

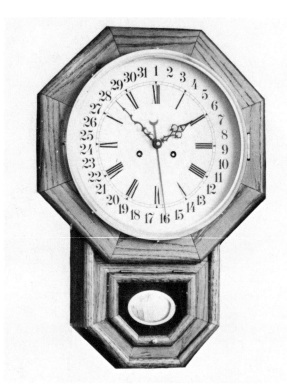

This wall clock is a classic design of the late nineteenth century, most often associated with schoolrooms but also seen in railway stations and mercantile establishments. The version offered here is an excellent reproduction and features a calendar dial with a separate hand to show the day of the month. It also has a pendulum movement with a chime that strikes the half hour and counts the hour.

Original clocks of this type are getting scarce and expensive, but any woodworker of moderate skill can build this heirloom piece. It's a challenging project that demands accurate cutting and joining, but the finished clock will be a lifetime source of pride and pleasure.

The builder is advised to have the dial, bezel, and movement on hand before beginning construction of the case. All components for this clock, including hardwood (oak, cherry, or walnut), bezel assembly, and decorative door glass can be ordered from the Mason & Sullivan Company (see the list of suppliers, p. 243, for the address). Their catalog offers a fine selection of clock parts and kits. We used their T-122 calendar movement that, like the bezel assembly, comes with installation instructions. For those readers who lack the time or inclination to build this clock from scratch, an identical clock can be assembled from a kit that contains complete instructions, hardware, and accurately precut parts.

Many of these clocks were built of oak, though cherry and walnut are also fine choices. The woodworker is urged, however, to use hardwood for the case as it can be machined to closer tolerances and is more appropriate for a good reproduction. Most of the case is built from ¾″ stock, and care should be taken to choose stock that is both clear and flat.

Begin construction with the back case, which houses the movement and provides for mounting of the dial and pendulum door assembly. Referring to Figures 1, 2, 3, and 4, and the bill of materials, you will see that the case consists of two sides (1), a top (2), and three pieces that make up the lower case (3). There are also two ¼″ plywood back panels (4 and 5).

Parts 1 and 3 can be cut from one piece ¾ x 3⅝ x 46″ (this allows a bit of extra length for the miter cuts). Shape one edge of this piece to a half-round profile before cutting it into the required five pieces. If you lack a router or shaper, the half-round molded edge can be shaped by hand by first cutting the corners off at 30 degrees, then rounding with file and sandpaper. A cardboard template will be useful for keeping the molding uniform over its entire length.

Miter the slanted sides and bottom (3) to an angle of 67½ degrees, as shown in Detail A. This angle may show on your miter gauge as 22½ degrees, depending on how the gauge is scaled. Also miter the lower end of each side (1) to 67½ degrees. It is strongly recommended that these miter cuts be done on scrap stock first, to check the accuracy of the gauge setting. A good fit between these parts is essential.

Again referring to Detail A, cut stopped grooves along each miter face to receive a ⅛″ plywood spline. Also cut a ¼ x ¾″ rabbet across the

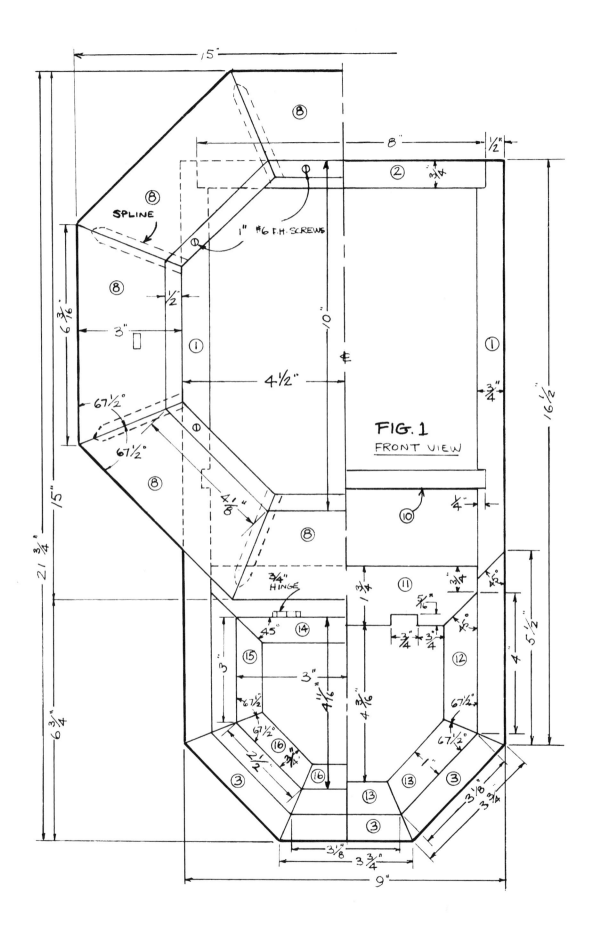

FIG. 1

FRONT VIEW

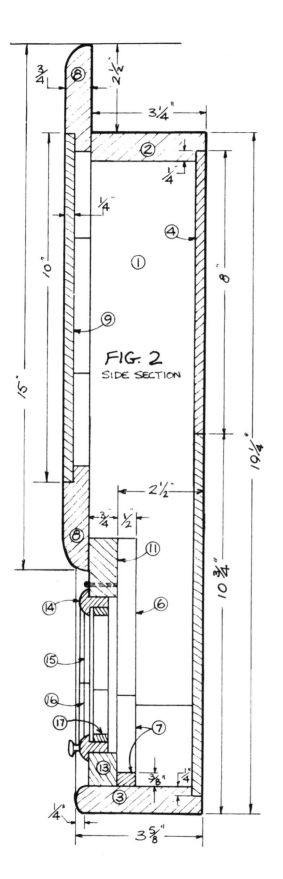

FIG. 2
SIDE SECTION

top inside face of the sides (1) to take the top (2), which is ¾ x 3¼ x 8″. All pieces, including the top, are rabbeted ¼ x ¼″ along the back edge to provide a recess for the two back panels.

Sides (1) are dadoed, as shown, for the chime-mounting shelf, and are also notched at an angle of 45 degrees to provide a ledge for the dial frame (8). Note that this notch will remove all but the lower 5½″ of molded edge along the front of each side. The notch is cut ⅜″ deep. Run the notch as far as possible on the table saw, and finish up with a sharp chisel and fine-tooth backsaw.

Finish sand all pieces and join with glue and splines. A flexible web clamp is extremely useful for clamping the case together. All clamping should be done on a flat surface (a pane of glass is ideal) and the case should be checked for squareness before the glue sets. Use extra care to wipe all glue drippings from the case to insure that the stain will penetrate evenly.

Cut the cleats (6 and 7) and glue and clamp them to the inside of the case as shown in Figure 3. These cleats provide a fastening surface for the pendulum-door frame. Referring to Figure 5, cut the parts for the pendulum-door frame. Note that three parts (13) are mitered 67½ degrees, while two parts (12) are mitered 67½ degrees on their lower ends, and 45 degrees on their upper ends. The top of the frame (11) is cut as shown, and dadoed to receive ¾″ butt hinges. All parts are grooved ⅛ x ¼″ to take plywood splines. Drill a ¼″ hole in the top edge of the bottom piece for a bullet catch as shown in Figure 5. Finish sand all frame parts, taking care not to round off sharp edges, and assemble the frame with glue and splines, securing it to the case by gluing and clamping to the cleats.

The pendulum door (Figure 6) is cut from ¾″-square stock. First cut the ¼ x ⁷⁄₁₆″ rabbet along one edge; then round off the outside edge as shown in Detail B. Cut the six separate pieces for parts 14, 15, and 16 to length and miter them to fit the door frame. These pieces should also be grooved ⅛ x ¼″ for splines. Sand well and join with glue and splines, clamping on a flat surface. When the assembly has thoroughly dried, run an outside ¼ x ⁷⁄₁₆″ rabbet around the door, to overlap the door frame which serves as a stop. Glue small hinge blocks to the top of the door and set the door aside for later installation.

The dial face frame (8) is cut from ¾ x 3″

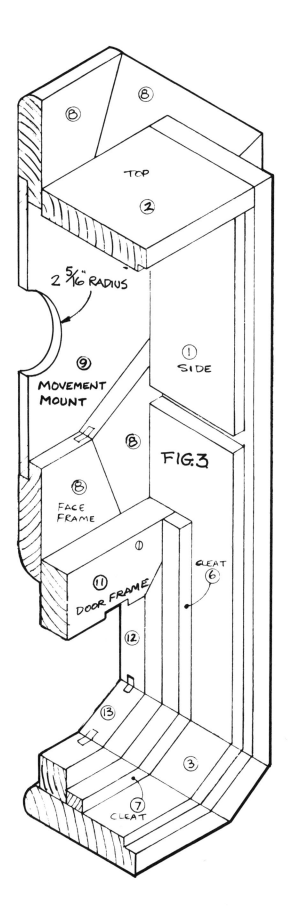

8 ⑧

⑧

TOP
② 2

2 5/16" RADIUS

⑨
MOVEMENT
MOUNT

① SIDE

⑧

FIG. 3

⑧
FACE
FRAME

①

⑪ DOOR FRAME

CLEAT
⑥

⑫

⑬

③

⑦ CLEAT

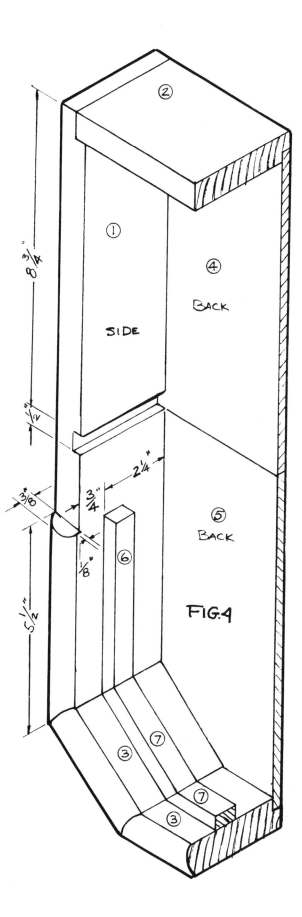

② 2

8 3/4"

① SIDE

④ BACK

1/2"

2 1/4"

3/8"

3/4"

⑤ BACK

1/8"

⑥

FIG. 4

5 1/2"

③ ⑦

③ ⑦

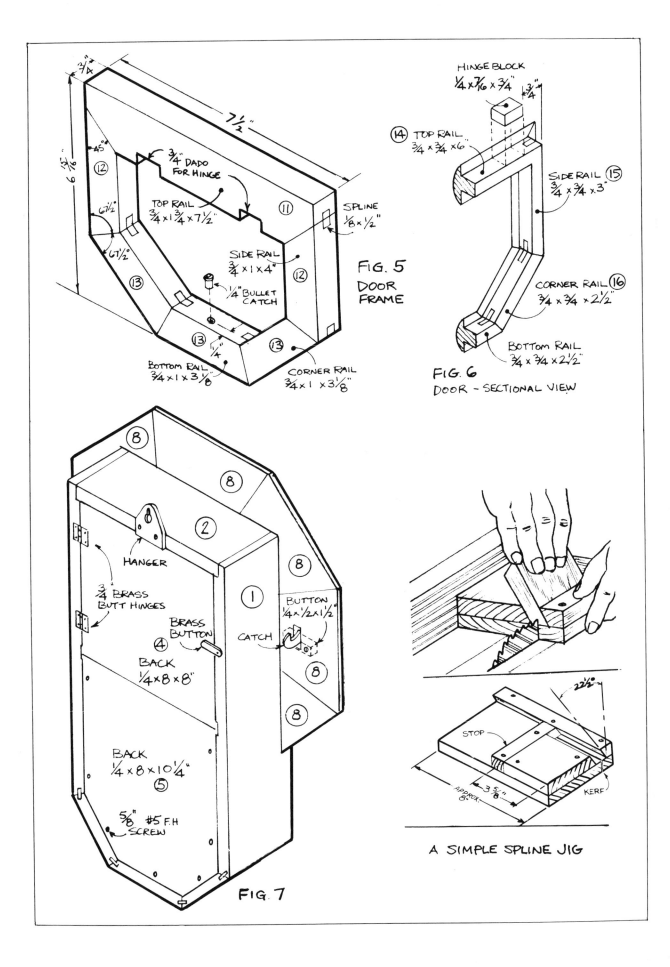

FIG. 5
DOOR FRAME

3/4"

7 1/2"

45°

6 1/16"

15"

67 1/2°

67 1/2°

3/4" DADO FOR HINGE

TOP RAIL
3/4 x 1 3/4 x 7 1/2"

SIDE RAIL
3/4 x 1 x 4"

1/4" BULLET CATCH

1/4"

SPLINE
1/8 x 1/2"

BOTTOM RAIL
3/4 x 1 x 3 1/8"

CORNER RAIL
3/4 x 1 x 3 1/8"

⑪ ⑫ ⑬

FIG. 6
DOOR – SECTIONAL VIEW

HINGE BLOCK
1/4 x 7/16 x 3/4"

3/4"

⑭ TOP RAIL
3/4 x 3/4 x 6"

SIDE RAIL ⑮
3/4 x 3/4 x 3"

CORNER RAIL ⑯
3/4 x 3/4 x 2 1/2"

BOTTOM RAIL
3/4 x 3/4 x 2 1/2"

FIG. 7

⑧ ⑧ ② ⑧ ① ⑧ ⑧

HANGER

3/4 BRASS BUTT HINGES

BRASS BUTTON
④

BACK
1/4 x 8 x 8"

CATCH

BUTTON
1/4 x 1/2 x 1 1/2"

BACK
1/4 x 8 x 10 1/4"
⑤

5/8" #5 F.H SCREW

A SIMPLE SPLINE JIG

22 1/2°

STOP

KERF

3 5/8"

APPROX. 8"

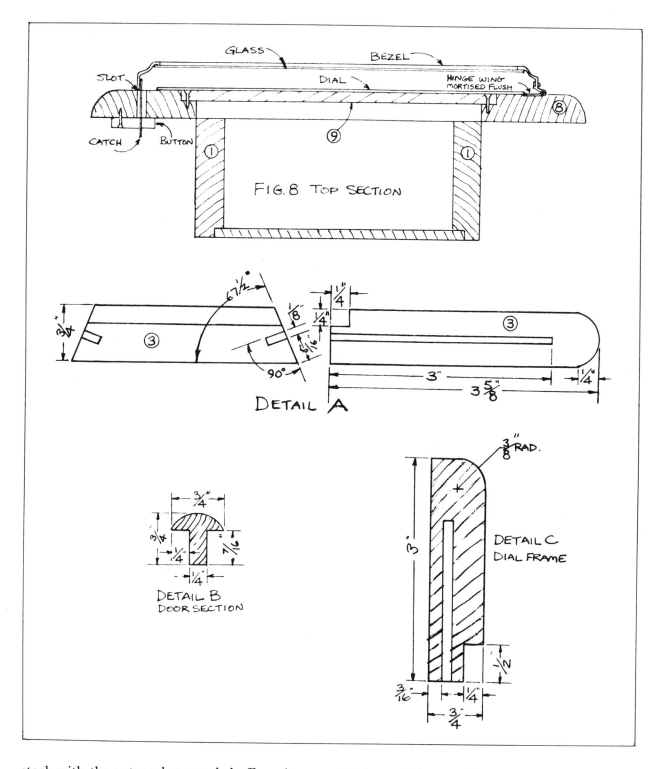

FIG. 8 TOP SECTION

DETAIL A

DETAIL B
DOOR SECTION

DETAIL C
DIAL FRAME

stock with the outer edge rounded off as shown in Detail C. The opposite edge is given a ¼ x ½″ rabbet to provide a recess for the ¼″ plywood movement mount (9). Each of the eight pieces of the face frame is cut to a length of 6³⁄₁₆″ and mitered to 67½ degrees. Again it is advisable to cut pieces from scrap first, and fit them together on a flat surface. Poorly fitted joints will most certainly spoil the overall appearance of the clock. Each piece must be given a ⅛ x ¼″ stopped groove for blind splines. After careful sanding, assemble the frame with glue and splines. Fasten the completed frame to the case with six 1″ #6 flat-headed screws through the rabbeted edge and into the case, and two 1¼″ # 7 flat-headed screws through the upper door frame (11).

27

Cut a ¼″ plywood movement mount (9) to fit the recess in the dial frame. A 2⁵⁄₁₆″-radius hole is drilled in the center for the movement and key winding shafts. The calendar movement recommended for this clock has four mounting ears, which are fastened to the plywood mount with small screws and washers. Instructions for mounting and regulating are included with the movement. A shelf is needed for mounting the coiled gong, and it can be cut from scrap hardwood and fitted into the dadoes cut in the case sides (1) as far forward as it will go.

The lower back panel (5) is cut from ¼″ plywood, and fastened to the case with six ⅝″ #5 flat-headed screws. The upper panel (4) is mounted with two ¾″ brass butt hinges as shown in Figure 7. The panel is held closed with a small turn button. The enameled metal dial face is fastened to the movement mount (9) with small wood screws. The brass bezel assembly comes complete with glass, mounting hinge, clasp, and instructions for mounting. It will be necessary to mortise the dial frame for the bezel hinge, and also to cut a small slot in the frame to take the catch. This process is shown in Figures 7 and 8, along with the ¼ x ½ x 1½″ turnbutton that holds the catch.

Remove the movement, dial, and bezel for finishing the case. Stain color is a matter of preference, and certainly the stain should be tried out on a scrap of similar wood to achieve the desired tone. Oak with its open, coarse grain requires a filler for a smooth finish. A golden oak finish is particularly handsome for a piece of this period, and can be achieved with a golden oak stain, followed by working a light brown filler into the grain. When the surface appears dull, wipe across the grain with a piece of burlap to remove excess filler. Allow the remaining filler to harden for 24 hours and then sand lightly with 400-grit paper, working with the grain.

The clock may be given a shellac, lacquer, or varnish finish. It's best to use a product and finishing schedule with which you are familiar. The synthetic varnishes in a satin finish are easy to apply, and will give very satisfactory results if used in a reasonably dust-free room and rubbed down between coats with 4/0 steel wool. Always use a tack cloth to remove all dust before adding additional coats.

After finishing, install butt hinges to the pendulum-door frame, then mark the locations of the hinges on the mounting blocks that were previously glued to the top of the door. The decorative door glass is secured by bradding small strips of pine or rubber molding to the door rabbets. Add a brass knob and small striker plate to the lower rail of the door, and insert a bullet catch into the hole previously drilled in the door frame's bottom rail. Finally, reinstall the dial, movement, and bezel assembly, and install a sturdy hanger at the top rear of the case. Refer to the instructions that come packed with your movement for getting the movement started and properly regulated.

BILL OF MATERIALS

Key	Part	Pcs. Req'd	T	W	L
1	sides	2	¾″	3⅝″	16½″
2	top	1	¾″	3¼″	8″
3	slant side, bottom	3	¾″	3⅝″	3¾″
4	upper back	1	¼″	8″	8″
5	lower back	1	¼″	8″	10¼″
6	cleat	2	⅜″	½″	4¾″
7	cleat	3	⅜″	½″	3⅛″
8	face frame	8	¾″	3″	6⁹⁄₁₆″
9	movement mount	1	¼″	10″	10″
10	chime shelf	1	½″	1¾″	8″
11	door frame, top	1	¾″	1¾″	7½″
12	door frame, sides	2	¾″	1″	4″
13	slant side, bottom	3	¾″	1″	3⅛″
14	door top	1	¾″	¾″	6″
15	sides	2	¾″	¾″	3″
16	slant side, bottom	3	¾″	¾″	2½″
17					

Hardware

¾″ butt hinges	4
wall hanger	1
turnbutton	1
bezel with glass	1
dial	1
⁵⁄₁₆″ brass knob	1
bullet catch	1
movement	1

glass retainers—as req'd

Tudor Birdhouse

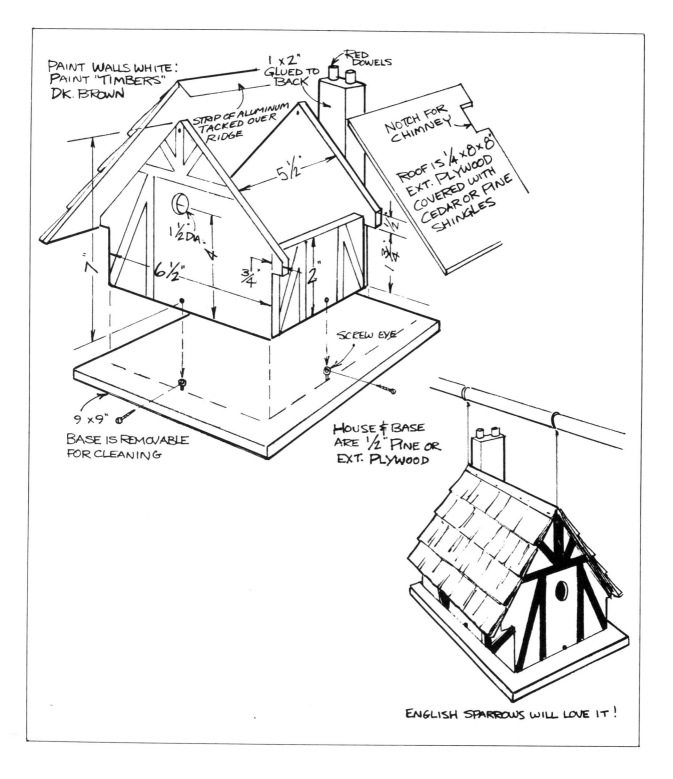

PAINT WALLS WHITE:
PAINT "TIMBERS"
DK. BROWN

1 x 2"
GLUED TO
BACK

RED
DOWELS

STRIP OF ALUMINUM
TACKED OVER
RIDGE

NOTCH FOR
CHIMNEY

ROOF IS 1/4 x 8 x 8"
EXT. PLYWOOD
COVERED WITH
CEDAR OR PINE
SHINGLES

5 1/2"

1 1/2 DIA.

6 1/2"

3/4"

2"

3 1/4"

SCREW EYE

9 x 9"

BASE IS REMOVABLE
FOR CLEANING

HOUSE & BASE
ARE 1/2" PINE OR
EXT. PLYWOOD

ENGLISH SPARROWS WILL LOVE IT!

Shaker-style Portable Chest

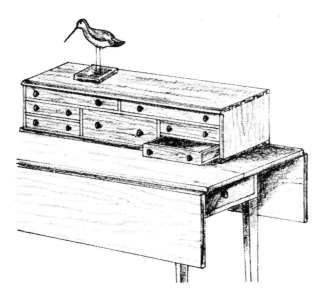

The original from which this piece was adapted was made at the Shaker settlement of Union Village, Ohio, sometime around 1830. It's a perfect example of the incredible amount of care and effort Shaker craftsmen put into the building of even relatively minor pieces. All four corners of the case are joined with half-blind dovetails, and the seven drawers are joined with through dovetails on all four corners. These were all cut by hand, and few modern craftsmen will be willing or able to find the time to do the same. For that reason we have offered the alternative of drawer sides rabbeted to fronts, and held with pegs. The dovetailing of the case provides much visual charm, however, and should be duplicated.

The original was made of walnut, though any cabinet-grade hardwood or pine may be substituted. Pine should be used for drawer sides and backs. Note that the case itself, as well as the drawer fronts, is of ⅝″-thick stock. If you cannot get your lumber planed to this thickness, ¾″ stock may be used, though it will necessitate some dimensional changes. All other parts of the chest are of ½″ stock. The back panel is also ½″ pine, but if the chest is to be wall hung, ¼″ plywood can be substituted. Drawer bottoms should be of thin plywood, preferably ⅛″ or ³⁄₁₆″. Dust panels salvaged from old chests of drawers are excellent for small drawer bottoms. Hardboard can be used, but it is really inappropriate for an antique reproduction.

Begin by cutting the top, bottom, and the two ends to size. Lay out dovetails on the end pieces, and cut these with a fine-tooth backsaw and chisel. Use the completed pins as templates to scribe sockets to the top and bottom pieces. Start the socket cuts with a backsaw, keeping within the scribed lines, and then clean up with a sharp chisel.

Choose your back-panel stock and cut ¼″ rabbets deep enough to allow the panel to come flush with the back edges of the case. The end pieces are rabbeted along their entire back edge, but the top and bottom pieces must have a stopped rabbet as shown in the detail. These can be run with a table saw and finished with a chisel. The molded front edge of the top may be shaped with a router and ½″ corner round and bead bit, or by running a ³⁄₁₆″ kerf in ½″ from the edge and planing the curve.

Ideally, partitions and drawer separators should be held in stopped dadoes, which cannot be seen from the front. This process involves a fair amount of careful layout and grooving, but if the piece is to be made of a fine cabinet wood, the extra effort will be worth it. If pine is used and facilities are limited, the various partitions can be cut and assembled as a unit with glued and nailed butt joints. This unit is then inserted into the case and held with small finishing nails driven from the outside. Whatever method is employed, great care should be exercised to see that all components are fitted squarely; otherwise, the drawers will be difficult to fit.

The back panel serves as a drawer stop and should be fastened with small nails before the drawers are constructed. Note that the drawer fronts are recessed slightly into the case. To determine the length of the drawer sides, measure from the back panel to the front edge of a case side, subtract ¹⁄₁₆″ plus ¼″ for the rabbeted drawer front, and cut all drawer sides to this dimension. Drawer construction as shown in Figure 1 and the detail is relatively simple. Fronts and sides are grooved to receive the bottom panel, which is

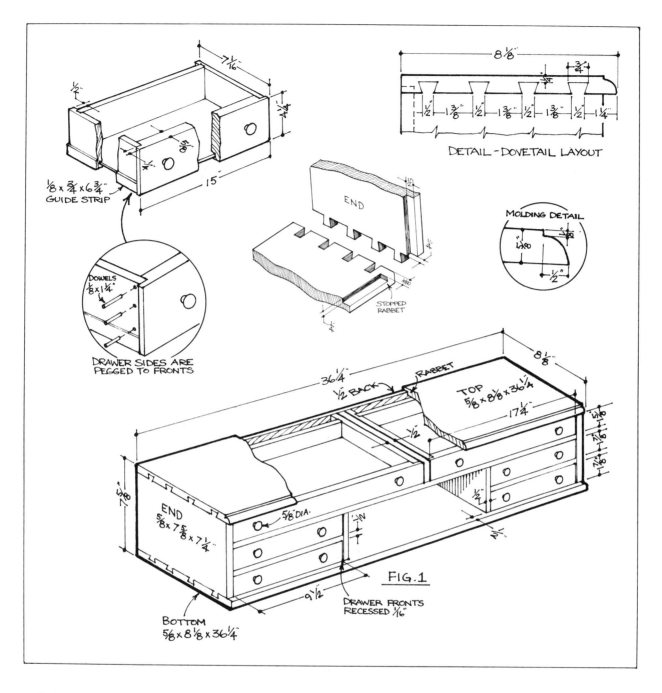

DETAIL – DOVETAIL LAYOUT

MOLDING DETAIL

½ x ¾ x 6¾"
GUIDE STRIP

DOWELS
⅛ x 1¼"

DRAWER SIDES ARE
PEGGED TO FRONTS

END

STOPPED
RABBET

½ BACK

RABBET

TOP
5⁄8 x 8⅛ x 36¼"

END
5⁄8 x 7⅝ x 7¼"

5⁄8 DIA.

FIG. 1

DRAWER FRONTS
RECESSED 1⁄16"

BOTTOM
5⁄8 x 8⅛ x 36¼"

nailed to the underside of the drawer backs. Sides may be fastened to fronts with glue and finishing nails, but the use of small pegs as shown in the detail is an attractive and permanent method. Thin guide strips are glued to the drawer sides flush with the drawers' front edges and set slightly above the bottom edges of the sides. Turned wooden knobs stained to match complete the project. These knobs were originally turned with slightly tapered pins and glued into the drawer fronts.

Walnut should be finished with boiled linseed oil thinned slightly with turpentine. Apply a coat, let it soak in for about 10 minutes, and then wipe off the excess. Allow this coat to dry overnight, then rub the piece down with 000 steel wool and repeat the process. Seal drawer sides, back, and bottom with two coats of shellac mixed half-and-half with wood alcohol.

If a stained finish is desired, apply the stain, and after 24 hours seal the piece with thinned shellac. Rub down with steel wool, remove all dust with a tack cloth, and apply several coats of satin-finish varnish.

Gossip Bench

Contemporary function coupled with Early American styling make this little gossip bench a most attractive piece. As the photograph shows, the small cabinet will hold a telephone and several directories. The drawer is handy for a personal directory, pencils, and paper.

The bench was built of nominal 2 x 6″ construction-grade pine (1⅝ x 5⅝″ actual), ¾″ white pine, and #3 pine shelving, with a small amount of red oak used for the spindles. Pine can be used for the turnings, but care and sharp tools are required to prevent tearing this soft wood.

Begin construction by turning seven pieces of 1¼″-square x 11¼″-long stock for the spindles. If no lathe is available, dowels or square-chamfered pieces may be substituted.

Select material for the seat and cut slightly longer than 36″, which will allow some squaring up of the seat after it has been glued up. A jointer or saw equipped with a molding head should be used on the 2″ edge of the stock to make almost invisible glue joints. If a planer is not available, the thickness of the boards should be reduced at this time. Alternate end-grain patterns as shown in Figure 1 to help prevent warping, and use four or more ½″ dowels to strengthen the glue joints. Apply glue and pressure with three or more pipe clamps, and set aside for 24 hours.

The feet and bench supports can be made fol-

lowing the details of Figure 2. Note that the feet are 1⅜″ thick, while the bench supports are 1⅛″ thick. Also, the ½″ notch is cut only from the feet, not from the bench supports. Make the mortise cuts in the feet and bench supports. Make the legs, lay out and cut tenons and stretcher mortises, and, finally, cut decorative chamfers as shown in Figure 2. The feet, legs, and bench supports can now be glued up.

While the glue joints are curing, continue work by cutting the arms to overall size (Figure 4). Drill the ½ x ½″ sockets in the left-hand arm (facing the bench) before cutting the contour of the arm. Cut the ¾ x ¾″ stopped rabbet in the right-hand arm, to receive the top and side of the cabinet.

Cut the backrest to overall size, then drill the ½ x ½″ spindle sockets 90 degrees to the surface, and make the 6-degree bevel cut on the backrest as shown (Figure 5). Cut the tenons and the contour of the backrest. The ends of the backrest should be worked by hand to fair into the arm height of 2⅝″.

Shape the stretcher, cutting mortises and small wedges to fit (Figure 6). If the glue joints in the seat have cured, square the seat to overall dimensions of 1⅝ x 18 x 36″. Drill the ½ x ½″ sockets along the left end and back, paying careful attention to the fact that the three holes for the armrest spindles are drilled 90 degrees to the surface, but the four holes for the backrest spindles are drilled at 84 degrees to the surface. Cut the stopped dadoes in the seat as shown (Figure 1), and use a hand plane or router with a ⅜″ rounding bit to round off the top edges of the front and two sides.

Assemble the stretcher and feet, and attach the assembly to the underside of the seat with two 1¾″ #8 countersunk wood screws into each support. Seat supports should be set back 1″ from the front edge and in 3″ from the ends before attaching. The stretcher is not glued into the legs but held in place with wedges.

Proceed to the construction of the cabinet that will receive the shelf and drawer. The sides, top, and shelf should be made from glued-up stock.

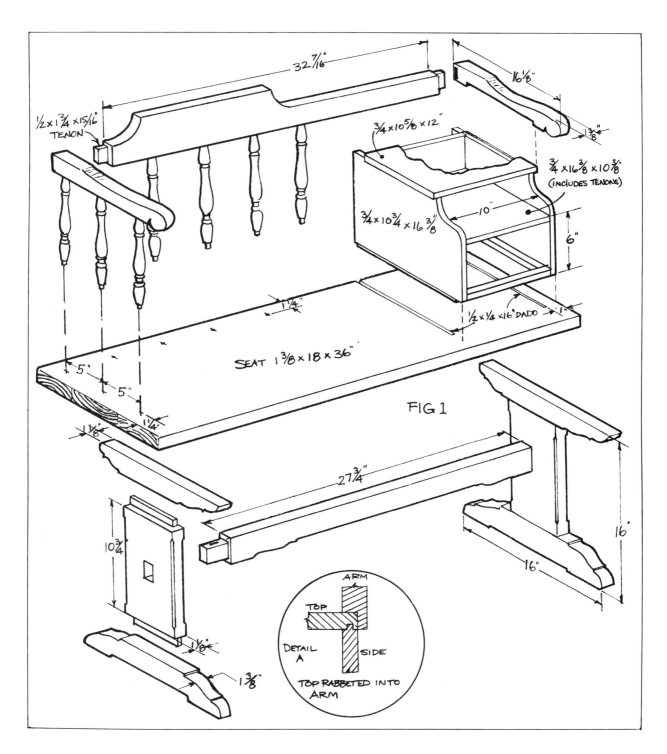

FIG 1

32 7/16"

16 1/8"

1/2 x 1 3/4 x 15/16" TENON

3/4 x 10 5/8 x 12"

3/4 x 16 3/8 x 10 3/8" (INCLUDES TENONS)

3/4 x 10 3/4 x 16 3/8"

10

6"

1 3/8"

1/4"

SEAT 1 3/8 x 18 x 36"

1/2 x 1/4 x 16" DADO

5"

5"

1 1/8"

1/4"

27 3/4"

16"

16"

16"

10 3/4"

1 1/8"

1 3/8"

DETAIL A

ARM

TOP

SIDE

TOP RABBETED INTO ARM

The overall size of the sides is 10¾ x 16⅜″. Cut the contour of the sides using the pattern (Figure 7). The sides are dadoed to receive the back and the shelf. The shelf is set into a dado that is stopped 1″ from the front edge of the cabinet to prevent showing the dado.

The top and bottom edges receive ¼ x ½″ tenons that fit into the bench seat and the top of the cabinet. A 1½″ notch cut is made in the top rear edge so the tenons will slip under the backrest. A simple butt joint is used between the back and the shelf. The top is made from a 10⅝ x 12″ piece, and made flush with the right side of the cabinet, extending ½″ over the left side and front.

There are two ½ x ¼″ stopped dadoes in the top to receive the tenons of the sides. The cabinet can be glued up separately and then glued to the bench, or it can all be glued up together, includ-

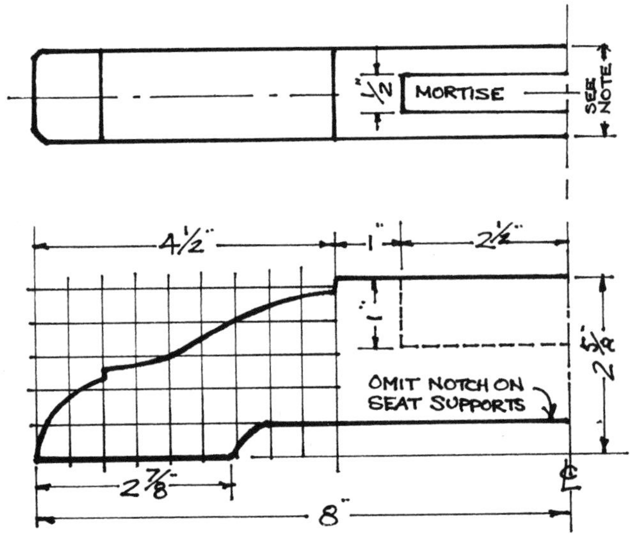
MORTISE
1/2"
SEE NOTE
4 1/2"
1"
2 1/2"
1"
2 5/8"
OMIT NOTCH ON SEAT SUPPORTS
2 7/8"
8"
℄

FIG. 2
SEAT SUPPORTS & FEET – 1/2" SQUARES
NOTE: FEET ARE 1 3/8" THICK
SUPPORTS ARE 1 1/8" THICK

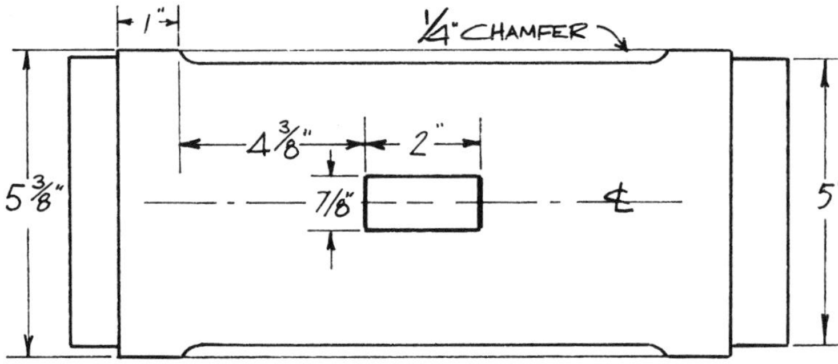
1"
1/4" CHAMFER
4 3/8"
2"
7/8"
℄
5 3/8"
5"

LEG – 5/4" PINE

FIG. 3

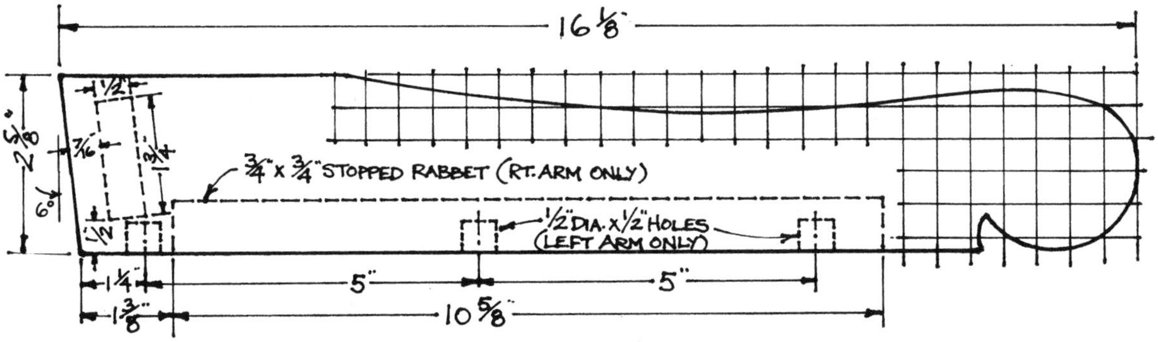
16 1/8"
1/2"
7/16"
3/4"
2 5/8"
6°
1/2"
3/4" x 3/4" STOPPED RABBET (RT. ARM ONLY)
1/2" DIA. x 1/2" HOLES (LEFT ARM ONLY)
1 1/4"
5"
5"
1 3/8"
10 5/8"

FIG. 4 ARM – SQUARES = 1/2"

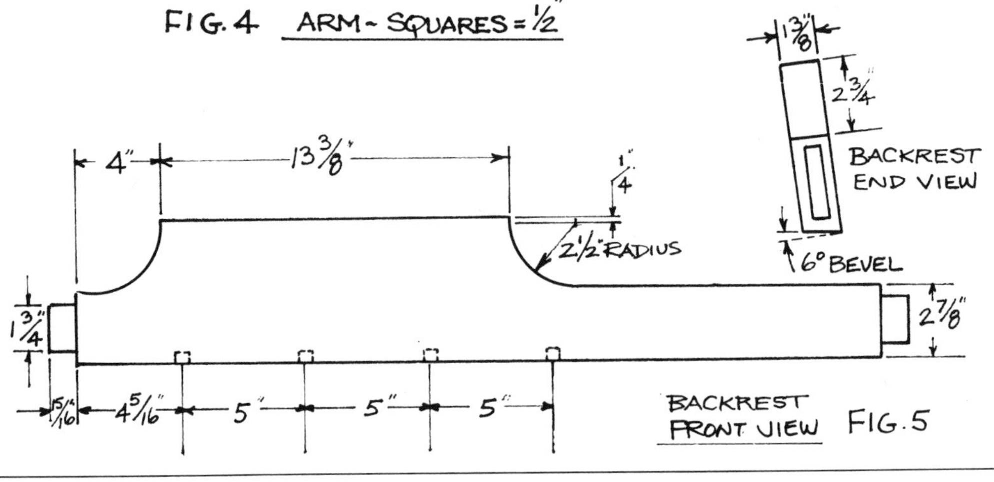
1 3/8"
2 3/4"
BACKREST END VIEW
6° BEVEL
4"
13 3/8"
1/4"
2 1/2" RADIUS
1 3/4"
2 7/8"
5/16"
4 5/16"
5"
5"
5"

BACKREST FRONT VIEW FIG. 5

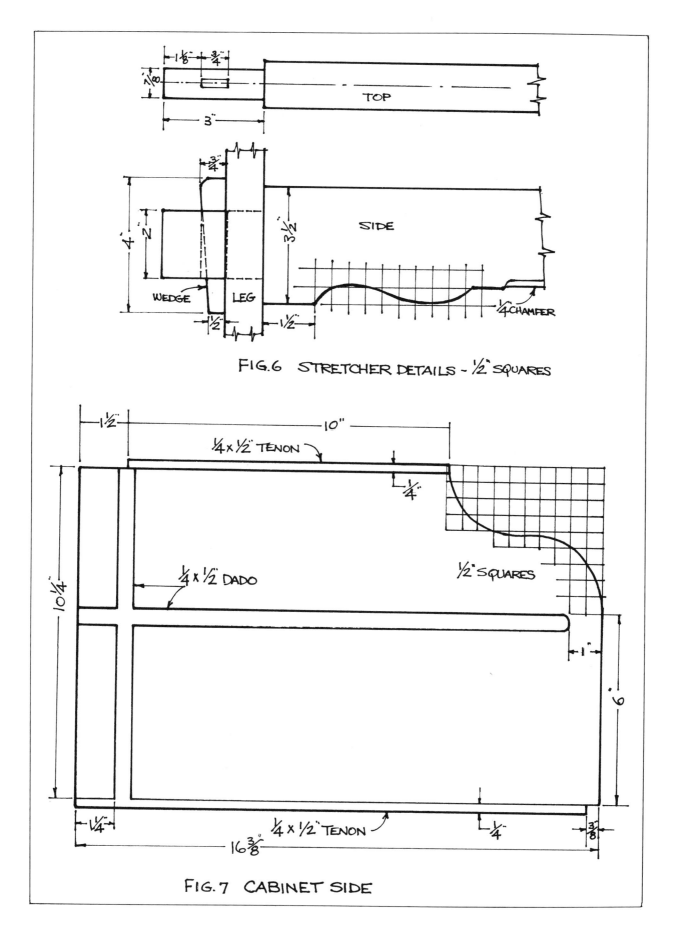

TOP

FIG. 6   STRETCHER DETAILS - ½" SQUARES

WEDGE   LEG

¼ CHAMFER

SIDE

¼ x ½" TENON

¼ x ½ DADO

½" SQUARES

¼ x ½" TENON

FIG. 7   CABINET SIDE

ing the arms and backrest. After the cabinet has been glued in place, the ¾ x ¾" drawer glides are added. The drawer is made to look like two drawers using the details of Figure 6. The drawer bottom is ¼" plywood or hardboard set into dadoes in all four members of the drawer. The bottom dadoes are set ½" up from the bottom edge of the drawer sides.

Finish sand the entire bench giving special attention to the arms and backrest, and rounding the top surfaces slightly. Apply your preferred finish. We used a sealer that was sanded lightly, followed by an oil-base stain, Plymouth Maple by Sears. This stain was covered with two coats of polyurethane and the final coat was rubbed with rubbing oil and pumice to give a satin finish.

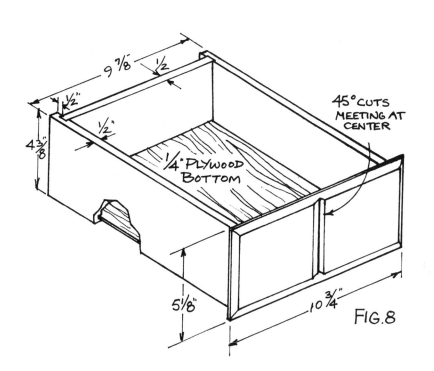

FIG.8

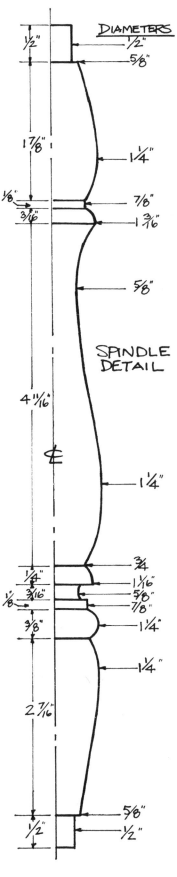

DIAMETERS

SPINDLE DETAIL

Colonial Dry Sink

The Early American dry sink is one of the most popular antiques for home workshop reproduction. There were a great many variations built through the eighteenth and nineteenth centuries, but they all basically served to store buckets of water drawn from the well. The upper "sink" compartment was usually lined with zinc to provide a watertight basin. This particular example is a large or double sink. The paneled ends and doors and the small counter with drawer are design features that help to make this an unusual and rewarding project.

Eastern white pine, which is a delight to work and takes stain beautifully, was used throughout. The back panel and recessed end and door panels were cut from a half sheet of ¼" knotty-pine veneered plywood.

Begin construction by edge joining 1" boards (¾" actual) to make up the 17¾ x 46½" bottom, the 18½ x 51" top, the 17¾ x 46½" shelf, and the 16⅜ x 20" countertop. Use ⅜" dowel pins for strengthening the glue joints, and be sure to allow for trimming and squaring up to finish size. After clamping, set the assembly aside to dry overnight, and begin work on the two framed end panels.

Refer to Figures 1 and 4 to determine the layout of the mortises, panel grooves, and rabbet for a recessed back panel. Bore the mortises by drilling a series of ⁵⁄₁₆" holes. Drill to a depth of 1¾" and clean out waste with a chisel. Tenons are 1⅝" long and their edges should be rounded to match the mortises.

Be sure to reverse the location of the back rabbet on the rear legs or you will end up with two left or right legs.

Assemble the framed panels with glue and clamps, but do not glue the ¼" plywood panel into its grooves. Lock each mortise and tenon joint with two ¼" dowel pins driven through and trimmed flush on both sides.

Cut and shape two front legs and fasten them to the sides with three counterbored wood screws. The counterbored holes should be ½" in diameter for matching plugs. After the front legs have been attached, join each framed end panel to the bottom with four counterbored 1½" screws. The bottom should be flush with the lower edge of each horizontal frame member. Add the top using four counterbored screws at each end. The upper and lower door frames are ¾ x 41½" and 1¾ x 41½" respectively. These are nailed to the top and bottom with finishing nails that are countersunk.

Fasten the shelf to the end frames with four screws in each end, and then add the center door divider, which is screwed to the upper and lower frames and nailed to the shelf. The addition of the ¼ x 47½ x 24¼" back panel completes the case.

The sink and drawer case are built next, and the assembly is screwed to the edges of the top. Check Figure 1 for screw locations. Figure 5 shows the drawer construction. The drawer front is 1" stock, while the sides and back can be cut from either 1" or ½" pine. The use of ½" stock will result in a lighter and more attractive drawer. When fitting the drawer try to maintain a uniform ¹⁄₁₆" clearance around the sides and top of the flush drawer front.

The final construction step is the cutting, mortising, and assembly of the two paneled doors. Refer to Figure 6 for the dimensions, and be sure to use a ⁵⁄₁₆" drill to start the mortises. Note that

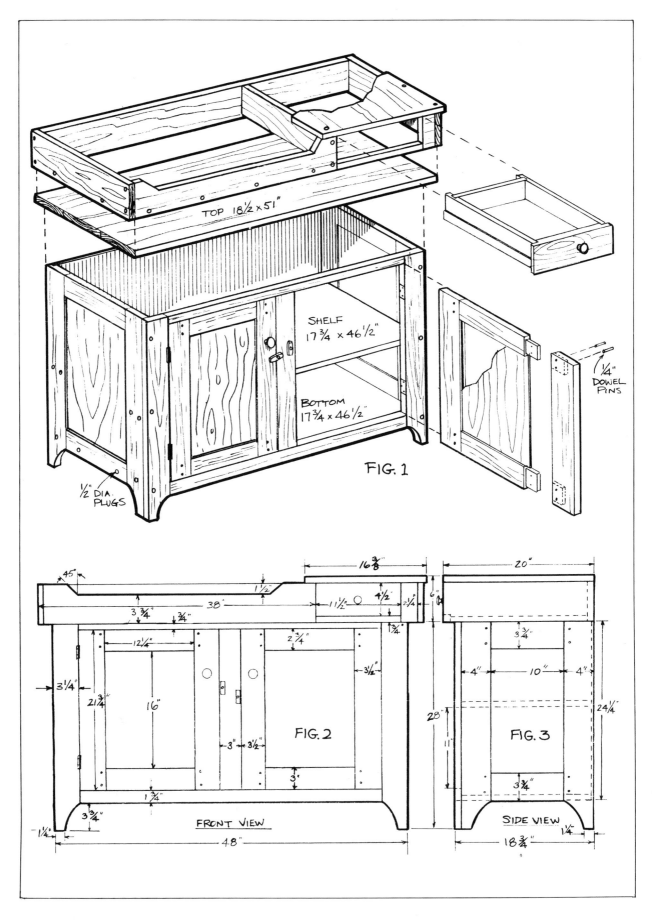

TOP 18½ x 51"

SHELF
17¾ x 46½"

BOTTOM
17¾ x 46½"

¼"
DOWEL
PINS

½" DIA.
PLUGS

FIG. 1

45

16⅜

20"

1½

38"

11½"

4½

2¼

6"

3¾"

¾"

1¾"

12¼"

2¾"

3½"

3¼"

21¾

16"

28

FIG. 2

FIG. 3

3½"

3"

11

24¼"

4"

10"

4"

3¾"

3"

3¾"

1¾"

3¾"

FRONT VIEW

48"

SIDE VIEW

18¾"

1¼"

¼"

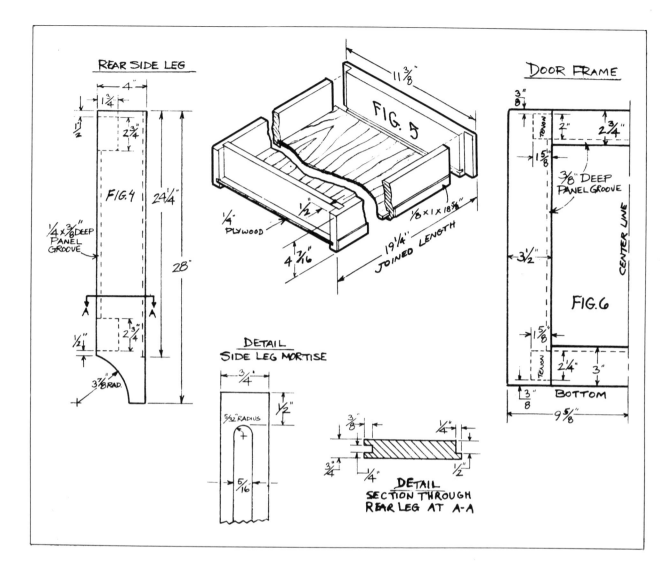

REAR SIDE LEG

FIG. 5

DOOR FRAME

FIG. 4

FIG. 6

DETAIL
SIDE LEG MORTISE

DETAIL
SECTION THROUGH
REAR LEG AT A-A

unlike the side legs, there's only ⅜ of an inch of wood between the mortises and the top and bottom edges of the frame sides. Thus, there is danger of splitting through at this point if you try to square off the mortise ends with a chisel. The ⅜″-deep panel groove will have to be cut to width according to the thickness of the plywood panel. There is some variation in these panels, and you may find that a ¼″ panel is actually 5/16″ thick.

Stain the panels before gluing and clamping the doors together—otherwise some shrinkage later on may expose part of the panel edges where the stain did not reach. The completed doors are hung with 2″ solid brass butt hinges, mortised into the doors and front legs. Antiqued black butterfly or HL hinges may also be used for a more rustic effect.

Round off the top edges of the sink to simulate years of wear. Plug all screw holes with dowel

stock or plugs cut from waste with a ½″ plug cutter. Fill the countersunk nail holes with fine sawdust mixed with a little glue, or wait until the piece is stained and fill the holes with a matching wax. Give the entire piece a finish sanding and dusting before staining.

We used one coat of Minwax Special Walnut oil stain, rubbing and toning the stain as necessary to accentuate the striking grain patterns. The stain coat was allowed to dry overnight and was then followed by a coat of satin-finish urethane varnish. When thoroughly dry, this was lightly sanded with 220-grit paper. The entire piece was dusted with a tack cloth before the second coat of varnish was laid on. This was followed by a rubdown with 5/0 steel wool, another dusting, and finally a thin coat of wax buffed to a soft luster.

Colonial Wall Box

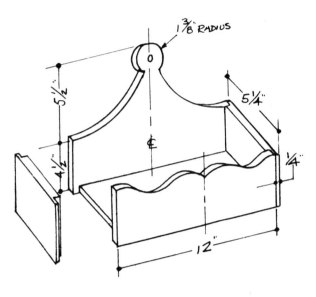

Probably the most popular of colonial-wall-box reproductions, the original pine box was most likely used for storing candles. There have been many variations, but this particular design has remained a favorite for well over two hundred years.

All parts of the box are made from ½″ pine. The box ends are rabbeted to receive the front and back and this joint is glued. The bottom is held with small finishing nails.

All parts of the box should be well sanded prior to assembly, and all edges well rounded to simulate many years of wear.

Many small household items of this type were painted. Our forefathers had a tendency to disguise pine, sometimes with a coat of milk paint, and sometimes with painted graining to simulate mahogany or other costly woods. Modern tastes run to antique pine stain protected with a coat or two of low-luster varnish.

Shaker-style Table Lamp

If you'd like to have a table lamp with a lot of Early American charm and you take pleasure in doing careful, close work, then this is the project for you. The lamp base is adapted from an early Shaker lantern design made of cherry. The old lantern often had a removable tray for the candleholder so that wax drippings could be more easily discarded. Sometimes, as in the Shaker original, the base contained a dovetailed slide that could be pulled out from the front.

You can build the lantern as a lamp base, or, with the addition of a candleholder and carrying handle, use it for its original purpose. It can also be easily adapted for an electric candle and used as a bracket-hung wall lamp. Clear white pine can be used, but cherry or walnut are better choices. Actually, very little material is needed for the lamp and you may have enough in your scrap bin to complete it.

If glass panes are used, the lamp should be constructed as shown in Figure 3, with pine retaining strips to hold the glass and permit replacement of broken panes. If Plexiglas or other plastic panels are used, the posts and rails can simply be grooved to hold the panels. In either

case, make sure that all cuts are square, for the lantern frame is butted and glued, and all joints must fit perfectly. A thin-kerf planer blade for the table or radial saw is very helpful for such fine work.

Forming the cornerposts and rails to hold the glass panes is perhaps the fussiest part of the job. To begin cut two 41½" lengths of ¾"-square strips. One length is for the posts; the other is for eight 5" rails. For glass installation, take a square strip and cut off two 5" lengths. These are for the upper and lower front rails, which do not hold glass. On the remaining strip cut a ¼ x ½" rabbet. Cut this into six 5" lengths. The other long strip is cut into two equal lengths, one of which is rabbeted the same as the rails. Cut this rabbeted piece into two 10" lengths for front posts. The remaining piece should be cut as shown in Detail A. The first two kerfs are made to hold the glass. The third and fourth cuts clean out the waste, providing the recess for the retaining strip.

A simple jig consisting of two ¾" boards clamped to the saw table, with the upper board overhanging the lower by ¾" and resting against the fence, will provide a safe tunnel for the strip to be pushed through and give support when the last cuts are made. Plastic windows require ¼"-deep grooves in four posts and six rails—one groove in each front post and the six rails, and two grooves in the rear posts. The kerfs should be wide enough to permit an easy fit of the glass or plastic.

Assemble the lantern by laying two rear corner posts and the upper and lower rails on a flat surface such as a sheet of glass. Insert the lantern glass to ascertain that the slots are deep enough to hold the glass. Size the end grain of the rails with a layer of glue, allow to dry, and recoat. Spread glue on corresponding points of contact on the posts. If plastic panels are used, they must be added at this point. Bring the four parts together and clamp, making sure that the assembly remains absolutely flat. Repeat the process, omitting the panels, with the front posts and rails.

Cut the 7½"-square base from ¾" stock, shape

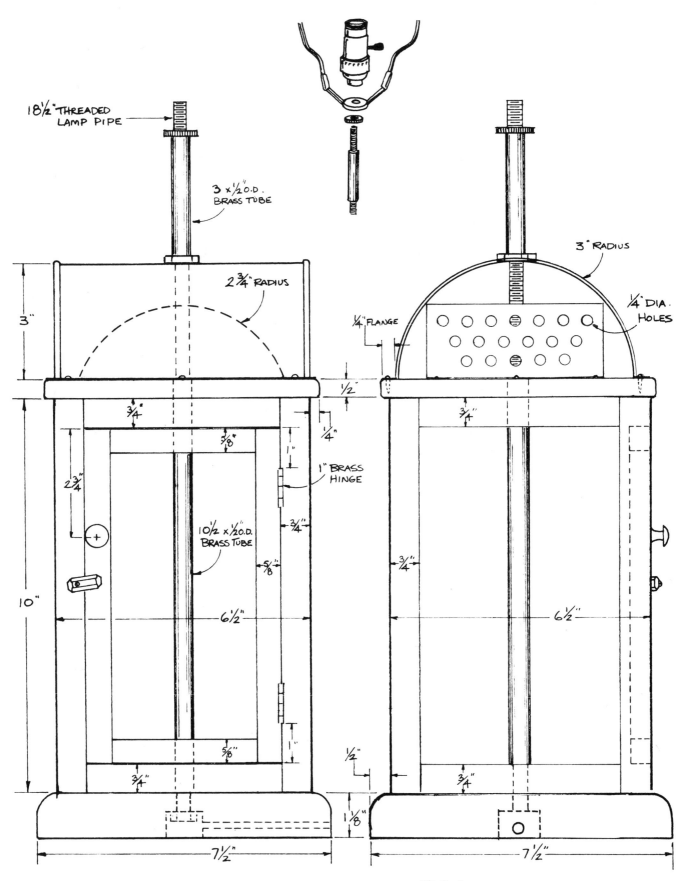

18½" THREADED LAMP PIPE

3 x ½" O.D. BRASS TUBE

2¾" RADIUS

3"

3⁄4"

3⁄8"

2¾"

10½ x ½" O.D. BRASS TUBE

6½"

5⁄8"

5⁄8"

3⁄4"

10"

3"RADIUS

¼" DIA. HOLES

¼"FLANGE

½"

3⁄4"

¼"

1"BRASS HINGE

3⁄4"

1"

3⁄4"

3⁄4"

6½"

½"

3⁄4"

1⅛"

7½"

7½"

FIG. 1   FRONT VIEW

FIG.2   SIDE VIEW

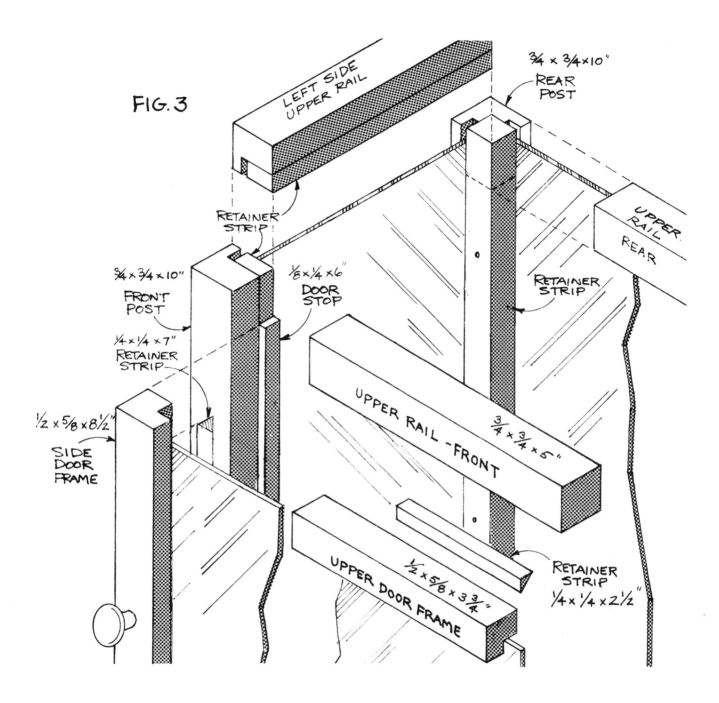

FIG. 3

LEFT SIDE UPPER RAIL

3/4 x 3/4 x 10"
REAR POST

RETAINER STRIP

UPPER RAIL REAR

3/4 x 3/4 x 10"
FRONT POST

1/8 x 1/4 x 6"
DOOR STOP

RETAINER STRIP

1/4 x 1/4 x 7"
RETAINER STRIP

UPPER RAIL - FRONT

3/4 x 3/4 x 5"

RETAINER STRIP

1/2 x 5/8 x 8 1/2"
SIDE DOOR FRAME

UPPER DOOR FRAME

1/2 x 5/8 x 3 3/4"

RETAINER STRIP
1/4 x 1/4 x 2 1/2"

the edges, and counterbore and drill the bottom for a threaded pipe, washer, and nut. Also bore a hole or rout a channel for the lamp cord. Cut the 7"-square lid from 1/2" stock and bore a 1/2" center hole for the pipe within a 1/2" brass tube. If the lantern is to be used for a candle or candle bulb, a 3"-diameter hole should be cut in the center of the lid. Plane and scrape upper and lower surfaces of the base and lid bottom as flat as you can get them.

Join the glued-up front and rear frames by adding the plastic panels and gluing and clamping the upper and lower side rails in place. The assembled frame is then glued to the base and lid. Run the threaded pipe through the assembly and clamp together with nuts at each end.

The door frame, which should fit with 1/32" clearance all around, is made of 1/2"-thick stock ripped to 5/8" width. All four parts are rabbeted 1/4 x 1/4", as shown in Detail B, then butted and

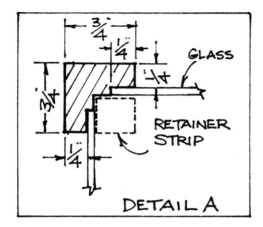

GLASS

RETAINER
STRIP

DETAIL A

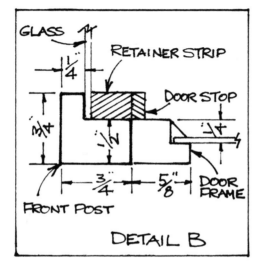

GLASS

RETAINER STRIP

DOOR STOP

DOOR
FRAME

FRONT POST

DETAIL B

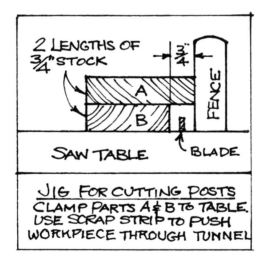

2 LENGTHS OF
3/4" STOCK

A

B

FENCE

SAW TABLE

BLADE

JIG FOR CUTTING POSTS
CLAMP PARTS A & B TO TABLE.
USE SCRAP STRIP TO PUSH
WORKPIECE THROUGH TUNNEL

glued together. Again, use a flat surface for clamping. Fasten the door with two 1″ brass butt hinges mortised into the door.

The inner and outer hoods are cut from sheet metal. Copper or brass is preferred, but tin cans can be used and look good when painted flat black. The inner hood perforations are purely decorative on the table lamp, but necessary for ventilation if a candle is used. Form a ¼″ mounting flange on each side of the hood and drill three holes in each flange for fastening to the lid with small screws or escutcheon pins. Also bore a ⅜″ hole for the threaded pipe. The outer hoods should have raw edges rolled into a small rim as shown in the front and side views.

Cut pine retaining strips to fit the rabbets and predrill the strips, posts, and rails for small brads, angling the holes at the rear strips to pass between the edges of the glass. Add glass panes and push the bradded strips into place with long-nose pliers.

The lamp should be stained if made of pine, while cherry and walnut look best if left unstained and given a penetrating oil finish. Brass or copper hoods should be polished and lacquered. Glue a thin strip of pine to the door jamb to serve as a stop. Cut the door glass for an easy fit. Fasten small triangular retaining strips by spot-gluing in place. Add a brass or wooden knob and small turnbutton.

Place a threaded pipe through the lamp and cover with brass tubing locked at the bottom with a lock washer and nut, and at the top with a flat brass nut. Thread lamp cord through the base hole and up through the center pipe. After the upper brass tube is added, a sufficient length of threaded pipe should protrude so that a knurled nut, lamp harp, and socket can be added. Wire up the socket and add a plug to the other end of the cord. When choosing and fitting a shade, the lower rim of the shade should come just below the bottom of the harp.

If the lantern is made for a candle, a brass candlestick socket can be purchased or lathe turned with a ⅞″ opening from hardwood. Fasten a heavy wire carrying handle through holes punched in the top of the outer hood.

Catboat Windmill

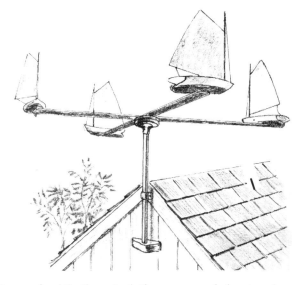

Around with the wind they go, each boat going through all the points of sailing in turn: beating, running, and reaching. Mounted on a pole in the yard or clamped to the gable end of a garage or utility shed, the salty-looking little catboat windmill provides an interesting and decorative means of judging wind strength.

We remember seeing one of these "wind machines" on New York's Long Island several years ago, and recently rediscovered the design in *Marlinspike Sailor,* a classic book on knots and ropework by Hervey G. Smith. We designed a hull that can be easily carved from soft pine and utilized a lazy-Susan bearing for the arms to pivot on.

To carve the catboat hulls, glue together (using water-resistant glue) two pieces of ¾ x 1½ x 8″ soft pine. Sandwich these between two pieces of ¾ x 1½ x 8″ pine, as shown in Figure 2. Cut a ¼ x ½″-deep groove down the center of the laminated block for the ¼ x 1 x 8″ plywood keel. Be sure to use waterproof exterior-grade plywood.

Bandsaw or rasp a sheer curve on the deck from stem to stern, then proceed to carve the hulls, using the illustration as a guide. When hulls have been shaped and sanded, the keels are glued in place, shaped to fair with the stem, and notched to receive the arm. Shape the masts, drilling holes for rings to hold the sails before gluing the masts into the deck sockets. String forestay wire from the mast to a small screw eye at the bow.

Sails are cut from sheet zinc or galvanized steel and painted white. Fasten the sail to the mast with heavy brass wire or soldered split rings. Adjust the mainsheet to allow the sail to swing freely to either side as shown in Figure 7. When the four hulls have been completed, cut two arms of ½″ hardwood, 1½″ wide x 36″ long. Half-lap these at the center as in Figure 6.

Cut two 5″ discs from ¾″ stock and fasten a lazy-Susan bearing between them. These bearings come with mounting instructions, and the 3″ size needed here sells for about one dollar. (It can be purchased from The Woodworker's Store; see p. 243 for the address.) The two catboat arms are screwed to the upper disc and a boat is fastened to the end of each arm with a screw driven through the arm and into the hull.

The catboat race can be pole mounted or fastened with pipe to the gable end of a garage, as shown in the illustration. It may also be fastened to a roof ridge by cutting equally spaced slots in the lower five inches of the pipe and bending the four fingers thus formed to conform with the roof pitch. Holes are then drilled near the ends of the fingers for mounting screws. Apply roofing tar or caulking compound over the holes before mounting. Lubricate the bearing periodically with bearing oil or pack it with light grease.

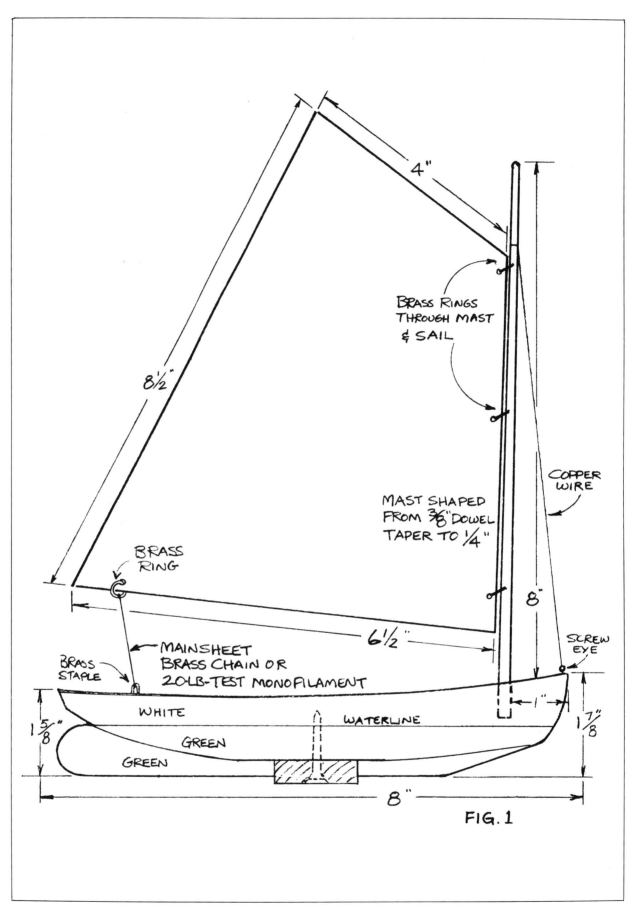

4"

8½"

BRASS RINGS
THROUGH MAST
& SAIL

COPPER
WIRE

MAST SHAPED
FROM ⅜" DOWEL
TAPER TO ¼"

8"

BRASS
RING

6½"

SCREW
EYE

MAINSHEET
BRASS CHAIN OR
20 LB-TEST MONOFILAMENT

BRASS
STAPLE

WHITE   WATERLINE

1⅝"

1⅞"

GREEN

1"

GREEN

8"

FIG. 1

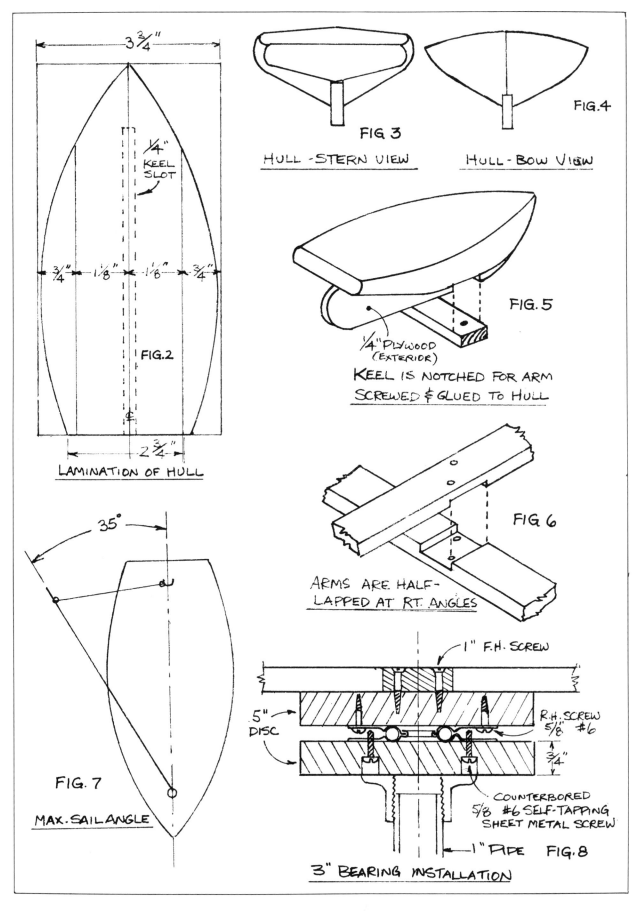

3¾"

¼"
KEEL
SLOT

¾" 1⅛" 1⅛" ¾"

FIG.2

2¾"

LAMINATION OF HULL

FIG 3

HULL - STERN VIEW

FIG.4

HULL - BOW VIEW

FIG. 5

¼" PLYWOOD
(EXTERIOR)

KEEL IS NOTCHED FOR ARM
SCREWED & GLUED TO HULL

FIG 6

ARMS ARE HALF-
LAPPED AT RT. ANGLES

35°

FIG. 7

MAX. SAIL ANGLE

1" F.H. SCREW

5" DISC

R.H. SCREW
5/8 #6

¾"

COUNTERBORED
5/8 #6 SELF-TAPPING
SHEET METAL SCREW

1" PIPE   FIG. 8

3" BEARING INSTALLATION

Pine Chair

Chairmaking is one area of woodworking where the novice may encounter some difficulty. The stresses placed upon a chair in normal use will soon reveal flaws in design and sloppy joinery. This particular design is about as simple as possible without appearing stiff or ungainly. The uncluttered appearance enables it to blend in with a wide range of styles, from Early American to contemporary. All phases of construction can be performed with hand tools, though a band saw and lathe will ease the work considerably.

Construction is begun with the seat, which is shaped from a 17″-square slab of 2″ pine (actual 1⅝″). It will be necessary to edge join and glue two pieces to achieve the width required. Use three ¾″ dowel pins to reinforce the glued joint. If several chairs are to be made, a cardboard pattern of the seat should be made up, complete with leg-tenon locations and back mortise.

Shape the seat as shown in Figure 1. Dishing out the top surface will improve the appearance

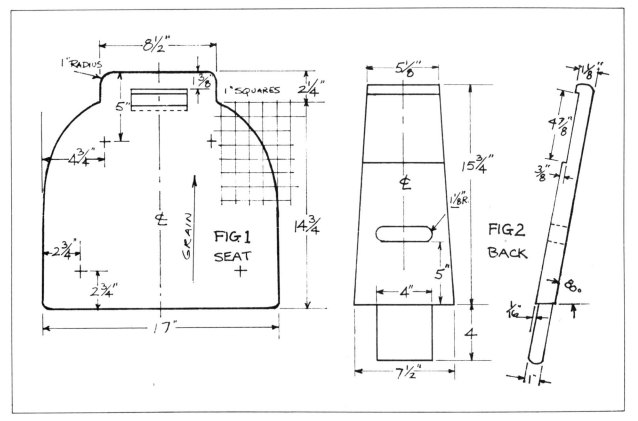

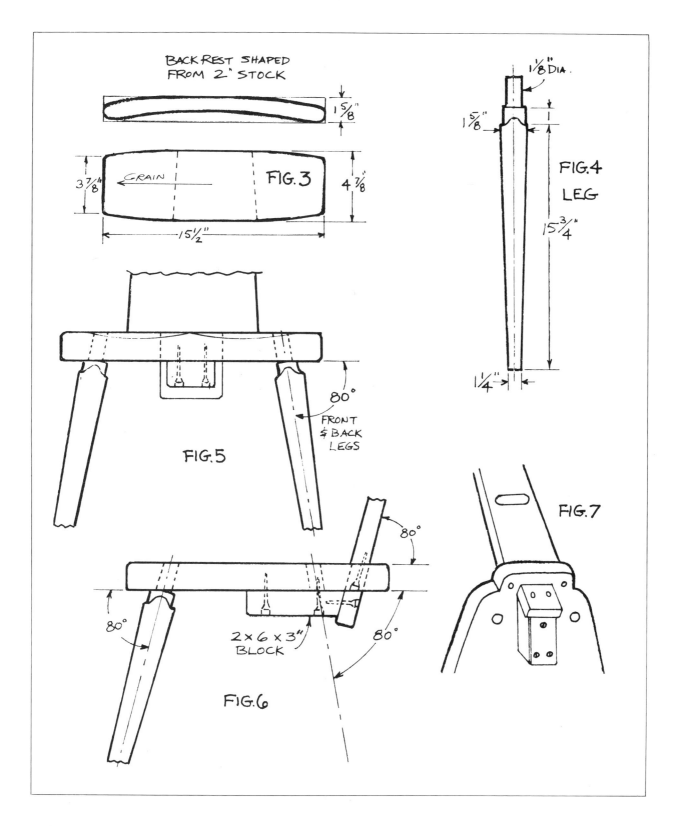

BACK REST SHAPED
FROM 2" STOCK

FIG.3

1 5/8"

3 7/8"   GRAIN   4 7/8"

15 1/2"

FIG.4
LEG

1/8" DIA.

1 5/8"

15 3/4"

1/4"

FIG.5

80°
FRONT
& BACK
LEGS

FIG.6

80°

80°

80°

2 × 6 × 3"
BLOCK

FIG.7

and comfort of the chair. This is best done with an in-shave (a special type of drawknife which has a curved blade), followed by sanding. Mark the locations of the leg tenons and cut out the mortise for the back upright. Cut this mortise by drilling out waste with a 1" auger, using a bevel gauge to guide the auger at an 80-degree angle. Clean up the mortise with a chisel.

Cut the upright (Figure 2) from ¾" stock (actual 1⅛"), forming the lower tenon and hand hold. The backrest (Figure 3) is shaped to a slight curve from a piece of 2″ stock, and here a band saw will do a nice job; otherwise use a spokeshave and rasp. When the backrest is completed, and well sanded, use it to lay out the wide dado in the upright (Figure 2). Cut this dado to a depth of ⅜″. The backrest is fastened in its slot with four 1¼″ #10 flat-headed (fh) screws, driven from the back into counterbored holes and hidden with ½″ dowel plugs.

The legs are shaped from 2″ stock cut to a length of 19″. Taper them as shown in Figure 4, and rasp or lathe turn the square to a round, 16″ up from the foot. One inch above this rounded portion, the seat tenon is shaped to a diameter of 1⅛″. Leave the tenon long to be trimmed flush with the seat later on.

A drill press is ideal for boring the leg-tenon holes, but, with care, the compound angles can be bored with a brace and bit. Use a bevel gauge to line up the auger, and remember that the legs splay 80 degrees to the front and rear, as well as to the sides (Figures 5 and 6). The best approach is to drill one front hole and then insert a leg tenon into the top side of the seat. Align the brace and bit with this leg, and proceed to bore the other front hole through from the top. A similar procedure is used for the rear legs.

Before fastening the legs, sand them, and give each corner a ¼″ chamfer for a lighter appearance. Cut a saw kerf in the top of each tenon for a hardwood wedge, which is driven at a right angle to the grain of the seat. Glue the tenons into their holes and carefully drive in glue-coated wedges. The tenons can now be trimmed and sanded flush with the seat surface.

Fasten the backrest assembly to the seat by driving the tenon into the seat mortise. Screw and glue a beveled reinforcing block (Figure 6) to the underside of the seat with three 2″ #12 screws, and screw the tenon stub to the block with two counterbored 1½″ #10 screws, covered with ½″ dowel plugs. Also counterbore the bottom of the seat for two 2″ #12 screws, to be driven up into the upright and plugged. These are shown in Figure 7.

Go over the assembled chair with a sander or rasp, and round off all sharp edges. Finish sand and apply the finish of your choice. We used a dark antique-pine stain, followed by thinned shellac sealer. After the shellac dries, give the entire piece a rubdown with 3/0 steel wool. Dust carefully and apply three coats of low-luster urethane varnish.

Now with this basic chairmaking experience, perhaps you'll be willing to tackle that elegant Windsor or Hepplewhite chair you've always wanted.

Colonial Spoon Rack

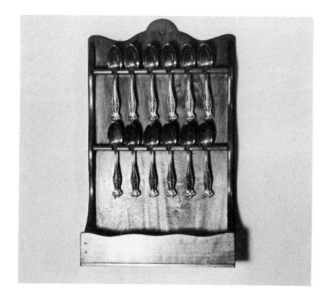

Any collection of fine silverware can be proudly displayed in this charming colonial spoon rack. Note that it is basically made up of seven parts: the back, two sides, the front, bottom, and two spoon holders. All are made from ⅜″ clear pine.

Since thin wide stock is hard to come by, the back will probably have to be made from two pieces of ½″ stock, edge glued together, then planed down to the ⅜″ thickness. After planing, transfer the grid patterns from the drawing to the stock and cut out.

Now cut out the two sides, again planing down the heavier stock and cutting the curves as shown in the pattern.

The front piece and bottom can be cut out next. Continue using the same procedure, taking care to make all cuts accurately.

The final two parts are the top and bottom spoon holders. Refer to the drawing for the dimensions needed to drill the holes and cut the grooves. You'll want a nice, clean hole here, so use a sharp drill bit. Cut the grooves so that they will be uniform in width.

Begin assembly by first attaching the back to the sides. Use wood glue and fasten from the back with small finishing nails. Next, attach the bottom to the back and sides. Use two decorative brass escutcheon nails on each side to attach the front. Finally, put the spoon holders in place and fasten from the back with finishing nails.

To finish, sand all surfaces completely and stain to suit. Apply two coats of satin varnish, rubbing down the final coat with 4/0 steel wool.

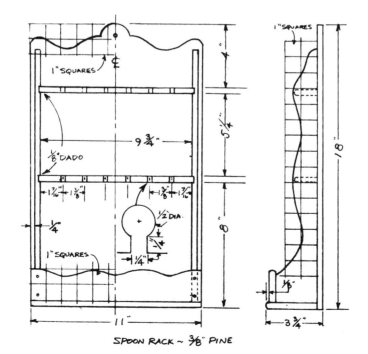

SPOON RACK ~ ⅜″ PINE

Aeolian Harp

The word "Aeolian" derives from Aeolus, the ancient Greek god of winds, but the principle of the wind harp goes back as far as King David and the Old Testament.

Basically, the harp consists of an oblong, hollow box over which strings are stretched and tuned to a single tone. When placed in a current of air, the harp produces full chords made up of the harmonics of the single tone. In a slight breeze, the harp gives off a droning hum, but as the wind increases in velocity, higher tones of the chord are produced and superimposed on the lower tones. Sudden bursts of gathering wind produce exhilarating crescendos which diminish quickly or continue as long as the wind holds.

This is a relatively simple project and even a crude job of joining will produce a working instrument. The harp box should be made of thin wood. Plywood of ⅛″ thickness is fine, and the basswood ply generally used for fretsaw work is adequate and available from many mail-order supply houses. The dust panels and drawer bottoms from old chests can also be used if long enough.

We built the harp from ⅛″ solid mahogany. However, this was not rigid enough for the lid, so there ½″ clear pine was used, planed down to ¼″ thickness. Spruce, which is used for guitar tops, would also be an excellent choice for the body of the harp, but on the expensive side.

Rip the top, bottom, and sides of the harp to about ³⁄₁₆″ wider than the finished size. When all parts are glued together, the overhangs can then be planed perfectly flush. The finished harp should be made just long enough to fit on a windowsill, preferably at a window that receives the prevailing wind.

Shape the two hard-maple pin blocks (which can be laminated from ¾″ stock) and sand all surfaces flat and smooth. Glue the pin blocks at each end of the bottom, then add the sides. After the glue has dried, trim the sides with a finely set block plane so that the top beveled edges match the slope of the pin blocks.

The interior braces are made by boring holes in a ½″ pine board and then cutting braces to fit between the harp sides. If you cut the braces first and then try to bore the holes, the wood may split. Glue the braces in position and after the glue has cured, plane the tops of the braces flush with the harp sides. The triangular pine glue strips (see the sectional end view) provide reinforcement and additional glue surface but are not absolutely necessary if plywood is used.

Before gluing the top in place, cut the 2½″-diameter hole in the top with a coping saw; then glue and clamp the top in place. Lay out the holes through the top and pin blocks for the tuning pins and finishing nails. Tuning pins can be purchased at many musical instrument shops. Ask for Autoharp or zither pins, and buy a small wrench to fit them (although if necessary, a standard adjustable wrench can also be used). One dozen pins are required. If not available locally, Autoharp pins can be ordered from Fretted Industries, 1415 Waukegan Rd., Northbrook, IL 60062.

The drilled holes for the tuning pins must be a tight fit or you will have trouble keeping the harp in tune. Use a ³⁄₁₆″ twist bit and a depth gauge set to drill all holes to a depth of ⅝″. Be sure to drill all holes vertically into the sloping blocks, and try to keep them uniform. The pins are tapped in with a hammer so that about ¼″ of the threaded portion still protrudes. When the strings are added, the pins will be twisted further into the block.

The block at the opposite end is drilled with undersize pilot holes for angled 4-penny finishing

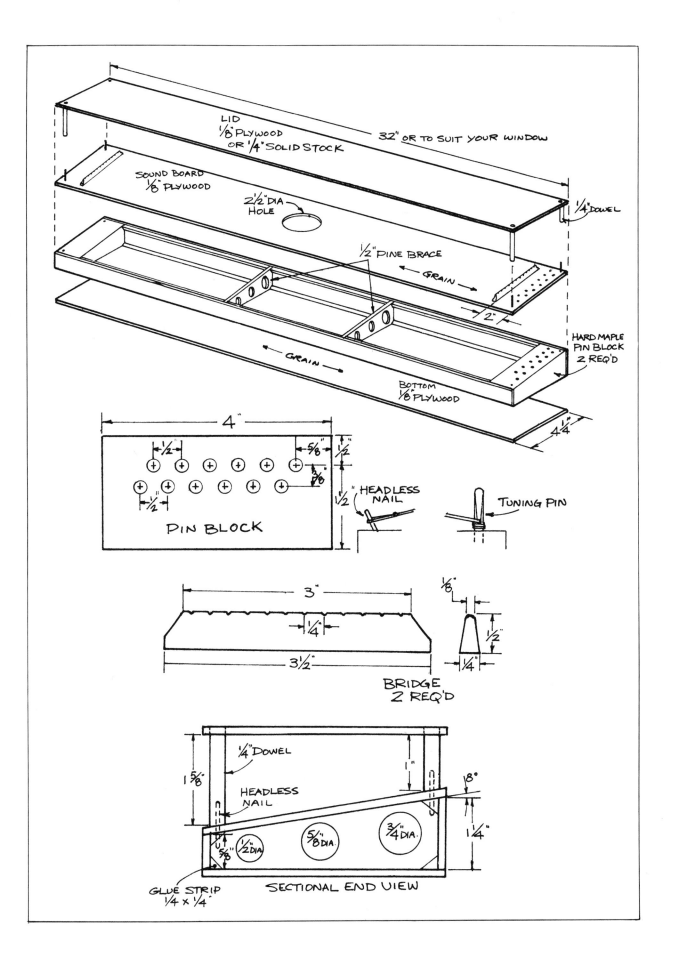

LID
1/8" PLYWOOD
OR 1/4" SOLID STOCK

32" OR TO SUIT YOUR WINDOW

SOUND BOARD
1/8" PLYWOOD

2 1/2" DIA
HOLE

1/4" DOWEL

1/2" PINE BRACE

GRAIN

2"

HARD MAPLE
PIN BLOCK
2 REQ'D

GRAIN

BOTTOM
1/8" PLYWOOD

4 1/4"

4"

1/2"   5/8"   1/2"

3/8"

1/2"   1/2"

PIN BLOCK

HEADLESS
NAIL

TUNING PIN

3"

1/8"

1/4"

1/2"

3 1/2"

1/4"

BRIDGE
2 REQ'D

1/4" DOWEL

1 5/8"

1"

8°

HEADLESS
NAIL

1/4"

1/2" DIA.   5/8" DIA.   3/4" DIA.

5/8"

GLUE STRIP
1/4 x 1/4"

SECTIONAL END VIEW

nails clipped to 1⅛″. Drive the nails with a nail set until about ⅝″ protrudes.

Cut two bridges about 4″ long from hard maple, taking care to keep them exactly equal in height. Taper them as shown in the bridge detail end view, but do not notch or install them until the harp is strung.

Twelve nylon guitar strings are needed, four each of G, B, and E strings. (These are strings no. 1, 2, and 3 on the classical guitar.) Starting at one side, tie small loops in the strings to fit over the nails, then lead each string to its proper pin. The pins have holes in them for attaching the strings. Leave enough slack in the strings to allow several windings around the pin and snip off the excess. Use the tuning wrench to turn each pin clockwise and down, and draw each string tight enough to rise about ¼″ off the harp top and ¼″ apart from the other strings.

File notches in the top edge of each bridge about ⅟₁₆″ deep and wide enough to hold the strings. Trim the bridges to finished length and position them at opposite ends, about 2″ away from the pins. It is not necessary to glue them in place.

Drill dowel holes in the lid stock to take ¼″ dowel lid supports. Cut the lid to finished size, glue the drilled dowels in place, and use them to locate the headless nails, which are driven into the harp and serve as retaining pins for the lid.

The harp may be stained to suit and should be given several coats of varnish. Tune the harp by bringing all the strings to one note: in other words, all strings should sound the same when plucked. If you have a piano, tune all the strings to the first G below middle C. New strings will stretch initially, and you will have some difficulty keeping the harp in tune, but keep retuning periodically and the strings will stabilize in about 24 hours.

Place the harp on the windowsill with the wide opening facing outdoors, then bring the window down on the lid to hold the harp in place. At the first breeze, you'll be rewarded with a heavenly sound and a lot of comment from friends.

Hutch Table

The constant struggle for survival through the early years of English settlement in the New World left little time for construction of anything other than the most rudimentary pieces of furniture. A table, chair, several stools, and a variety of chests and cupboards were, for the most part, all these early settlers had. Within a generation with the influx of skilled craftsmen, houses evolved from simple one-room dwellings to structures of more imposing design and dimensions. As living space increased, so did the need for more furniture.

Of necessity the early dining table consisted of simply hewn planks laid across trestles that were stored against a wall when not needed. The tilt-top table then followed, and it was only logical to construct the base so that it served also as a seat. The next step was to construct a box seat with a lid so that a storage area was added. Thus, the table became a seat and a hutch as well. Early usage of the word "hutch" referred to chests or boxes for storage. These tables were marvelous examples of multi-use furniture.

We are no longer so pressed for living space, and upholstered chairs are much more comfortable to sit in, but the hutch table remains a charming and useful accessory for the home with early colonial furnishings. It's also perfect for the small apartment.

Eastern white pine is the proper wood to use for this project, and knotty stock is the best, as long as the knots are tight. Start construction with the legs, which are cut to shape from ¾″ stock. Edge glue two boards with ½″ dowels to achieve the required width. Lay out and cut two ¾ x 2½″ tenons on each. Next, shape the feet from solid or glued-up stock, and scribe mortises directly from the leg tenons. Cut the mortises 1½″ deep.

Assemble the legs and feet temporarily, and tack a brace across them while you lay out the front and back panel dovetails. Cut dovetails on the front and back panels and scribe the shape to the legs. Disassemble the legs and feet and cut dovetail notches in the legs. Shape scrolls on the lower edges of the front and back panels and fit

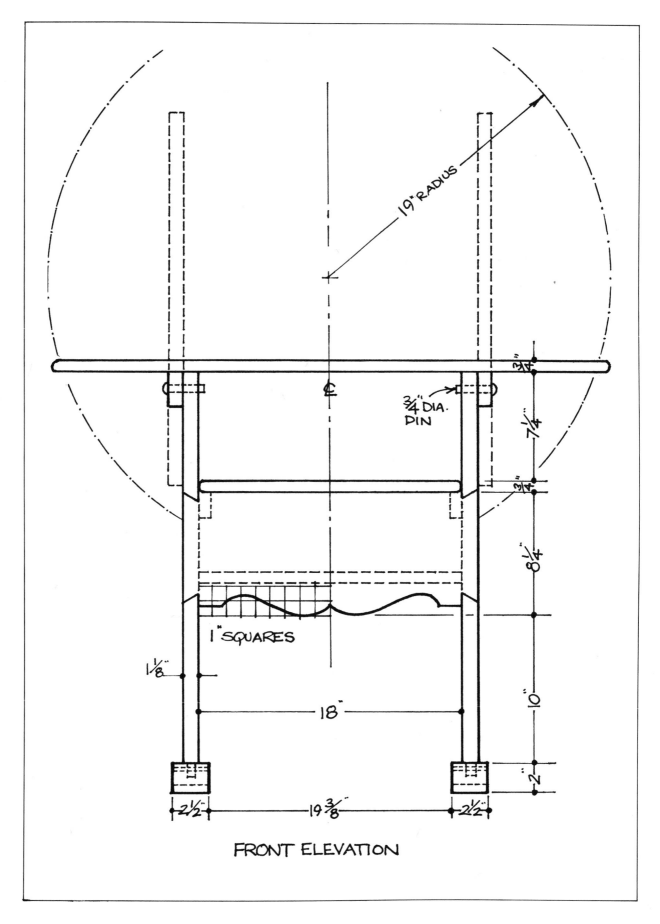

19" RADIUS

3/4" DIA.
PIN

3/4"

7 1/4"

3/4"

8 1/4"

1" SQUARES

1 1/8"

10"

18"

2"

2 1/2"

19 3/8"

2 1/2"

FRONT ELEVATION

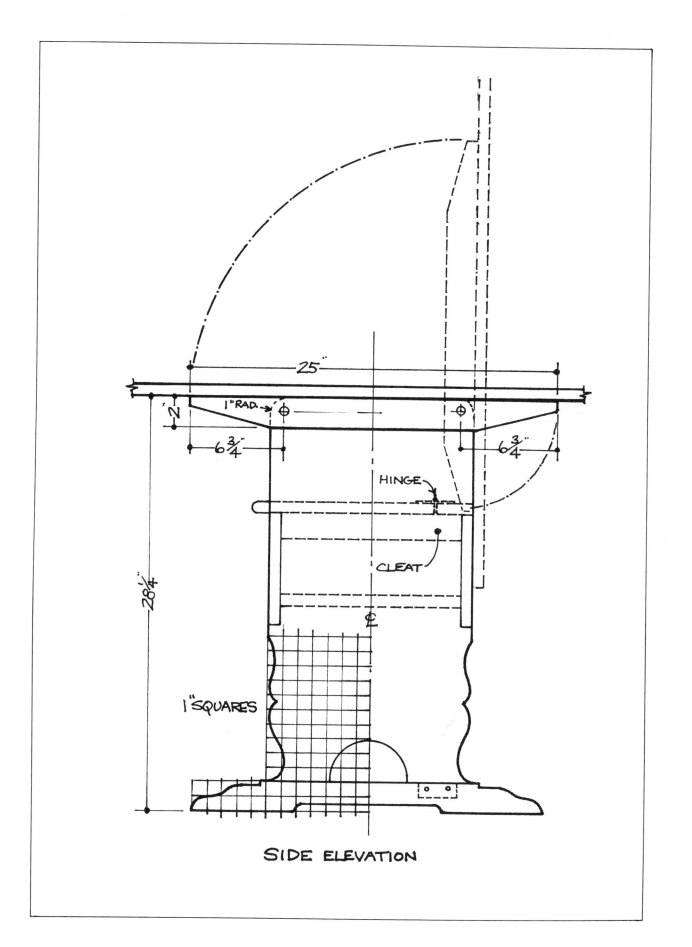

25"

1"RAD.

2"

6 3/4"

6 3/4"

HINGE

CLEAT

28 1/4"

℄

1" SQUARES

SIDE ELEVATION

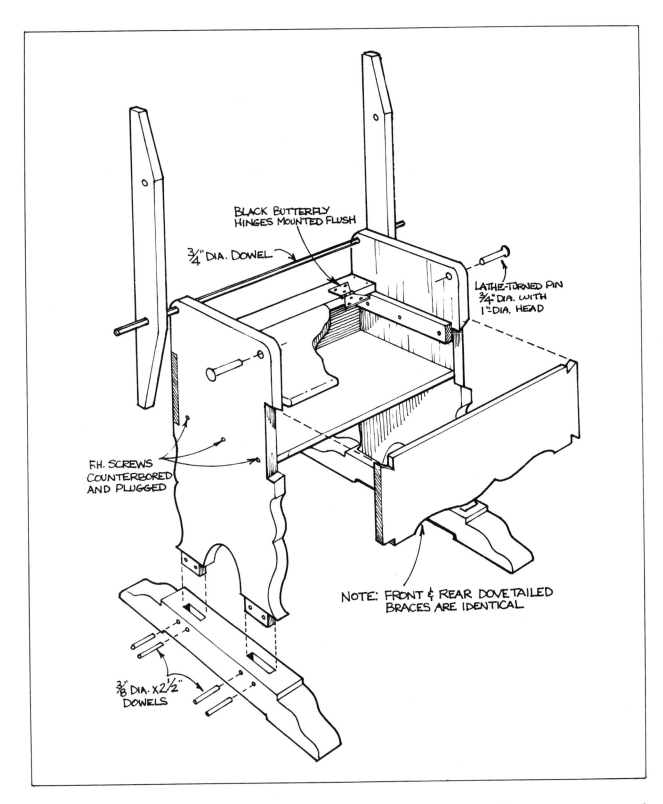

BLACK BUTTERFLY
HINGES MOUNTED FLUSH

¾" DIA. DOWEL

LATHE-TURNED PIN
¾" DIA. WITH
1" DIA. HEAD

F.H. SCREWS
COUNTERBORED
AND PLUGGED

NOTE: FRONT & REAR DOVETAILED
BRACES ARE IDENTICAL

⅜" DIA. X 2½"
DOWELS

the panels to the legs. The exploded view shows the seat-box bottom fastened to the legs with screws and plugs, but it is much more workman-like to dado the bottom into the legs and the front and back panels. With the panels fastened temporarily to the legs, a line can be scribed around the interior surfaces for accurate alignment of the dadoes. Cut these to a depth of ⅜"; then cut the bottom to size, glue it into the dadoes of the legs, and add the panels. Clamp the assembly, tacking on braces to maintain squareness. The dovetailed ends of the panels are secured to the legs with counterbored wood screws covered with ⅜" plugs.

The feet can now be joined permanently to the legs with ⅜" dowel pins driven almost, but not quite, through from the outside. Allow the pins to protrude slightly and round off for an antique pegged effect. Seat-support cleats can now be cut to fit between front and back panels. These are screwed into place from the inside.

The seat lid is made up of two pieces: a narrow hinge cleat, 2½" in width, which is fastened to the top of the back panel with blind dowels or plugged screws; and the lift-up lid, which extends about 1" beyond the legs. Round off the front edges of the seat and install with a pair of 2" black butterfly hinges mounted flush.

The top support cleats are of ¾" stock x 2 x 25". Cleats can be made of 1" stock if you prefer. Shape the cleats and clamp them flush with the top edges of the legs to drill ¾" pin holes through both cleats and legs. Use a backup block to prevent splintering. Shape two front pins from 1"-diameter x 2½" dowel with a knob on one end as shown. Most of these tables had tops that pivoted at the rear on one long dowel that went clear through both cleats, and the example shown employs this arrangement; but you may use two short pins as are used for the front.

The top is made of ¾" stock, edge glued with ⅜" dowels or stopped ¼" plywood splines for strength. Joint the boards, but before locating the dowels, lay the boards out in position, arranging them for the most pleasing grain effect. Locate a 38"-diameter circle. Then plan your dowel or spline locations so that they will not appear at the edges when the top is cut to shape.

After gluing up the slab, take a thin pine batten about 21" in length, and drill a small hole through the center about 1" from one end. Measure 19" from this hole and drill another small hole, big enough for the point of a pencil to ride in. Now fasten the batten to the center of the slab with a small brad through the first hole, and swing the batten in a full circle, scribing the circular shape with the pencil. Cut the top to shape with a saber saw and carefully rasp and sand edges, rounding them off to simulate wear.

Distress surfaces, if so desired, and round off all outer edges of the base with a rasp before sanding with medium to very fine paper. A dark-toned oil stain looks most authentic on this piece, and it is suggested that final finishing be done with a penetrating oil finish, such as Watco Danish Oil or Minwax Antique Oil. This is a simple quick finish that will give the table the soft glow of old, well-worn wood that originally would not have received a hard-surface finish. This type of finish can be applied with a cloth or with the hands, and it is certainly easier than cleaning up and caring for varnish brushes. As with any sealer, though, be sure to cover all surfaces, including inside the seat, to minimize absorption of moisture.

Pine Wall Shelf

This small shelf unit is a pleasant project and will provide an attractive background for display of pewterware, figurines, plants, or perhaps some richly bound old volumes. Construction is entirely of ½″ white pine, with the exception of the drawer bottoms, which are of ⅛″ plywood.

Start by laying out 1″ squares on cardboard or a scrap of Masonite, and enlarge the shapes of the upper back and shelf sides. Use a jigsaw to cut the two templates and then transfer the designs to the pine stock. Cut the sides first and run the three dadoes across each. The upper back edges are given a stopped rabbet as shown. A router makes this work easy, but a fine job can be done with a straightedge and sharp chisel.

Next, cut the two shelves, bottom, scrolled back, and drawer divider to finish size. Don't forget to locate and cut dadoes for the drawer divider. Sand all parts thoroughly before assembling with glue. Be sure to double-check for squareness after clamping, and if you prefer to stain later, remove all glue drippings with a damp cloth.

Although the drawers are small, the woodworker should exercise care in their construction. Shortcut methods, such as nailing the bottom directly to the sides, only detract from the quality of your workmanship. The method of construction shown is a good approach for most light-duty pine drawers. Grooves for the drawer bottoms should be cut wide enough to allow the drawers to slide freely. Use glue and finishing nails to join drawer sides to fronts. After the drawers are completed, glue small stop blocks in each drawer opening, located so that the drawer fronts will come flush with the shelf sides. Install ¾″-diameter wooden or porcelain knobs.

Distress the piece a bit and round off all sharp edges before giving it a finish sanding. Apply an antique pine stain, and after 24 hours finish with a couple of coats of low-luster synthetic varnish. Rub down with 4/0 steel wool to provide an even sheen; then finish off with paste wax.

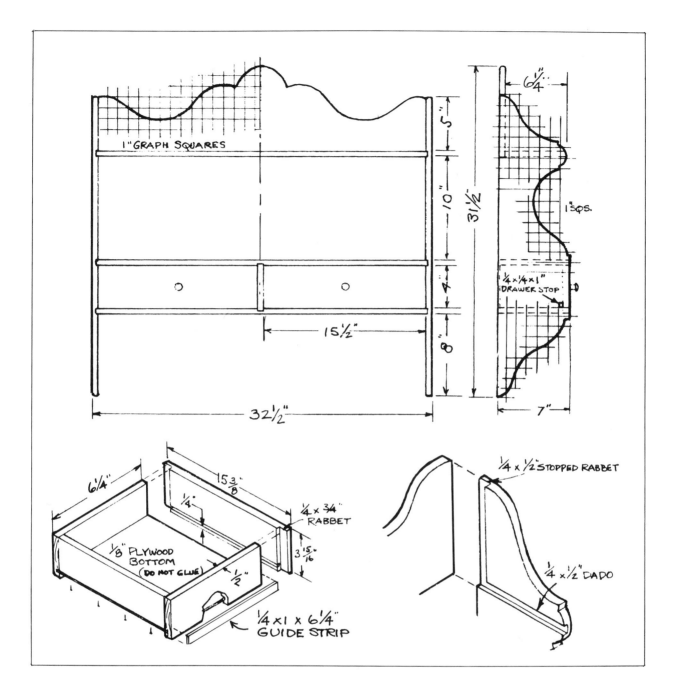

1" GRAPH SQUARES

5"

10"

31½

4"

8"

15½"

32½"

6¼"

1" SQS.

¼ x ¼ x 1"
DRAWER STOP

7"

6¼"

15⅜"

¼"

¼ x ¾"
RABBET

3 15/16"

½"

⅛" PLYWOOD
BOTTOM
(DO NOT GLUE)

¼ x 1 x 6¼"
GUIDE STRIP

¼ x ½ STOPPED RABBET

¼ x ½" DADO

Contemporary Candle Lantern

This lantern was designed to harmonize with contemporary furnishings and yet provide a bit of old-fashioned charm for those who would like the best of both worlds. The basic design probably dates back to sixteenth-century northern Europe and so-called Swedish farm lanterns. Similar examples existed in New England in the late 1600s, and were designed to make use of the very small panes of glass available at the time for diamond-pane casement windows.

Since there is no separate hinged door, construction is quite simple. The only problem you will encounter will be the recessing of the four sides to hold the panes of glass. This operation is simple for those who own an electric router but, if you lack this tool, the job can be accomplished by rough chiseling of the area to be recessed. The bottom of the recess can be leveled off by sharpening the head of a large flat-headed wood screw and driving it far enough into a beam so that the sharpened screw head can be used to plane down the irregularities, as shown in the detail.

Begin by cutting the front and back from ½″ (actual) walnut, cherry, or pine to a finish size of 6 x 10″. Lay out the pane openings and, after clamping both pieces together, use a jigsaw to cut the openings. Next, cut the two sides to 5 x 10″ and again lay out and cut the openings.

The back side of each lantern side must be recessed to a depth of ⁹⁄₁₆″ to hold the glass panes, which are secured either with small brads or short lengths of ⅛ x ⅛″ retaining strips spot glued or bradded in place. The area to be recessed on each side should extend about ³⁄₁₆″ beyond the cutout all around and the center pane divider should be completely recessed, as only one pane of glass is fitted to each side.

Before adding the glass and assembling the lantern, sand all parts carefully and round off edges. Stain, paint, or other finish should then be applied. Use stain or enamel on pine and penetrating oil finish on walnut or cherry.

Fasten the glass in place, apply glue to the butting surfaces of the four sides, and lightly clamp together. When the glue has dried, drill all corners for ⅛″ pegs, which reinforce the joints and provide a decorative touch if they are of contrasting wood.

Cut top and bottom pieces to fit exactly between the sides and drill the various holes shown on the plan. Use the ⅜″ corner holes in the top and bottom to lay out the exact length of the candleholder, which is cut from ½″ stock. Cut this piece at least an inch longer than needed to prevent splitting when drilling the end holes, which are then shaped into slots.

The rod used for lifting the candleholder should be glued into a hole in the holder. The part of the rod that protrudes through the lantern top should be slightly tapered. A brass or wood knob or ball screwed to the top adds a decorative touch, though it is not necessary. Sand the rod so that it slides easily through the top hole. The candle is impaled on a small screw driven through the holder, or you can use a small candle cup or a piece of brass tubing.

Join the top and bottom with glue and ⅜ x 10″ corner rods. Add the candleholder and fasten the entire assembly inside the lantern with eight countersunk brass screws. A piece of brass rod or heavy wire forms the carrying handle, which is secured to the lantern with two screw eyes.

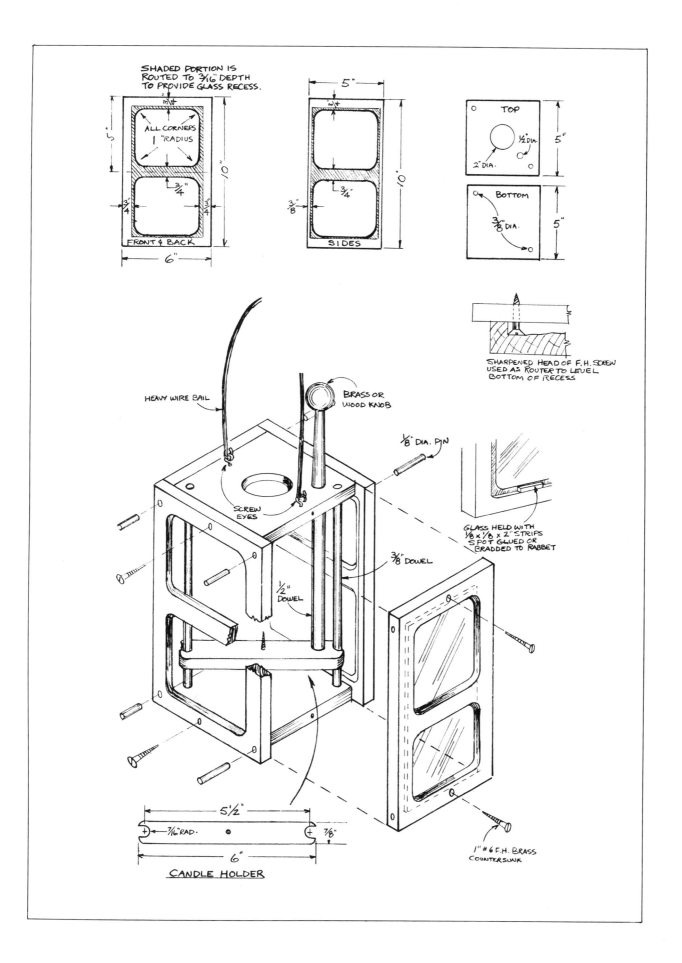

SHADED PORTION IS
ROUTED TO 3/16" DEPTH
TO PROVIDE GLASS RECESS.

3/4"
ALL CORNERS
1" RADIUS
5"
10"
3/4"
3/4"   3/4"
FRONT & BACK
6"

5"
3/4"
10"
3/4"
3/8"
SIDES

TOP
2" DIA.
1/2" DIA.
5"

BOTTOM
3/8" DIA.
5"

SHARPENED HEAD OF F.H. SCREW
USED AS ROUTER TO LEVEL
BOTTOM OF RECESS

HEAVY WIRE BAIL

BRASS OR
WOOD KNOB

1/8" DIA. PIN

SCREW
EYES

GLASS HELD WITH
1/8 x 1/8 x 2" STRIPS
SPOT GLUED OR
BRADDED TO RABBET

3/8" DOWEL

1/2"
DOWEL

5 1/2"
3/16" RAD.
7/8"
6"

CANDLE HOLDER

1" # 6 F.H. BRASS
COUNTERSUNK

Doll Cradle

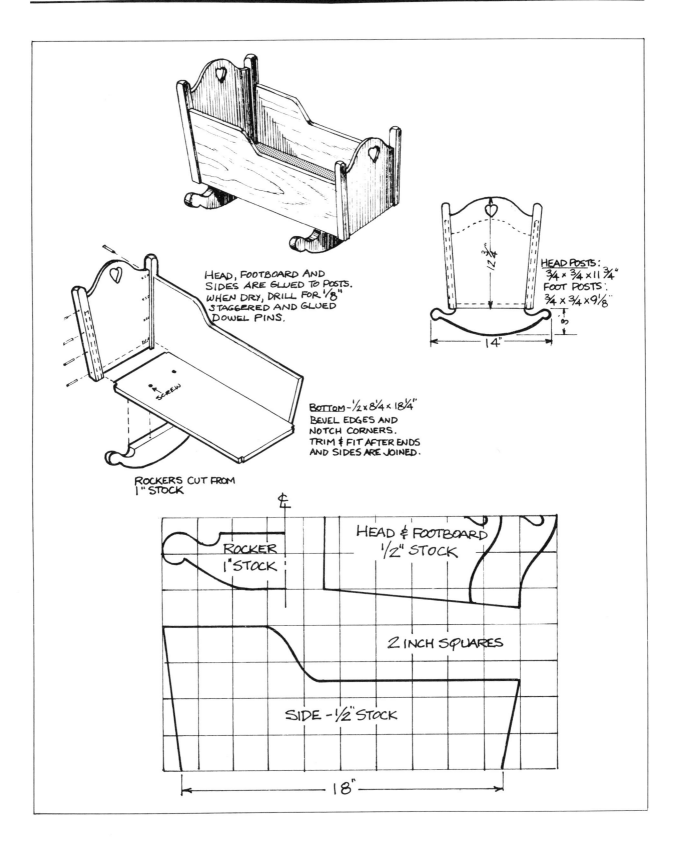

HEAD, FOOTBOARD AND
SIDES ARE GLUED TO POSTS.
WHEN DRY, DRILL FOR 1/8"
STAGGERED AND GLUED
DOWEL PINS.

HEAD POSTS:
3/4 × 3/4 × 11 3/4"
FOOT POSTS:
3/4 × 3/4 × 9 1/8"

12 3/4"

14"

SCREW

BOTTOM — 1/2 × 8 1/4 × 18 1/4"
BEVEL EDGES AND
NOTCH CORNERS.
TRIM & FIT AFTER ENDS
AND SIDES ARE JOINED.

ROCKERS CUT FROM
1" STOCK

ROCKER
1" STOCK

HEAD & FOOTBOARD
1/2" STOCK

2 INCH SQUARES

SIDE — 1/2" STOCK

18"

Collector's Pier Cabinet

This little cabinet, or étagère, will provide an elegant setting for small collectibles. Used alone, or in pairs on a wall or sideboard, it is a decorative accent, and displays keepsakes to best advantage. A fine cabinet wood, such as cherry, is recommended for the outside surfaces. Black walnut, though expensive, will put the piece in an heirloom category. Since the cabinet is relatively small, you may want to consider a fancy veneer treatment of flat surfaces with hardwood moldings stained to match.

The joinery is fussy enough to provide an interesting challenge for the experienced woodworker, but the project is by no means beyond the ability of a careful novice. Most of the case is constructed of ½" stock, while the drawer front and top and bottom panels are of ¾" stock. Pine may be used wherever it will not be seen, including the drawer sides and back.

The best approach is to cut the sides to length first. If a power saw is used, set the blade to 4

degrees for cutting the bevel on the bottom and top edges of each side. The two upper shelves should be joined to the sides with ¼" tenons resting in stopped dadoes. Note that the shelves are set back ¼" from the front edges of the sides. Lay out the sides together and mark ⅛ x ⅛"-deep dadoes 5" in length from the back edge. Cut the dadoes with the blade set 4 degrees from vertical. Next, reset the blade to zero and cut a ¼" rabbet along the back edge of each side to provide for a recessed back panel.

Cut and shape the upper trim piece as shown in Figure 1 and rabbet each end to fit over the ½" sides. Cut this trim a bit long, and after it is joined to the sides with glue it can be trimmed exactly flush with the sloping sides. With the upper trim piece in place, you will have established the width of the cabinet top. Next, prepare the lower shelf from ¾" stock, cutting 6" wide x 11" long. Take care to insure that all cuts are perfectly square to avoid later problems in fitting the moldings. Rabbet both edges of the shelf, as shown in Detail B, and join the shelf to the sides with glue and countersunk 3-penny finishing nails. Undersized pilot holes should first be drilled in hardwood.

After the sides are joined to the bottom shelf, the two upper shelves can be cut for an exact fit. Cut the shelves ¼" longer than the measurement between sides to allow for a ¼ x ⅛" lip on the top edge to match the 5" dadoes previously cut in the sides. All cuts should be made with the saw blade inclined to match the 4-degree slope of the sides. The shelves are 5½" deep and butt against the back panel. Carefully round off the front edges before gluing the shelves in place.

The rabbeted drawer-case sides are glued to the lower shelf as shown in Detail B. Glue a ⅜ x ½" spacer strip to the bottom of the shelf between the sides. The drawer front will stop against this strip. The case bottom is cut from ¾" stock, rabbeted, and joined to the sides as shown in Detail C. Pine can be used for this piece as well as the sub-bottom, as these pieces will be covered by molding. Glue and nail the sub-bot-

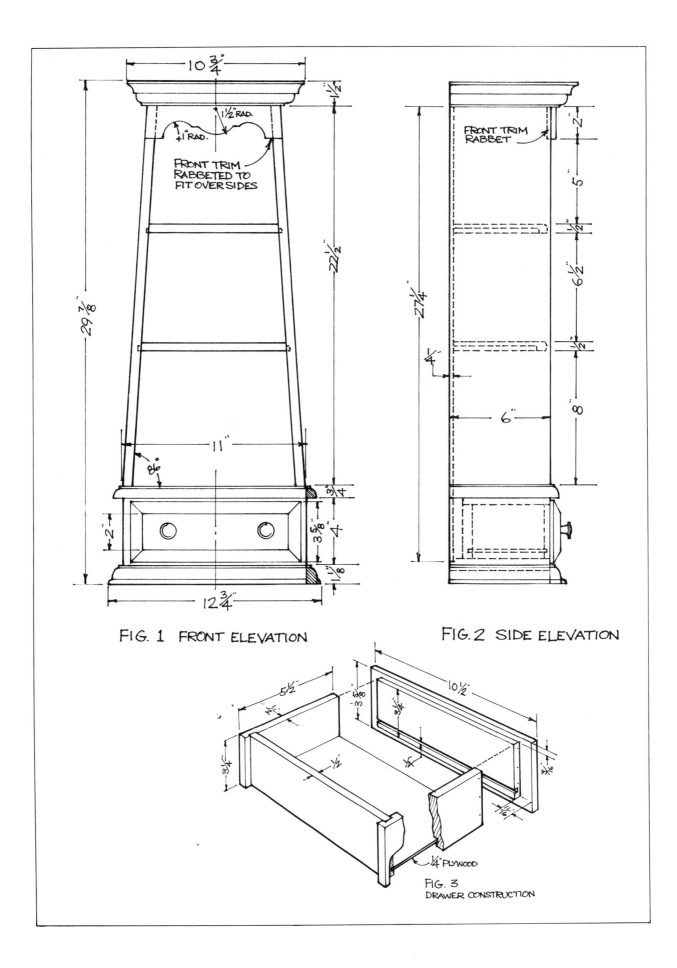

10 3/4"

1/2"

1 1/2" RAD.

1" RAD.

FRONT TRIM
RABBETED TO
FIT OVER SIDES

22 1/2"

29 7/8"

11"

8°

3/4"

3"

3 5/8"

4"

2"

1 1/8"

12 3/4"

FIG. 1 FRONT ELEVATION

FRONT TRIM
RABBET

2"

5"

1/2"

6 1/2"

1/2"

27 1/4"

1/4"

8"

6"

FIG.2 SIDE ELEVATION

5 1/2"

2 1/2"

3 3/8"

10 1/2"

3/4"

3/4"

3 1/2"

1/2"

1/4"

3/16"

1/16"

1/4" PLYWOOD

**FIG. 3
DRAWER CONSTRUCTION**

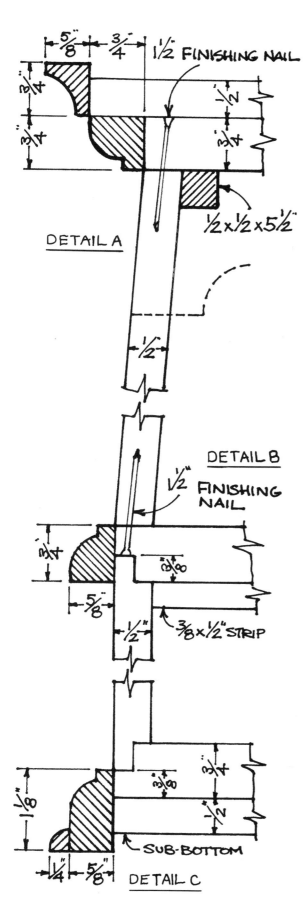

DETAIL A

5/8" 3/4" 1/2 FINISHING NAIL

3/4"

3/4"

1/2"

3/4"

1/2 x 1/2 x 5 1/2"

1/2"

DETAIL B

1/2"

1/2 FINISHING NAIL

3/4"

3/8"

5/8"

1/2"

3/8 x 1/2" STRIP

1/8"

3/8"

3/4"

1/2"

SUB-BOTTOM

1/4" 5/8"

DETAIL C

tom in place, making all edges exactly flush with the bottom.

Shape ⅝ x 1⅛″ molding with a router or by hand, and carefully miter and glue it and the quarter-round molding to the base assembly as shown in Detail C. Assemble the top by gluing two ½ x ½ x 5½″ pine strips to the underside of a ¾ x 8 x 6″ piece of pine. The strips are set in ½″ from each side as shown in Detail A, and must be beveled to fit against the sides of the cabinet. The top assembly is then glued in place and finishing nails driven down through the top into the cabinet sides. Now add the ¾ x ¾″ molding, gluing it to the top with mitered corners. Cut a piece of ½″ pine to fit flush with the outer edges of the molding. This is glued in place as a base to provide support for the upper cove molding.

The back panel can now be cut to shape and glued and bradded into its recess. Use stained ¼″ plywood, or you can paint the back panel. Black, dark green, or Chinese red are excellent colors when used with stained cherry. Consider the possibility of covering the back panel with a fancy wallpaper or veneer.

The drawer front is shaped from ¾″ stock, while the sides and back are of ½″ pine. After beveling the drawer front for a raised panel effect, cut an 11/16″-wide x ¼″-deep rabbet along both ends, and a 3/16″-wide x ¼″-deep rabbet along the top and bottom edges. Groove the back to take a ¼″ plywood bottom, and use this groove to locate matching grooves in the drawer sides. After cutting the grooves, join the back and sides. The bottom is slipped into its grooves, and the front is joined to the sides with glue and finishing nails.

Sand all surfaces of the cabinet thoroughly, working down to a very fine grit. If cherry was used, it will take a stain very evenly because of the density of the wood. The particular shade is up to you, but a darker stain will give the cabinet an "old world" look and accent the items on display. Follow the stain with a sealer coat of shellac mixed half-and-half with alcohol. Sand lightly after the sealer dries, and apply two or three coats of a satin-finish varnish; the final coat should be rubbed down with 4/0 steel wool. Walnut looks best with a penetrating oil finish applied according to the manufacturer's directions. Finally drill holes and add two ¾″ brass knobs to the drawer front.

Butler's Tray Table

This fine mahogany table is based on an eighteenth-century English design. The tray top with hand grips can be removed for serving and features a handsome scrolled rim. The tabletop and tray bottom are of ¼″ mahogany plywood; all other stock is solid Honduras mahogany.

Eighteenth-century English cabinetmakers worked with mahogany cut in the West Indies and Central America. This variety, referred to as Honduras mahogany, is the proper type for reproduction of fine period English and American furniture. Many lumber dealers stock Philippine mahogany, which is not really a mahogany but a type of tropical cedar called Luan or Bataan. This is a lightweight, soft wood, not suitable for most furniture. It is good for shelving, veneering of flush door panels, and boat planking. You may also come across African mahogany, a tough, hard wood, quite handsome with its dark reddish color. This type is often used in boat construction.

Begin construction by gluing and clamping together two lengths of ¾″ mahogany to form the legs—or use solid 1½″ stock. Shape the top of the legs as shown in Detail A. Legs are cut to 16½″ length. Cut the table front, back, and end rails from ¾″ stock and rabbet the upper inside edges of all pieces as shown in Detail B. In addition to the upper edge rabbet, the front and back rails

are rabbeted ¾″ to receive the end rails. Glue and clamp these pieces together taking care to keep the assembly square. Drill pilot holes and glue, clamp, and screw the legs in place as shown in Detail C, using 1¼″ #8 flat-headed screws. Cut a ¼″ plywood top very slightly oversize and plane for a good final fit before gluing and clamping it in place.

The stretchers are cut from ¾″ stock, cut to length and half-notched to receive the lower cross-rail. Glue this assembly together and then glue and clamp it in place between the legs, with its lower edges 5″ up from the bottom of the legs. After the glue has thoroughly dried, mark and drill for ¼″ dowels. Drill the dowel holes 2¼″ in depth. Cut the dowels slightly long and groove them to release trapped air before driving them into the glued holes with a soft mallet. Chisel off the excess dowel.

Cut four rim pieces for the tray from ½″ stock. Run ½″ rabbets on the ends of the front and back rim pieces, and a ¼″ rabbet on the lower inside edge of all the pieces to hold the tray bottom. Enlarge the grid drawings and transfer the pattern to the back and side pieces. Shape with a saber saw. Next drill 1″ holes at each end of the hand grips and remove stock in between with a saber or coping saw. Rasp and sand all curves smooth and round off top edges. Glue and clamp the tray together, again taking care to keep the assembly square. Cut and plane the plywood bottom for a snug fit and attach it with glue and brads.

Sand the entire piece carefully with medium, fine, and very fine sandpaper, rounding the top edges of the tabletop and tray and breaking sharp corners on the legs and stretcher assembly. Dust the piece and apply mahogany stain to the desired tone. After the stain has dried, brush on a wash coat of thinned shellac. For a very smooth finish on open-grained woods such as mahogany, a paste wood filler should be used. Choose a wood filler that is color-tinted to match the mahogany and apply according to the manufacturer's directions. It is best to work a small area at a time, using a short-bristled brush and following the

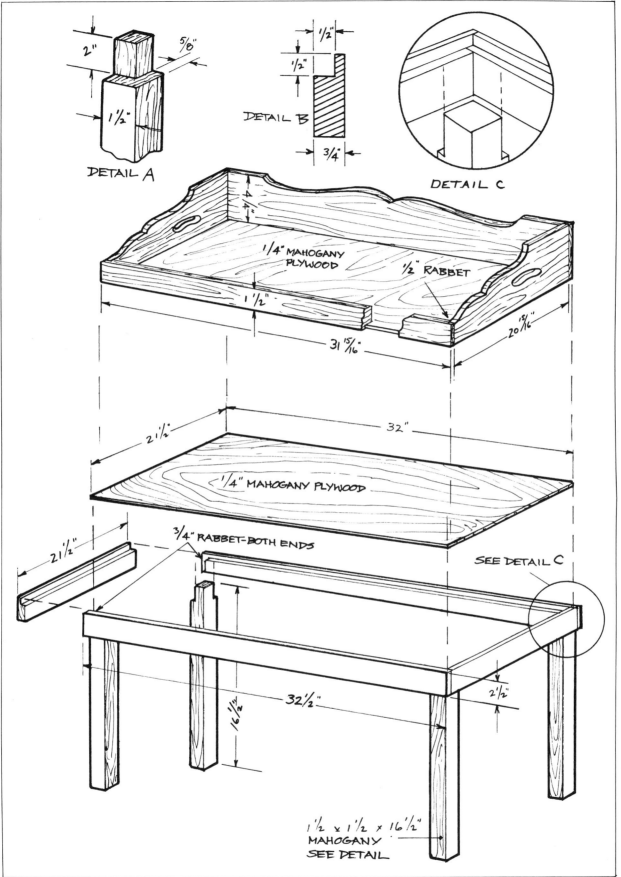

DETAIL A

2"
5/8"
1 1/2"

DETAIL B

1/2"
1/2"
3/4"

DETAIL C

4 1/4"
1/4" MAHOGANY PLYWOOD
1/2" RABBET
1 1/2"
31 15/16"
20 15/16"

21 1/2"
32"
1/4" MAHOGANY PLYWOOD

21 1/2"
3/4" RABBET-BOTH ENDS
SEE DETAIL C
2 1/2"
16 11/2"
32 1/2"

1 1/2 x 1 1/2 x 16 1/2"
MAHOGANY
SEE DETAIL

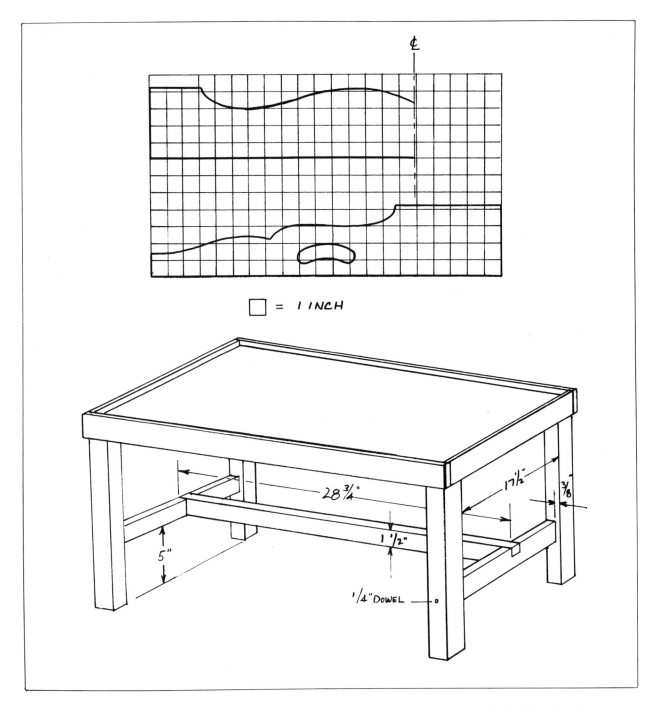

☐ = 1 INCH

grain of the wood. When the filler begins to lose its shine, wipe it off with burlap pads, rubbing across the grain. Follow this by rubbing lightly with a clean cloth until all surplus filler is removed. Allow to dry for at least 24 hours before applying a sealer coat of a half-and-half mixture of varnish and turpentine. When the sealer coat is dry, sand lightly and go over the piece with a tack cloth before laying on a final coat of full-strength satin-finish varnish.

Early American Cupboard

If your kitchen is large enough for it, this country-style cupboard will provide considerable storage space while adding a good deal more charm than additional wall cabinets. It's also a fine dining room piece for storing that set of fancy dishes that is used only occasionally. This is a project that will take quite a few hours to complete, but the joinery is uncomplicated; all phases of construction can be handled by a woodworker with modest skill and equipment. It's a very rewarding piece to build.

White pine is used for the entire project, with the exception of drawer bottoms and upper and lower back panels, which are of ¼" plywood.

Start construction by gluing up ¾" boards to form the sides of the cupboard. Use ⅜" dowel pins to reinforce the joints. After the sides have been glued up, ¾" dadoes are cut for the bottoms of the upper and lower cabinets. A ½" dado is also cut to receive the upper drawer support, and the top edge is rabbeted ¼ x ¾" for the top. To receive the ¼"-thick top and bottom plywood backs, a ¼ x ⅜" stopped rabbet is cut along the inside back edge of the cupboard side (see Figure 1B).

Next the upper and lower front frames are constructed of ¾" pine as shown in Figure 3. All joints are secured with ¼ x 1½" dowel pins, with the exception of the lower door divider and the horizontal drawer rail, which are half-lapped together. Great care must be used in constructing both frames to make them perfectly square with good, tight joints. A doweling jig is a must for this phase of the work.

The lower cabinet bottom is glued up from two boards and trimmed to width to fit in its dadoes; it should be flush with the front edges of the sides and the back of the rear rabbet. Cut the upper drawer support shelf from ½" pine with a rabbet to receive the back panel, and cut the upper cabinet bottom from ¾" pine. These pieces are dadoed to receive the two drawer dividers, which are cut from ¾" stock.

Slip the shelves into their respective dadoes, and join the lower frame to the sides with glue and finishing nails. Screws are better but the screw holes must be counterbored deep enough to insert ⅜"-diameter plugs to hide the screws. Add the plywood back panels and top to help square up the assembly before clamping. Double-check for squareness before applying pipe clamps and letting the glue dry. If you have enough pipe clamps, add the upper frame also; otherwise, do one at a time.

Next, begin work on the upper and lower doors. Details A, B, and C of Figure 2 show the specifications for construction of the raised panel doors. Cut all door frames, allowing for the ⅜" lip, and groove them as shown to receive frame tenons and panels. Cut tenons on each end of the

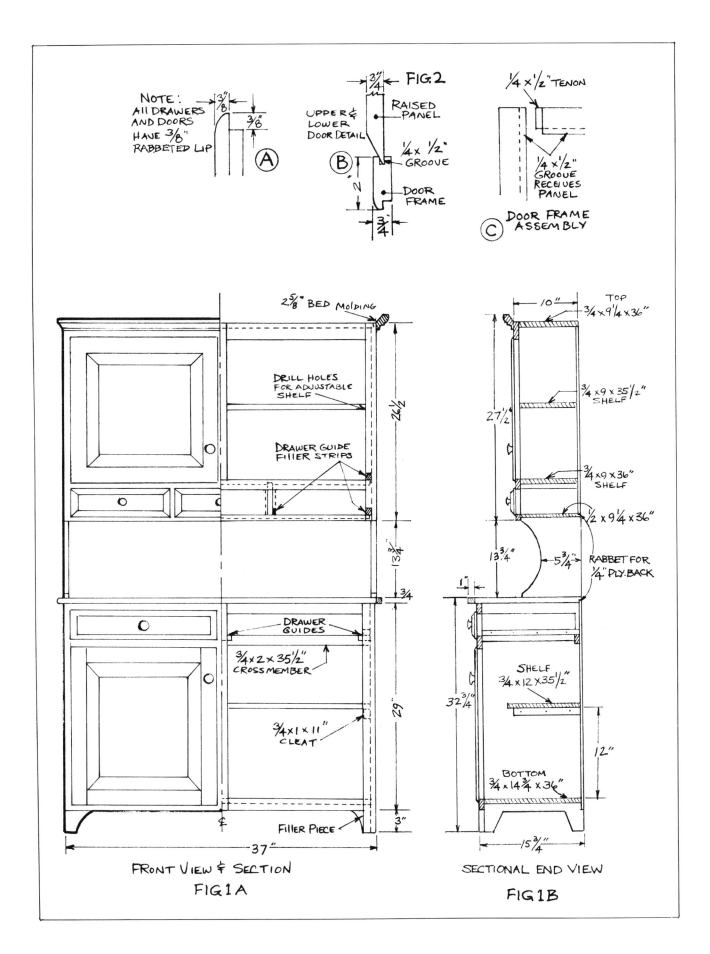

NOTE:
All DRAWERS
AND DOORS
HAVE 3/8"
RABBETED LIP

3"/8

3/8"

(A)

FIG. 2

3"/4

RAISED PANEL

UPPER & LOWER DOOR DETAIL

(B)

1/4 x 1/2" GROOVE

DOOR FRAME

2"

3/4"

1/4 x 1/2" TENON

1/4 x 1/2" GROOVE RECEIVES PANEL

(C) DOOR FRAME ASSEMBLY

2 5/8" BED MOLDING

DRILL HOLES FOR ADJUSTABLE SHELF

DRAWER GUIDE FILLER STRIPS

26 1/2"

13 3/4"

3/4"

DRAWER GUIDES

3/4 x 2 x 35 1/2" CROSS MEMBER

29"

3/4 x 1 x 11" CLEAT

FILLER PIECE

3"

37"

FRONT VIEW & SECTION
FIG 1A

10"

TOP
3/4 x 9 1/4 x 36"

3/4 x 9 x 35 1/2" SHELF

27 1/2"

3/4 x 9 x 36" SHELF

1/2 x 9 1/4 x 36"

13 3/4"

5 3/4"

RABBET FOR 1/4" PLY. BACK

1"

SHELF
3/4 x 12 x 35 1/2"

32 3/4"

12"

BOTTOM
3/4 x 14 3/4 x 36"

15 3/4"

SECTIONAL END VIEW
FIG 1B

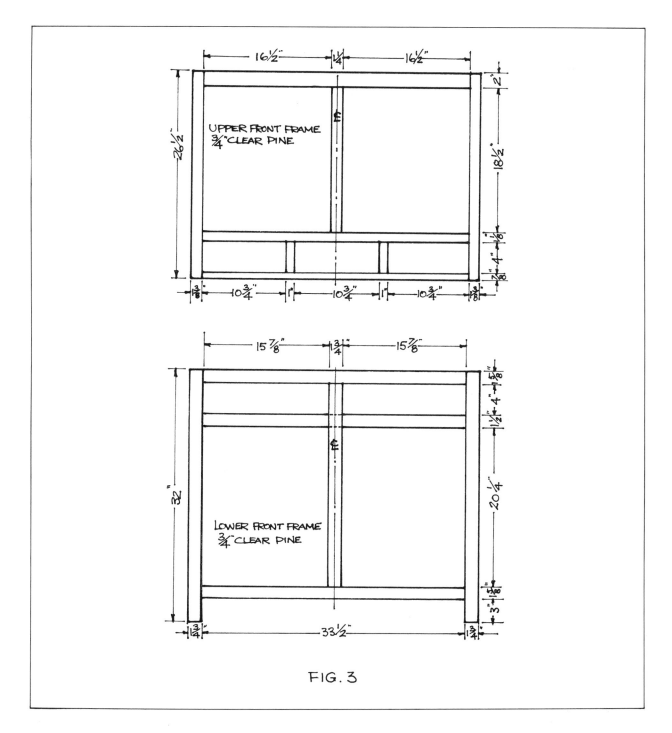

UPPER FRONT FRAME
¾" CLEAR PINE

LOWER FRONT FRAME
¾" CLEAR PINE

FIG. 3

horizontal frames to match the grooves. Panels are glued up to width and run through the table saw with the blade inclined at 18 degrees. When gluing up the doors, apply glue to the tenoned corner joints, but do not glue the panels; they should be free to contract and expand in their grooves. After the glue has dried, run a ⅜″ rabbet around all edges of the doors, then round off the outer edges.

Glue ¾″ stock together to form the countertop.

Carefully cut notches in each end to fit around the cupboard sides and cut a ¼ x ⅜″ rabbet in the back edge for the back panel. Before adding the countertop and its trim, the lower drawer guides and shelf cleats should be installed. The back supporting crossmember is fastened level across the plywood back with screws driven through the plywood. The three drawer supports, which are each made up of two pieces, are then cut, glued, and nailed together so that the upper piece,

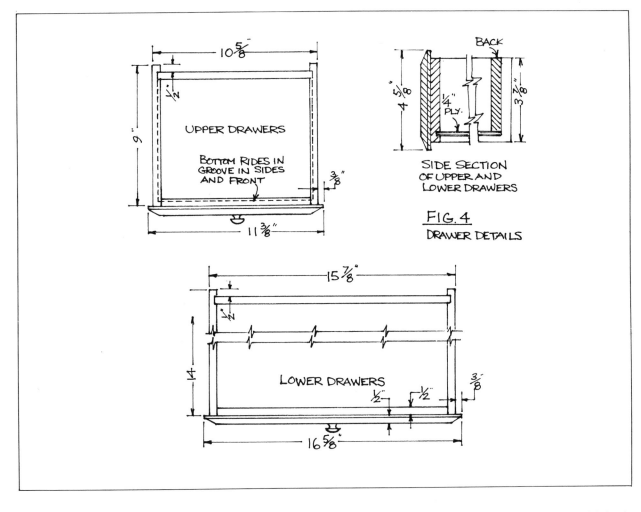

UPPER DRAWERS

BOTTOM RIDES IN GROOVE IN SIDES AND FRONT

SIDE SECTION OF UPPER AND LOWER DRAWERS

FIG. 4
DRAWER DETAILS

LOWER DRAWERS

which is ¾″ longer, can be screwed to the rear crossmember. (This is shown in the exploded view and Figure 1B.) The center support must be wide enough to support both drawers. Cut it to fit snugly between the crossmember and the front frame, and drill two ¼″ holes through the frame and into the support. Drive two dowel pins in to firmly attach this member. Side supports are screwed to cupboard sides, as are lower shelf cleats. You can now install the countertop, gluing and nailing it to the sides and front frame. Cut 1″ trim and fasten it to the counter and sides with glue and finishing nails. The front corners of the trim should be mitered.

Drawers are all lipped, with beveled fronts; Figure 4 gives construction details. Drawer fronts are made up of two pieces of ½″ pine, glued together to allow a ⅜″ lip at top and bottom and a ⅜″ lip at both ends. Drawer bottoms can be either ¼″ plywood or Masonite.

Finally, a length of 2⅝″ bed molding is mitered and nailed to the top of the cupboard to provide

a handsome trim. Crown molding, which is shown in the exploded view, can also be used. The photo shows the cupboard with a bed molding, which is a bit more difficult to miter.

Obviously, there's a lot of sanding work involved in finishing the piece, but some planing and distress marks will add character, so don't overwork yourself trying to remove every little defect. Our cupboard was sanded with medium-grit paper before assembly, and after assembly a fine-grit paper was used; but various dents and gouges which accumulated in the construction process were left. All edges were rounded a bit and one coat of Minwax Early American stain was applied; this was followed by a coat of full-strength urethane varnish. The entire piece was then given a light sanding followed by dusting with a tack cloth. A final coat of satin urethane varnish was applied. All nail holes were filled with color-matched wax, and wooden knobs and black H hinges were installed.

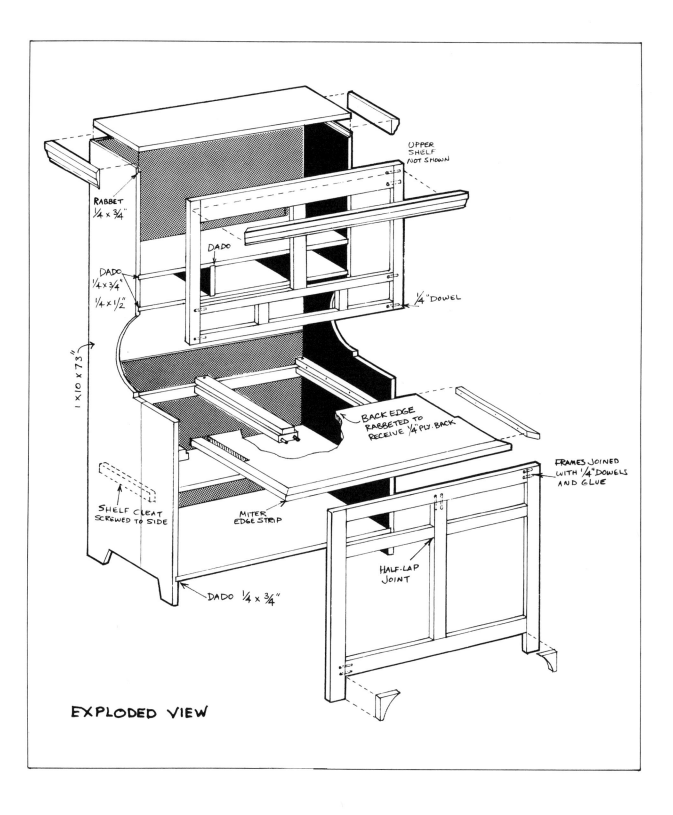

RABBET
¼ × ¾"

UPPER
SHELF
NOT SHOWN

DADO

DADO
¼ × ¾"

¼ × 1½"

¼" DOWEL

1 × 10 × 73"

BACK EDGE
RABBETED TO
RECEIVE ¼" PLY. BACK

FRAMES JOINED
WITH ¼" DOWELS
AND GLUE

SHELF CLEAT
SCREWED TO SIDE

MITER
EDGE STRIP

HALF-LAP
JOINT

DADO ¼ × ¾"

EXPLODED VIEW

Two Duck Decoys

One thousand years ago, American Indians tied bundles of reeds and grasses together to form lifelike duck decoys. The art of handcrafting wooden decoys flourished in the mid- and late nineteenth century, when professional market hunters armed with huge bore shotguns inflicted a fearful toll on the wild duck population. Old decoys have since become prized collectors' items, and most now serve as decorative pieces.

The decoy designs offered here can be used either for hunting or as decoration. However you intend to use them, we're sure that you will find them most enjoyable and surprisingly easy projects, as no great carving skill is required.

While many craftsmen prefer cedar for decoys, you'll find that white pine is entirely satisfactory, and much easier to work with as it does not splinter as easily as cedar. About 8 feet of ½ x 8″ pine is needed for the body of the mallard, which is the bigger of the two designs. The head is carved from a separate block that can be solid or glued-up stock.

Enlarge and transfer the shape of each layer to cardboard, or plywood patterns if you wish to make a number of the decoys. If you have one, a band saw is ideal for sawing several identical pieces at once; otherwise, use a coping or saber saw. Note that certain layers have a central cutout that forms a hollow cavity within the decoy. This cavity helps make the decoy buoyant and reduces the weight of the decoy—no small matter when a dozen have to be transported to the hunting site.

After the layers have been cut out and drilled for ⅜″ dowels, assemble them as shown in Figure 5. Be sure to use waterproof glue between the layers if you intend to use the decoys for hunting. Clamp the stack and allow to dry overnight. The dowels should be cut about 2″ longer than necessary, and the excess length extended beyond the bottom layer. A length of 2 x 4″ drilled to receive the dowels will provide a convenient means of securing the decoy in a vise or clamping it to a work surface for easier shaping.

Pencil the outline of the head on a block of pine and drill the ⅜″ hole for mounting the head. Rough cut the head to shape and mount it on the front dowel. To carve the body to shape, merely remove stock until all the edges disappear. A Stanley Surform® does an excellent job of quickly removing excess wood. Follow up with a bastard file, which will give the slightly rough effect needed for a natural appearance. Fair the neck into the body with small circular and half-round files, and carve the head to shape with a sharp knife and files. The head should be somewhat narrow on top, flaring out to the cheeks. Authentic glass eyes look best and can be purchased from a local sporting goods dealer or from a taxidermy supply house. Check the classified section of the hunting and fishing magazines for these suppliers. You can also drill holes for black beads or small glass marbles which would then be epoxied in place.

After the decoy has been shaped, apply a couple of coats of sealer and paint the plumage with flat outdoor enamel or oil paint. Figure 6 provides a general guide for the final painting, but your best bet is to examine other decoys, or check with the local library for a book showing the drakes in full color.

If the decoys are to be used for decorative pieces, trim the projecting dowel stubs off and cover the bottom of the decoy with green felt; or leave about one inch of the stubs and mount the decoy on a 1½″- to 2″-thick base. Figure 7 shows how the decoy can be mounted on a pine or hardwood oval or rectangle with hardware added to

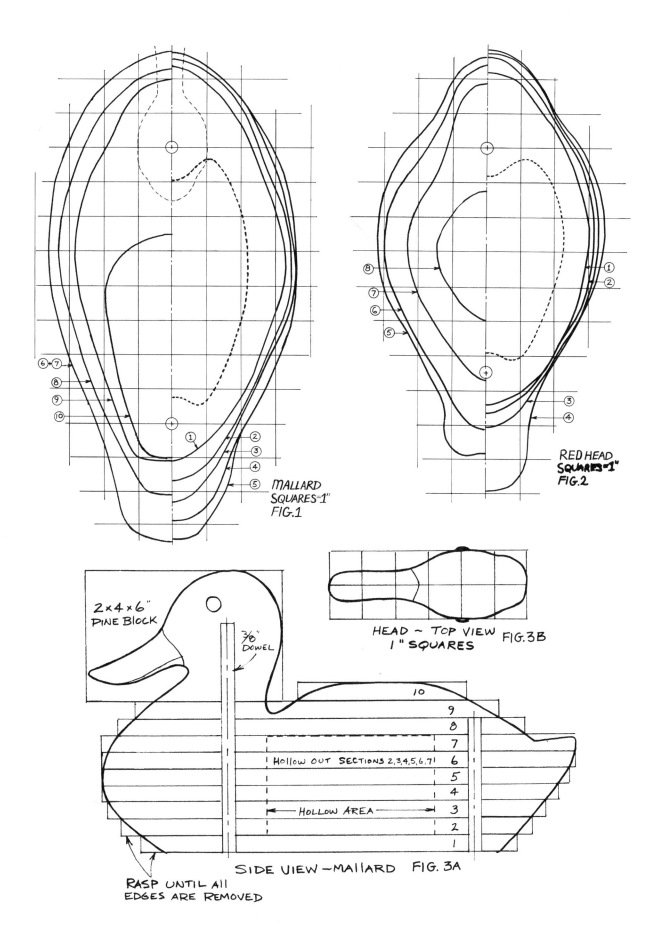

MALLARD
SQUARES=1"
FIG.1

⑥・⑦
⑧
⑨
⑩
① ② ③ ④ ⑤

RED HEAD
SQUARES=1"
FIG.2

⑧ ⑦ ⑥ ⑤
① ② ③ ④

2×4×6"
PINE BLOCK

3/8"
DOWEL

HEAD ~ TOP VIEW   FIG.3B
1" SQUARES

10
9
8
7
Hollow out sections 2,3,4,5,6,7   6
5
4
HOLLOW AREA   3
2
1

SIDE VIEW – MALLARD   FIG. 3A

RASP UNTIL All
EDGES ARE REMOVED

77

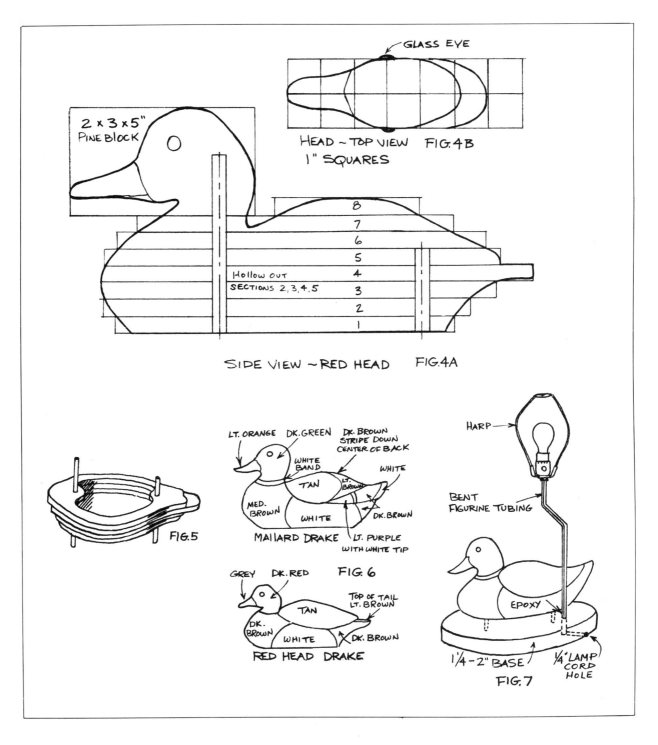

GLASS EYE

HEAD ~ TOP VIEW   FIG.4B
1" SQUARES

2 x 3 x 5"
PINE BLOCK

8
7
6
5
Hollow out   4
Sections 2,3,4,5   3
2
1

SIDE VIEW ~ RED HEAD   FIG.4A

FIG.5

LT. ORANGE DK.GREEN DK. BROWN
STRIPE DOWN
CENTER OF BACK
WHITE
BAND
TAN   WHITE
LT.
BROWN
MED.
BROWN
WHITE   DK. BROWN
MALLARD DRAKE   LT. PURPLE
WITH WHITE TIP

FIG. 6

GREY   DK. RED   FIG. 6
TAN
TOP OF TAIL
LT. BROWN
DK.
BROWN
WHITE   DK. BROWN
RED HEAD DRAKE

HARP

BENT
FIGURINE TUBING

EPOXY

1¼-2" BASE   ¼" LAMP
CORD
HOLE
FIG. 7

convert it into a lamp that will be a most handsome addition to the den or family room. If the decoys will be used for hunting, it will probably be necessary to add a strip of lead to serve as a keel. This can be secured with a flat-headed screw and a screw eye which will hold the mooring line. The floating characteristics of the decoy will determine how much lead is needed.

Countinghouse Desk

This desk is representative of the type generally used in mercantile establishments in the early nineteenth century. There were many variations, some with an impressive array of pigeonholes and drawers, and, of course, a matching high stool. Admittedly, the need for these desks went out with handwritten ledgers and eyeshades, but they still have great charm as decorative furniture with considerable storage space. If a mirror is fitted to the underside of the lid, the desk makes a most unusual vanity or dressing table.

Construction is relatively straightforward, and although the example shown is made of white pine, cherry or maple may be used for an equally handsome natural finish. The legs are cut from 2″-square stock (actually 1¾″) and they are tapered on all four sides, down to 1″ square at the foot. The taper should begin about 7″ from the top end, just below the drawer frames. A taper jig will be helpful in roughing out the legs, though they should be finish planed after being cut with a table or radial arm saw.

The drawer frames and the upper rail are cut from ¾″ pine (actual). The front and rear drawer frames are secured to the legs with two ⅜″ dowel pins. Side rails are glued and clamped between the front and rear leg assemblies, and the center rail drawer support is doweled to the front and rear frames. The top rail is glued in place flush with the tops of the front legs. Be sure to set side drawer frames in ⅛″ from the outer surfaces of the legs to allow for the addition of side panels, which are inset ⅛″.

The side panels are added next and are glued and nailed to the lower side frames. Use finishing nails and set them below the surface. The counter may now be glued to width from two or three boards. The front to rear dimension of the countertop is exactly the same as the distance between the outer edges of the front and rear legs. The counter is fastened in place overhanging the front legs by ¾″ leaving a ¾″ space at the rear for the backboard.

Cut the box sides and front as shown in the detail and join to the counter with blind ⅜″ dowel pins. The front of the slanted box can be joined to the sides with two dowel pins at each corner as shown, but a dovetailed box joint at this point will add considerable visual interest to the piece. A chest lock and escutcheon should be added to the front of the box. The mortising for this hardware can best be accomplished before the front is joined to the sides. The rear box top is glued and nailed to the sides.

Enlarge the pattern for the backboard and transfer the shape to a ¾ x 10″ board. After shaping the backboard, fasten it to the rear counter edge and box sides with glue and finishing nails. The upper sides of the desk can now be shaped and fastened to the counter edges and backboard. The front edge of the counter should extend about ¼″ beyond the front ends of the upper sides.

The upper drawer supports are cut from ½″ pine for a snug fit, and fitted in place with glue and nails. The pigeonhole shelf is assembled separately to fit snugly inside the box, and is fastened by gluing and clamping the plywood top to

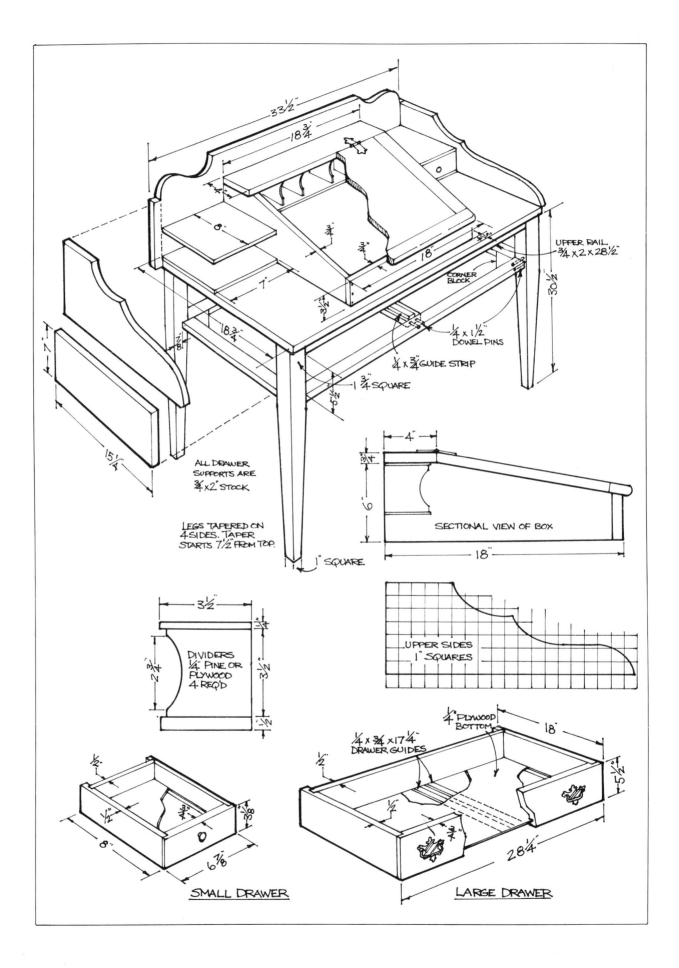

33½"

18¾"

UPPER RAIL
¾ x 2 x 28½"

18"

CORNER
BLOCK

30½"

¼ x 1½"
DOWEL PINS

¼ x ¾ GUIDE STRIP

1¾" SQUARE

7"

7/8"

18¾"

15¼"

ALL DRAWER
SUPPORTS ARE
¾ x 2" STOCK

LEGS TAPERED ON
4 SIDES. TAPER
STARTS 7½" FROM TOP.

1" SQUARE

4"

¾"

6"

SECTIONAL VIEW OF BOX

18"

UPPER SIDES
1" SQUARES

3½"

2¾"

3½"

DIVIDERS
¼" PINE OR
PLYWOOD
4 REQD

½"

¼"
PLYWOOD
BOTTOM

18"

¼ x ¾ x 17¼"
DRAWER GUIDES

½"

5½"

½"

¾"

SMALL DRAWER

8"

6⅞"

3/8"

28¼"

LARGE DRAWER

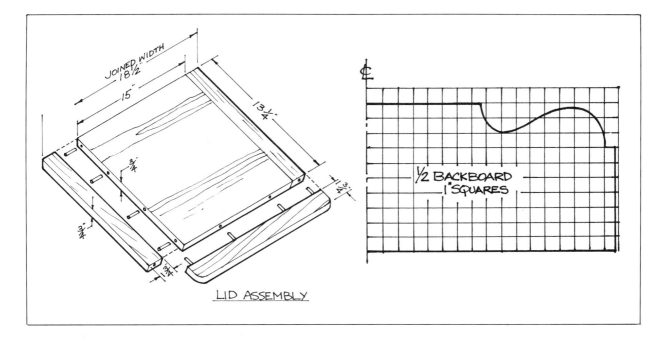

JOINED WIDTH 18½"

15"

13¾"

¾"

¾"

4⅛"

¾"

¾"

LID ASSEMBLY

₵

½ BACKBOARD
1" SQUARES

the underside of the box top. The ¼″ partitions are best cut by resawing from a thicker board. If plywood is used, the problem of hiding the plies can be solved by omitting the curved front edge and gluing a thin strip of pine over the plywood edge. If you wish to take the time, the partitions are best fastened by cutting stopped dadoes in the top and the bottom shelf; otherwise join the pieces with glue and brads.

The lid consists of a glued-up slab of ½″ stock with the grain running as shown. Edge cleats are of ¾″ stock and are fastened with ¼″ blind dowel pins. The ¼″ recess thus formed on the underside of the lid can be used to hold a vanity mirror secured with small moldings bradded in place. The back edge of the lid should be planed to a bevel. Brass hinges of the type shown are found at most hardware stores, and look very attractive against stained wood.

The large drawer and two smaller drawers are made up with ¾″ fronts, rabbeted and grooved to receive ½″ pine sides and ¼″ bottoms. Glue the sides to the fronts, and when they are dry drill through the sides into the fronts for three ¼″ dowel pins per side. This process makes a sturdy joint without resorting to dovetails.

Sand the entire piece carefully and round off

all sharp edges. If you have used pine, a little distressing with a tire chain and awl will add character to the piece. Distressing should be done before the stain is applied. Brush or wipe on the stain of your choice, looking for areas where glue smears prevent the stain from getting to the wood. Small glue-smeared areas can be shaved off with a chisel or gouge down to the bare wood for restaining. Do this before the stain on adjoining surfaces dries to facilitate blending of the patched area. Small gouged areas will blend in with the overall distressing.

After the stain has dried, seal the entire piece with a thinned sealer such as shellac mixed half-and-half with alcohol. Next, sand lightly to cut raised grain "whiskers." Finish the piece with at least two coats of satin varnish. After allowing plenty of time for drying, go over all visible surfaces with 4/0 steel wool to remove dust specks and give the piece an even, soft sheen. Finally, add the hardware of your choice. The Chippendale drawer pulls shown on the example are not really authentic for a nineteenth-century piece, but they certainly look good with a dark stain. You may wish to consider Hepplewhite embossed oval pulls for the large drawer, and small round brass knobs for the small drawers.

Shaker-style Step Stool

This small step stool with its lidded storage compartment is a handy addition to any household, whether decorated in traditional or contemporary style. The piece is pure Shaker, combining sturdy construction with clean, functional design. Pine, oak, and maple are all appropriate woods for building the step stool. Just be sure to use well-seasoned, flat stock or you will have some problems cutting the dadoes.

Begin construction by cutting the sides of the step stool from ¾″ stock. Lay out the dadoes on both pieces side by side so that the slots will coincide exactly. Note that the horizontal dado is ¼ x ¾″, while the vertical dado is ¼ x ½″. Cut the dadoes with a saw and chisel or with power equipment. Next, lay out and cut notches for the ½″ back panel, and then lay out and cut the front and bottom curves.

The back and front panels are cut from ½″ stock, while the lid and step are of ¾″ stock. Cut all parts squarely and sand carefully before joining with glue. Keep the assembly clamped overnight if possible so that the glue has plenty of time to cure. Cut the lid and cleat to size, and glue and nail the cleat to the top edge of the front, using countersunk finishing nails.

Before adding hinges, go over the piece, breaking all sharp corners with sandpaper to give it a worn look; then apply the stain of your choice. At least three coats of a tough urethane satin finish will keep the step stool looking good for years. Be sure to seal all surfaces, including the storage compartment and the underside.

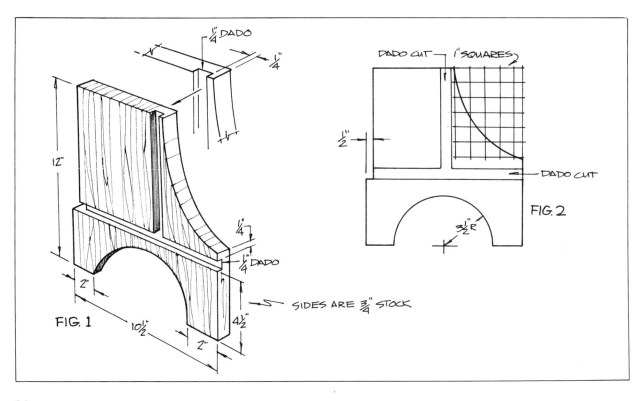

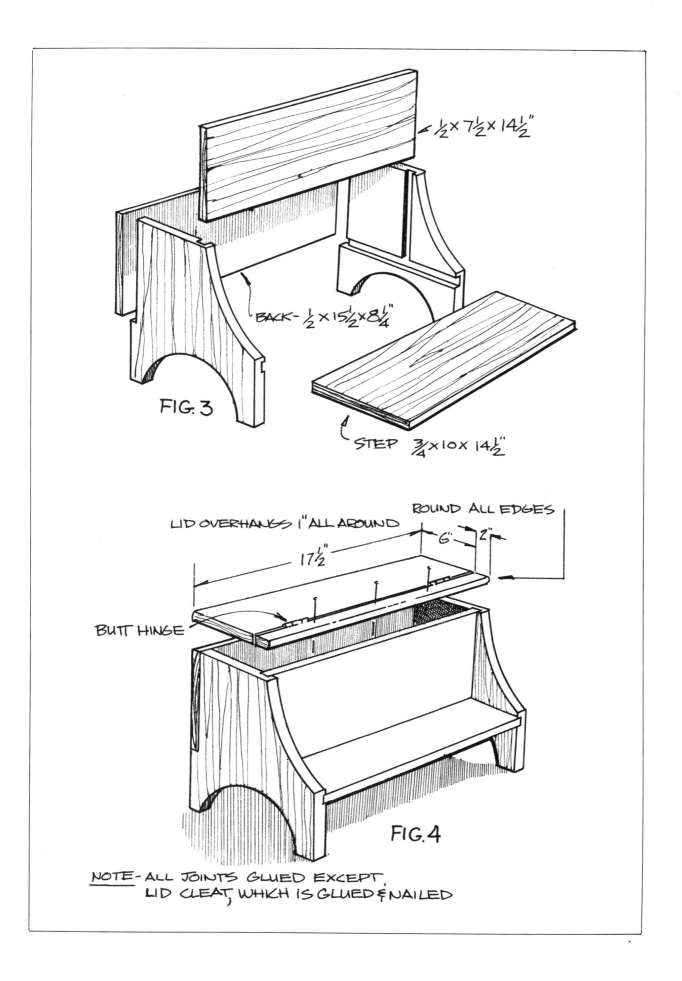

$\frac{1}{2} \times 7\frac{1}{2} \times 14\frac{1}{2}"$

BACK— $\frac{1}{2} \times 15\frac{1}{2} \times 8\frac{1}{4}"$

FIG. 3

STEP $\frac{3}{4} \times 10 \times 14\frac{1}{2}"$

LID OVERHANGS 1" ALL AROUND

ROUND ALL EDGES

6"

2"

$17\frac{1}{2}"$

BUTT HINGE

FIG. 4

NOTE— ALL JOINTS GLUED EXCEPT
LID CLEAT, WHICH IS GLUED & NAILED

Cube Table

This smartly styled contemporary table is mounted on casters for mobility. The lower portion is open at both front and back, and will hold a good number of books or magazines. It is made of ¾″ plywood and covered in plastic laminate in whatever color or wood grain that appeals to you.

Samples of plastic laminates are available at most building supply dealers and come in a wide variety of colors, textures, and wood grains, such as walnut and Brazilian rosewood. A handsome effect can be achieved using the maple butcher-block laminate with the drawer front and bookcase interior enameled in a bright, contrasting color. Of course, the plywood surface can also be painted, or covered with real wood veneer.

Begin construction by cutting the four sides, top, and bottom panels to the sizes indicated. Note that the side panels are narrower than the front and back ones in order to butt between them. Cut out the drawer and book openings in the front panel, and the book opening in the back panel, using a keyhole or saber saw and clamped guide strip to insure straight cuts.

Run ¼″ dadoes along the bottom edges of both side panels to hold the bottom, which is set with its upper surface flush with the book opening. Assemble the components with glue and finishing nails, or better still, with blind dowel pins. Leave the top off until the drawer runners have been installed.

Drawer construction is shown in the detail. The drawer front is shaped from ¾″ clear pine with a lip on all edges. The drawer sides are fastened to the front with glue and brads. When assembling the drawer, make sure that it's perfectly square and flat. Drawer runners are cut from ¾″ pine to fit between the table's front and back panels. A rabbet is cut for the drawer sides to ride on. Fit the drawer runners accurately by laying the table on its side, inserting the drawer, and while the drawer is in place, gluing in the runners, lightly touching the bottom edges of the drawer sides. When the glue has dried, secure the runners with three 1¼″ #6 flat-headed countersunk wood screws. Now add on the top with glue and finishing nails, and carefully sand all panel surfaces and adjoining edges to provide a flat surface for the laminate, veneer, or other finish.

If you decide to use laminate, cut the pieces a bit oversize to allow trimming. Work one surface at a time using contact cement according to the manufacturer's instructions. Trim each laminate panel before going on to the next adjoining panel. The top covering is added last. Seal and paint the drawer front and bookcase interior. The inside of the drawer should be sealed with varnish to keep a clean appearance, and swelling problems will be reduced if both wide surfaces of the drawer sides are sealed as well. Choose a contemporary-style drawer knob and fasten it to the drawer front.

Mount plate-type casters by screwing them to the plywood bottom at each corner. Be sure to allow each caster enough room to swivel freely. Casters of 1¼″ size are usually 1⅝″ high, so this allows ⅜″ clearance between the floor and the bottom edges of the table. If you have very deep pile or shag carpeting, it may be better to omit the casters.

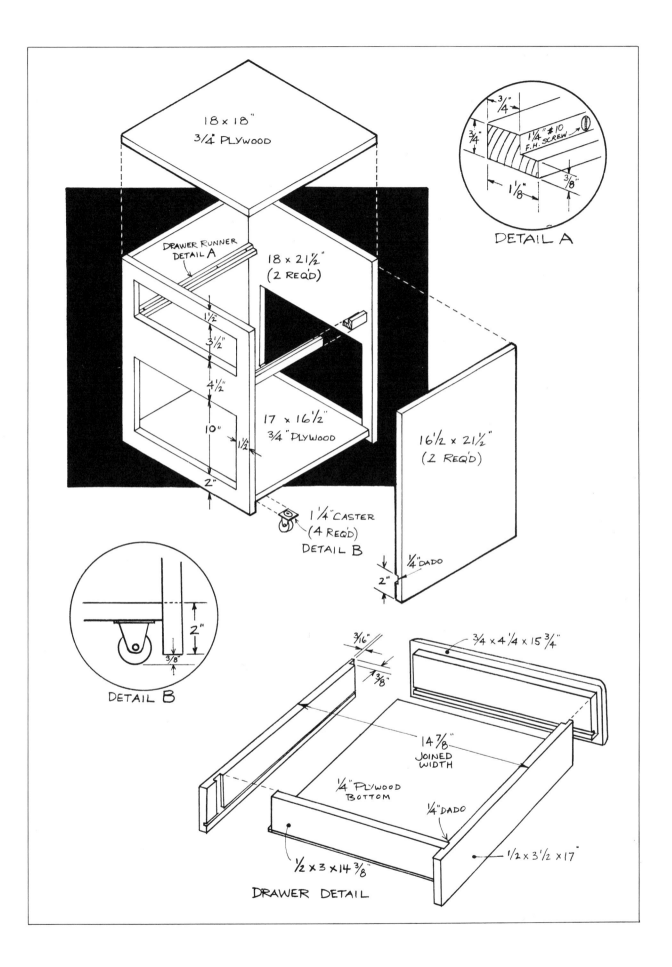

18 x 18"
3/4" PLYWOOD

DRAWER RUNNER
DETAIL A

18 x 21½"
(2 REQ'D)

1½"
3½"
4½"
10"
1½"
2"

17 x 16½"
3/4" PLYWOOD

16½ x 21½"
(2 REQ'D)

1¼" CASTER
(4 REQ'D)
DETAIL B

3/4"
3/4"
1¼" #10
F.H. SCREW
3/8"
1⅛"

DETAIL A

2"
3/8"

DETAIL B

¼" DADO
2"

3/16"
3/8"
3/4 x 4¼ x 15¾"

14⅞"
JOINED
WIDTH

¼" PLYWOOD
BOTTOM

¼" DADO

½ x 3 x 14⅜

½ x 3½ x 17"

DRAWER DETAIL

Parsons Table

The Parsons table has become a twentieth-century furniture classic. Simple uncluttered lines, perfect proportions, and great versatility insure that its popularity will continue for generations. This table can be built for dining, as a coffee or end table, bedside table, or, in a small version, as a bunching table that can be arranged to meet any need. Incidentally, the name has nothing to do with the clergy. The table derives its name from the renowned Parsons School of Design, which originated it in the 1930s.

This particular version makes use of an inset top of whatever material suits your fancy. The drawings show the table with a flush top of 12"-square decorative floor tiles. By all means, use any other appropriate material, or even make removable panels so that you can have a variety of tops. Consider parquet flooring, gauged slate, marble, or a fancy veneered panel. If your tastes run to very contemporary furniture and you enjoy the visual impact of very graphic styles, these tables can be enameled in bright colors, or even covered with fabric. The possibilities are almost limitless.

This table is 24½" square and 22" high. These dimensions may be changed, but to preserve the basic design the side aprons and legs should be the same width. Use extreme care in building this table, particularly if it is to receive a clear finish, as all joints must fit perfectly for a clean, smooth look. A hardwood is preferred as it can be machined more accurately to close tolerances than soft pine. Birch is an excellent choice if a light, natural finish is desired. If the table is to be painted, use poplar or kiln-dried fir.

Glue up stock for the legs and lay out notches on the tops. Keep cuts to the waste side of lines, making a check first, followed by cuts into the end grain. The distance from the notch to the top of the leg is 2¾" less the thickness of the plywood panel and top covering. If ³⁄₃₂" flooring tile is used, this dimension will be 2⁵⁄₃₂". Trim the legs to a finish length of 21½".

The side aprons are shaped next. The depth of the rabbet on these aprons will also be determined by the thickness of the material used for the top, plus the ½" plywood. As insurance, cut the aprons a bit wide, to 2⅛". This extra rabbet depth will provide a slight lip that can be planed down later to be perfectly flush with the top.

The aprons are glued and clamped to the legs while they are rested upside down on a flat surface. Work with one leg and two aprons at a time, rather than trying to glue and clamp the entire assembly together at once. When the frame is dry, measure and cut the ½" plywood panel for an easy fit. A hole is counterbored ¾" into each corner of the panel. This hole should be big enough at least to take the socket wrench needed to tighten the lag screws. Then drill a pilot hole through the panel and into the top of each leg. Wax or soap the threads of the 2" lag screws and drive them home, with washers, so that their heads do not protrude above the panel.

Go over the entire piece, sanding joints to achieve a smooth flush surface all around. Finish sand with medium, fine, and very fine paper and apply a finish of your choice. The plywood panel can then be covered with tiles or other material, using the type of adhesive recommended by the manufacturer, or, if you planned for it, a removable panel can be inserted in the recess.

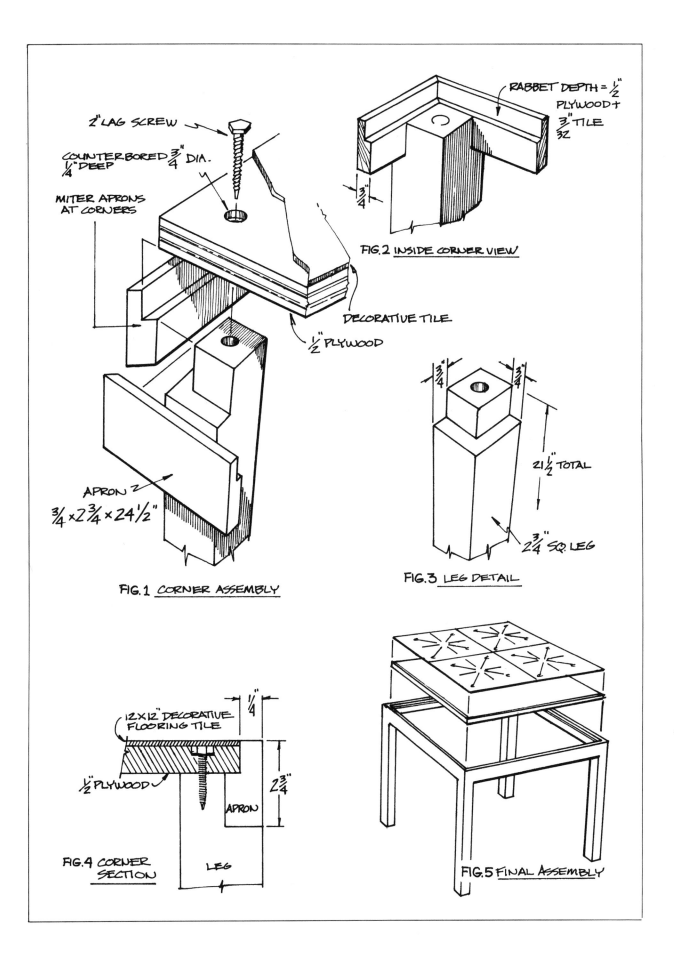

2" LAG SCREW

COUNTERBORED $\frac{3}{4}$" DIA.
$\frac{1}{4}$" DEEP

MITER APRONS
AT CORNERS

APRON
$\frac{3}{4} \times 2\frac{3}{4} \times 24\frac{1}{2}$"

FIG. 1 CORNER ASSEMBLY

RABBET DEPTH = $\frac{1}{2}$"
PLYWOOD +
$\frac{3}{32}$" TILE

$\frac{3}{4}$"

FIG. 2 INSIDE CORNER VIEW

DECORATIVE TILE

$\frac{1}{2}$" PLYWOOD

$\frac{3}{4}$" $\frac{3}{4}$"

$21\frac{1}{2}$" TOTAL

$2\frac{3}{4}$" SQ. LEG

FIG. 3 LEG DETAIL

12 × 12" DECORATIVE
FLOORING TILE

$\frac{1}{4}$"

$\frac{1}{2}$" PLYWOOD

$2\frac{3}{4}$"

APRON

LEG

FIG. 4 CORNER
SECTION

FIG. 5 FINAL ASSEMBLY

Toy Riverboat

Few children nowadays will ever have the opportunity to see a real river stern-wheeler. These shoal-draft vessels, once common on our large river systems, have all but vanished from the scene. Small children couldn't care less about nostalgia, and generally see anything that floats as a "boat," but we guarantee that they'll love this jaunty little vessel with its splashing paddle wheel.

We designed this toy for quick and easy construction. By stacking the material for sawing and drilling, large numbers of them can be turned out in a short time for sale at craft fairs and other outlets.

The hull is cut from ¾ x 4 x 9½" white pine. Form the bow and cut out a 2 x 2¼" notch for the paddle wheel. The roof sections are ⅛" thin pine sliced from a thicker piece. If you lack the machinery to do this, you can use exterior-grade ¼" plywood, though it gives the superstructure a bit of a top-heavy appearance. Don't use ⅛" plywood drawer bottoms or dust shields from an old chest, as this material will quickly delaminate from exposure to moisture.

Clamp the two roof sections to the hull in proper position, and drill all holes for ⅛" columns and a ⅜" stack. The cabin is glued up from two pieces of ¾" pine with a ⅜" hole drilled through the center to receive the stack. Before assembly sand all parts carefully, removing all sharp edges. Glue the cabin to the hull, fitting the roof sections temporarily to make sure that the stack hole lines up. Give all components a couple of coats of a good sealer and attach the superstructure to the hull with a spot of Weldwood plastic resin glue at each column. Tack the lower roof to the cabin with a couple of small galvanized finishing nails. Incidentally, plastic resin glue is highly water resistant for all practical purposes except in hot water (over 120 degrees), so save yourself some money and don't buy the very expensive Resourcinal waterproof glue just for this project.

The pilothouse is shaped from a block of pine or 1" dowel planed flat on one side. Glue this to the roof.

The paddle wheel is cut according to the detail, half-notched together, and glued. A rubber band around the wheel is stretched between the two ¼" stanchions to provide a splashy though short-lived propulsion. A small screw eye may be added at the bow for the addition of a tow cord.

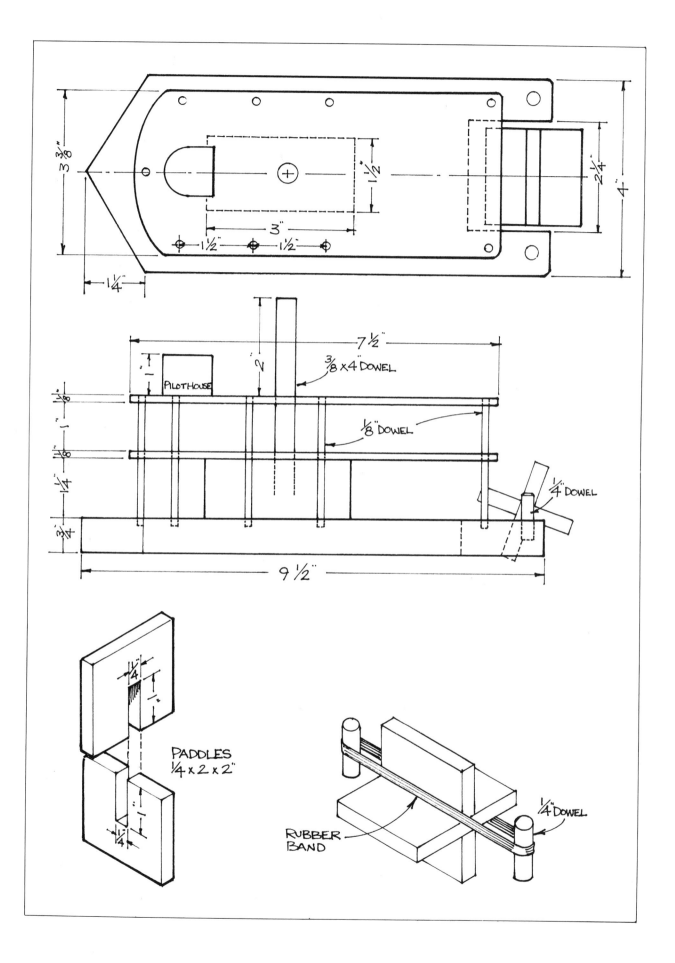

3 3/8"

1 1/2"

3"

1 1/2" — 1 1/2"

1 1/4"

2 1/4"

4"

7 1/2"

PILOTHOUSE

3/8 x 4 DOWEL

2"

1/8"

1"

1/4"

1/8" DOWEL

1/4" DOWEL

3/4"

9 1/2"

PADDLES
1/4 x 2 x 2"

1/4"

1"

1"

1/4"

RUBBER
BAND

1/4" DOWEL

Pine Trestle Table

Over the years we've seen more trestle table designs than we can remember. They range from ornate and massive sixteenth-century Spanish tables shaped from 2″ stock to the long and lean Shaker communal dining tables with gracefully arched maple feet. The table we're presenting here combines what we feel are some of the best features of many designs. Posts and rails are enhanced with stopped chamfers; the feet are long, narrow, and nicely shaped. Locking wedges are of cherry, which contrasts with the natural pine. The turned-spindle center support is a feature occasionally found in long seventeenth-century American tables, but not often seen in reproductions. If you lack a lathe, substitute a post of 1⅝″-square stock with stopped chamfers. With the square center post and a natural finish, as shown in the photograph, this table has an elegant Scandinavian look that will fit in well with contemporary or antique furnishings.

Begin construction by jointing four ¾ x 8 x 72″ pine boards for the top, alternating the grain direction. These boards are joined with glue and ⅜″ dowel pins spaced about a foot apart. The boards should be cut slightly longer than 6′ and trimmed to length after the glue has dried. You'll need five bar or pipe clamps 4′ in length for the top. They should be applied on alternate sides of the

slab to prevent distortion. Don't be upset if you find that the top is a bit wavy when the clamps are removed. It will be flattened between battens later when you are ready to attach it to the support cleats.

Next shape three support cleats and two feet from 2″ pine (actual thickness is 1¾″). Pair up the two feet and matching cleats and lay out mortises and tenons. Be sure to mark each set carefully so that each tenon can later be inserted in its particular mortise. We cut the tenons to shape using a tenon jig on the table saw, but, of course, they can be done very nicely by hand with a tenon saw. Carefully center the tenons on the feet and cleats to scribe mortises, which are drilled out and then cleaned up with a sharp chisel or cut with a drill press or router. Note that the mortise in the feet does not go all the way through; this is a bit more trouble to clean out, but provides more gluing area.

When the mortises and tenons have been cut and fit to your satisfaction, the long stretcher can be laid out and cut with tenons on each end and a ¾″-diameter hole drilled in the top center to hold the spindle. Cut mortises in the posts for the stretcher tenons, taking care to get a good fit without splintered edges, particularly on the outside surfaces that are not covered by the shoulder of the tenon.

Next, lathe turn the center support post, or chamfer a square post. For turning, start with a 1⅞″ turning square and lay out the turned portions with a square at each end. Reduce turned portions to a cylinder and cut beads and coves. The square portions can be planed down after the turning is completed. Use the parting tool and calipers to cut ¾″ pins at each end. Note that the rail that will hold the turned post is 1¾″ thick, but the chamfers reduce its thickness to 1⅝″. Therefore, the bottom square of the turned post should be no wider than 1⅝″, while the top square fits into a 2″ cleat, so it doesn't matter if it is left oversize. Drill a ¾″ hole in the center cleat and glue the spindle into it, but do not use glue for the bottom pin. If you failed to get a snug fit of the pins in their sockets, cut a slot in

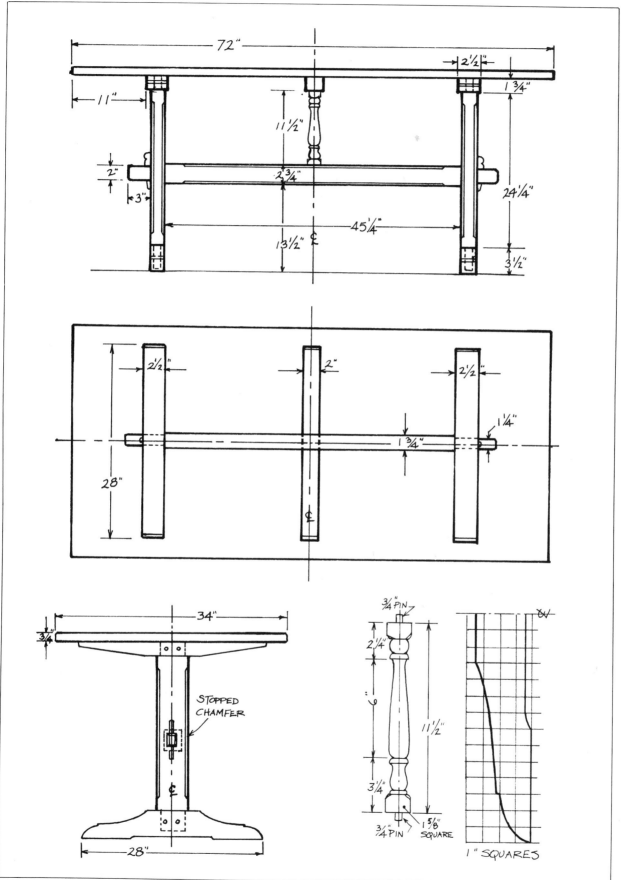

72"

2½"

1¾"

11"

11½"

2"

2¾"

3"

24¼"

45¼" ¢

13½" ¢

3½"

2½"

2"

2½"

1¾"

1¼"

28"

34"

¾"

STOPPED CHAMFER

28"

¢

¾" PIN

2¼"

6"

11½"

3¼"

¾" PIN

1⅝" SQUARE

N⅞

1" SQUARES

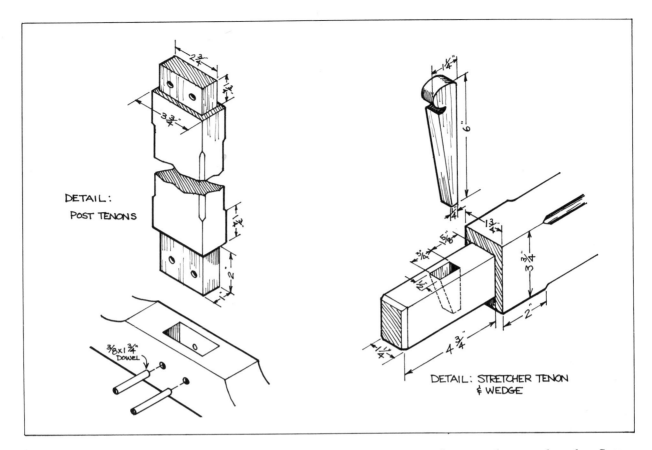

DETAIL:
POST TENONS

3/8 x 1 3/4"
DOWEL

DETAIL: STRETCHER TENON
& WEDGE

the pins and tap in a small hardwood wedge to spread them a bit.

Fit together all components of the trestle assembly on a flat surface to make sure it is square and sits solidly. Drive posts tightly against the shoulders of the long stretcher and mark mortises for locking wedges. These mortises should be cut with a taper from ¾" on top to ½" on the bottom. Take care at this point not to split the ends of the rails. Drill out waste first with a ½" drill bit and clean up with a ½" chisel and three-cornered file. Wedges were shaped from cherry scrap, but any hardwood can be used. Sand the wedges and break sharp corners slightly before tapping them into place. Some fitting will probably be necessary at this point, to get the wedges to fit equally. Do not pound them in, as the stretcher may split.

Glue the posts into their respective mortises in the feet and cleats and lock them in place with ½" dowel pins glued and driven all the way through both parts. Trim the pins flush. Do not use glue on the stretcher-post joint. Drill four ¼" holes through each cleat, 2" and 8" from each end.

Prepare the top for mounting by planing and sanding both sides flat. If the top is a bit wavy,

clamp two stout battens along each end to flatten it. After clamping the battens, lay the top upside down across two sawhorses and locate the trestle assembly 11" in from each end and evenly spaced from front to back. Drive a 1¼" #12 round-headed wood screw with washer through the holes nearest the ends of the cleats and into the top. If you cut the cleats to the proper thickness, the screws should penetrate ⅝" into the top. There's not much room for error here, so be careful to see that the screws do not protrude through the other side, and that they grip the top tightly. Drive 2" #12 round-headed screws with washers into the remaining holes.

With all the cleats firmly screwed to the top, remove the battens. The top should now remain flat and you may proceed with finishing, which consists of a careful sanding followed by stain, if you desire, and two coats of polyurethane finish on the trestle assembly and three coats on the top. Lightly sand between coats and don't forget to seal the underside of the top with at least one well-applied coat. A coat of furniture wax and a good buffing will add additional depth and protection to the finish.

Pecking Bird

Pendulum-operated toys date back to ancient times. This particular version originated in central Europe sometime in the fifteenth century.

Cut a 1 x 1 x 2¼″ soft-pine block for the body and cut ¼ x ³⁄₁₆″ notches in both ends. Locate and drill a ³⁄₁₆″ dowel hole and two small pinholes for wire brads, as shown. Round the body by carving and sanding.

Trace the head and tail from the full-size drawing and transfer to ³⁄₁₆″ pine. Drill pinholes, then jigsaw the shapes. Make the handle from ³⁄₁₆″ pine and locate and drill three ³⁄₁₆″-diameter holes.

Thread a 10″ length of heavy thread through the pinhole of the head piece and fasten it at the notch. Tie another length to the tail piece, then fasten the head and tail to the body with small headless brads.

Glue a short length of ³⁄₁₆″ dowel into the body and handle. Cut and drill the pendulum block and thread both strings through the holes in the handle and block, knotting them together at the bottom of the block. The block should hang about 3″ below the handle.

To activate the bird, hold the handle and move it in a circular direction, causing the pendulum to swing. The bird will tip its head and tail alternately, as if feeding.

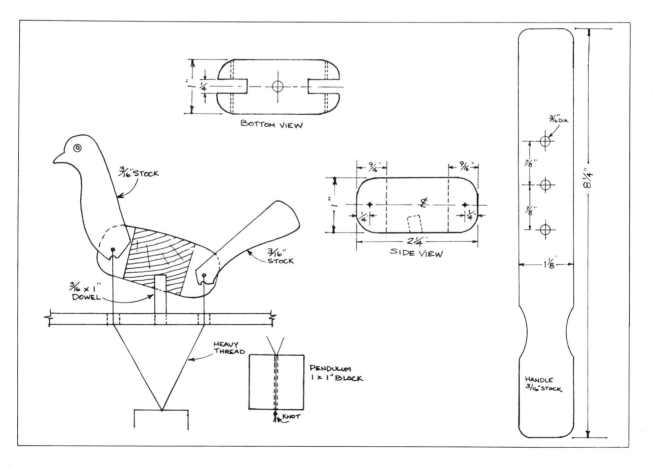

Toy Train

A few evenings in the shop will be sufficient to turn out this ever-popular toy—a fair exchange for the hours of fun it will provide. Note that all bases are of the same dimensions, except for the engine tender, which is 1″ shorter, so you can knock them out quickly. Make a template for the axle holes to insure uniformity, and use a doweling jig if you have one. The holes should be drilled slightly oversize to allow the ¼″ axles to turn freely. Axles are glued to 2″ discs of pine.

The locomotive boiler is shaped from a block of glued-up pine, planed round. The engine cab is a glued-up block with a cove cut on a table saw

or bandsaw, or gouged by hand. The roofs of the engine cab and caboose are simply ¾″ pine stock planed round.

Join the car bodies to bases with glue and finishing nails. The tender and gondola bodies are of ¼″ stock that can be resawed either from thicker stock or plywood. Drill pilot holes through the bases for finishing nails to secure these thin parts accurately, and make sure that no nail tips poke through.

Dowels of various sizes are shaped for the boiler dome, smokestack, engine face, and log carrier. Couplings are formed from ½″ dowel and shaped according to the detail. Each car, except the engine, should have one of each type of coupling. Again, use a stiff paper template to mark each base for coupling holes.

The entire train should be given an exceptional sanding. Work over each piece until it's as smooth as you can get it with the edge grain showing clearly and well-rounded edges. The train may be sealed with shellac and enameled in various bright colors, but we prefer a natural finish, sealed with several coats of shellac or clear penetrating oil. Enamel the engine's eyes white, and when dry dab a spot of black on each, using a ¼″ dowel end. Paint the nose red.

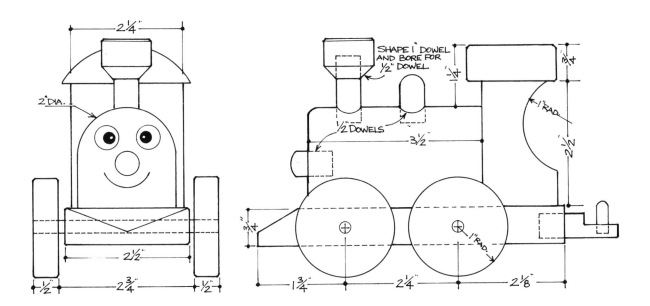

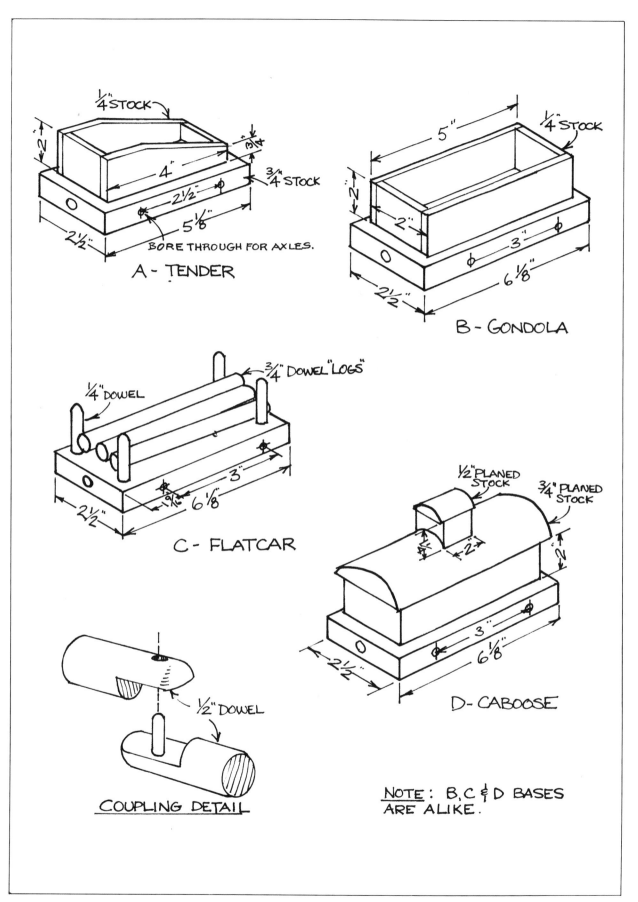

¼" STOCK

2"

4"

3/4"

¾" STOCK

2½"

2½"

5⅛"

BORE THROUGH FOR AXLES.

A - TENDER

5"

¼" STOCK

2"

2"

3"

2½"

6⅛"

B - GONDOLA

¾" DOWEL "LOGS"

¼" DOWEL

3"

2½"

6⅛"

C - FLATCAR

½" PLANED STOCK

¾" PLANED STOCK

2"

2"

2"

3"

2½"

6⅛"

D - CABOOSE

½" DOWEL

COUPLING DETAIL

NOTE: B, C & D BASES ARE ALIKE.

Butterfly-Wing Table

The design of this useful table dates back to the seventeenth century, when living space was generally cramped and one or two rooms served for cooking, eating, socializing, and sleeping. Drop-leaf tables, trestle tables with removable tops, and gate-leg designs were popular because they saved space. The butterfly-wing table derives its name from the shape of the leaf supports, which resemble butterfly wings, although we have seen tables with similar supports referred to as "Rudder tables."

This particular design is similar to one featured by Lester Margon in his fine book *American Furniture Treasures*. Our design has been scaled down for use as an end or occasional table, and the joinery has been revised to include the use of dowel pins instead of the original mortise-and-tenon construction. Skilled woodworkers who enjoy the challenge of the more difficult mortise-and-tenon joinery may substitute these joints, keeping in mind the fact that the mortises for the end rails must be cut in at an angle of 84 degrees to the inside face of each leg. This operation can best be done with a drill press. Tenons must also be mitered to butt against the adjoining tenons of the side rails.

Construction is begun with the legs, which are best turned from maple stock 1½" square (Figure 1). Legs are 20¾" in length and should be cut longer to allow for the angled cut of 84 degrees at the top. All dowel holes should be laid out on the square stock, and holes drilled before turning. Dowel-location lines should be left on the square sections of the legs to serve as guides for the location of the corresponding holes in the upper and lower rails. It's best to cut a full-size template of the leg profile to insure producing four identical legs. With the large gouge, rough the turned section of each leg to a cylinder with a diameter of 1⁷⁄₁₆", then smooth down to 1⅜" with a skew chisel. Coves and beads are then marked off with the help of the template and cut to final depth. Sand the turnings while they are in the lathe with medium to very fine sandpaper. Plane a ¼" chamfer on each corner of the upper and lower legs and cut the tops to the proper angle, taking care to make the cuts in correct relation to the dowel holes.

Both upper and lower rails are of ¾" stock, preferably maple. The two upper end rails are cut to 2 x 4⅛". Set the miter gauge to 84 degrees to cut angled sides. Drill two holes for ⅜" dowels in each end, using the leg holes as a guide for marking (Figure 2A). The lower end rails are also of ¾" stock and are cut to 1½ x 7¼", with ends angled to 84 degrees and one dowel hole drilled in each end (Figure 2B). The two lower side rails are ¾" stock and are cut to 1½ x 13". Drill both dowel holes and a pivot-pin hole as shown in Figure 2C. Dowel pins in the lower end and side rails should extend 1" into the legs. It is necessary to cut the end of each pin at a 45-degree angle so that adjoining pins will not interfere with each other when they are driven home.

Prepare a full-size pattern of the butterfly wings and transfer it to ½" maple stock. Cut out the wings with a saber or coping saw. The outboard or curved portion of each wing should be worked into a well-rounded edge. Drill the top and bottom of each wing for a ¼" hickory pin. Care should be taken to drill holes perpendicular to the long axis of the wings. The table frame can now be assembled with glue and clamps. Upper end rails should be planed flush if they protrude above the tops of the legs.

We turn our attention now to construction of the top, which consists of three separate sections of ¾″ maple. Dowel and glue the maple stock together to form each leaf and the center section. At this point you must decide whether a rule joint will be milled on the top sections as shown in Figure 3B. If you have a router with matching cutters, the joint can be cut easily. The joint may also be formed with hand tools by first cutting a bevel to remove excess stock, and then using a gouge to shape the cove along the end of each drop leaf; but this will require considerable care and patience. The original table had a center section and drop leaves with plain square edges. Either way will be authentic, but the rule joint is more attractive. If you use the rule joint, just remember to add an extra inch to the 9¾″ dimension shown in Figure 3B. When doweling stock to make up the leaf sections, make sure that the joints are parallel to the hinged joint. In other words, the grain of the entire top should run in the same direction as the long side rails.

The top is in the shape of an ellipse, as was the original, and although this is more difficult to lay out than an oval, it somehow looks more elegant. We have laid out the ellipse for you and come up with the measurements you will need to make a pattern of one-quarter of the top. This can then be used to scribe the entire top. Referring to Figure 4, tape a piece of heavy paper square to the edge of a drawing board or table, and with a T square or framing square, draw baseline AC 12 13/16″ long. Perpendicular to AC draw line AB 10 7/16″ high. On line AC carefully mark off distances of ⅛, ¾, 1⅞, 3¾, 6⅛, and 9¼″. Number these points from 1 to 6. On line AB mark off heights of 1½, 3⅜, 5¼, 7, 8¾, and 10″. Number these from 1 to 6. Connect lines AC and BD with a T square and triangle by drawing perpendicular lines from points 1 through 6. Connect lines AB and CD in the same manner. At the point where each corresponding set of lines intersects, place a dot. The dots, when connected, will give you one-quarter of the ellipse. Cut out this pattern and after temporarily clamping the top sections together, transfer the shapes to the top by flopping the pattern along lightly scribed centerlines.

The top sections may then be shaped with a saber saw. The outer edge of the top should be well rounded. Hinges are located by placing the three top sections underside up on a flat surface. Clamp lightly with a bar clamp and mark the lo-

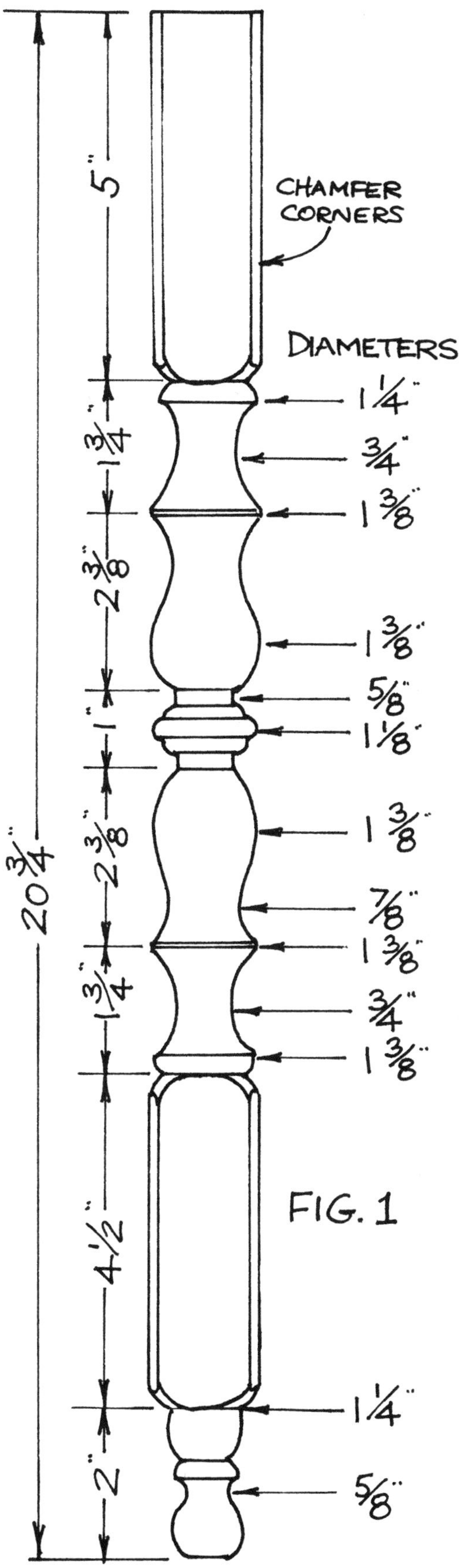

CHAMFER CORNERS
DIAMETERS
5"
1¾"
2⅜"
1"
2⅜"
1¾"
4½"
2"
20¾"
1¼"
¾"
1⅜"
1⅜"
⅝"
1⅛"
1⅜"
⅞"
1⅜"
¾"
1⅜"
1¼"
⅝"

FIG. 1

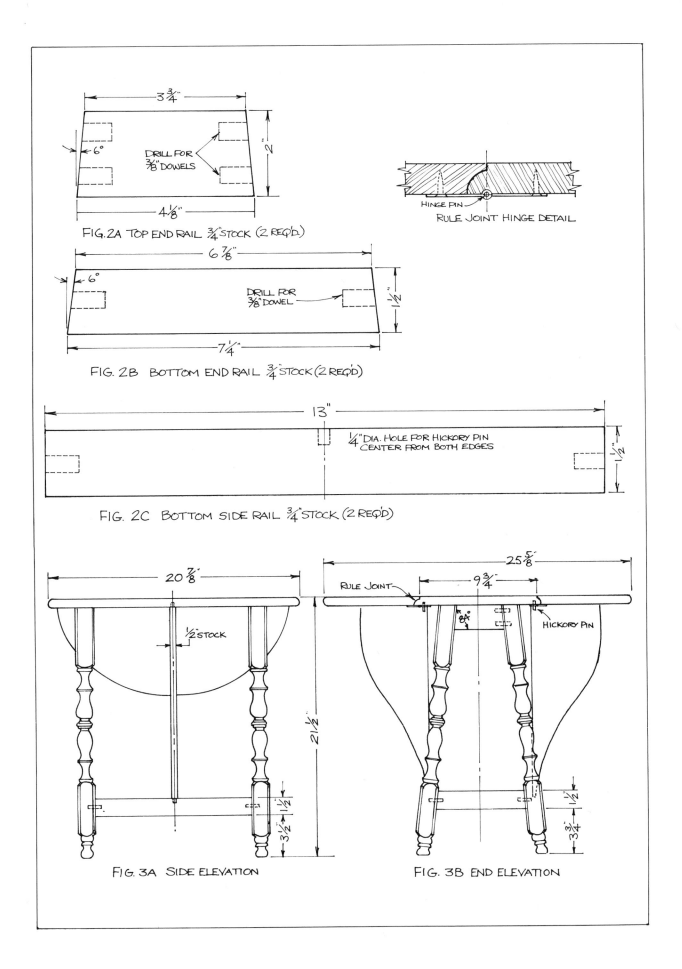

FIG. 2A TOP END RAIL ¾" STOCK (2 REQ'D.)

3¾"

6°

DRILL FOR ⅜" DOWELS

2"

4⅛"

RULE JOINT HINGE DETAIL

HINGE PIN

FIG. 2B BOTTOM END RAIL ¾" STOCK (2 REQ'D)

6⅞"

6°

DRILL FOR ⅜" DOWEL

1½"

7¼"

FIG. 2C BOTTOM SIDE RAIL ¾" STOCK (2 REQ'D)

13"

¼" DIA. HOLE FOR HICKORY PIN CENTER FROM BOTH EDGES

1½"

FIG. 3A SIDE ELEVATION

20⅞"

½" STOCK

21½"

½"

3½"

FIG. 3B END ELEVATION

25⅝"

RULE JOINT

9¾"

8°

HICKORY PIN

½"

¾"

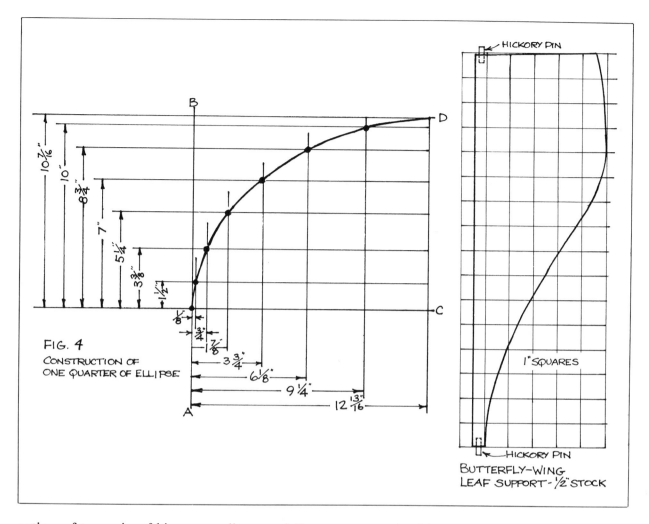

FIG. 4

CONSTRUCTION OF
ONE QUARTER OF ELLIPSE

HICKORY PIN

1" SQUARES

HICKORY PIN

BUTTERFLY-WING
LEAF SUPPORT-½" STOCK

cations of two pairs of hinges equally spaced. To set the hinge leaves flat it will be necessary to gouge a groove to recess each hinge barrel, as shown in the detail. After the top has been hinged, place the assembled table frame, with leaf supports, on the underside of the top and mark the locations of the pivot-pin holes. The top is fastened to the frame by drilling and counterboring two holes in each upper end rail for wood screws to be driven up into the top. Drill undersized pilot holes in the top to receive these screws.

Select a desired stain and apply sufficient coats to achieve the shade you want. Wipe off excess stain between coats. Allow stain to dry for 24 hours before applying a sealer. When the sealer is thoroughly dry, sand lightly and apply a good grade of low-luster varnish, sanding lightly between coats.

Adirondack Lawn Chair

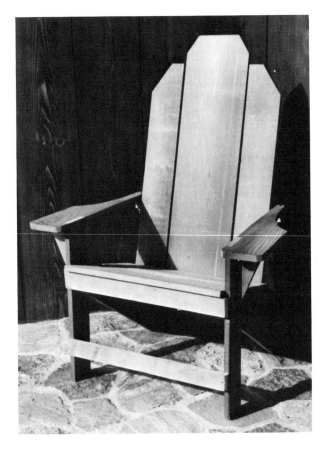 

If you'd like something more substantial and attractive than the usual aluminum-tubing-and-plastic lawn chairs, then consider this version of an old-time favorite which can be disassembled for winter storage. These chairs were popular at such famous gilded watering holes as Saratoga Springs at the turn of the century. One can imagine the linen-clad "sports" taking their leisure in them on the front lawn with tall drinks, Havana cigars, and racing forms. Gingerbread decoration was in fashion then, and the front aprons of these chairs were likely to be cut in elaborate scrolls.

Modern construction employs redwood, an easy wood to work and very tolerant of exposure to the elements. This design is worked out for 1″ (¾″ actual) stock for the sake of economy and light weight. If you're a heavyweight then consider using ⅝″ stock. The design is also adaptable to a double-length settee with the addition of a center leg. This would require ⅝″ stock.

Start by cutting the rear leg-seat supports, laying out on 8 x 32″ stock. Cut these together, if possible, to make them exactly identical. Cut two front legs to 3⅝ x 22¾″, and notch the tops for armrests. Clamp the legs to the seat supports and drill holes for ¼ x 2″ carriage bolts. The narrow front edge of the seat supports should be flush with the front edges of the legs.

Tack a temporary batten across the rear legs to hold them so their inside faces are 20″ apart. Then cut three seat boards 3½ x 20½″, and arrange them across the seat supports so there is a ¼″ space between each, and the front board butts against the edges of the front legs. Screw these in place in countersunk holes and then add the fourth board, which should extend about 1¼″ beyond the front legs. This seat board will be wider than the other three and ½″ shorter to fit between the front legs.

Cut slotted cleats to hold the chair's back, lo-

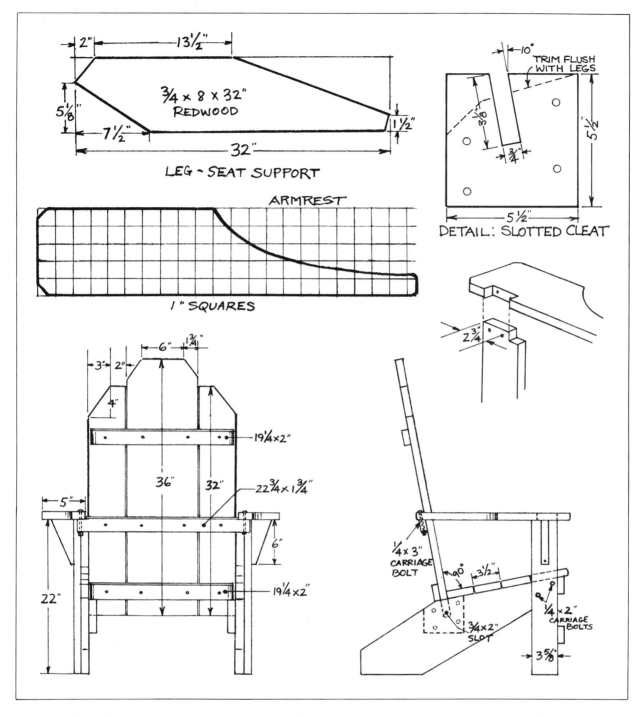

LEG - SEAT SUPPORT

$\frac{3}{4}$ x 8 x 32"
REDWOOD

ARMREST

1" SQUARES

DETAIL: SLOTTED CLEAT

TRIM FLUSH WITH LEGS

$\frac{1}{4}$ x 3"
CARRIAGE
BOLT

$\frac{3}{4}$ x 2"
SLOT

$\frac{1}{4}$ x 2"
CARRIAGE
BOLTS

cated so that the slots are at right angles to the seat. Trim these flush with the upper edges of the seat supports, and fasten them with four screws each. Cut the back boards to length and fasten them with upper and lower cleats. Round off the ends of the cleats for a better appearance. Mount the back assembly into the slots, and cut and shape the armrests as indicated The armrests should extend about 1½″ beyond the chair back. Cut the center cleat and bevel the top edge to fit

snugly up against the armrest. Clamp these together and drill for ¼ x 3″ carriage bolts.

Add triangular arm braces with two screws in each, and finally the front apron and lower leg brace. Round off the ends of these members with a rasp or Surform®. Tighten all screws and carriage bolts, drag the chair out into the sun, and enjoy a tall, cold drink. Sorry about those Havana cigars.

Swan Rocker

Building this lovely rocker is in itself a pleasurable pastime, but the real reward comes from seeing a happy child seated between the graceful swans. It's a piece that will most likely become a treasured family heirloom, delighting generations of children. Unlike some of the plywood and pressed-board versions being produced commercially, this rocker is made of ¾″ solid pine. Given a fine finish and appropriate upholstery, it's a plaything that will grace any room.

Enlarge the swan on a 1″ grid pattern. This can be done on brown wrapping paper, which is then cut to shape and the outline drawn on the stock. We used a dressmaker's pattern wheel to go over the lines, leaving small indentations in the wood that were connected with a pencil line.

Joint the boards to be glued up, but before doweling, transfer the pattern and locate the ⅜″ dowels so they will not be exposed when the swan is cut out. Try to locate one dowel in the narrow part of the neck. This area will be reinforced con-siderably with the addition of the curved brackets.

After cutting the swans and brackets, clamp them together and round all edges with a rasp and sandpaper. Drill ½″ holes for the eyes. Then cut the three seat sections, beveling adjoining edges of the seat and leg rest for a good joint. Arrange the seat parts on one side and mark the seat location on the swan with a pencil line. Also locate the ⅝″ dowel sockets. Drive small headless brads along the pencil line, spaced every 2″ apart and protruding about ⅛″. Also drive brads into the centers of the dowel locations. Now align the swans and press them carefully together so that the brad points will transfer the seat outline and dowel locations to the opposite side. This process will guarantee that everything is level and parallel.

Remove the brads and glue and screw quarter-round molding to both sides. Beg, borrow, or steal a Forstner bit to cut the dowel sockets—or, as a last desperate measure, drill the holes with an auger bit—and hide the holes on the other side caused by the feed screw with small plugs.

Now assemble the rocker, gluing the dowels into their sockets, screwing the seat to its supports, and adding the curved brackets and the small tray, which is fastened with two screws driven up through each end of the bottom into the curved brackets.

Give the entire piece a careful sanding, making sure there are no sharp edges or splinters, and stain if you wish. A low-luster finish is best, and you may seal with varnish, shellac, or one of the polyurethane finishes, or take the easy way and use one of the penetrating oil finishes.

Upholster the seat with 1″ foam rubber cut to shape and covered with fabric. The fabric can be fastened to the seat edges with tacks and covered with matching tape. However, the best arrangement is to make removable cushions for ease in cleaning.

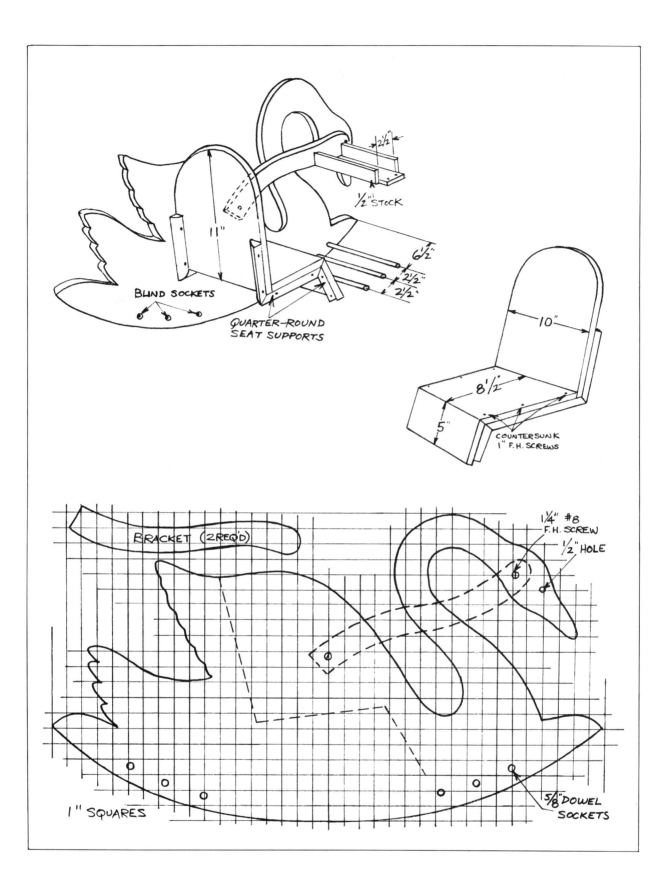

2½"

½" STOCK

11"

BLIND SOCKETS

QUARTER-ROUND
SEAT SUPPORTS

6½"

2½"

2½"

10"

8½"

5"

COUNTERSUNK
1" F.H. SCREWS

BRACKET (2 REQ'D)

1¼" #8
F.H. SCREW

½" HOLE

1" SQUARES

5/8" DOWEL
SOCKETS

Small Shaker-style Table

This Shaker-inspired table has a sprightly, long-legged look that will enable it to fit in well with either period or contemporary furnishings. It's particularly suited for use as a bedside table. The design is spare and clean, as is typical of Shaker pieces. The long slender legs are tapered on all four sides, a departure from the usual Shaker practice of tapering square legs on the inside surfaces only.

Cherry would be a particularly fine choice of wood to use in the construction of this piece. The original was made of pine, with clear stock used for the legs. Of course, pine or fir can be used if the table is to be painted. Just be sure to select clear, straight stock for the legs.

Begin construction by squaring four pieces of stock to 1¼" for the legs A. These are 24¾" long and may be glued up from two pieces of ¾" stock. Using a table saw or hand plane, cut a taper on

all four sides starting 4½" down from the top of each leg. The legs taper from 1¼" to ¾". A taper jig is useful here, if you have a table saw; otherwise it's not much of a job to do the tapering with a hand plane.

Next, cut two side aprons B and join to the legs with two ⁵⁄₁₆" dowel pins per joint. Locate the dowel holes by driving two headless brads into the apron ends, allowing about ⅛" to protrude; then use these points to mark corresponding holes in the legs. Be sure to set aprons in ¹⁄₁₆" from the outside faces of the legs. Drill dowel holes for pins 1½" in length, and score the dowels before coating them with glue and tapping in place.

Join the other legs and side aprons in the same way, then connect the back and front aprons C and D. One dowel pin in each end of the front apron is sufficient. Side- and back-apron dowel pins should be staggered so as not to interfere with each other. Clamp these joints and check the squareness of the assembly, tacking scrap braces to the legs if necessary to maintain squareness while the glue is drying.

The drawer runners E are next cut from ¾" pine to 1 x 13⅛". They are notched to butt against the front and back legs and the front and back aprons. They should also be flush with the top of the front apron. Secure the runners with glue and 1¼" #8 flat-headed screws.

Next, cut two side cleats F and one back G cleat from ½" pine. These should be 1 x 12¼". The back cleat should be notched around the side cleats for a neat fit. Drill three countersunk holes through the side of each cleat for mounting to the aprons with ¾" #6 flat-headed screws. Also drill three countersunk holes up through the bottom of each cleat for 1½" #6 screws, which will be driven into the top.

Glue up ¾" stock to form the top, which is 17" deep x 18" wide. Dowel pins or stopped splines will insure that the boards comprising the top stay together permanently. While the top is drying, cut four corner blocks I from ¾" pine. Fasten these with glue and finishing nails. Filler strips H should be glued to the side aprons to help guide the drawer. These strips should be cut

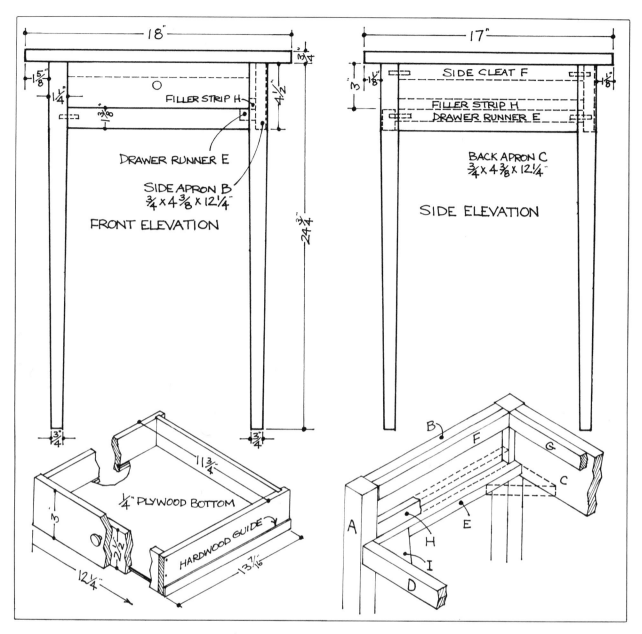

to fit and will be from ¼″ to ⁵⁄₁₆″ thick, depending on the actual thickness of the aprons and legs.

Drive screws up through the bottoms of the side and back cleats so that the screw points protrude slightly. Now temporarily fasten the cleats to the aprons, and place the top in its proper position. Press down on the top so that the tips of the cleat screws will register the locations of the pilot holes. Before fastening the top, stain the underside and give it a couple of coats of sealer. Then fasten the cleats to the top, set the top on the frame, and screw and glue the cleats to the aprons.

The detail offers a suggestion for drawer construction from ½″ pine with a ¼″ plywood bottom

let into grooves all around. The sides are fastened with glue and nails to the front, which in turn is glued to a false front. Thin hardwood strips may be glued to each side as drawer guides. Sand all drawer components well before assembly.

Finish the table by breaking all sharp edges with sandpaper and thoroughly sanding all surfaces, working down from medium to very fine paper. Dust carefully and apply one or more coats of the stain of your choice, following the manufacturer's directions. After the stain is dry, apply a sealer coat followed by light sanding to remove raised "whiskers." Dust or use a tack cloth before applying finishing coats. A final rubdown with 4/0 steel wool will give a soft sheen.

A Picture-Framing Primer

The picture in the illustration is a Currier and Ives print framed in a standard crown molding purchased at the lumberyard. This was just thick enough to allow a rabbet to be cut that would contain the glass, print, and thin cardboard backing. If the inner edge of molding used is too thin to provide a ¼″ rabbet, it will be necessary to construct a subframe of pine. This can be cut ¼″ less in width than the molding and glued to it as shown in Figure 4.

Producing custom picture frames in your home shop is a pleasant way to earn a substantial extra income. It's also a great convenience to be able to make your own frames as needed. Moldings made especially for frames can be purchased at frame shops or by mail from firms specializing in framing equipment. Better still, use standard lumberyard moldings if you can, and the total cost for frames will be very low. Be sure to choose straight, unwarped moldings without sap streaks.

There are a few general rules that will help you choose a suitable molding for the picture you wish to frame. Always keep in mind that the frame should complement the picture rather than dominate it. Large ornate frames look best with large, dark, oil paintings. Landscapes depicting rugged scenes such as seascapes or mountains look good when framed in natural oak, wormy chestnut, or driftwood. Paintings or prints in an abstract style look best with relatively flat moldings in solid colors or finished natural.

If a colored frame is desired, or a combination of colored and naturally finished moldings, look for an accent color in the picture, one that is rich and deep and generally used sparingly in the composition. Mats and glass are rarely used with oil paintings. Prints and watercolors almost always look better with the addition of a mat, and glass is needed for protection from dust, smoke, and insects. The outside dimensions of the mat will determine the outside dimensions of the rabbet cut in the back of the frame, and the size of glass needed.

Most home craftsmen are familiar with the technique necessary to produce clean miter cuts for picture frames. A simple miter box used with a backsaw will be adequate if locked firmly in the workbench vise. A very handy jig for cutting perfect 45-degree angles with a table saw is detailed in Figure 1. This jig can also be used for halving discs. Cut the jig platform as shown, taking dimensions from your particular table saw. Set jig slides in the saw table slots, making sure they rest against the outboard sides of the slots, and then clamp the slides to the platform. Turn the platform over and secure the slides with screws before releasing the clamps. Run the platform into the saw blade to form the center slot. It's best to use a hollow-ground satin-cut blade for glass-smooth cuts. Lay out the position of the plywood guides using the saw slot as a centerline. When screwing the guides in place, use a framing square to maintain a perfect 90-degree angle. All shop jigs should be carefully sealed to prevent moisture from destroying accuracy.

Mitered frame sections should be sanded and finished before joining. Size end-grain cuts with a thin film of glue and drill undersized pilot holes for the proper size finishing nails. Put a dab of glue on mating pieces, lock one piece in the vise, and join together, holding firmly while tapping in the finishing nail. Remove the assembled joint from the vise and set the nailhead and fill with matching filler. Frames can also be conveniently joined using the simple wedging jig shown in Figure 2. If you do much frame work, several of these jigs can be secured permanently to the bench top.

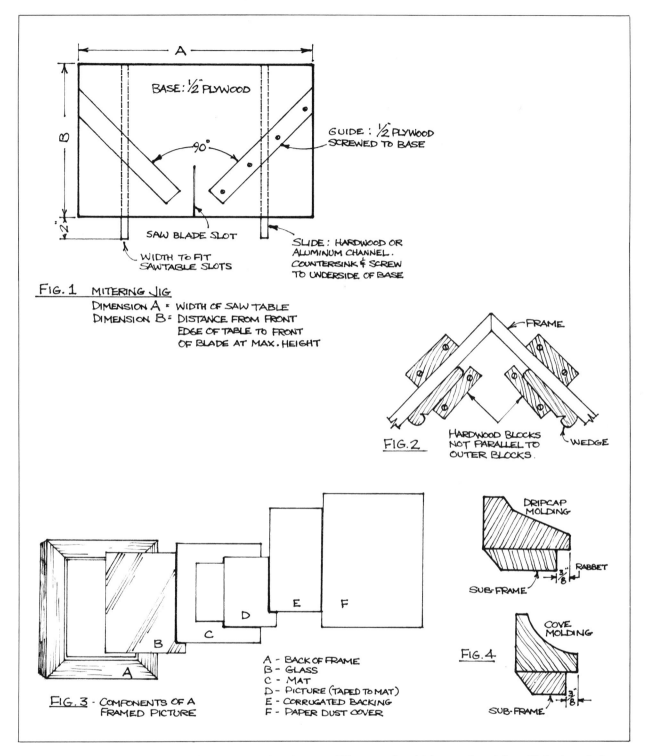

FIG. 1 MITERING JIG
DIMENSION A = WIDTH OF SAW TABLE
DIMENSION B = DISTANCE FROM FRONT
EDGE OF TABLE TO FRONT
OF BLADE AT MAX. HEIGHT

BASE: ½" PLYWOOD

GUIDE: ½" PLYWOOD
SCREWED TO BASE

90°

SAW BLADE SLOT

WIDTH TO FIT
SAWTABLE SLOTS

SLIDE: HARDWOOD OR
ALUMINUM CHANNEL.
COUNTERSINK & SCREW
TO UNDERSIDE OF BASE

FRAME

HARDWOOD BLOCKS
NOT PARALLEL TO
OUTER BLOCKS.

FIG. 2

WEDGE

FIG. 3 - COMPONENTS OF A
FRAMED PICTURE

A - BACK OF FRAME
B - GLASS
C - MAT
D - PICTURE (TAPED TO MAT)
E - CORRUGATED BACKING
F - PAPER DUST COVER

DRIPCAP
MOLDING

RABBET

³⁄₈"

SUB-FRAME

FIG. 4

COVE
MOLDING

³⁄₈"

SUB-FRAME

Mat board comes in a wide variety of colors and textures and you'll have to select the best combination for your picture. The window opening in the mat must be cut carefully for a clean, neat effect. Keep in mind that the bottom border width should be about 15 percent wider than the top and side borders; a typical mat has a 3½″ bottom border and 3″ borders at the top and sides.

The cut should be made with a slight bevel showing, using a sharp utility knife and a steel straightedge. If you've never framed your own pictures before, chances are you'll be so pleased with the results that you'll want to invest in a mat cutter. These are not too expensive and are available at artists' supplies stores.

After cutting the mat to size and cutting out

the opening, remove any slight ragged edges of mat board with fine sandpaper. The beveled edge may be tinted with a watercolor wash of the picture's accent color, and a neat border line of black, gold, or the accent color can be drawn ½″ to ¼″ from the window edge using a ruling pen or a fine felt-tip pen.

Figure 3 shows how the components are fitted into the frame. Picture glass should not be a tight fit in the frame rabbet. When all is adjusted to your satisfaction, and well centered, drive two or three retaining brads into each side of the rabbets. Work carefully with a tack hammer to avoid cracking the glass. Better yet, push the brads in with long-nose pliers. When everything has been secured within the frame, run a thin film of white glue around the back of the frame. While the glue is getting tacky, cut a sheet of brown paper roughly one inch bigger than the frame all around, and sponge one side with enough water to dampen without soaking. Place the paper dry side down on the glued frame and smooth it down, working from the center outward. As the paper dries, it will shrink drumtight and provide a neat, professional-looking backing for your picture. Trim excess paper from the frame by rubbing fine sandpaper along the edges. This method is much better than trying to trim it with a razor.

Country Cupboard

This unpretentious little cupboard is an ideal project for those woodworkers with limited experience and equipment. The simple nailed butt joints, which advanced workers may consider crude, are quite appropriate and in harmony with this rustic and utilitarian design.

Given care in cutting and finishing, the piece is rewarding and quite lovely, considering the relatively small amount of effort required to build it. It will provide excellent storage and lend warmth to a country-style kitchen or dining room. It's also perfect for the vacation cottage.

With the exception of the drawer bottoms, the piece is built from 1 x 8″ shiplap pine. The shiplap joints can be seen in Figure 2 at the edge of

the countertop. All shiplap joints are butted without glue.

Start with the base ends E, which are 11¼″ in width and made of two boards held together with top cleats N and shelf cleats F. To achieve the required width, it will be necessary to rip the boards, removing one shiplap edge from each. If an equal amount is ripped from each board, the joint will appear as shown in the center of each end.

If you lack a table saw, use a marking gauge to scribe the ripping line and a portable circular saw or hand saw to rip, keeping 1/16″ on the waste side of the line. Then clamp the board in a bench vise and plane the rough edge down to the line. Remember to sand all parts completely before joining.

Cut four ¾ x 1½ x 11¼″ N cleats and set two aside for later use. Fasten the remaining two flush with the top edges of the base ends, using three countersunk 1¼″ flat-headed screws. The two ¾ x 1½ x 11¼″ F cleats are fastened so that the top of shelf G will be 9″ from the floor.

Next, use finishing nails to fasten two boards to the F cleats to form shelf G, which is 1 x 11¼ x 25½″. Cut two upper rails J to 1 x 1½ x 27″, and two front trim pieces H to 1 x 2 x 24″.

Lay the ends on their back edges on a flat surface with the shelf in place, and mark locations, then glue and nail parts J and H to the edges. Add two 1 x 2 x 4″ filler strips K and the 1 x 1½ x 8½″ part M, which is glued and clamped to rails J. Divider L, ¾ x 1½ x 4″, is then glued and clamped to M.

Rip three boards for a 1 x 14 x 29½″ countertop. Join these with two center cleats N, screwed to the underside with 2″ countersunk flat-headed screws. These cleats should be located as shown in Figure 1 and exactly flush with the back edge of the countertop.

Add the countertop to the base, driving finishing nails through the top and into end cleats N and upper rail J. Also nail through upper rail J into the ends of the N cleats, two nails per cleat. Set all nail heads.

Shiplapped backboards D are ripped to give a

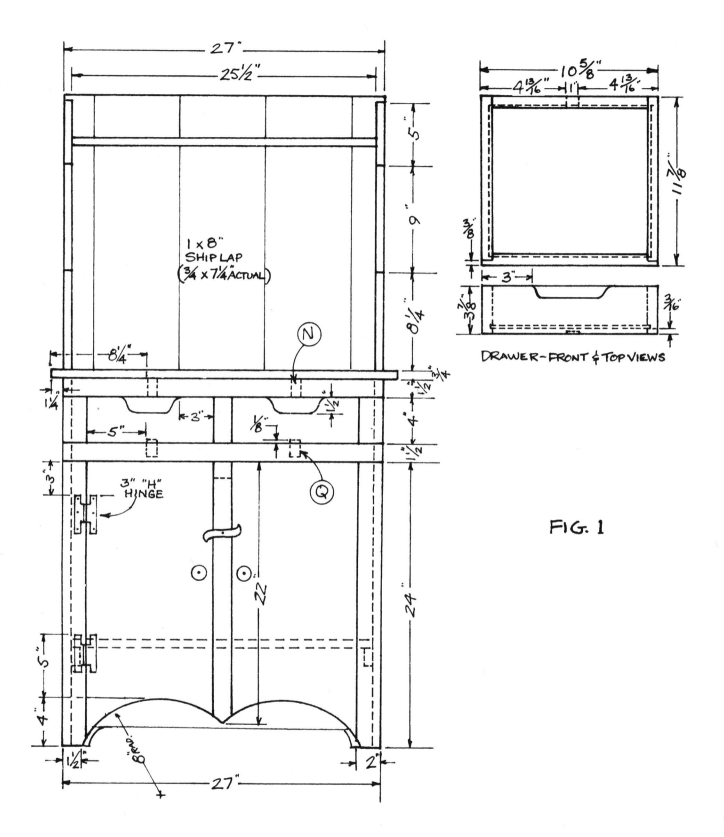

27"

25½"

1 x 8"
SHIP LAP
(¾ x 7¼" ACTUAL)

5"

9"

8¼"

8¼"

N

¾"

½"

1¼"

3"

5"

⅛"

Q

3" "H"
HINGE

22

24

5"

4"

8" RAD.

1½"

2"

27"

10⅝"

4¹³⁄₁₆" 1" 4¹³⁄₁₆"

11⅞"

3⁄8"

3"

7⁄8"
3⁄8"

3⁄16"

DRAWER—FRONT & TOP VIEWS

FIG. 1

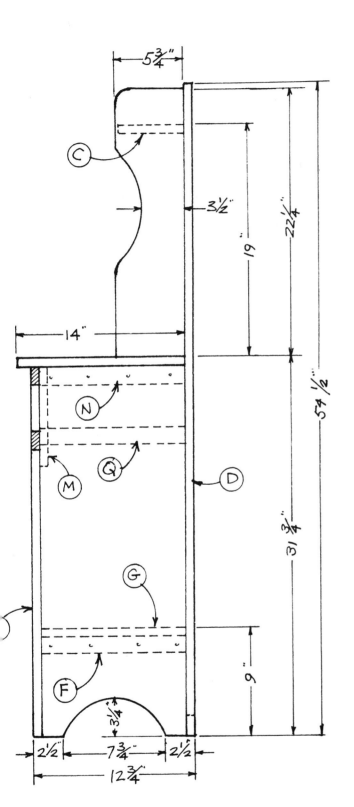

total joined width of 27″. Figure 1 shows three full-width boards used with a narrow ripped board at each end. If you prefer, you can use 1 x 6″ boards so all boards will be of more uniform width.

Turn the base over and fasten the back boards with common nails driven through the back into the edges of E, G, and A. Use a saber saw to cut a portion of the lower edge away as shown in Figure 2. This operation will help the cupboard to stand solidly on slightly uneven floors.

Upper sides B are cut to size and shaped with the saber saw. Fasten 1 x 5½ x 25½″ upper shelf C to the sides with finishing nails, then nail through the back boards into ends B and the back edge of shelf C. The back boards should extend ½″ higher than the sides. Drive one finishing nail through the front edge of each side and angled into the top as shown in Figure 2.

Join shiplap boards for two 1 x 10⅝ x 23″ doors held together with 1 x 1½ x 8″ cleats P, screwed in place as shown. Cut center divider I, which is ¾ x 1½ x 24″. Lay out both doors on a flat surface with I in between. Allow a ⅟₁₆″ space between the doors and I by placing finishing nails between them.

Prepare a beam compass by drilling a ⅛″ hole for a pencil point near the end of a ¼ x 1 x 10″ strip. Exactly 8″ from that hole drive a finishing nail through the center of the strip and into a scrap block of stock the same thickness as the doors. Move this block about until you can scribe two arcs that will mark the doors and intersect at the center of I as shown in Figure 1. Use a saber saw to shape the bottoms of the doors and part I.

Mount the doors with 3″ black H hinges. Allow about ⅟₁₆″ clearance between the doors and trim parts H. Then add the center divider by gluing and clamping to M and nailing to the lower shelf. Trim the lower ends of parts H to fair with the curves cut in the doors.

The drawer guides Q, which are of 1 x 1½ x 11¼″ stock, must be very carefully located. Their upper edges should extend ⅛″ above rail J to form a guide upon which a corresponding notch in the drawer back can ride. The guides must also be parallel to the cabinet ends and level from front to back. Use a framing square and level to locate the guides and pencil around their ends butting against the back and rail J.

111

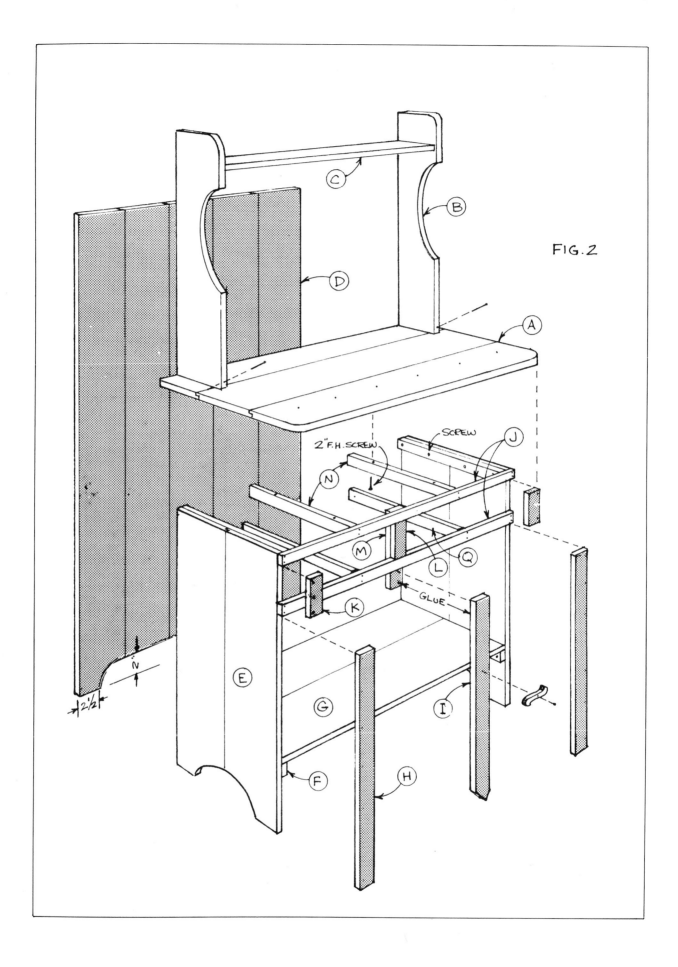

FIG. 2

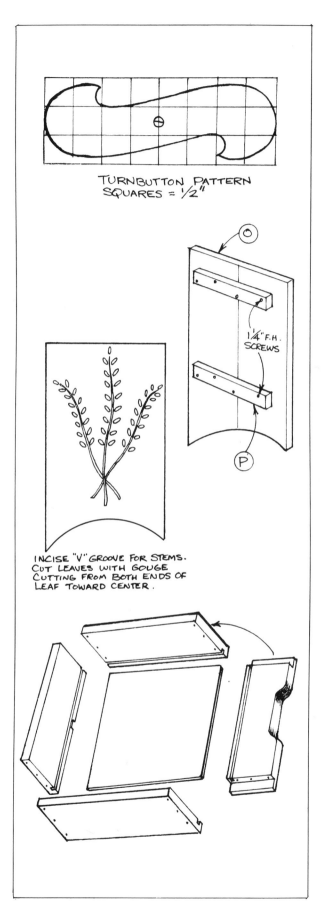

TURNBUTTON PATTERN
SQUARES = 1/2"

1/4" F.H.
SCREWS

INCISE "V" GROOVE FOR STEMS.
CUT LEAVES WITH GOUGE
CUTTING FROM BOTH ENDS OF
LEAF TOWARD CENTER.

Using a headless brad chucked in the drill, bore two small pilot holes centered in the outline and through the back. Then drive two common nails through these holes from the back and into the ends of the guides. Also drive two finishing nails through J and into the guides.

The drawers are of 1″ pine, except for the bottoms, which are of ¼″ plywood. Front, back, and sides are grooved to take the bottom. Refer to the drawer detail in Figure 1 for all dimensions.

In the old days, a plow plane would have been used to cut these grooves. They can still be cut by hand by clamping hardwood guide strips along the scribed lines, allowing for the thickness of the saw blade, and running a back- or panel saw along the guide strips to cut the sides of the groove. Then the groove is cleaned out with a ¼″ chisel.

Cut ⅜ x ¾″ rabbets on the drawer fronts to take the sides. The back should be given a ⅛″-deep x 1″ notch located to ride over the guide rail. Assemble the drawers with glue and nails but do not glue the bottom in the grooves. Make sure the drawers are flat and square before the glue dries. The turnbutton is cut using the pattern and fastened with a blued 1¼″ right-handed screw.

If you would like to try your hand at simple decorative carving, this is a good opportunity. The stems can be carved easily with a veiner chisel or even a sharp penknife. Use a small gouge to cut the leaves. If you have never tried surface carving before, practice first on a scrap of pine.

Round off all edges that would normally receive wear, and then give all outside surfaces a final sanding using 220-grit production paper. Apply an oil stain that will give the appearance of antique pine. Allow the stain to dry for 24 hours and then apply a penetrating oil finish such as Watco Danish Oil, which is very easy to use. If a clear surface finish is preferred, avoid high-gloss varnishes, which are not in keeping with the character of this simple piece. Two ¾″ porcelain or wood knobs complete the project.

Little Red Wagon

Any small child will be delighted to receive this toy wagon. It's been a favorite plaything for generations and we're sure that it will still be around in much the same form one hundred years from now.

This is a toy wagon. It is not big or strong enough to haul children; rather it was meant to haul Teddy Bear and Raggedy Ann, and for that purpose it is admirably suited. The basic design can be enlarged into a functional wagon to haul heavier loads. Just beef up the materials and use ½″ to ¾″ oak for the box, hard maple for axle supports, and steel instead of wooden axles. Of course, rubber-tired wheels will help things along. The wagon, as detailed, is an enjoyable project for a rainy, raw Saturday, and you may have sufficient scrap available to build it without having to run to the lumberyard.

The wagon box is constructed entirely of ¼″ plywood, and it is preferable that it be exterior grade as the wagon is bound to be left outdoors sooner or later. Take extra care to sand the box thoroughly so there is no danger of splinters. Fasten the sides to the ends with glue and 1″ common nails. Note that the ends of the box are inset just a bit for appearance—about ⅛″ will do it. The plywood bottom is glued and nailed all around. Make sure that none of the nails pokes through the sides as it can inflict a nasty cut.

Front and rear axle supports are 1 x 2 x 7½″ fir. Cut curved notches out of each end of the front support and drill a slightly oversize hole for a ¼″ kingbolt. Now slice the support in half to form the two identical parts of the steering assembly. The upper part is secured to the wagon bed with ¼ x 1″ machine screws, washers, lock washers, and nuts. The rear axle support is fastened to the bed with three 1″ flat-headed screws countersunk flush.

Axles are ⅜″ dowel stock and are fastened to the axle supports either by driving heavy staples over them or by drilling axles and fastening with 1½″ common nails. Wheels are cut from ¾″ exterior plywood or 1″ pine stock. Drill slightly oversize holes for the axles, drill for ⅛″ pegs, and mount a large washer, then a wheel, followed by another washer and a peg.

The wagon tongue can be fabricated from almost anything available, including dowel stock. Fasten it to the lower steering support with small metal angles screwed to the support and fastened to the tongue with a machine screw, washer, and nut. A piece of ⅜″ dowel serves as a handle.

Sand all parts of the wagon and give it a couple of coats of sealer. Now you can go ahead and paint your wagon—red, of course.

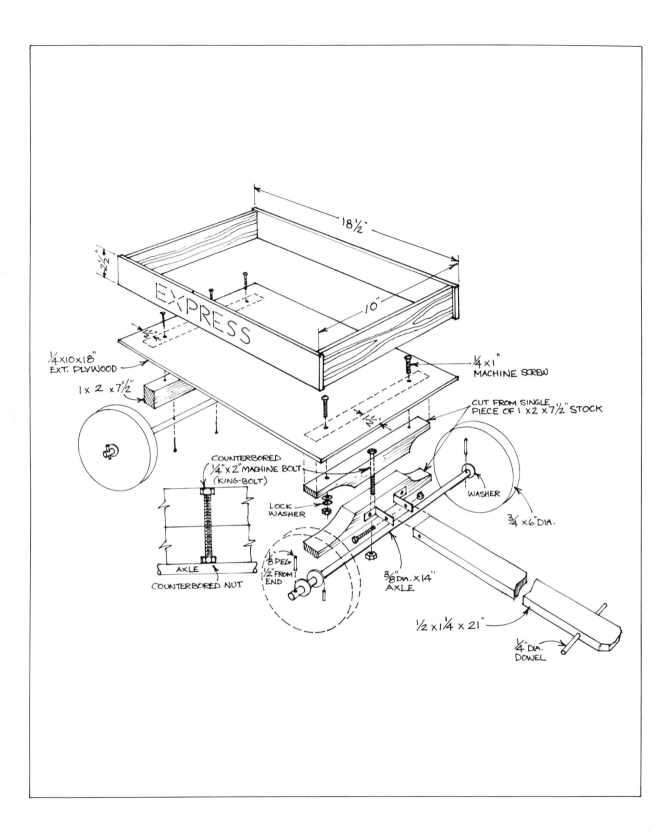

18½"

2½"

EXPRESS

10"

¼ x 10 x 18"
EXT. PLYWOOD

1 x 2 x 7½"

¼ x 1"
MACHINE SCREW

CUT FROM SINGLE
PIECE OF 1 x 2 x 7½" STOCK

COUNTERBORED
¼" x 2" MACHINE BOLT
(KING-BOLT)

WASHER

¾ x 6" DIA.

LOCK
WASHER

AXLE

COUNTERBORED NUT

⅛ PEG
½" FROM
END

⅜" DIA. x 14"
AXLE

½ x 1¼ x 21"

¼" DIA.
DOWEL

Butcher-block Table

State health codes have required restaurants to replace those fine old maple chopping blocks and food preparation counters with modern, non-absorbent surfaces. As a result, a lot of well-worn but still functional maple tables have found their way into private homes. Perhaps this has provided impetus for the growing popularity of butcher-block furniture. We've seen the butcher-block influence in just about every kind of furniture imaginable, with the possible exception of baby cribs. A good mellow work surface of maple is still a very handy thing to have in the home kitchen and, of course, is very pleasant to look at.

This table does not have a solid-maple end-grain top, but rather it is an inverted box of 1″ maple set on solid legs. This method of construction avoids the considerable expense, not to mention the tedious effort, required to build up a 2″ to 3″ slab of maple with 10″ aprons. Nevertheless, it is a handsome and durable piece, and will be light enough to move easily about the kitchen or out into the backyard for barbecues.

You'll need 8 board feet of 1″ hard maple for the top assembly, plus a piece 1½ x 24″ for the knife rack. If you want to use solid 2½ x 2½″ legs, you'll probably have to have them planed down from thicker stock. For this reason, it may be more economical to glue the legs up from three pieces of 1″ stock. This will give you legs of 2¼″

to 2⅛″ square, depending upon how thick the 1″ stock actually is when purchased. The nominal size rough cut is 1″ but, of course, finish planing will remove some stock, resulting in an actual thickness of from ¾″ to ⅞″.

The top is made up of edge-glued stock to a final dimension of 22½ x 24″. If you have a router, the most secure means of joining individual boards is with a glued spline joint of ¼″ plywood. However, the spline grooves on the top and the front and back aprons should not be run to the edges, as the spline will then show in the finished piece. This is no problem with the side aprons (one of which holds the knife rack), as all edges are concealed. If you lack a router, join the boards with ⅜″ dowels of at least 2″ length.

Front and back aprons are glued up and cut to a final size of 11 x 24″. Side aprons, which are fastened between the front and back, are 11 x 10¾″. Assemble the aprons by carefully aligning and clamping each joint, and drilling and counterboring for three 1¼″ #8 flat-headed screws and dowel plugs. After the holes have been drilled, remove the clamps, apply glue, re-clamp, and drive home screws at least ¼″ below surface. The top is fastened to the aprons with six screws driven through the top into both side aprons, and six screws driven through the front and back aprons into the edge of the top. A belt sander should be used to level all irregularities in the top assembly, and break all sharp edges.

Legs are cut to 30¼″ and fastened to the aprons with fabricated-steel flat stock, which can be purchased in 3′ lengths at most hardware stores. Bend the strap to conform to the exact width of the legs plus a 1¼″ tab on each end, as shown in Detail A. Drill ¼″ holes in each tab and fasten the legs to the aprons with two ¼″ full-thread carriage bolts, washers, and nuts, as shown in Detail B. Carriage bolts, if too long, can be hacksawed if you get the kind that are threaded all the way to the square shoulder.

The knife rack is then laid out and cut to size. The ⅜″ holes at each end are drilled out and the knife slots can be cut with a router or by drilling a series of ⅜″ holes and cleaning out waste with

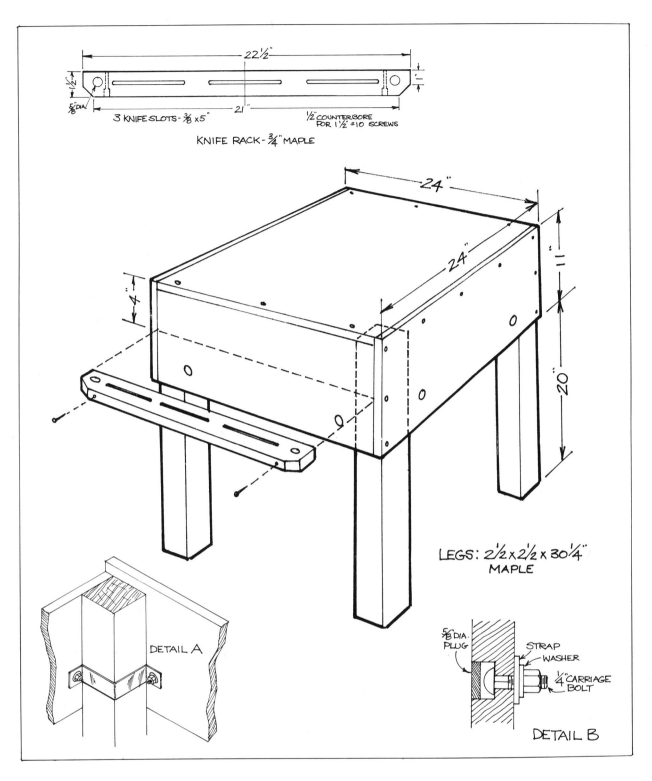

22½"

½"

⅝" DIA.

3 KNIFE SLOTS - ⅜ x 5"

21"

½" COUNTERBORE
FOR 1½" #10 SCREWS

1"

KNIFE RACK - ¾" MAPLE

24"

24"

4"

11"

20"

LEGS: 2½ x 2½ x 30¼"
MAPLE

DETAIL A

⅝" DIA.
PLUG

STRAP

WASHER

¼" CARRIAGE
BOLT

DETAIL B

a chisel. The ends of the slots should be rounded off with a file. The rack is secured to the side apron with two counterbored 1½" #10 flat-headed screws and glue.

Plug all screw holes with dowels or plugs cut with a plug cutter, and chisel off flush. Give all surfaces a careful sanding and break the sharp edges on the legs. The top and aprons should be given a clear, nontoxic finish such as that used for salad bowls. A clear, hard finish of this type can be obtained from Craftsman Wood Service Company (see p. 243 for the address). The legs may be finished with the same type of sealer or any other clear, durable finish.

117

Apothecary Chest

A perennial favorite among collectors of early Americana, the apothecary chest is a rare and very appealing piece. Original chests were generally much larger than this piece. Our adaptation is simply a small chest of drawers that has been given the compartmented look by adding dummy dividers to the drawer fronts. There are actually only three large drawers.

The home craftsman will find this an enjoyable project, as all parts of the chest can be cut from standard 1 x 12″ white pine. There is no need to joint and edge glue boards to form the case sides or top. Solid drawer dividers are used rather than drawer frames, so shrinkage and expansion should be the same between case sides and dividers, provided all are cut from the same equally seasoned boards.

Choose well-seasoned, flat ¾″ pine boards and cut the top, case sides, and dividers. Note that the dividers are ¼″ less in width than the sides to allow for the inset back panel. Lay out and cut the ¼ x ¾″ rabbets and dadoes on each case side and the ¼ x ¼″ rabbet for the back panel. Attach the top divider to the sides, flush at front edges, with glue and 2″ finishing nails. Spread glue in dadoes and insert the bottom divider, and then add the remaining dividers.

Add the plywood or Masonite back panel, gluing and nailing with ¾″ nails. Attach drawer stops with glue, and the front filler strip with glue and small finishing nails. The top is fastened flush at the back, with a ⅝″ overhang at the front and sides. Use six 1¼″ #8 wood screws driven through the top divider and into the top.

Enlarge the patterns for the base front and sides, and transfer to ¾″ pine. Cut scrolls, round off upper edges, and sand well. Miter the front corners and test for a good fit before fastening with 1¼″ #8 screws driven from the inside.

Follow Figure 2 for drawer construction details. Guide strips are glued to the drawer sides, and the drawer bottom extends ½″ beyond, and is nailed to the drawer back. Drawer sides and front are dadoed to receive the bottom. Note that the drawer fronts are grooved to receive dummy dividers, and are finish sanded before the divider strips are glued in place. Round the front edges of the dividers, and distress them a bit before adding them to the drawer fronts.

This piece will look good if distressed a bit with a tire chain, awl, or other tool. Rasp signs

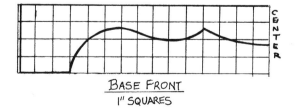

BASE FRONT
1″ SQUARES

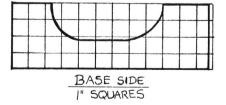

BASE SIDE
1″ SQUARES

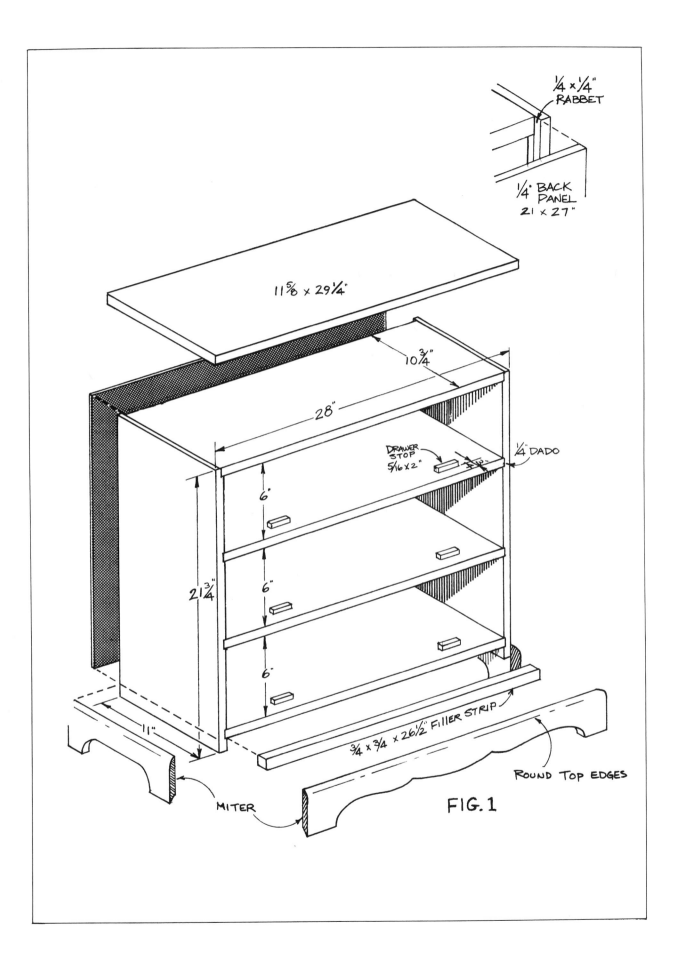

¼ x ¼" RABBET

¼" BACK PANEL 21 x 27"

11⅝ x 29¼"

10¾"

28"

DRAWER STOP 5/16 x 2"

¼" DADO

6"

6"

6"

21¾"

11"

¾ x ¾ x 26½" FILLER STRIP

ROUND TOP EDGES

MITER

FIG. 1

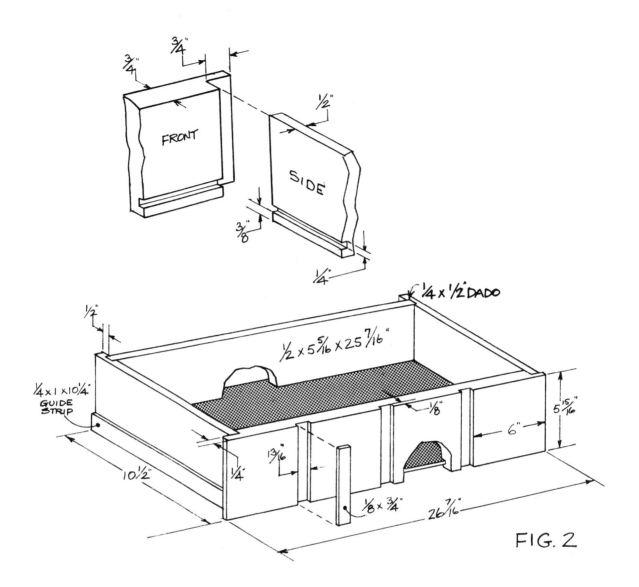

FRONT

SIDE

¾"

¾"

½"

⅜"

¼"

¼ x ½ DADO

½"

½ x 5⁵⁄₁₆ x 25 ⁷⁄₁₆"

¼ x 1 x 10¼"
GUIDE
STRIP

¼"

13⁄16"

⅛"

⅛ x ¾"

26⁷⁄₁₆"

10½"

6"

5¹⁵⁄₁₆"

FIG. 2

of wear along the top edges and front corners and then give the piece a final sanding. The chest in the photograph was given one coat of Minwax Early American stain. When this dried, full-strength satin-finish urethane varnish was applied. After drying, this was sanded lightly to a uniform dull finish. A second coat of urethane was then applied, followed by a rubdown with 5/0 steel wool.

One-inch-diameter porcelain knobs look the best, but twelve of them will cost about $17. If you have some glossy white enamel on hand, you can save a few dollars by painting wooden knobs, or just staining them to match the chest. We personally feel that any furniture project worth building deserves the best hardware you can purchase.

Tumbling Toby

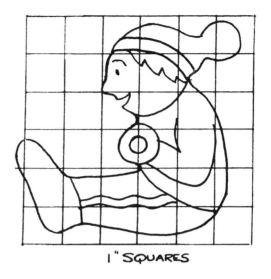

1" SQUARES

Here's a simple wooden toy that's guaranteed to delight youngsters and intrigue grownups as well. Toby is counterbalanced so that a light tap will set him somersaulting back and forth along the parallel bars, and he'll keep going for some time.

This toy can be made quickly from just a few scraps of pine and dowel. Low in cost and easily mass-produced, it's an ideal item for sale to gift and toy shops.

Start by enlarging the pattern squares to 1" on heavy paper. Then transfer the figure to the enlarged grid. Cut out the pattern, and use it to trace the figure on ½" pine. Jigsaw to shape and drill a ¼" hole through the hands. Insert a 3" length of dowel so that it protrudes an equal dis-

tance on each side and glue in place.

The parallel bars are shaped from ¾" pine. Rasp a gentle curve along the top of each bar as shown. Drill holes in the bottom edge of each bar for ⅜" dowel uprights.

Cut two base pieces and drill three ⅜" holes in each, two for the upright supports and one for the long stretcher. Sand all parts carefully and assemble the parallel bars with glue. Temporarily place a spacer block between the bars while the glue dries to keep them parallel and spread about an inch apart.

Finish the toy with a couple of coats of thinned shellac. Toby can be left natural or painted with enamels or colored with felt-tip pens.

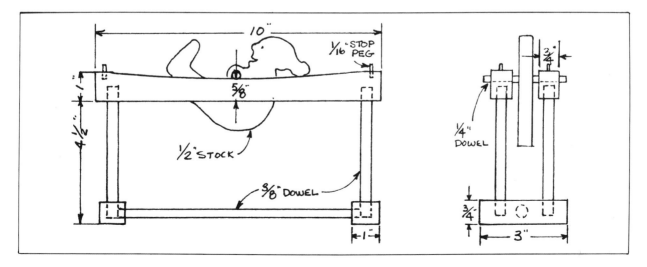

Coffee Table

Crisp, uncluttered lines and an interesting contrast between elegant walnut and natural maple make this table a worthy project for the woodworker of moderate skill.

The top is an assembly consisting of a ½″ walnut plywood panel, edged with maple strips. The lower leg assembly is made entirely of hard maple.

Legs are shaped from 2″ nominal stock and are 1¼″ square at top and bottom. Cut the two long stretchers to overall length from ¾ x 1¾ x 36½″ stock, and shape tenons on each end. A tenon length of 1¼″ is about right. Note that the stretchers are tapered from 1¼″ at each end to a midpoint width of 1¾″. The end rails are shaped from ¾ x 1½ x 15½″ stock, and are not tapered.

Make an identifying mark on all legs, rails, and stretchers so that tenons and dowel pins mate with the parts for which they were individually fitted. Lay out and cut mortises, and bore the legs for ⅜″ dowel pins to fasten the end rails.

Sand all parts thoroughly to remove machin-

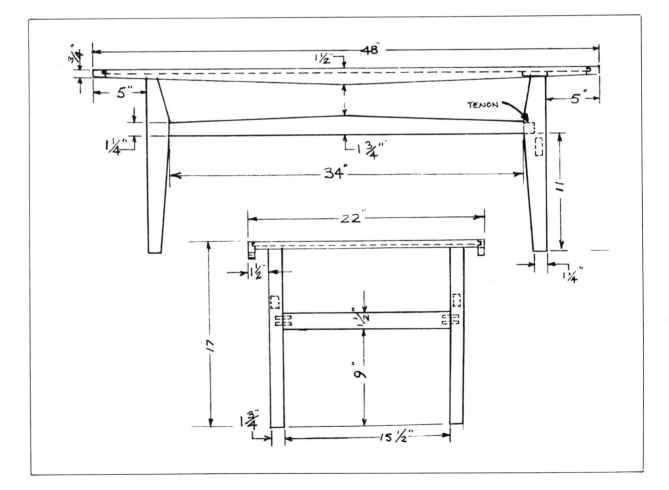

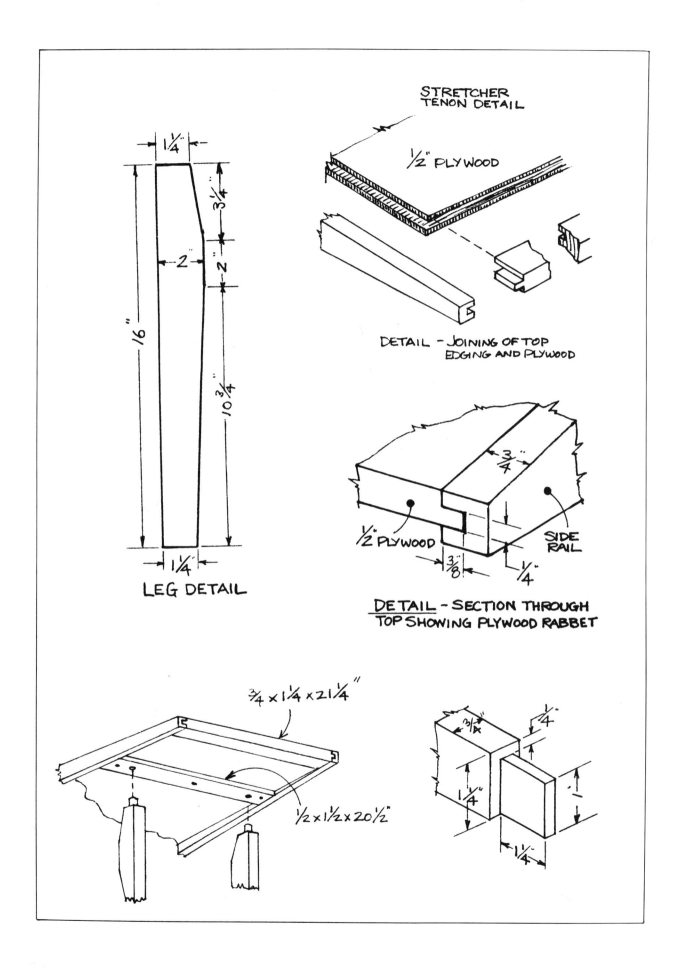

STRETCHER
TENON DETAIL

½" PLYWOOD

DETAIL – JOINING OF TOP
EDGING AND PLYWOOD

1¼"

3¾"

2

2"

16"

10¾"

1¼"

LEG DETAIL

¾"

3¾"

½" PLYWOOD

3⁄8"

¼"

SIDE
RAIL

DETAIL – SECTION THROUGH
TOP SHOWING PLYWOOD RABBET

¾ x 1¼ x 21¼"

½ x 1½ x 20½"

3⁄4"

¼"

1¼"

1¼"

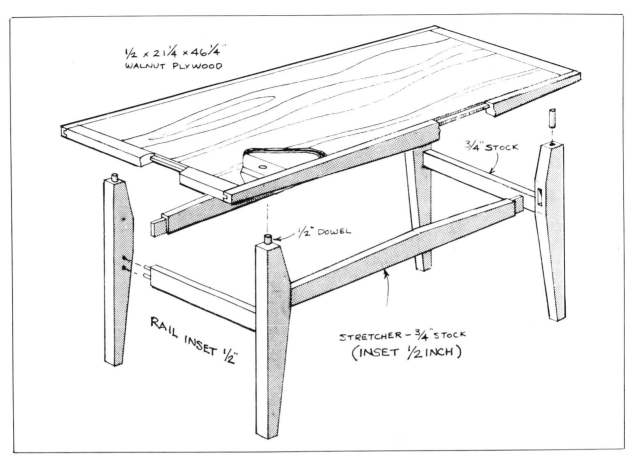

1/2 x 21/4 x 461/4"
WALNUT PLYWOOD

3/4" STOCK

1/2" DOWEL

RAIL INSET 1/2"

STRETCHER — 3/4" STOCK
(INSET 1/2 INCH)

ing marks before assembling the frame with glue and clamps.

Next, the plywood panel for the top is cut to overall size and rabbeted around all four edges. Use a plywood-cutting blade with your table or radial saw to produce a smooth, nonsplintered cut.

Shape the two tapered edge strips for the top from 3/4" maple, then cut the two end strips. Set up a dado cutter, and run a 1/4 x 3/8" groove along all edging strips. Also cut 1/4 x 3/8" tongues on both ends of the wide strips. Assemble the top with glue and clamp overnight.

When the top has dried, cut two cleats to fit across the underside. Drive a small headless brad into the top center of each leg and use these brads to punch marking holes in each cleat to locate dowel sockets. Bore the legs to a depth of 1" to take 1/2 x 1 3/8" dowel pins. Groove the pins to release trapped air and glue, and drive them into the legs so that 1/2" protrudes. Bore a 1/2" hole through the cleats, using the punch marks as centers, and glue the cleats to the legs.

Complete the assembly by turning the top upside down and placing the frame assembly on it.

When it is centered, fasten the cleats to the top with countersunk 3/4" #10 wood screws.

While many prefer the contemporary look of open-grain oiled walnut, a tabletop such as this, which may be subjected to spilled drinks and wet glasses, is best given a paste wood-filler treatment prior to sealing. Use a walnut-toned paste wood filler, and mix with turpentine according to the manufacturer's directions. Apply the filler to the panel with a brush, and work only a small section at a time. When the wet appearance is gone, rub the filler well into the pores of the wood, using a pad of burlap. Rub first across the grain and then with it. Remove all traces of surface filler before it begins to harden, as it is difficult to remove once it sets up. For that reason, don't try to do the entire top at once.

Sand the panel lightly, taking care not to go across the grain of the end strips. Dust the surface and use a tack cloth to pick up all traces of dust. Finish the top with at least three coats of urethane varnish, rubbing down with 4/0 steel wool between coats. The lower frame and underside of the top should each receive at least two coats.

124

Money Printer

Here's a clever magic trick that youngsters will have a lot of fun with. Insert a blank piece of paper between the rollers of the "press," crank the handle, and out comes a real honest-to-goodness dollar bill!

The secret is in the black ribbon that forms an S curve around the two rollers. When a real dollar bill is fed into the rollers, it is wrapped around the lower roller out of sight under the ribbon. As blank paper is fed in from the other side, it dis-appears and the bill comes out, giving the illusion that the blank paper is being printed into a dollar bill.

This is a good project for the novice woodworker. The base is made by shaping the uprights and drilling both at the same time for ⅜" holes for the roller shafts. The rollers are 1" dowels turned on a lathe with ⅜" axles, or drilled to receive dowel axles.

The dowel on the upper axle should be shouldered to fit a ¼" hole in the crank arm, though in a pinch it can be tapered instead.

Glue black ribbon one full turn around each roller to cover them completely, as shown. Assemble the rollers to the base and add a wooden knob, which can be a drilled-out cabinet knob.

To use the money printer, insert a real bill between the rollers from the side away from you when the crank is to your right. Turn the wooden knob toward you until the bill is just hidden between the rollers. You're now ready to "print" by inserting a blank into the side nearest you and turning the crank toward you. As the blank feeds in, the bill comes out the other side.

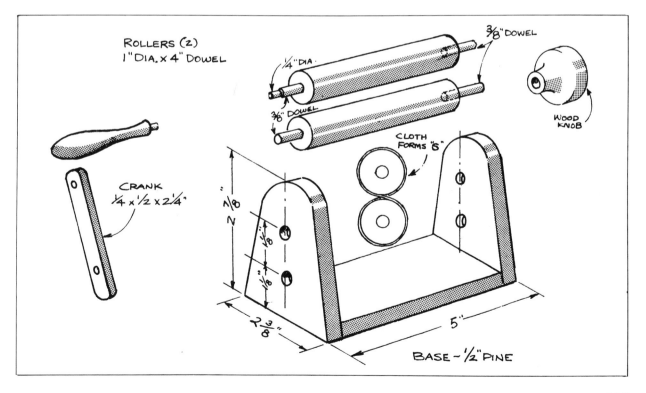

Gun Cabinet

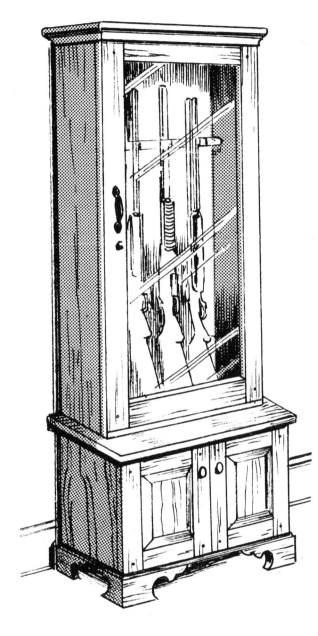

upper section is high enough to hold most rifles and shotguns. The plans show a wood frame and glass door, which are relatively economical and easy to make. If you are willing to spend about an additional $50, an eight-light sash makes a very handsome door and can be ordered through your building supply dealer. These pine sashes are available in 1⅛ x 24 x 54″, and should require only a bit of planing of the lower rail to fit the cabinet as dimensioned.

Start construction with the base unit by cutting the six bracket feet according to the pattern. Four of these are joined in pairs with splined miters to form the front feet. The remaining two are rabbeted and glued to the notched rear pieces.

The base molding is best shaped with a router, though a separate molding can be glued to a length of ¾ x 2¼″ stock. This molding is cut into three parts and mitered as shown. Glue the base molding to the feet, flush with the outer edges, and reinforce the joint with glue blocks.

Next, cut the lower-cabinet bottom, sides, and top to size from glued-up stock. Rabbet the lower edges of the sides to fit around the bottom. The back edges of the sides are also rabbeted to hold the recessed ¼″ back panel. Join these parts with glue and countersunk finishing nails. Use 2-penny common nails to fasten the back panel.

Align this assembly on the base so that the back of the panel is flush with the back ends of the base. The front edge of the base molding should extend 1½″ beyond the front edge of the cabinet bottom. This allows for the addition of the two small doors, which are ¾″ thick.

Fasten the cabinet to the base with glue and countersunk finishing nails. Shape the rounded trim from a length of ¾ x ¾″ pine, mitering the ends and fastening it around the cabinet top with small countersunk finishing nails. Cut the plywood back panel to size and fasten with small nails.

Cut the rails and stiles for both lower doors. These can be easily tenoned and grooved with the bench saw. The beveled panels are shaped for an easy fit in the grooves. Assemble the doors dry to ascertain that all parts fit well before finish sand-

This good-looking pine cabinet was designed primarily for the storage of rifles, shotguns, and fishing rods, with a lower cabinet for related gear. If you're not inclined to hunt or fish, you will find that with the addition of adjustable shelves, it will serve most admirably as a curio cabinet.

The cabinet is made in two parts, both for ease of construction and for moving. The lower section has a shelf and plenty of storage space, while the

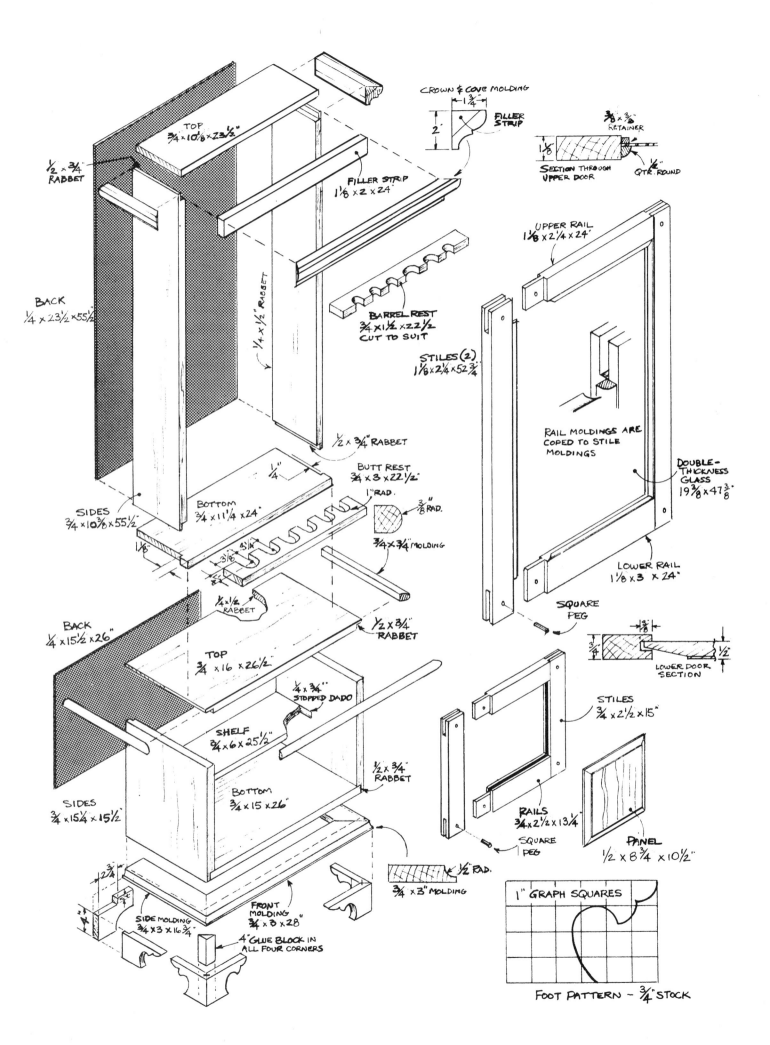

TOP
¾ × 10⅝ × 23½"

½ × ¾ RABBET

CROWN & COVE MOLDING
1¾
2'
FILLER STRIP

⅜ × ⅜ RETAINER
1⅛
SECTION THROUGH UPPER DOOR
¼" QTR. ROUND

FILLER STRIP
1⅛ × 2 × 24"

BACK
¼ × 23½ × 55½"

¼ × ½" RABBET

BARREL REST
¾ × 1½ × 22½
CUT TO SUIT

UPPER RAIL
1⅛ × 2¼ × 24"

STILES (2)
1⅛ × 2¼ × 52¾"

RAIL MOLDINGS ARE COPED TO STILE MOLDINGS

DOUBLE-THICKNESS GLASS
19⅜ × 47⅜"

½ × ¾" RABBET

SIDES
¾ × 10⅝ × 55½"

¼"

BUTT REST
¾ × 3 × 22½"

1"RAD.

BOTTOM
¾ × 11¼ × 24"

1⅛

⅜

¾

1" RAD.
⅜" RAD.
¾ × ¾ MOLDING

LOWER RAIL
1⅛ × 3 × 24"

SQUARE PEG

¼ × ½" RABBET

½ × ¾" RABBET

BACK
¼ × 15½ × 26"

TOP
¾ × 16 × 26½"

¼ × ¾" STOPPED DADO

SHELF
¾ × 6 × 25½"

½ × ¾" RABBET

SIDES
¾ × 15¼ × 15½"

BOTTOM
¾ × 15 × 26"

⅜
¾
½
LOWER DOOR SECTION

STILES
¾ × 2½ × 15"

RAILS
¾ × 2½ × 13¼"

SQUARE PEG

PANEL
½ × 8¾ × 10½"

2¼

4"

SIDE MOLDING
¾ × 3 × 16¾"

FRONT MOLDING
¾ × 3 × 28"

4" GLUE BLOCK IN ALL FOUR CORNERS

½ RAD.
¾ × 3" MOLDING

1" GRAPH SQUARES

FOOT PATTERN - ¾" STOCK

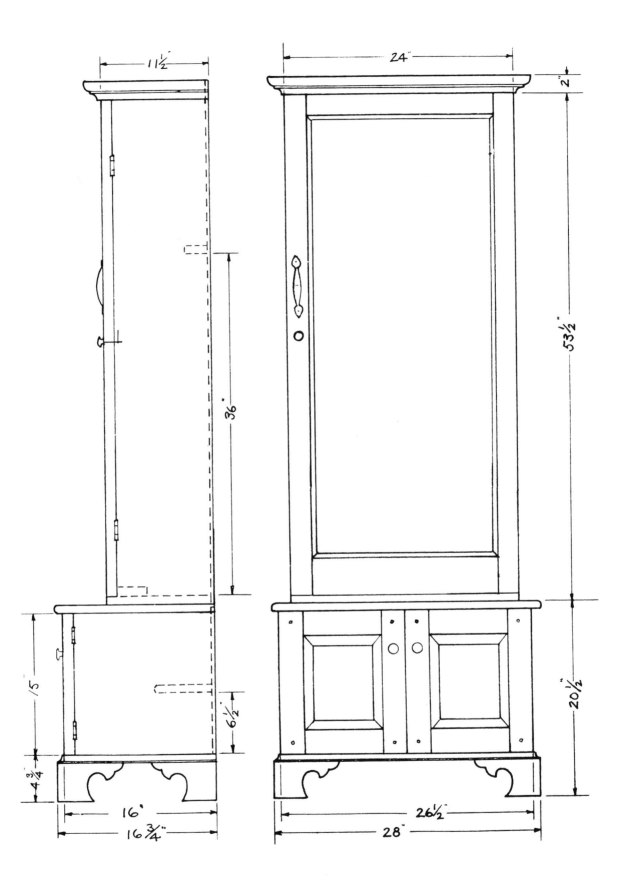

ing, gluing, and clamping. Do not glue the panels in place. They should be left free to move in the door-frame grooves. Drill the corner joints to receive a ⅜″-square peg, which locks the slip joint and provides a decorative touch.

The parts for the upper cabinet are next cut to size, sanded, and assembled. Glue and nail the sides to the top and bottom, making sure that the assembly is square as the glue sets. Add the shelf and back panel, nailing at 8″ intervals. The panel fits into side rabbets and covers the back edges of the cabinet top and bottom. The 1⅛″ filler strip is cut slightly long, nailed to the top and sides, and is then trimmed flush with the sides.

Cut a triangular strip and glue it to a 4′ length of crown molding as shown in the detail. This molding is then cut, mitered, and nailed around, flush with the top edge of the cabinet.

Rails and stiles for the upper door are cut, tenoned, and grooved as shown. It's best to take the overall door measurements from the completed upper cabinet, and make the door frame very slightly oversize. Later it can be planed to an exact fit. Make sure the door is square and flat after gluing joints and clamping. As was done with the lower doors, the corners should be locked by driving in ½″-square pegs.

The double-thickness window glass rests in a rabbet formed by nailing a ½″ quarter-round molding to the door frame as shown. The ends of the upper and lower moldings should be coped to fit neatly over the side moldings.

Lay the glass in place and add square retainer strips that have had undersize pilot holes predrilled in them. To avoid cracking the glass, push brads through the retainer strips and into the frame with long-nose pliers. For a neat appearance, these strips should be mitered at the corners.

Cut the butt and barrel rests and glue them in place. The barrel rest must be cut to suit your particular weapons. Cover the cutout portions of the rests with strips of green felt, cemented on to protect the butts and barrel bluing.

Finish sand the cabinet and remove all dust before staining the interior and exterior. Seal all surfaces with three coats of satin varnish, rubbing down each coat with fine steel wool, and using a tack cloth before adding the next coat.

Install magnetic catches for the lower doors. A cupboard latch, engaging a slot in the cabinet side, can be used for the upper door. If there are children in the house, install a cam-type cabinet door lock.

Serving Tray

Patterned after a lovely Shaker original, this serving tray can be made of pine, mahogany, or walnut. The ⅜″ thickness of the sides and ends is no problem, as these parts are narrow enough to be easily resawed from thicker stock.

It's best to prepare the bottom first as its final thickness will determine the width of the grooves in which it rides. Basically, the bottom is ¼″ plywood or hardboard, veneered on both sides to match the rest of the piece. Mahogany and white pine veneer cost about the same while walnut is a bit more. The veneer is simply contact cemented to the plywood, the excess trimmed off with a veneer knife. Sand the veneered panel carefully.

Next cut stock for the ends and lay out and run the grooves ³⁄₁₆″ deep and wide enough to take the bottom in an easy slip fit. Enlarge the pattern for the curved top edge on heavy paper and cut out and trace the outline on the stock. Jigsaw to shape, round off the top edges carefully, and sand.

Cut the sides to length and width, and groove them the same as the ends. Round off the top edges. Use glue and clamps to join the ends and sides but do not glue the bottom in its groove. Give the pieces a final sanding and finish with clear sealer or a penetrating oil finish.

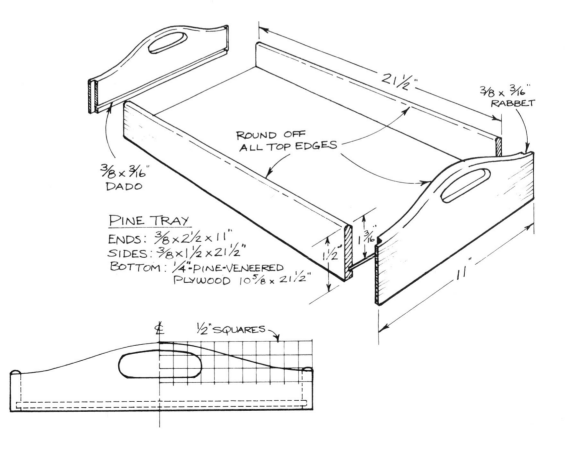

21½″

⅜ x ³⁄₁₆″ RABBET

ROUND OFF ALL TOP EDGES

⅜ x ³⁄₁₆″ DADO

1½″ 1 ³⁄₁₆″

11″

PINE TRAY
ENDS: ⅜ x 2½ x 11″
SIDES: ⅜ x 1½ x 21½″
BOTTOM: ¼″-PINE-VENEERED PLYWOOD 10⅝ x 21½″

½″ SQUARES

Chopping-block Table

This handsome chopping-block table features a cutlery drawer, double utensil rack, and storage shelf. The top consists of twenty-eight lengths of hard maple, laid on edge, glued, and bolted. Maple, poplar, clear fir, even pine can be used for all other parts.

Begin by hand or power jointing twenty-eight pieces of ¾ x 2 x 21″ maple for the top. Lay twenty-six pieces flat with ends carefully aligned, and with a framing square scribe a line across all pieces, 2½″ in from each end to locate holes for the ⅜″ threaded rods.

Using a ⁷⁄₁₆″ auger and doweling jig, bore the two holes through all twenty-six pieces, taking care to keep all holes perfectly aligned. The two outer pieces are counterbored with a ¾″ bit to a depth of ⅝″; the remaining thickness is drilled through at ⁷⁄₁₆″ as shown in the detail in Figure 2.

Apply glue to all mating surfaces, thread the rods through, and clamp together by placing lock washers and nuts on each end of the threaded rods. After the top has dried, it can be belt sanded flat and the four holes plugged with slices of ¾″ dowel.

The legs can be either solid stock or glued up from two or more thicknesses, carefully jointed for an inconspicuous glue line. Cut three aprons B and C and upper and lower front rails H and I, and join them to the legs using two ⅜ x 1¾″ dowels at each apron end, and one ⅜ x 1½″ dowel at each rail end. Glue and clamp the assembly.

Next cut the drawer rails F. Note that these are notched at each end to fit around the legs and butt against the aprons. Counterbore the drawer rails and fasten them to the aprons with three 2″ #8 flat-headed screws per rail.

Cut two guide strips G to fit between the front and back legs, butting against the aprons and flush with inboard edges of the drawer guides. Secure these with three 1¼″ #8 flat-headed screws per guide.

In order to fasten the top, three ¾ x ¾ x 14½″ cleats D and E are cut to fit between the legs. Predrill and countersink for two 1½″ #10 flat-headed screws up through each cleat, as shown in Figure 1. The cleats are fastened to the aprons with three 1¼″ #8 flat-headed screws per cleat. Triangular blocks J are added to each corner of the frame to provide additional rigidity. Fasten these with glue and finishing nails driven into undersize pilot holes.

The parts for the upper utensil rack are next cut to size. Note that the uprights receive ⅜ x 2″ rabbets to half-lap into notches cut in each side of the top slab. The upper ends of the uprights are notched to receive the 3½″-wide front and back pieces, which are drilled for heavy wire S hooks.

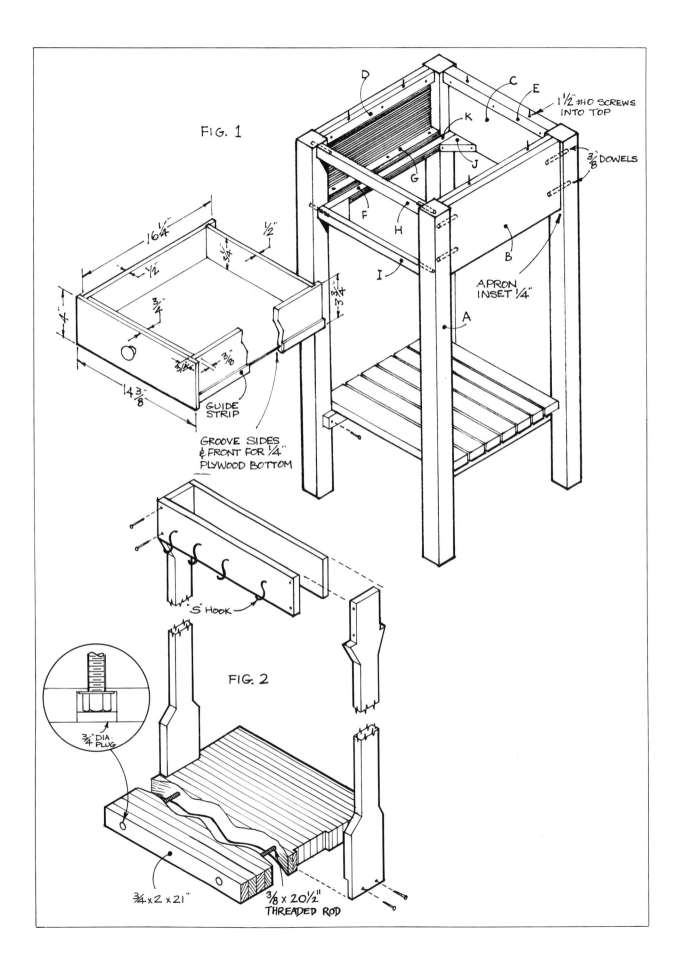

FIG. 1

16¼"

½"

¾"

½"

4"

¾"

3½"

14⅜"

3/8

¾"

3/8

GUIDE STRIP

GROOVE SIDES & FRONT FOR ¼" PLYWOOD BOTTOM

D

C

E

1½" #10 SCREWS INTO TOP

3/8" DOWELS

K

J

G

F

H

I

B

APRON INSET ¼"

A

S HOOK

FIG. 2

¾" DIA. PLUG

¾ x 2 x 21"

3/8 x 20½" THREADED ROD

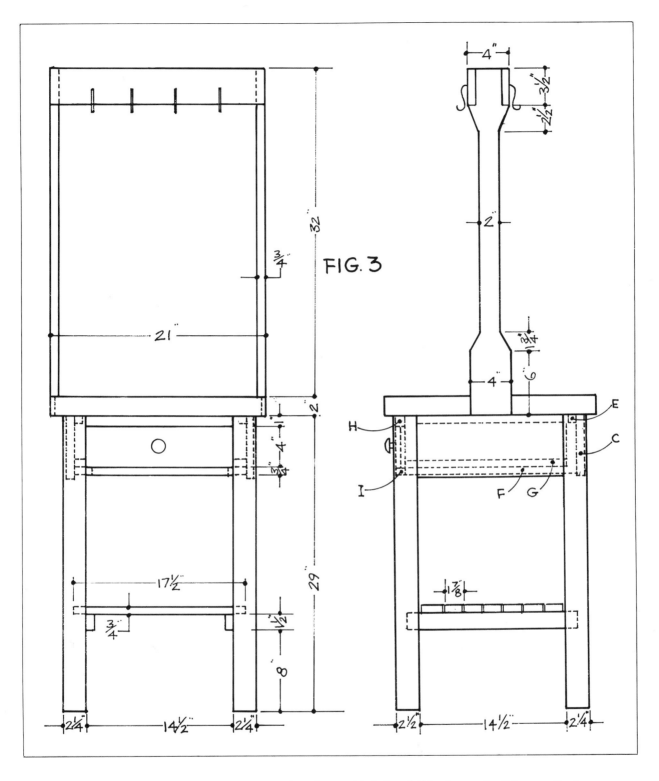

FIG. 3

The lower shelf consists of seven lengths of ¾ x 1⅛ x 17½″ stock resting on cleats which are screwed between the front and back legs. Allow equal space between the slats, and fasten them to the cleats with a screw at each end.

The drawer front is rabbeted along the top and ends to receive the 3¾″-wide sides. The bottom, which is of ¼″ plywood, slides easily in grooves cut ¼″ up from the lower edges of the front and sides. The drawer back is glued into dadoes in the sides, and the bottom is nailed to the assembly.

After the drawer is assembled, it should be inserted, and when the front is flush with the upper and lower rails, short lengths of ⅜″ dowel K are glued into holes bored into the rails to serve as drawer stops.

Center the leg assembly upside down on the underside of the top and mark locations for eight screws to be driven up through cleats D and E and rail H into undersize pilot holes in the top.

Finish the top with either an application of warm salad oil, or better still, the special non-toxic finish made especially for salad bowls. The remainder of the table and rack should be given two or three coats of a urethane finish. Sand lightly and dust well between coats.

If you wish, casters can be added to the legs so that the unit can be moved about the kitchen. In this case, it may be necessary to cut the legs a bit shorter.

BILL OF MATERIALS

Key	Part	Pcs. Req'd	T	W	L
A	leg	4	2¼″	2¼″	29″
B	side apron	2	¾″	6″	14½″
C	back apron	1	¾″	6″	14½″
D	side cleat	2	¾″	¾″	14½″
E	back cleat	1	¾″	¾″	14½″
F	drawer rail	2	¾″	1¾″	17″
G	guide strip	2	¾″	1¼″	14½″
H	upper rail	1	¾″	1″	14½″
I	lower rail	1	¾″	¾″	14½″
J	triangular glue block	4			
K	drawer stop		2 ⅜″ dowel		

Eighteenth-Century Mirror

paper, cut along the outline and trace around this template, transferring the design to the stock. Use a saber saw to cut the scroll. Rasp and plane a bevel around the back edge and drill two holes for heavy cord, which is looped over a wall hanger.

Distress the back and frame and sand, finishing with 220-grit paper. Stain to suit and finish with thinned shellac or satin varnish. Fasten the mirror with glazier's points or brads and nail the frame to the backboard. We duplicated antique nails by filing the heads of box nails to a rectangular shape.

A smaller version of this charming piece appeared in *The Pine Furniture of Early New England* by Russell H. Kettell (Dover, 1929). We designed ours a bit larger to use a standard 8 x 10″ mirror.

Rip four feet of ¾ x 1⅜″ clear pine for the frame. Resaw this strip to ⅝″ thickness and cut a 1¼ x ¼″ rabbet along one edge. Plane the strip to the rounded profile shown and cut it into four pieces, which are then mitered and joined with glue.

The backboard is ¾″ pine planed to ½″ to ⅝″ thickness. Enlarge the scroll pattern on heavy

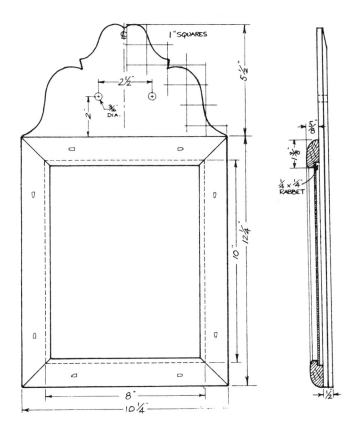

135

Wall Cabinet

This nicely proportioned cabinet has a good deal of charm, whether painted or stained. It is so practical you'll probably want to make more than one, especially since it can be used in any room of the house. We use one as a medicine chest alongside a large antique mirror hung over the lavatory.

Although you can build the shutters yourself, it's a lot quicker to buy them ready-made. We used a pine standard size of ¾ x 8 x 20″, available at any home improvement center. The ones we used have movable louvers that can be opened and closed by a wooden bar on the back side.

The sides are first cut to length and width and the curves transferred from a full-size template. Lay out and rout three ¼″-deep dadoes in each piece. The exact width of the dadoes will depend on the thickness of the shelf stock, so have the material on hand for accurate measurement.

Workers with power equipment will have no problem routing these dadoes. If you only have hand tools, clamp hardwood strips to the stock and use them to guide the backsaw. Cut two par-

allel kerfs or grooves and then clean them out with a chisel.

The plywood back fits into a rabbet, which properly should be stopped at the lower edge of the wide bottom shelf. If you plan to paint the cabinet, use ordinary ¼″ fir plywood. If the cabinet is to be stained and sealed, don't use fir plywood, as it almost always looks horrible when stained. Instead use ⁵⁄₁₆″ knotty-pine-veneered plywood. This veneered plywood is sold in full 4 x 8′ sheets. However, half sheets or smaller pieces can usually be obtained wherever unfinished kitchen cabinets are sold, or can be ordered by your local supplier. Incidentally, this plywood is very useful for paneled cupboard doors, case backs, and many other applications.

Again, if you have just hand tools, use a hardwood guide strip to guide a sharp utility knife and score the side of the rabbet with repeated passes, then chisel out the waste. The bottom can be cleaned up with a flat bastard file.

Cut three stationary and one adjustable shelves and drill a series of small holes for pegs to support the adjustable shelf. Sand all parts, working with at least three grits of papers starting with medium and working down to very fine.

If you plan to stain the piece, it's best to stain first before assembly to avoid having glue drips cause uneven staining. The shelves are glued into place and the back is fastened with small nails.

Check the case carefully to make sure it stays square, and use clamps or temporarily nailed braces if necessary. The doors are shaped at the tops as shown and fastened with overlay hinges mounted as shown. Two small knobs complete the project.

In finishing our cabinet we tried something a bit different and it worked out quite well. We wanted to color the piece but let the grain show through, so we chose a Lexington green stain by Minwax. As it came from the can, it seemed much too bright, so we mixed a bit of Minwax walnut stain in with it. The resulting color was a very attractive muted or antique green. This was allowed to dry for several days and the piece was then given two coats of satin-finish urethane varnish.

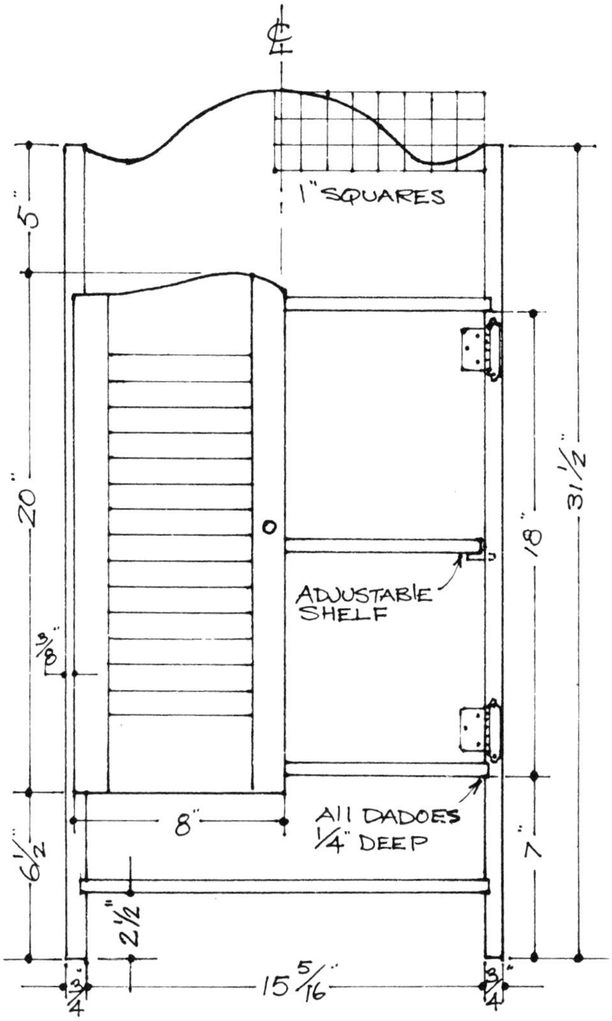

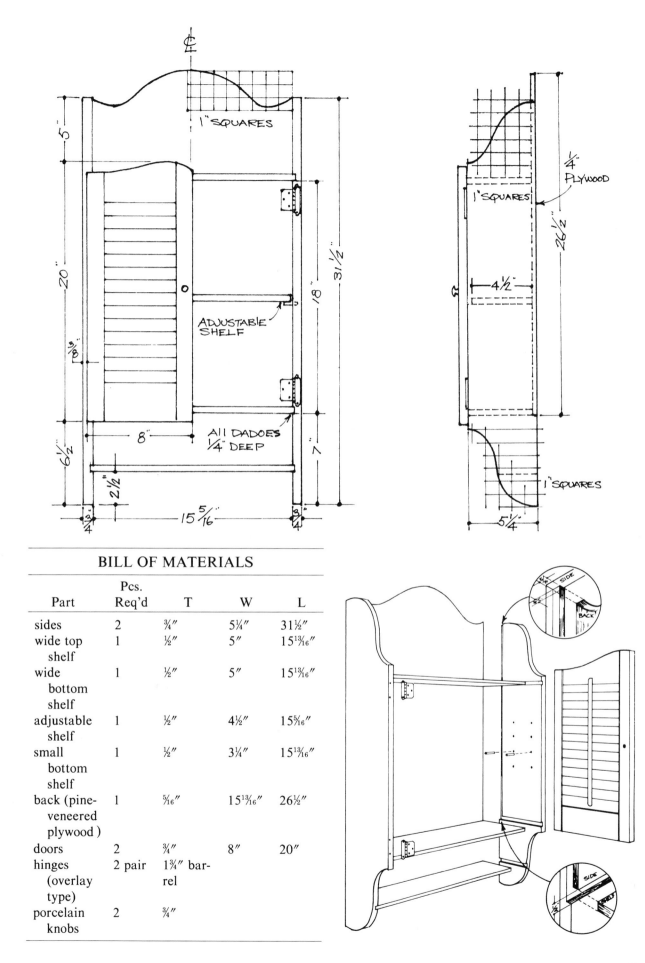

1" SQUARES
5"
20"
18"
31 1/2"
ADJUSTABLE SHELF
3/8"
8"
All DADOES 1/4" DEEP
6 1/2"
7"
2 1/2"
15 5/16"
3/4
3/4"

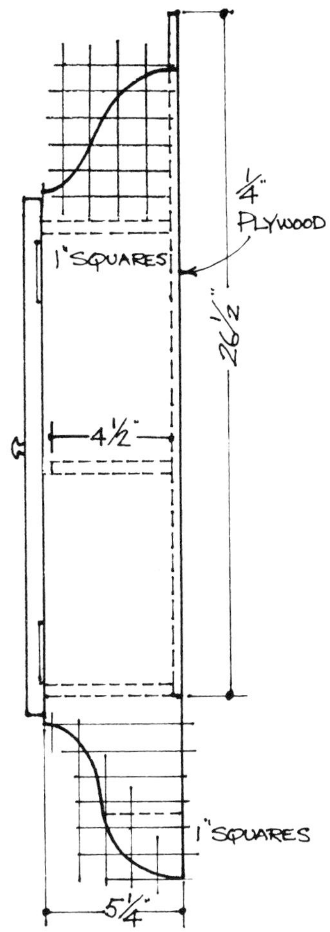

1/4" PLYWOOD
1" SQUARES
26 1/2"
4 1/2"
1" SQUARES
5 1/4"

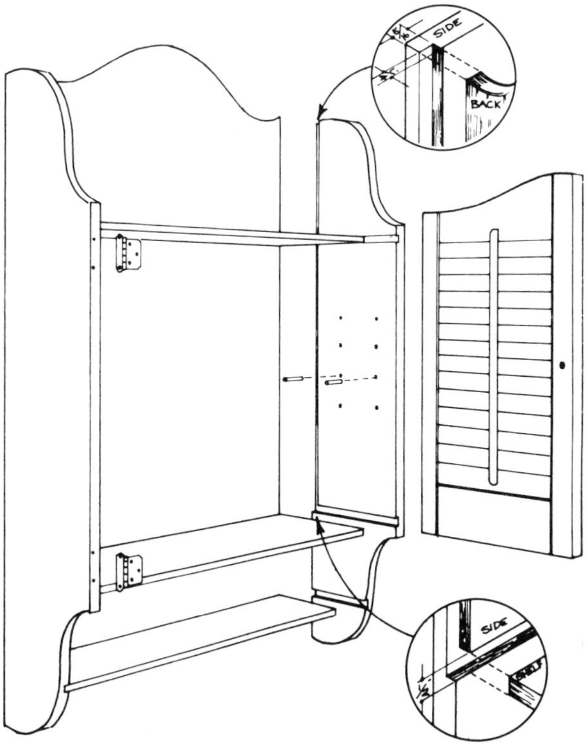

SIDE
BACK
SIDE
SHELF

BILL OF MATERIALS

Part	Pcs. Req'd	T	W	L
sides	2	¾″	5¼″	31½″
wide top shelf	1	½″	5″	15¹³⁄₁₆″
wide bottom shelf	1	½″	5″	15¹³⁄₁₆″
adjustable shelf	1	½″	4½″	15⁵⁄₁₆″
small bottom shelf	1	½″	3¼″	15¹³⁄₁₆″
back (pine-veneered plywood)	1	⁵⁄₁₆″	15¹³⁄₁₆″	26½″
doors	2	¾″	8″	20″
hinges (overlay type)	2 pair	1¾″ barrel		
porcelain knobs	2	¾″		

Animal Mobile

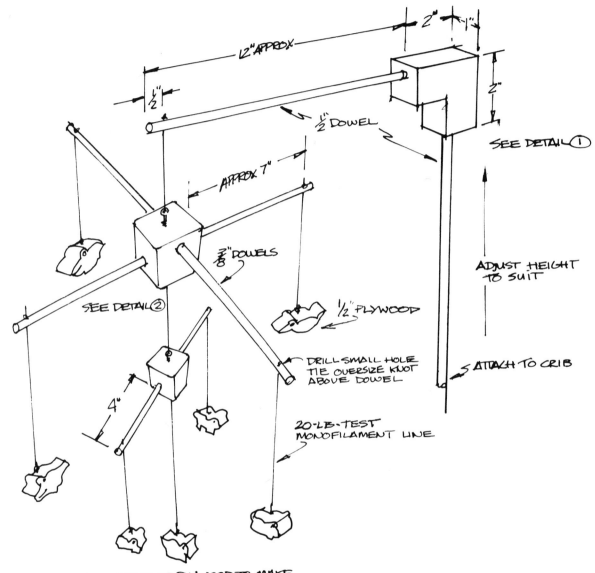

12" APPROX

2"

1"

1/2"

1/2" DOWEL

2"

SEE DETAIL 1

APPROX 7"

3/8" DOWELS

ADJUST HEIGHT TO SUIT

SEE DETAIL 2

1/2" PLYWOOD

DRILL SMALL HOLE TIE OVERSIZE KNOT ABOVE DOWEL

4"

20-LB-TEST MONOFILAMENT LINE

ATTACH TO CRIB

USE GOOD GRADE OF PLYWOOD TO MAKE ANIMALS AS MOST SOLID WOODS WILL SPLIT THROUGH THIN SECTIONS

CRIB ATTACHMENT CAN BE ELIMINATED AND MOBILE HUNG FROM CEILING

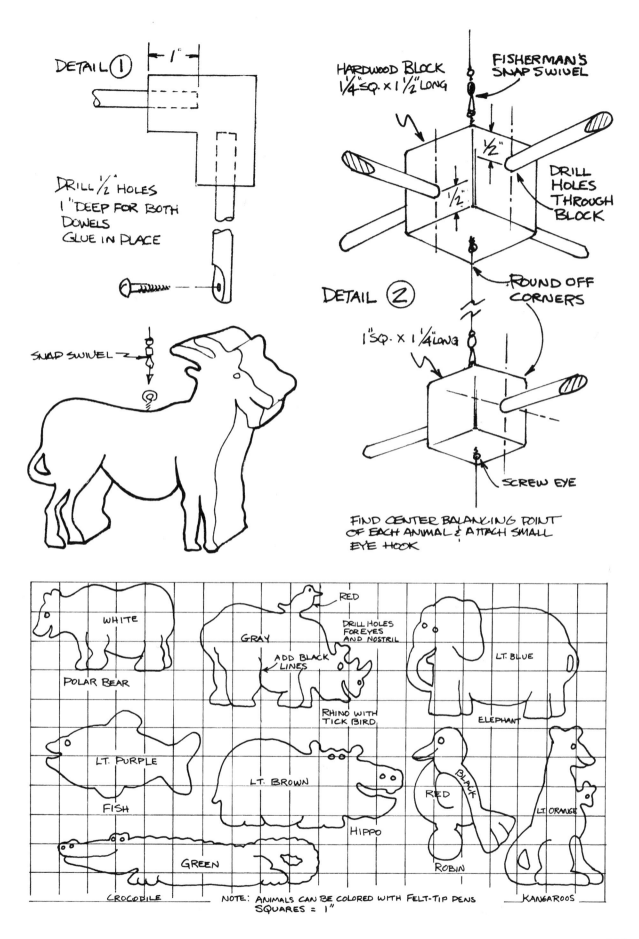

DETAIL ①

1"

DRILL ½" HOLES
1" DEEP FOR BOTH
DOWELS
GLUE IN PLACE

SNAP SWIVEL

HARDWOOD BLOCK
1¼"SQ. X 1½" LONG

FISHERMAN'S
SNAP SWIVEL

½"

½"

DRILL
HOLES
THROUGH
BLOCK

DETAIL ②

ROUND OFF
CORNERS

1" SQ. X 1¼" LONG

SCREW EYE

FIND CENTER BALANCING POINT
OF EACH ANIMAL & ATTACH SMALL
EYE HOOK

WHITE

POLAR BEAR

RED

GRAY

ADD BLACK
LINES

DRILL HOLES
FOR EYES
AND NOSTRIL

RHINO WITH
TICK BIRD

LT. BLUE

ELEPHANT

LT. PURPLE

FISH

LT. BROWN

HIPPO

RED   BLACK

ROBIN

LT. ORANGE

GREEN

CROCODILE

NOTE: ANIMALS CAN BE COLORED WITH FELT-TIP PENS
SQUARES = 1"

KANGAROOS

Bookcase

A well-filled bookcase is a decorative asset to any room and although built-in bookcases are found in many homes, there is frequently a need for additional storage space. A small unit such as the one featured here fits nicely in a student's room or small apartment.

The design is Early American with a "Country Chippendale" styling. Pine or maple of ¾″ thickness are appropriate woods, although oak or even redwood can be used. Nice construction features include stopped dadoes to support the shelves, and molded bracket feet. Shelves and sides are cut from standard 1 x 10″ boards so no edge gluing is necessary.

Begin construction by ripping the sides to a uniform 9½″ width and 40½″ length. Note that the sides rest on the floor and support all weight; the bracket feet are mainly decorative. Both side pieces are rabbeted along their inside rear edges, as shown, to enable the back panel to fit flush with the sides.

There are four dadoes to be cut across each side. The lower dado, which receives the bottom, is run all the way across the board as it is hidden by a molding. All other dadoes are stopped ⅜″ short of the front edge. By notching the shelf ends and setting them back ⅛″ from the front edge of the sides, you will avoid later problems if uneven shrinkage occurs between shelves and sides. A power router is one of the most convenient tools for cutting stopped dadoes, but the job can be done with a power saw or an old-fashioned router plane. When both pieces are laid out side by side, the dado grooves should line up perfectly. Finish the sides by cutting the curves on top and front.

Next, cut the shelves to the dimensions shown on the front view. The bottom is ⅜″ wider than the next two shelves, and the upper back edge is given a ¼ x ¼″ rabbet to support the back panel. The other shelves are notched to fit the dadoes and are butted against the back panel.

It's advisable to thoroughly sand the sides and shelves and stain them before assembly; otherwise, there are bound to be glue drippings and smears to cause unsightly marks if the staining is done later. Allow the oil stain to dry for a couple of days, then you can wipe off the glue with a damp sponge without removing the stain.

Size the end grain of the shelves with glue and allow to dry before applying another coat to shelves and dadoes. Insert the shelves and use at least four pipe clamps to draw the joints up tight. Wipe off all glue drippings immediately and use a try square to check the case for squareness. Make sure that the upper shelves are flush with the side rabbets and set in ⅛″ from the front.

Allow the assembly to dry overnight and then measure and cut the back panel to fit with a slight "breathing space" all around. This is fastened with small box nails. Cut the scrolled top and rabbet the ends as shown. The scrolled top rests on the upper shelf and back panel and is held with glue and small finishing nails into the sides.

A ¾ x ¾ x 34½″ support strip is glued and clamped to the front lower edge of the bottom to serve as a backing for the front trim. Cut the

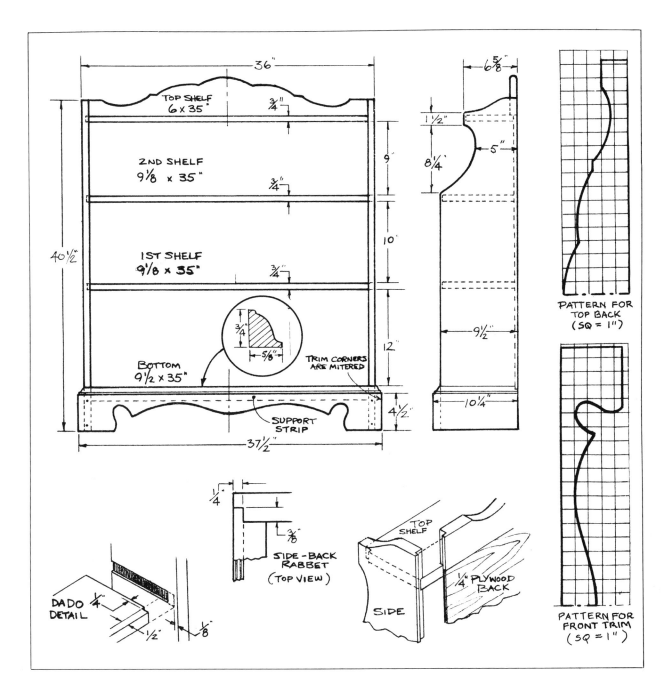

front and side trim to width and length allowing for the 45-degree miter cuts on each piece. The molded top edge can be cut directly on the trim with a router and ¼″ Roman ogee bit, or if you lack a router, a suitable small lumberyard molding can be added.

Transfer the pattern for the bracket feet to the front trim and cut with a jigsaw. It's best not to stain the trim until after it is attached, as the mitered joints may require a bit of sanding. Glue and clamp the side-trim pieces in place, and after the glue dries, drive two 1¼″ screws through the sides and into each trim piece. Fasten the front trim using countersunk finishing nails and glue.

The trim is then stained and the entire bookcase is given two or three coats of urethane varnish. Use a satin-type finish and sand lightly with well-worn 220-grit paper between coats. The final coat may be left as is or waxed and buffed. Be sure to apply finish to all surfaces, including the underside of the bottom and upper shelves. Fill nail holes with a matching filler wax, sold in stick or crayon form. Excess wax is buffed off with a soft cloth.

Candle Sconce

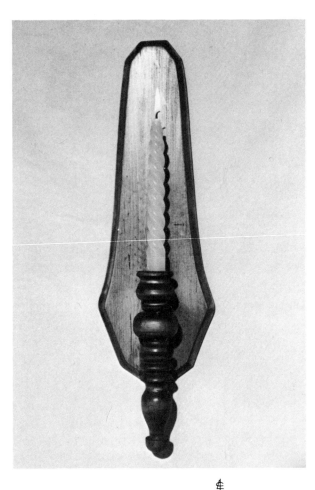

This sconce will make a most welcome gift. Chances are you'll want to make a pair for yourself also; they look very attractive flanking a pine mirror.

Prepare a turning blank 2¼″ square x 12″ long. This length will permit turning both the candleholder and the short, tenoned mounting arm in one operation. After roughing a cylinder to 2⅛″ diameter, the various elements of the turning can be cut with small and large gouges and a ½″ skewed chisel.

Sand the turnings at slow speed and burnish to a soft glow with a thin strip of maple before removing them from the lathe and separating the parts. Drill out a ¾″-diameter socket for the candle and drill a ½″-diameter socket in the turning for the mounting stub.

Prepare a template to transfer the shape of the back and run a cove-molded edge around using a router and ⅜″ coving bit. Sand the back and stain the turning and back to suit. Drill the back to take the turned stub, which is glued into the turning and back. Drill an angled hole near the top edge of the back to hang on a finishing nail and finish with several coats of satin urethane varnish.

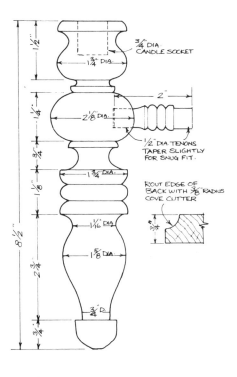

Onion Cutting Board

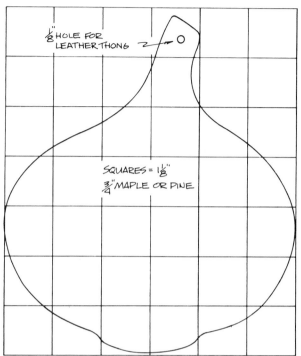

⅛" HOLE FOR
LEATHER THONG

SQUARES = 1⅛"
¾" MAPLE OR PINE

This whimsical little cutting board is shaped like an onion, and the shape pretty well explains its function. Use it only for slicing onions and spare your regular board the pungent aroma associated with raw onions.

Construct a full-size penciled grid of 1⅛" squares on a piece of cardboard and transfer the onion pattern to the grid. Cut out the cardboard onion shape and use it as a template to draw the onion on a board. Use a close-grained wood such as pine or maple. Clamp the board to the work surface and cut around the outline with a saber saw. Bore a ⅛" hole for a leather hanging thong, and then sand both surfaces and round the edges slightly. The board may be left natural or finished by rubbing down with hot olive or salad oil.

Contemporary Tier Table

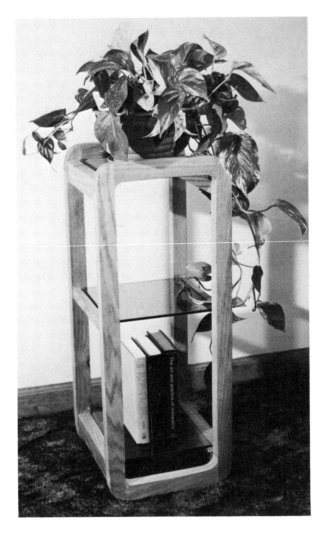

Pleasing curves and clean lines, complemented by the rich look of natural-finish oak and smoked glass, result in this handsome three-tier stand. Use it to highlight your favorite curios, books, and perhaps that special flowering houseplant.

The exposed mortise-and-tenon joints add both strength and interest to the overall design. Five-quarter-inch red-oak stock is used throughout.

Make the front and back frames first. Note that each frame is made up of two stiles and two rails joined by exposed mortise-and-tenon joints at each corner. Cut the stiles to ⁵⁄₄ x 1½ x 30″, then carefully lay out and cut the ⅜ x 2½″ mor-

tise. To make this cut, we used a table-saw tenon jig, setting the saw-blade depth to 2½″, and ran the stock (on end) through the blade. About three passes are needed to get the ⅜″-wide mortise.

Next cut the frame rails to ⁵⁄₄ x 2½ x 12″. The rail thickness must be 2½″ to account for the 1″ radius at each frame corner. The excess stock will be cut out later. Lay out and cut the ⅜ x 2½″ tenons on each frame rail end. This joint is going to show, so use care here, making sure each tenon fits tightly with its mating mortise.

After all mortise-and-tenon joints have been cut, the stiles and rails can be joined to make the frame. Apply a thin layer of glue to all surfaces of each joint, then assemble and check for squareness. Apply clamps both horizontally and vertically, recheck for squareness, then set aside to dry thoroughly.

Next, cut the four top and bottom side rails to ⁵⁄₄ x 2 x 10¾″. A ³⁄₁₆ x ⅜″ rabbet is cut along one edge of each piece. The two center rails (⁵⁄₄ x 1 x 10¾″) can also be cut now. Each center rail also has a ³⁄₁₆ x ⅜″ rabbet.

When the frame has thoroughly dried, remove the clamps, then lay out and drill holes for all ⅜ x 1½″ dowel pins as shown in the drawing. Note that the top and bottom side rails each have two dowel pins while the center rails have one. Be sure to keep in mind that the rails are inset ⅛″ (see Detail A).

Next, use a compass to lay out and mark the 1½″ outside and 1″ inside radius on each corner of the front and back frames. A band saw, saber saw, or coping saw can be put to use to make the curved cut. Try to make each cut as clean and square as possible.

Before final assembly, thoroughly sand both frames and all side rails. Use special care on the curves, as these make the piece especially pleasing. Use fine sandpaper to lightly round all edges.

To assemble all components glue and clamp the six side rails to the front and back frames, again checking for squareness. Use enough

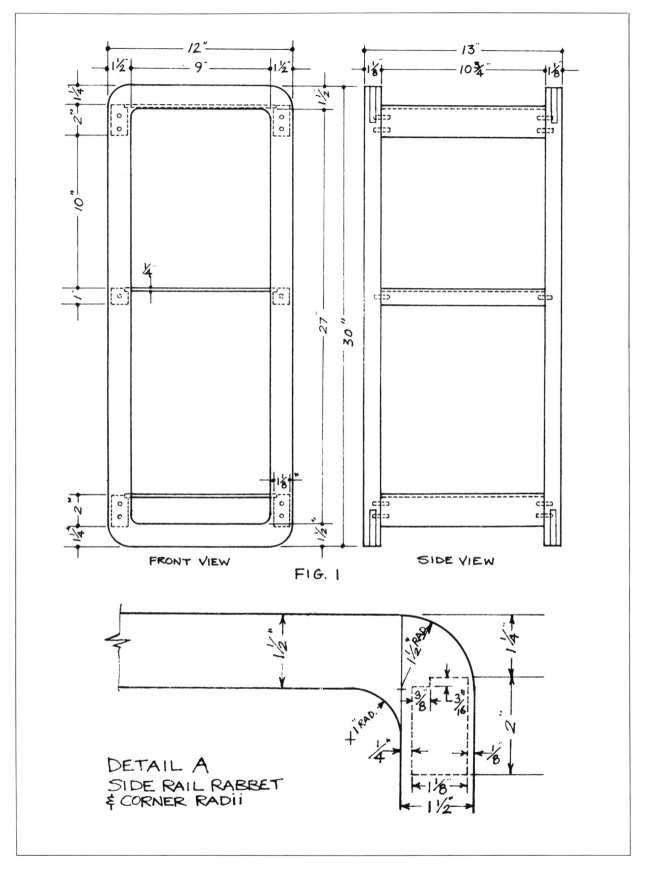

FRONT VIEW

SIDE VIEW

FIG. 1

DETAIL A
SIDE RAIL RABBET
& CORNER RADii

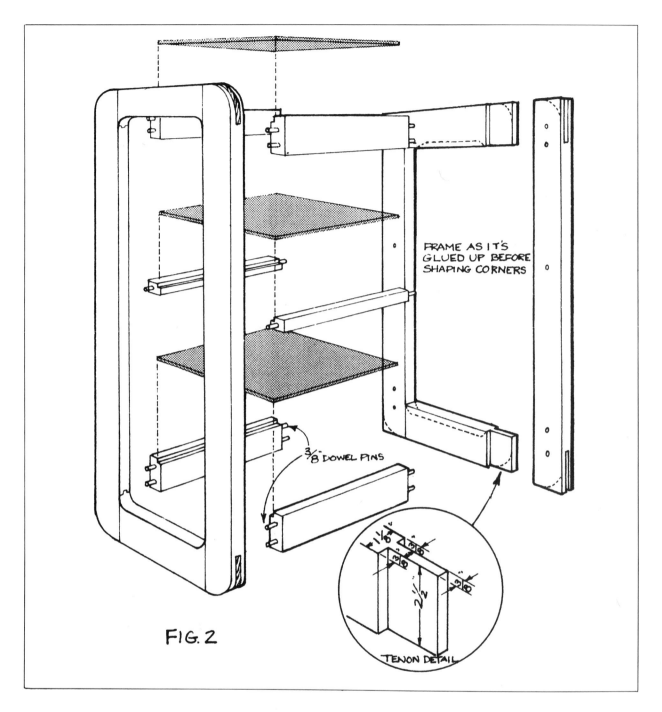

FRAME AS IT'S
GLUED UP BEFORE
SHAPING CORNERS

3/8" DOWEL PINS

FIG. 2

TENON DETAIL

clamps to insure that the joints will be tight, and it's always a good idea to use clamp pads to protect the wood surface.

The shelves are ¼″ smoked glass, available at most glass dealers, who will also cut it to size (10⅛ x 10⅝″). Make sure they remove the sharp edges.

For a final finish, we applied two coats of pure tung oil finish. After thorough drying it was rubbed down with 4/0 steel wool.

146

Pine Medicine Cabinet

If you're adding a bathroom or remodeling an old one, here's a wall-mounted medicine cabinet that's low in cost to build and has far more charm than most in-wall metal cabinets commercially available. The size was based on a 12 x 18″ mirror we purchased for $4.00 and stripped of its plastic frame. This particular cabinet, which will not span the studs usually located in back of a lavatory, was firmly attached with two toggle bolts through the cabinet back and into a paneled plasterboard wall.

The cabinet back was made from glued-up ½″ pine. Plywood can be used, but when it is stained the curved top will be noticeably different from the rest of the cabinet unless it is covered with a pine veneer.

Cut sides to width and length and lay out the curves, back-edge rabbet, and ¼″-deep x ¾″-wide dadoes. If desired, the dadoes can extend completely across the sides. Stopping them short of the front edges and notching the shelves is extra work but is a more refined technique. Don't forget to drill a series of spaced ¼″ holes for an adjustable shelf. The shelf can be of glass or ½″ pine and will be supported on four pegs pushed into the holes.

The towel bar is turned from a length of pine, but if you lack a lathe, square or dowel stock can be used. Drill ¼″-deep sockets in both sides to hold the towel bar.

Assemble cabinet sides, shelves, back and tower bar, using glue in the dadoes and small box nails to fasten the back. With the case assembled, you can get an exact measurement of the door and drawer openings.

The door parts are cut to size, rabbeted to form the door lip, and notched for the half-lap joints at each corner. The front edges of the frame are rounded off as shown in the sectional view A-A.

Glue and clamp the frame together on a flat surface. After the glue dries, use a ¼″ router bit with pilot to run a ¼ x ½″ rabbet around the back of the frame to hold the mirror, backing, and retaining strips. Use a chisel to square off the rounded corners of the routed rabbet.

Cut ⅛″ plywood or hardboard backing to fit easily into the rabbet and rip pine retaining strips, which are bradded in place. The 5⁄16″ lipped drawer front is cut from ¾″ stock. Drawer construction is as illustrated, with the sides glued and nailed or pegged to the drawer-front rabbet.

The cabinet in the photo was stained with one coat of walnut oil stain and given three coats of low-luster urethane varnish, rubbed down between coats with 4/0 steel wool. The door was fitted with a 1″-diameter wooden knob and magnetic catch. Drawer pulls are ⅜″ in diameter and can be of wood, brass, or white porcelain.

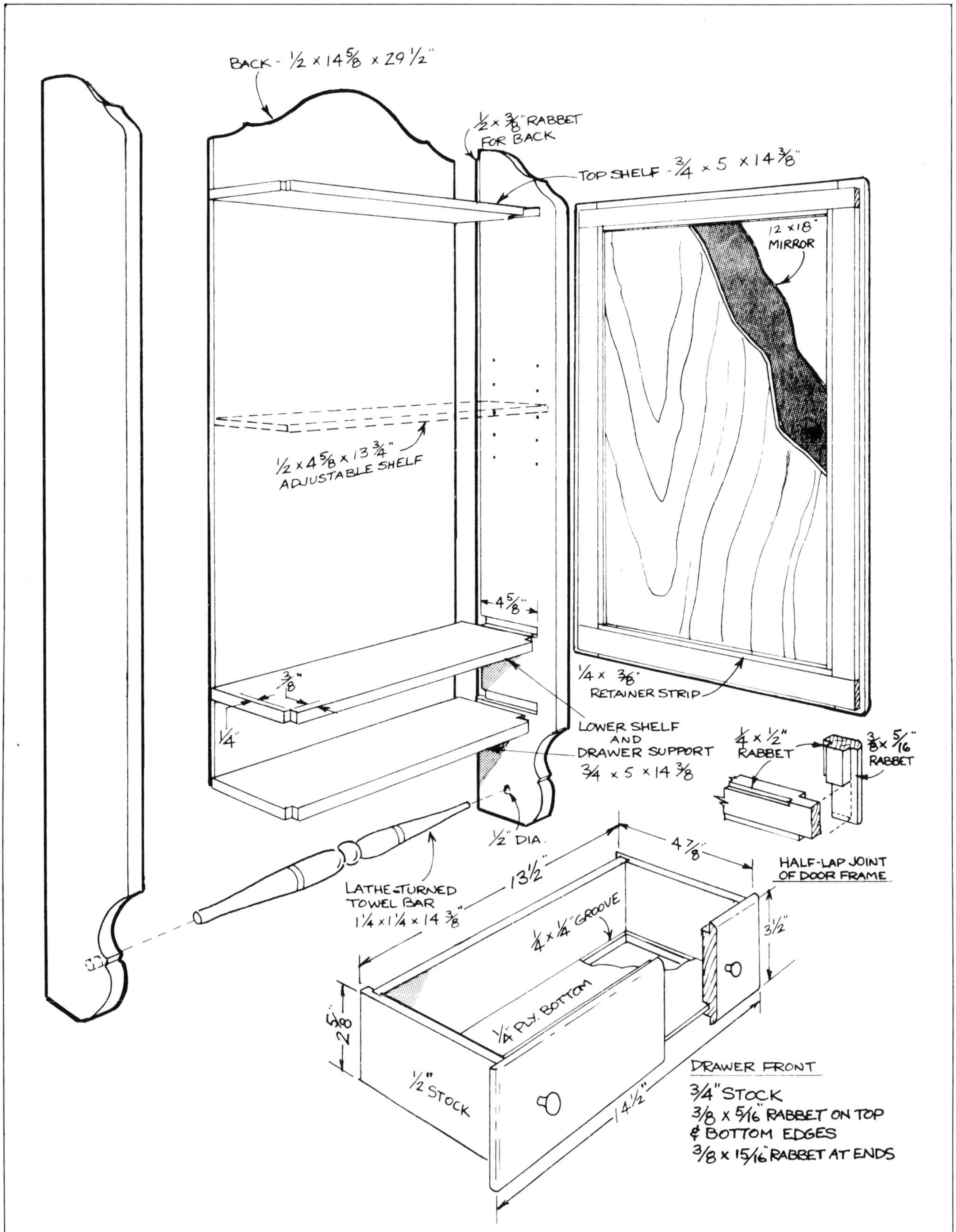

BACK - 1/2 x 14 5/8 x 29 1/2"
1/2 x 3/8" RABBET FOR BACK
TOP SHELF - 3/4 x 5 x 14 3/8"
12 x 18" MIRROR
1/2 x 4 5/8 x 13 3/4" ADJUSTABLE SHELF
4 5/8"
3/8"
1/4"
1/4 x 3/8" RETAINER STRIP
LOWER SHELF AND DRAWER SUPPORT 3/4 x 5 x 14 3/8
1/4 x 1/2" RABBET
3/8 x 5/16" RABBET
HALF-LAP JOINT OF DOOR FRAME
1/2" DIA.
LATHE-TURNED TOWEL BAR 1 1/4 x 1 1/4 x 14 3/8"
13 1/2"
4 7/8"
1/4 x 1/4" GROOVE
3 1/2"
2 5/8"
1/4" PLY. BOTTOM
1/2" STOCK
14 1/2"
DRAWER FRONT
3/4" STOCK
3/8 x 5/16" RABBET ON TOP & BOTTOM EDGES
3/8 x 15/16" RABBET AT ENDS

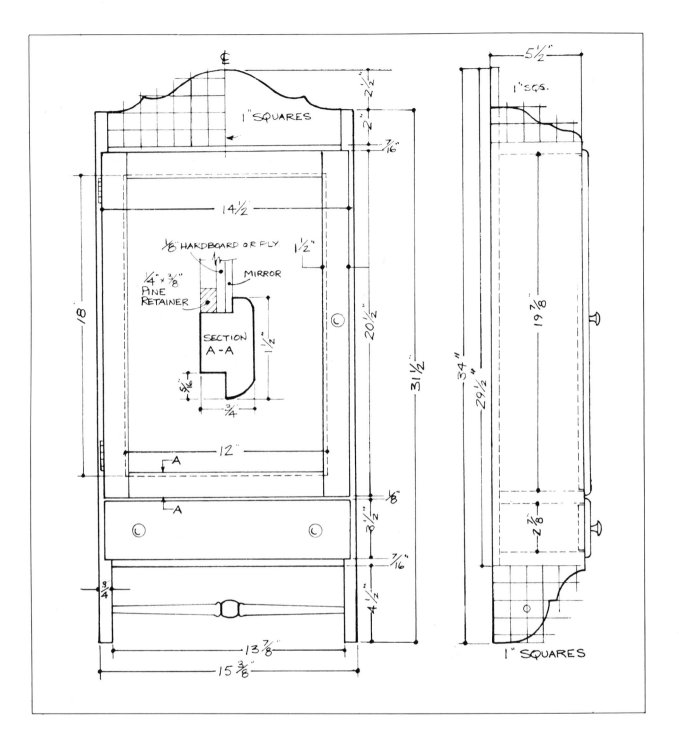

C̶

1" SQUARES

2½"

2"

7/16"

14½

⅛" HARDBOARD OR PLY.

1½"

¼" × ⅜" PINE RETAINER

MIRROR

SECTION A-A

½"

5/16"

¾"

18

20½"

31½"

12"

A

A

⅛"

3½"

7/16"

4½"

¾

13⅞"

15⅜"

5½"

1" SQS.

19⅞

34"

29½"

2⅞"

1" SQUARES

Divided Patio Settee

Pine, fir, or redwood can be used for this project. We selected redwood for ours because it needs no preservatives, does not rot, and is generally unaffected by the elements.

No matter what kind of wood is used, though, be sure to use plated carriage bolts and galvanized nails. Unprotected hardware will quickly rust out. It's also important to use water-resistant glue for all glue joints.

The first step in construction will be to assemble the base frame, which consists of two long front and back frame rails A and four short frame rails B. This base serves as the foundation for all other members of the settee, so try to use lumber that's free from splits, checks, knots, and warp.

Cut the long front and back frame rails A to length, then lay out and drill 1″-diameter holes for the short rail tenons L. When drilling the holes be sure to keep the drill bit square so that later the round tenon will fit up without difficulty.

Cut the four short frame rails to length. On each end lay out and drill a 1″-diameter x 2″-deep hole, and as before, keep the drill bit square. The short rail tenons L are made from 1″-diameter closet pole cut to a length of 4″ and are inserted in the frame rail ends (see Detail A). Be sure to use sufficient water-resistant glue.

Now the four short frame rails B with tenon ends can be inserted into the front and back long frame rails A as shown. Again use sufficient glue to insure a firm bond. Clamp the frame together, and check to make sure the corners all fit up square.

Cut the eight back supports I to length from 1″-diameter closet pole. Now, cut the four back posts D to the rough length (29″), then lay out and drill the 5/16″-deep x 1″-diameter back-support sockets, as shown. Using the dimensions given in Detail B, cut the angled half-lap joint in the ends of each of the back posts.

The back supports I can now be glued and clamped to the back posts D. After drying fit

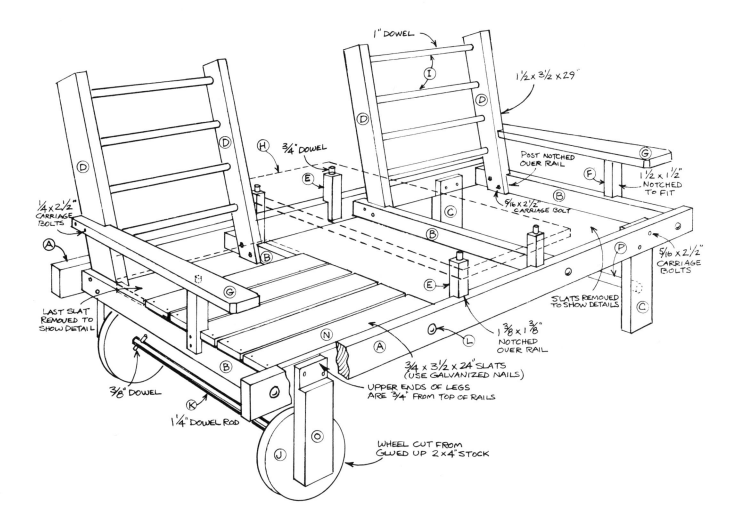

1" DOWEL

I

D

D

1½ x 3½ x 29"

POST NOTCHED OVER RAIL

G

F

1½ x 1½"
NOTCHED TO FIT

H   ¾" DOWEL

E

5/16 x 2½"
CARRIAGE BOLT

B

B

D

¼ x 2½"
CARRIAGE BOLTS

A

B

E

P

5/16 x 2½"
CARRIAGE BOLTS

G

C

LAST SLAT REMOVED TO SHOW DETAIL

SLATS REMOVED TO SHOW DETAILS

N

A

L

J

1⅜ x ⅞"
NOTCHED OVER RAIL

B

¾ x 3½ x 24" SLATS
(USE GALVANIZED NAILS)

3/8" DOWEL

K

UPPER ENDS OF LEGS
ARE ¾" FROM TOP OF RAILS

1¼" DOWEL ROD

O

J

WHEEL CUT FROM
GLUED UP 2 x 4" STOCK

each of the angled back posts into place on the base frame; then drill holes for two 5/16" x 2½" carriage bolts, located as shown in the drawing.

The two armrest posts F are cut to length, then half-lapped and joined to the base frame with 1½" #12 flat-headed screws. The armrest G is cut to the dimensions shown in Detail D. After cutting the angled half lap, attach the arm to the post top with a ½"-diameter blind dowel. The angled half lap is assembled to the back post D with two ¼ x 2½" carriage bolts, as shown.

Next, the twelve seat slats N can be cut to length and width and nailed into place (use galvanized nails). One board on each seat will have to be notched to fit around the armrest post F. Allow about ¼" between each board. In order to fit, the board that butts against the back posts D will have to be ripped to a width narrower than the other slats. Note that the seat slat ends will

overlap the short frame rails B about 5/16" on each end.

Cut the four table posts E to size, then half-lap one end. Glue and screw them to the frame as shown. Cut the tabletop H to the dimensions shown and join the individual boards with the two tabletop cleats M. Finally, attach the tabletop to the table posts with ¾"-diameter blind dowels. If desired, drill a hole in the tabletop center to accept an outdoor lawn umbrella.

Next, cut stretcher P to the length shown. Then cut the two stationary legs C to length and drill the ½"-deep stretcher sockets. Half-lap one end of each leg, then assemble the stretcher and attach it to the base frame using two 5/16" carriage bolts. Cut the wheel legs O to length and half-lap one end. Referring to Detail C, assemble the wheel axle K to the wheels J.

Give the entire project a thorough sanding,

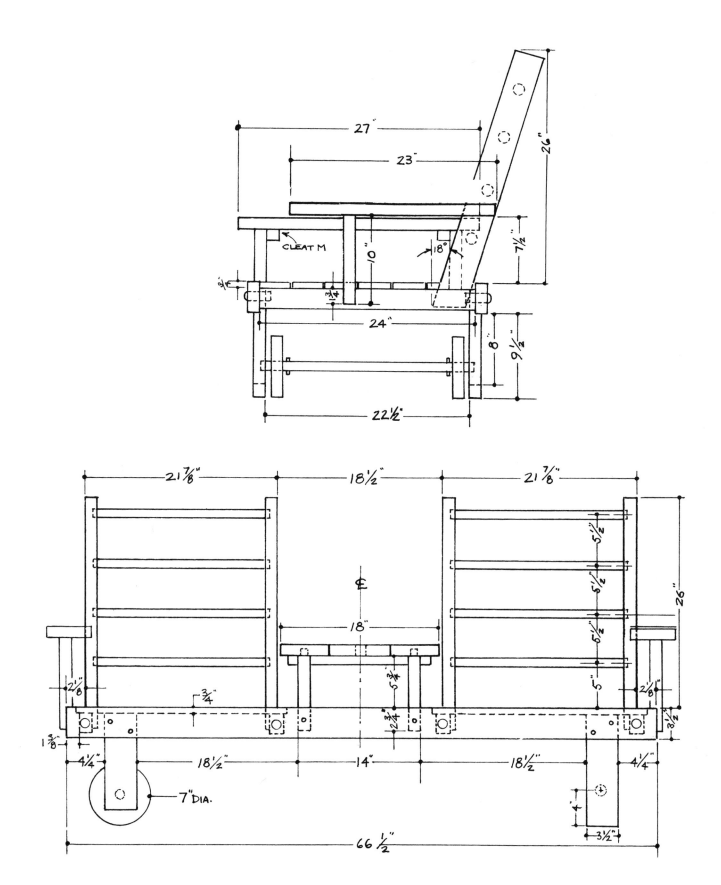

152

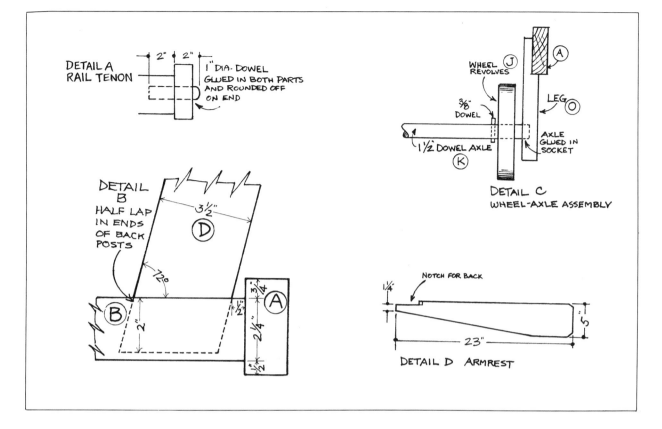

DETAIL A
RAIL TENON

2" | 2"
1" DIA. DOWEL GLUED IN BOTH PARTS AND ROUNDED OFF ON END

DETAIL B
HALF LAP IN ENDS OF BACK POSTS

3½"
Ⓓ
12°
Ⓑ
2"
Ⓐ
2¼"
½"
3¼"
½"
½"

WHEEL REVOLVES Ⓙ   Ⓐ
3/8" DOWEL
LEG Ⓞ
1½" DOWEL AXLE Ⓚ
AXLE GLUED IN SOCKET

DETAIL C
WHEEL-AXLE ASSEMBLY

NOTCH FOR BACK
1¼"
23"
5"

DETAIL D ARMREST

making sure to round all sharp edges. If the settee is made from pine or fir, finish with a good-quality redwood stain applied according to the manufacturer's instructions.

If redwood is used, then no special finishing techniques are necessary.

The chair cushions are standard size and can be purchased in most stores where outdoor furniture is sold.

BILL OF MATERIALS

Key	Part	Pcs. Req'd	T	W	L
A	long frame rails	2	1½"	3½"	66½"
B	short frame rails	4	1½"	2¼"	24"
C	stationary legs	2	1½"	3½"	12¼"
D	back posts	4	1½"	3½"	29"
E	table posts	4	1⅜"	1⅜"	8½"
F	armrest posts	2	1½"	1½"	10"
G	armrest	2	1½"	5"	23"
H	tabletop	1	1½"	18"	27"
I	back supports	8	1" dia. x 19½"		
J	wheel	2	1½" x 7" dia.		
K	wheel axle	1	1¼" dia. x 23½"		
L	tenons	8	1" dia. x 4"		
M	cleats	2	1½"	1½"	16"
N	seat slats	12	¾"	3½"	24"
O	wheel leg	2	1½"	3½"	10¾"
P	stretcher	1	1" dia. x 23½"		
Q	carriage bolts	16	5/16" x 2½"		

Treasure Chest

This fine case can be adapted to hold almost any small prized possession, perhaps an antique set of measuring instruments or a jewelry collection. The case shown in the photograph was made for an 1861 Colt Union Army revolver and the velvet is appropriately dark blue.

This is a deceptively simple project. Considerable care will be required to achieve neat and tight joints, but much of the beauty of the case lies in its well-fitted dovetail and rabbeted joints. Take your time on this one, handling your tools with affection, and you will turn out a piece that will bring a feeling of pride every time you look at it.

All stock is ½" thickness (actual). The original case is pine, but walnut would be an excellent choice. The top and bottom are identical, and each is made up of three jointed and edge-glued pieces, cut to size and planed dead flat. It is important that these pieces be flat in order to cut rabbets accurately. Run the ½" rabbets around all four edges, leaving a lip ³⁄₁₆" to ¼" thick.

Next, cut stock for the sides of the case and lay out the dovetails. A cardboard template of the dovetails will assure uniformity. Lay out the male pins and cut with a fine dovetail saw and

razor-sharp chisel. You will note that the pins are quite narrow, a style that gained in popularity toward the middle of the nineteenth century. After completing a set of pins, stand them against the adjoining case side and scribe around the pins with a small, sharp knife to transfer the exact shape for the corresponding sockets. Cut out the sockets and identify each completed set with a light pencil mark as you proceed, so that each set of pins can later be fitted to their particular sockets.

After all dovetail joints are cut, the case is assembled with glue. After drying, a cut is made completely around the box 1¼" down from the best surface selected to be the top. If this operation is performed on a table saw, use a blade that will cut as narrow a kerf as possible. After the lid has been cut off, cut a slab of 2" Styrofoam to fit inside the box. Lay out the treasures the case is to contain and outline them on the Styrofoam with a felt-tip pen; then, using a gouge or even a sharpened spoon, cut out the Styrofoam to the depth and shape necessary to contain the item to be displayed.

Velvet in the color of your choice is then wrapped around the Styrofoam much as you would wrap a package. Excess material is folded neatly and flapped underneath where it can be secured with staples or thread. Leave sufficient slack in the velvet covering so it can be pushed down into the shaped depression.

When the Styrofoam is covered to your satisfaction, set it aside and sand and stain the case. Apply sealer to all surfaces of the case, sanding lightly between coats. Three or four well-laid-on coats of varnish and a final rubbing with 4/0 steel wool followed by paste wax and buffing will give the piece a finish with depth and durability. Small corner pads or felt may be fastened to the bottom if desired. Finally, mount solid brass hinges and a hasp or lock with an escutcheon plate.

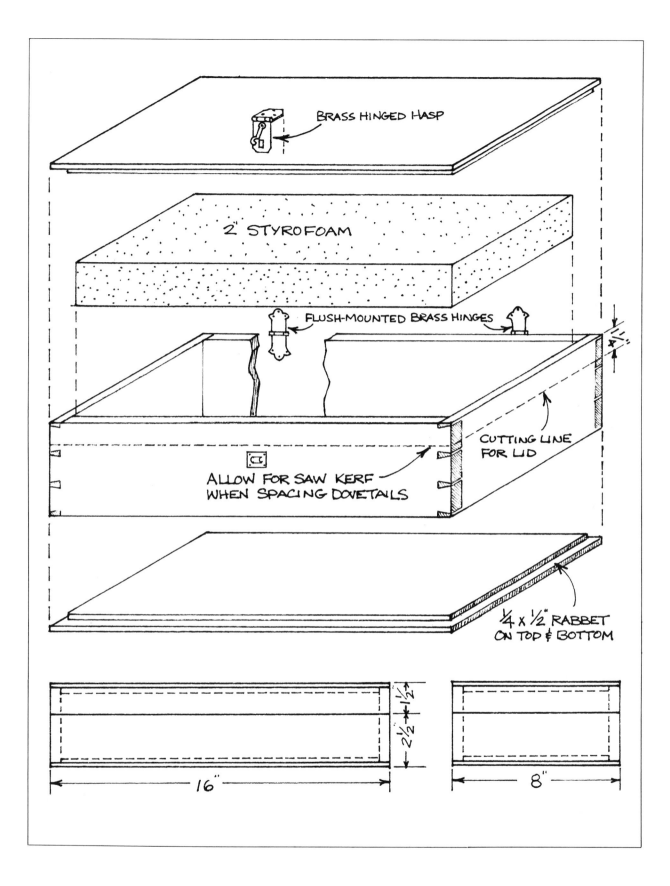

BRASS HINGED HASP

2" STYROFOAM

FLUSH-MOUNTED BRASS HINGES

CUTTING LINE FOR LID

ALLOW FOR SAW KERF WHEN SPACING DOVETAILS

¼ x ½" RABBET ON TOP & BOTTOM

16"

8"

2½"

1½"

Contemporary Coffee Table

This attractive contemporary table has a light and elegant look, and will present no unusual problems in joinery as it is basically a doweling job. A methodical approach in cutting the various parts will insure accurate and clean joints. All cuts must be absolutely square, so adjust your equipment beforehand. If you intend to cut pieces by hand, you will need a jig such as a miter box to achieve square cuts.

A doweling jig is very helpful for this project, and you will need some sort of depth gauge to insure that you drill all holes to a uniform depth. Any cabinet hardwood is suitable for this table. If you prefer a light finish, use maple or birch. The top can be either solid stock, veneered panel, or plywood with veneered edges. The top sits ½″ above the legs and all dowels can be seen. You may wish to stain these supporting dowels a contrasting color, or paint them black. Another nice touch would be to cover the dowels with collars of lacquered brass tubing.

The frame will require 21 feet of 1½″-square stock. All joints in the frame are held with glue and two ⅜″-diameter x 1½″-long dowel pins.

The dowels that support the top are ¾″ diameter. You'll need a total of twelve: six pieces 1¾″ long for the legs, two pieces 2¾″ long for the end rails, and four pieces 4¼″ long for the front and back rails.

Saw all frame stock to exactly 1½″ square. Next cut six legs to 14½″, two end rails and one middle rail to 19″ each, and two front and two back rails to 26¾″. Sand all pieces thoroughly. Make an identifying mark on each leg, then lay out, mark, and drill ⅜″-diameter x ¾″-deep dowel holes for all frame joints. You will have to keep your wits about you to drill all the legs with the proper number of holes in the proper locations. Before assembling the frame, it's best to drill the twelve ¾″-diameter holes for the top support dowels. These holes are ¾″ deep and must be drilled uniformly so that the top will seat securely on each.

Join the front and back leg units first, then connect the three assemblies with front and back rails. Seat the large dowels and lay a straightedge over them to insure that they are all of the same height. Set the frame aside to dry while the top is being glued up. When the top is completed, turn it underside up, and set the frame upside down on it. All edges of the top and frame should be flush. Carefully scribe around each dowel and then punch a starting hole in the exact center of each dowel location. Drill twelve holes ¾″-diameter x ½″-deep in the bottom of the top. Here you will be faced with the possible problem of having the screw on the end of your auger or spade bit emerge through the good side. A Forstner bit is perfect for this situation, but it is expensive. The alternative is to let the tip of your bit punch through and plug the holes later with pegs of matching wood.

If you want to cover the supporting dowels in lacquered brass tubing, cut the required number of tubes to length. Use a file to remove any burrs and apply a thin coat of lacquer to prevent tarnishing. Slip the brass tubes on the ¾″ dowel posts, apply wood glue, then assemble and clamp to the top. Allow to dry.

Sand and stain to suit and give the entire table several coats of a good alcohol-proof sealer, carefully sanding between coats. Be sure to seal the underside of the top also, especially if it is made up from solid stock.

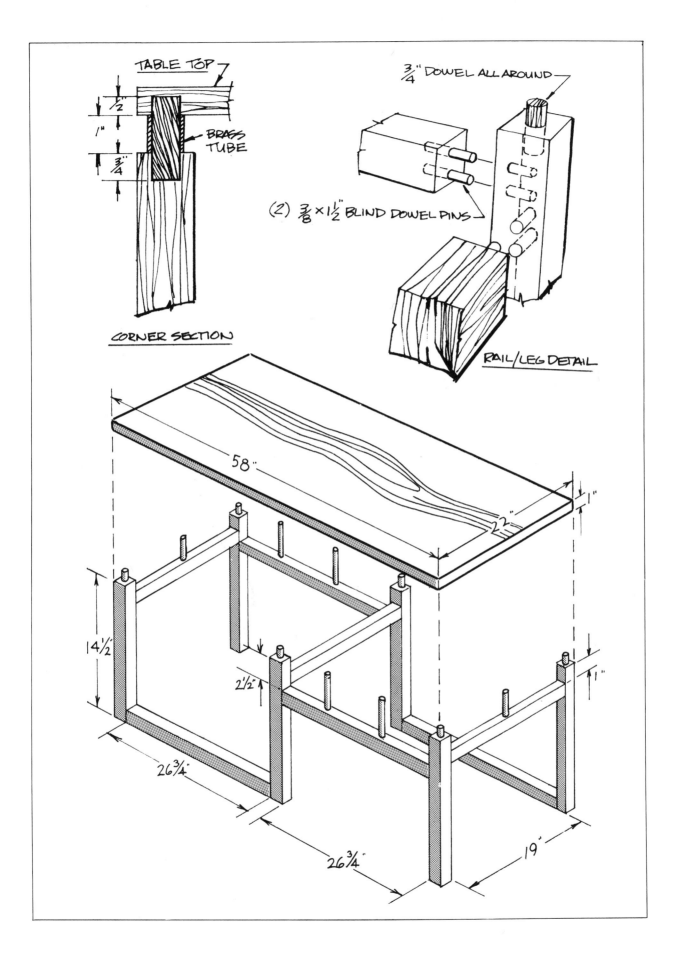

TABLE TOP

½"

1"

¾"

BRASS
TUBE

CORNER SECTION

¾" DOWEL ALL AROUND

(2) ⅜×1½" BLIND DOWEL PINS

RAIL/LEG DETAIL

58"

1"

2"

14½"

2½"

1"

26¾"

26¾"

19"

Contemporary End Table

A contemporary table like this should be made using a good cabinet hardwood. For a light, natural finish either maple or birch would be a good choice. Walnut is always popular if a darker finish is desired. If you've already made the coffee table (see the preceding project), you'll undoubtedly want to use a matching wood for the end table.

Note that the piece is essentially made up of nine basic parts: the four legs, a front and back rail, two side rails, and the top. The top can be either solid stock, veneered panel, or hardwood plywood with veneer-taped edges.

Start construction by cutting the four legs from 1½″-square stock to a length of 20¼″. Next, from the same size stock, cut the front and back rails 22″ long and the side rails 14″ long.

Lay out, mark, and drill holes for ⅜ x 1½″ blind dowel pins for all frame joints (refer to the detail shown with the coffee table project, p. 157). Al-

ways keep the drill bit perpendicular to the work surface in order to insure proper alignment and fit of the dowel pins.

Next, lay out, mark, and drill holes in the legs and rails for the ¾″-diameter support-post dowels. These holes are ¾″ deep and must be drilled uniformly so that the top will be level when assembled and glued. A total of ten ¾″-diameter dowels are required (four pieces 2¼″ long for the legs, two pieces 3¼″ long for the side rails, and four pieces 4¼″ long for the front and back rails). Glue and seat the dowels to the legs and rails as shown (refer to the detail on p. 157). Lay a straightedge over them to insure they are all the same height. Make adjustments as necessary.

The legs and rails can now be glued and clamped. Make sure that all joints are square. Set aside and allow to dry overnight.

When the top is completed, turn it underside up, and set the frame upside down on it. All edges of the top and frame should be flush. Carefully scribe around each dowel and then punch a starting hole in the exact center of each dowel location. Drill dowel holes in the bottom of the top to a depth of ½″. If you use an auger or spade bit, you will be faced with the problem of the screw point breaking through the top of the good side. If this occurs, the most practical solution is to plug the holes with pegs of matching wood. If you have one, the ideal bit to use here is a Forstner bit.

The dowels may be stained a contrasting color, painted, or covered with pieces of brass tubing, as described in the coffee table project (p. 156).

Sand and stain (if desired) to suit. Apply several coats of a good quality sealer, carefully sanding between coats.

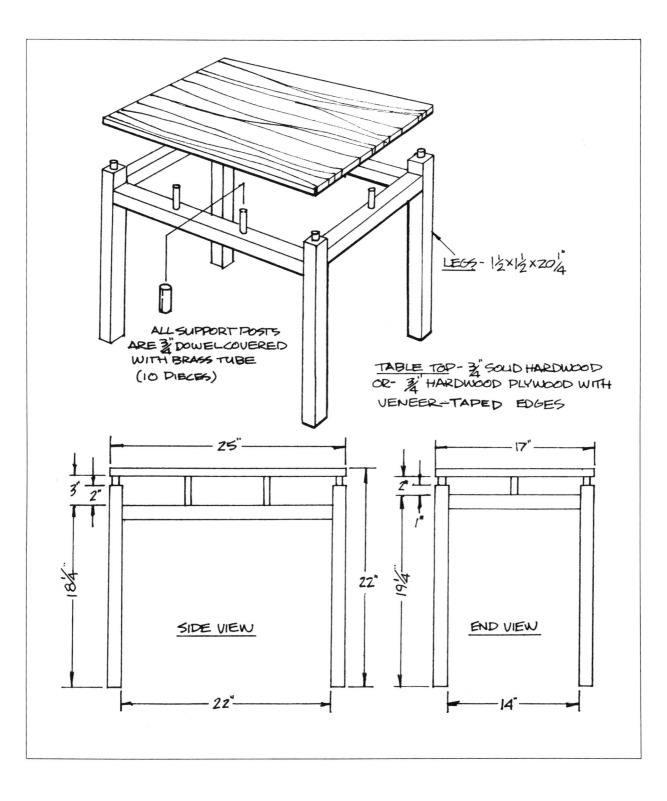

LEGS - $1\frac{1}{2} \times 1\frac{1}{2} \times 20\frac{1}{4}$"

ALL SUPPORT POSTS
ARE $\frac{3}{4}$" DOWEL COVERED
WITH BRASS TUBE
(10 PIECES)

TABLE TOP - $\frac{3}{4}$" SOLID HARDWOOD
OR - $\frac{3}{4}$" HARDWOOD PLYWOOD WITH
VENEER-TAPED EDGES

25"

3"
2"

18$\frac{1}{4}$"

22"

22"

SIDE VIEW

17"

2"

1"

19$\frac{1}{4}$"

14"

END VIEW

Curio Table

Prized stamps, coins, butterflies, dueling pistols, or just about any collection of small items can be attractively displayed in this fine little curio table. Besides providing protection for your collection, the table is the right size for use as an occasional or end table in the den or family room.

The nicely detailed turned legs give the piece a traditional look, but if you lack a lathe or would prefer a more contemporary design, simply substitute square or tapered legs. The table shown was built of pine, but cherry or maple are also good choices.

The legs (Detail A) are turned from 1¾ x 1¾ x 19″ clear stock, either solid or glued up. It's a good idea to lay out and cut the mortises in each leg while they are still in the square. Allow a bit of extra length at the foot end so that the foot can be shaped without interference with the lathe tailstock. In order to insure that all legs are turned alike, prepare a template of the leg profile and use this to lay out the various turnings. A good hand with the skew chisel and gouge will do most of the tapering, coves, and beads. Finish sand the legs while they are lathe-mounted at slow speed, working down to 220-grit paper.

The aprons are cut from ¾″ stock allowing 1½″ extra length for a ¾″ long tenon at each end. You will need easy access to the items stored in the table, and one way to provide for this is to cut a small opening in the back apron and fit it with a hinged door. This should be done before the apron is joined to the legs.

Dry-fit all joints before applying glue and clamping. After the glue has dried, drill each joint for two ¼ x 1½″ dowel pegs, which are glued in place and later trimmed off flush.

Referring to the sectional view of Detail B, shape four molded strips E and brad them to the bottom edge of the aprons. These strips provide a decorative bead and also support the table bottom, which can be cork board, ½″ plywood, or ⅝″ particle board. Cut the bottom F for an easy fit with about 1⁄16″ clearance all around, and notch it to fit around the legs. The bottom can be painted, veneered, covered with green felt, or otherwise treated in a way that will provide an attractive background for the curios.

After the bottom is in place, cut the small strips G and brad them in place to conceal the loose joint between the aprons and bottom. These strips butt up against the legs.

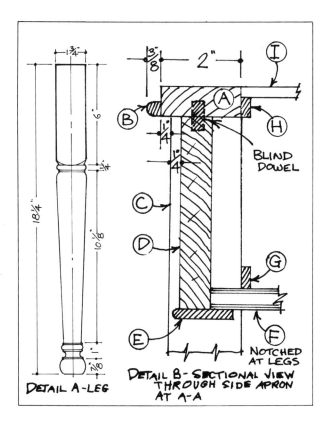

DETAIL A-LEG

DETAIL B-SECTIONAL VIEW THROUGH SIDE APRON AT A-A

BLIND DOWEL

NOTCHED AT LEGS

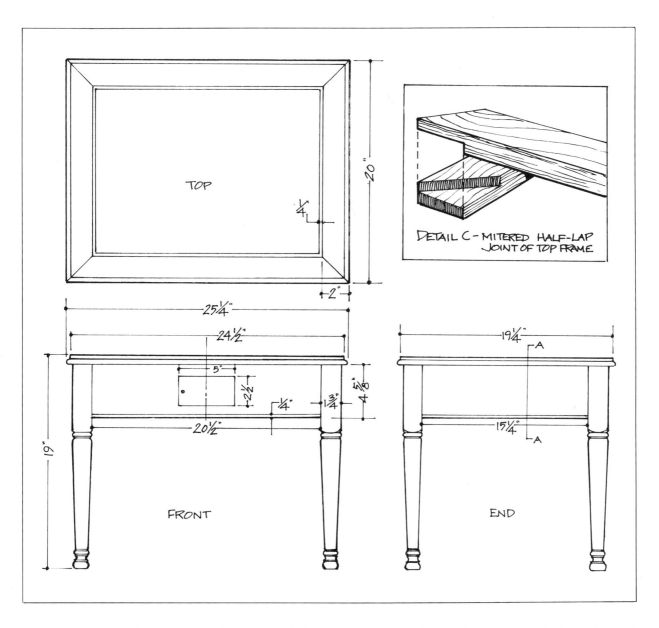

DETAIL C — MITERED HALF-LAP JOINT OF TOP FRAME

TOP

FRONT

END

The top frame is made of ¾″ stock, and the corners are joined with mitered half laps as shown in Detail C. Sand the frame parts carefully before assembly. Glue the corner joints and double-check for squareness before the glue sets. The frame is trimmed with a half-round molding, mitered at the corners, which provides a nice decorative touch and conceals the end grain of the joints. Cut and fit the small door to the apron opening. Mount the door with small brass hinges and fasten a small knob and turnbutton.

The ¼″ plate glass should be cut for an easy fit within the frame. It rests on four small strips H that are glued to the frame. These strips are mitered at the corners.

Stain the table to suit and finish with at least three coats of varnish, well rubbed with 4/0 steel wool between coats. A final coat of wax, buffed to a soft shine, completes the project.

BILL OF MATERIALS

Key	Part	Dimensions
A	top frame	¾ x 2″
B	half-round molding	⅜″
C	leg	1¾ x 1¾ x 18¼″
D	apron	¾ x 4⅜″
E	molding strip	¼ x 1½″
F	bottom	½″ plywood, etc.
G	inside trim	¼ x ½″
H	glass ledge strip	¼ x ½″
I	plate glass	¼″

Pine Lap Desk

Though now primarily collectors' pieces, the little lap desk of the nineteenth century is still very useful for personal correspondence and check writing. This example is a bit more elaborate than most; in addition to the usual large storage compartment for writing paper, it has an upper compartment for envelopes, canceled checks, and letters. A tiny drawer, originally for an inkwell, is handy for postage stamps.

The desk is a nice decorator item and will look quite elegant sitting on a small table or stand. Construction is not tricky, but the builder is advised to start with good flat ½″ stock, and make sure that all cuts are perfectly square. Pine, preferably clear, is a good choice, but cherry or mahogany are better if they are available.

Start construction by jointing and gluing up stock of sufficient width for the large lid and bottom. Allow extra length and width for trimming

later to exact size. Cut two sides B, and lay out and cut a drawer opening in one side. Cut the front C, divider E, and back F. Shape rabbets in the front and sides, and notch the divider to fit between the sides. Don't forget the ¼″ groove in the side to take a removable partition I.

Attach the back and front to the sides with glue. Clamp the assembly and check carefully to make sure that it's square. Fasten the bottom with small finishing nails driven through the front, sides, and back. Add divider E, which should fit snugly between the sides. Glue the rabbeted joints and nail through the sides into the ends of the divider.

The drawer is constructed with ¼″ plywood sides and bottom. The drawer back and front are of ½″ stock. The front has a ¼″ lip around all four edges and the sides are fastened with glue and brads to the rabbet thus formed. In order to keep the drawer from falling out, one side is extended 4″. This extension is grooved to slide on a wood screw driven into the filler piece K.

Cut the filler piece to length and width, and glue and clamp it to the back, butting it against the desk side. If you don't have a clamp with a throat deep enough to reach the far end, cut a couple of pieces of pine scrap to wedge between divider E and the filler piece.

Now insert the drawer and bore a 1″ hole through divider E to insert a screwdriver, which is used to drive the round-headed screw through the slotted side and into the filler. After the drawer is fastened, you can add the compartment

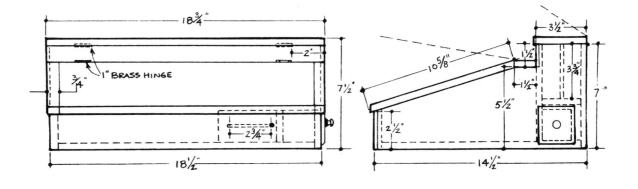

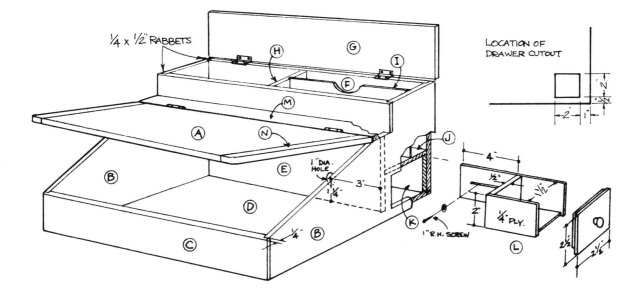

bottom J, which is pressed into place and rests on the top edge of the filler. Fasten by nailing through the divider and back. You can now add divider H and removable partition I.

Cut the top lid G to size and mount with two small brass hinges mortised into the top edge of the back. Add ledge M, which overhangs each side by ⅛″. Finally, cut the large lid to size, glue on edge strips N and bevel the front and back edges of the assembled lid. Fasten the lid with 1″ brass butt hinges.

Round all corners slightly with sandpaper and finish the exterior surface with stain and a shellac or varnish. Seal the interiors of the main box and upper compartment, and either cover the bottom of the desk with felt or add a small felt disc to each corner.

BILL OF MATERIALS

Key	Part	T	W	L
A	lid	½″	10⅝″	17¼″
B	sides (2 req'd)	½″	7″	14¼″
C	front	½″	2¾″	18½″
D	bottom	½″	13½″	17½″
E	main divider	½″	6½″	18½″
F	back	½″	7″	18″
G	upper lid	½″	3¾″	18¾″
H	divider	½″	2½″	3¾″
I	partition	¼″	3¾″	9¼″
J	pigeonhole bottom	½″	2½″	17½″
K	filler	½″	2¼″	7″
L	drawer	———	———	———
M	ledge	½″	1½″	18¾″
N	lid edge strips	½″	¾″	10⅝″

Contemporary Table

This versatile table with light, uncluttered legs and frame should appeal to those who prefer contemporary designs with the warmth of wood. The size can be varied to suit whatever purpose you have in mind, from a small lamp or occasional table to a good-size cocktail or patio table. The design shown is offered as a departure point.

The top can be made in several ways: either from glued-up ¾″ solid hardwood with a well-sanded edge; from a piece of ¾″ cabinet-grade solid-core plywood with matching veneer-taped edge; or from common ¾″ fir plywood with laminated plastic top and edging in a wood grain such as teak or walnut.

Rails are shaped from solid ¾″ hardwood and may be lightened if desired by cutting out the shape shown in the drawings. The blind mortise-and-tenon joints shown are merely a suggestion; through tenons exposed on the outside of the legs will provide additional visual interest to the piece.

The legs, which are shaped from ¾ x 1½ x 8″ hardwood, are tapered on the inside edge only, the taper starting just below the point where the rails join the leg. Cut the mortise first and then cut the taper on a bench saw with a tapering jig and bevel or round off the tops of the legs.

If the top is made from ¾″ solid stock, boards of 4″ to 6″ width should be edge joined with ⅜″ dowels and glue.

Cabinet-grade ¾″ plywood makes a fine top if a matching veneer tape is glued on very carefully to conceal the edges. Allow the tape to slightly overhang the top edge of the table, then trim off flush with a finely set plane. Needless to say, the top must be cut in a perfect circle and the edges sanded square with no valleys or high spots. A band saw used with a circle-cutting jig is best, but a portable saber saw fitted with a pivoted beam will handle the job.

Economical ¾″ fir plywood can be used for the top. A low-grade veneer can be applied to the bottom and a nicely figured veneer to the top and edge, or just a wood-grained plastic laminate could be used on top. The selection of plastic laminate is extensive, with styles from rosewood to simulated maple butcher block available. Use contact cement for fastening the edging first, plane off the overhang, then add slightly oversized laminate and apply plenty of roller pressure from the center out to bond the plywood and plastic. Trim the excess with a plane.

The top can be fastened to the frame-leg assembly by drilling small pilot holes up through the rails and counterboring these holes with a ⅜″ bit to take eight 1½″ #8 flat-headed screws.

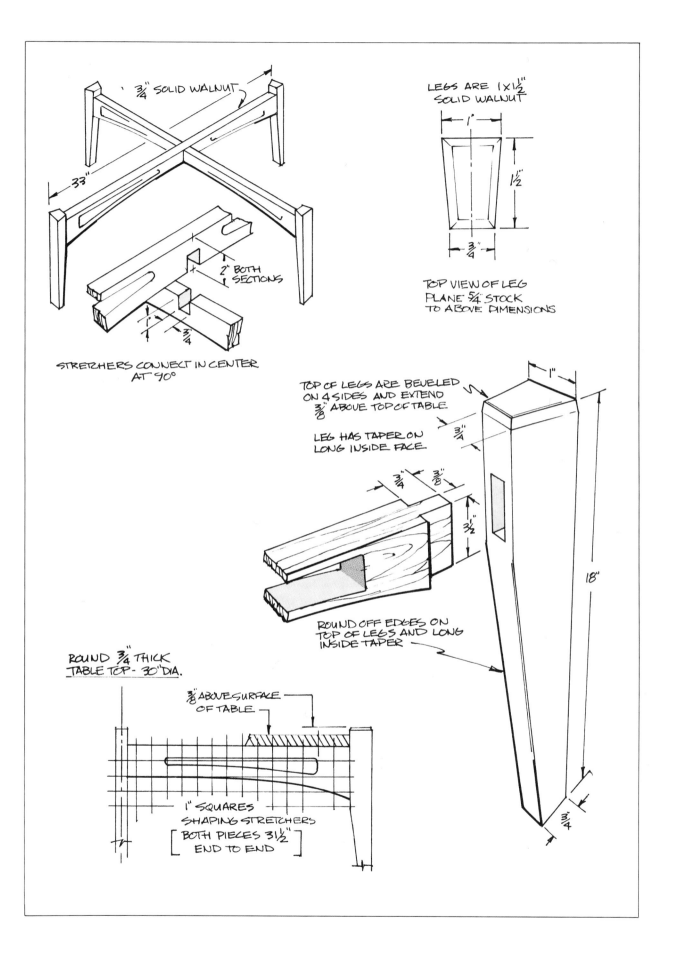

¾" SOLID WALNUT

33"

2" BOTH SECTIONS

¾"

STRETCHERS CONNECT IN CENTER AT 90°

LEGS ARE 1x1½" SOLID WALNUT

1"

1½"

¾"

TOP VIEW OF LEG
PLANE 5/4 STOCK
TO ABOVE DIMENSIONS

TOP OF LEGS ARE BEVELED
ON 4 SIDES AND EXTEND
⅜" ABOVE TOP OF TABLE

LEG HAS TAPER ON
LONG INSIDE FACE.

1"

¾"

¾"   ⅜"

3½"

18"

¾"

ROUND OFF EDGES ON
TOP OF LEGS AND LONG
INSIDE TAPER

ROUND ¾" THICK
TABLE TOP - 30" DIA.

⅜" ABOVE SURFACE
OF TABLE

1" SQUARES
SHAPING STRETCHERS
[BOTH PIECES 31½"
END TO END]

Eighteenth-Century
Half-Round Table

This beautifully proportioned little table is a reproduction of an early eighteenth-century piece. People who enjoy traditional woodworking will be pleased to note that there isn't a single nail or screw used in the construction. All joints are pegged as in the original. Clear pine was used for the original, but cherry or maple can certainly be substituted with equally pleasing results.

Begin by edge joining two or more ¾"-thick boards to form a rectangle of about 14¼ x 28¼". Lay out the half circle of the top and locate ⅜ x 1½" dowel pins at the joints. Drive in glue-coated grooved pins, and glue and clamp the boards together to dry overnight.

Cut the two aprons and two front rails to width and lay out tenons on each end. The legs are ripped from thick stock and mortises are located so that the rails and aprons will be set back ⅛" from the outer faces of the legs.

It will be necessary to miter the apron tenons that enter the front leg so that they will just clear each other. The tenons on the rails are ¼" shorter than the apron tenons and do not need to be mitered.

The back legs are notched to receive the back rail, and a bit of care is required here for a well-fitted joint. The notches can be cut by mounting each leg in a V-block jig, which is nothing more than two 45-degree beveled strips nailed to a base. Use this jig to hold the leg while you cut the notch with a dado cutter mounted on a table or radial saw. The notch is cut just deep enough to contain the rail with its edges flush with the leg surface. Cut the back rail longer than needed and later, when it is fitted into the leg notches, it can be trimmed exactly flush.

Now, lay out the chamfers on each leg. Use a chisel to start and stop each chamfer and remove stock in between with a spokeshave or plane. Take care to keep the chamfers uniform and cleanly cut, as they contribute considerably to the charm and light appearance of the table.

Dry-fit the legs, aprons, and rails. Draw the joints closed with clamps while you drill 1"-deep holes for ¼"-diameter pegs. Cut the pegs longer than needed and drive them in just far enough to lock the assembly together for fitting the top.

Next, drive a small brad into the top center of each leg and place the leg assembly upside down on the underside of the top. When the top is centered, bear down on the legs and the brads will punch small holes in the top which will serve as centers for ½" dowel pegs driven through the top and into the legs.

Disassemble the table and finish sand all parts, taking care not to round off the edges of the chamfers. The table shown was given one coat of Minwax Early American stain, which was allowed to dry for 24 hours. The final finish consisted of two applications of Minwax Antique Oil, a penetrating-type finish that can be buffed to a soft luster.

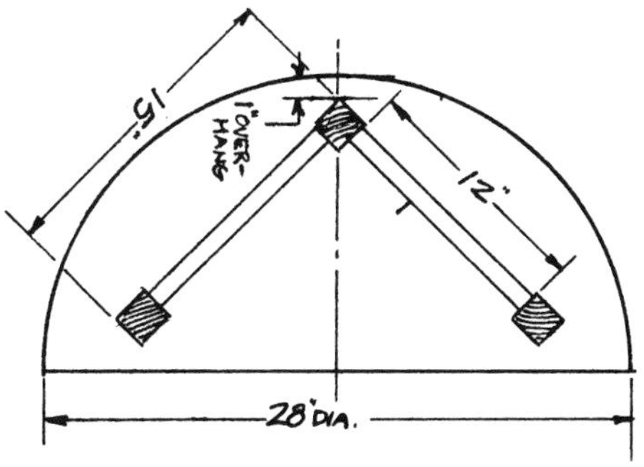
15"
1" OVER-HANG
12"
28" DIA.

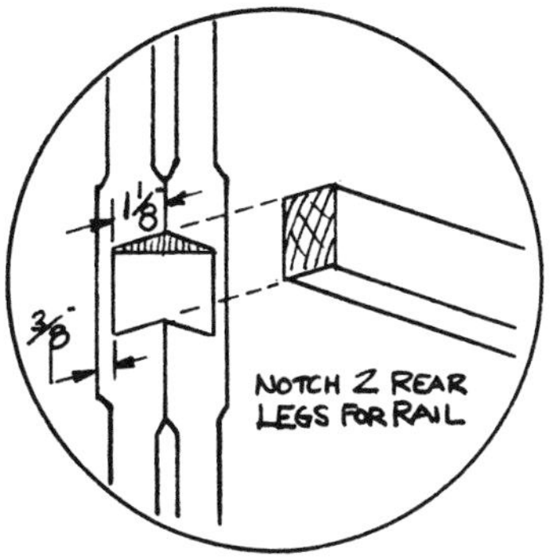
1 1/8
3/8"
NOTCH 2 REAR LEGS FOR RAIL

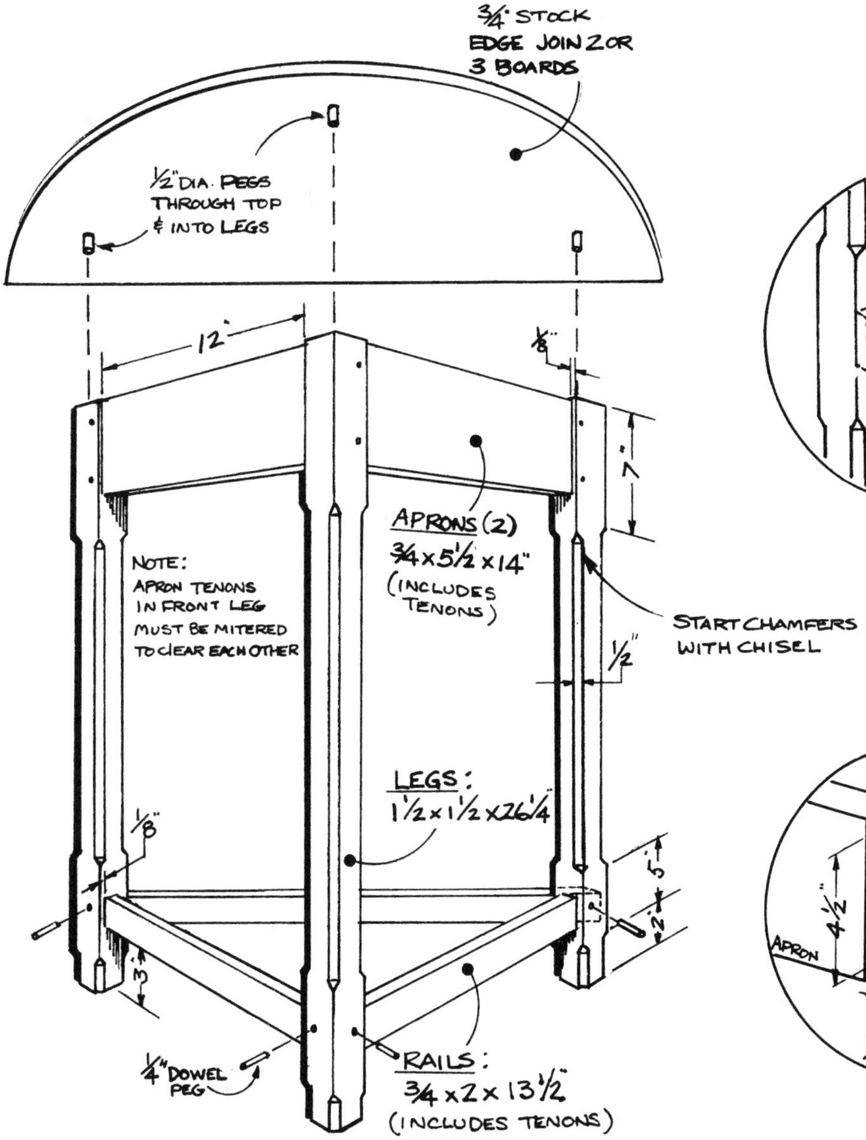
3/4" STOCK
EDGE JOIN 2 OR 3 BOARDS
1/2" DIA. PEGS THROUGH TOP & INTO LEGS
12"
1/8"
7"
APRONS (2)
3/4 x 5 1/2 x 14"
(INCLUDES TENONS)
NOTE:
APRON TENONS IN FRONT LEG MUST BE MITERED TO CLEAR EACH OTHER
START CHAMFERS WITH CHISEL
1/2"
LEGS:
1 1/2 x 1 1/2 x 26 1/4"
1/8"
5"
2"
3"
1/4" DOWEL PEG
RAILS:
3/4 x 2 x 13 1/2"
(INCLUDES TENONS)

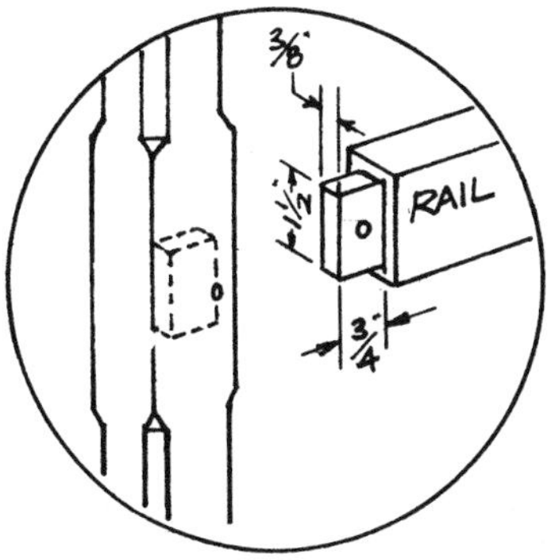
3/8"
1 1/2"
RAIL
3/4"

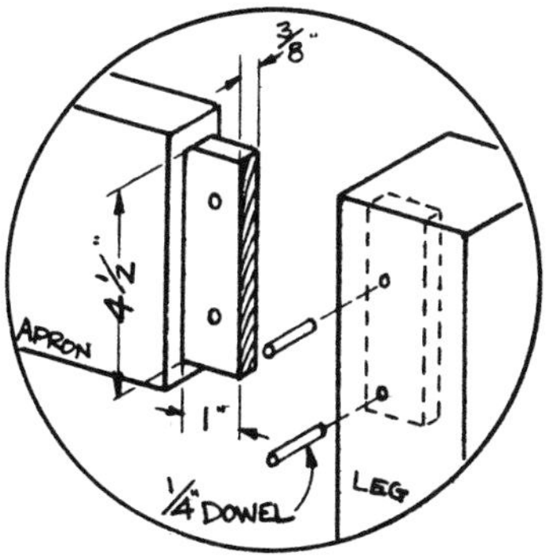
3/8"
4 1/2"
APRON
1"
1/4" DOWEL
LEG

Stereo/End Table

Here's a contemporary furniture design that can be used to house your stereo equipment stylishly, or if you prefer it can easily be adapted to create a handsome end table.

The stereo-speaker wings can be folded up and out of the way if space is at a premium in your home or apartment. No matter which way you choose to make it, though, it's sure to be a most useful and attractive piece of furniture.

Ideally, you should use hardwood for this project. We wanted our table to have a dark natural finish so we selected walnut; however, birch or maple would also be fine choices, especially if a light, natural finish is desired.

Begin this project by making the four legs A, the front and back top rails B, and the front and back bottom rails C. Referring to Figure 2, make the table-front frame by doweling and gluing the two front legs to the top and bottom front rails as shown.

Make the back frame by repeating the process with the two back legs and the top and bottom back rails. Next, on each frame lay out, mark, and cut the 1¼″ radius, the 2¼″ width, and the foot taper (Figure 1).

The top should be made next. Note that it is basically a mitered frame D, rabbeted to take a plastic-laminated or veneered ½″ plywood panel. Start by cutting the plywood E to size. We used black plastic laminate to cover the top surface of our table. Plastic laminate is available in a wide range of solid colors and simulated wood grains, and can provide an attractive, easy-care finish, particularly for a contemporary piece such as this. Apply the laminate according to the manufacturer's directions and trim off excess at the edges of the plywood.

Of course, if you enjoy veneer work, this is a good opportunity to practice. If veneer is used, it's advisable to veneer the underside of the panel with a lesser grade of veneer to equalize stresses.

The mitered and rabbeted frame D is made

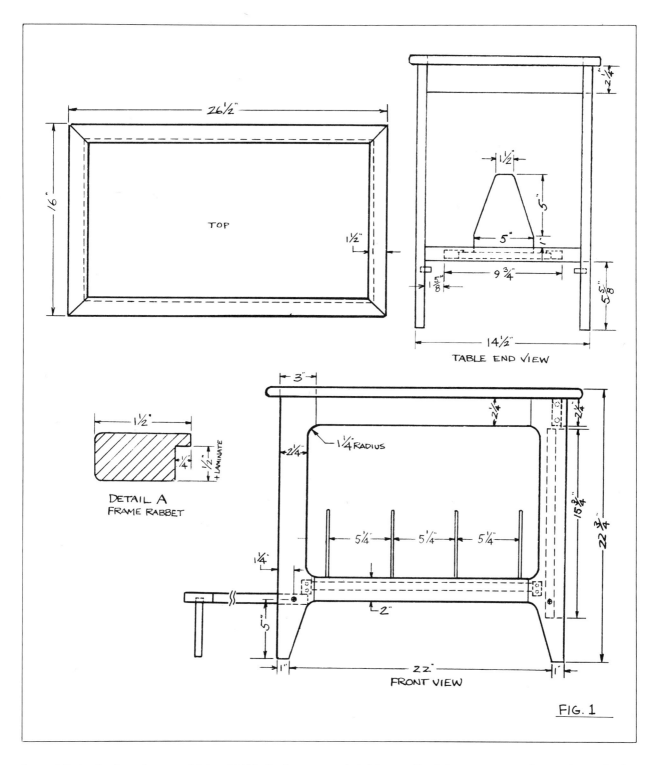

TOP

26½"

16"

1½"

TABLE END VIEW

2¼"

1½"

5"

5"

1"

9¾"

5⅝"

5⅝"

14½"

DETAIL A
FRAME RABBET

1½"

½" + LAMINATE

¼"

FRONT VIEW

3"

2¼"

1¼ RADIUS

2¼"

2¼"

2¼"

5¼" 5¼" 5¼"

15¾"

22¾"

1¼"

5"

2"

1"

22"

1"

FIG. 1

from 1″ stock ripped to a width of 1½″. Refer to Figure 1 and Detail A for the frame dimensions. We used a blind-doweled miter joint at each corner to provide added strength. You'll want an attractive joint here, one that's clean and tight, so make measurements and cuts with special care. Use a miter box if you have one. Glue and clamp the frames and secure the laminated panel with finishing nails driven at an angle up through the panel and into the frame. It's best to drill undersize pilot holes for the nails.

The bottom shelf (record rack) can be made next. The record dividers may be eliminated if you plan to use this piece as an end table. Cut the ½″ plywood F to size. Referring to Figure 1, rout ¼″-wide x ⅜″-deep x 5″-long grooves across

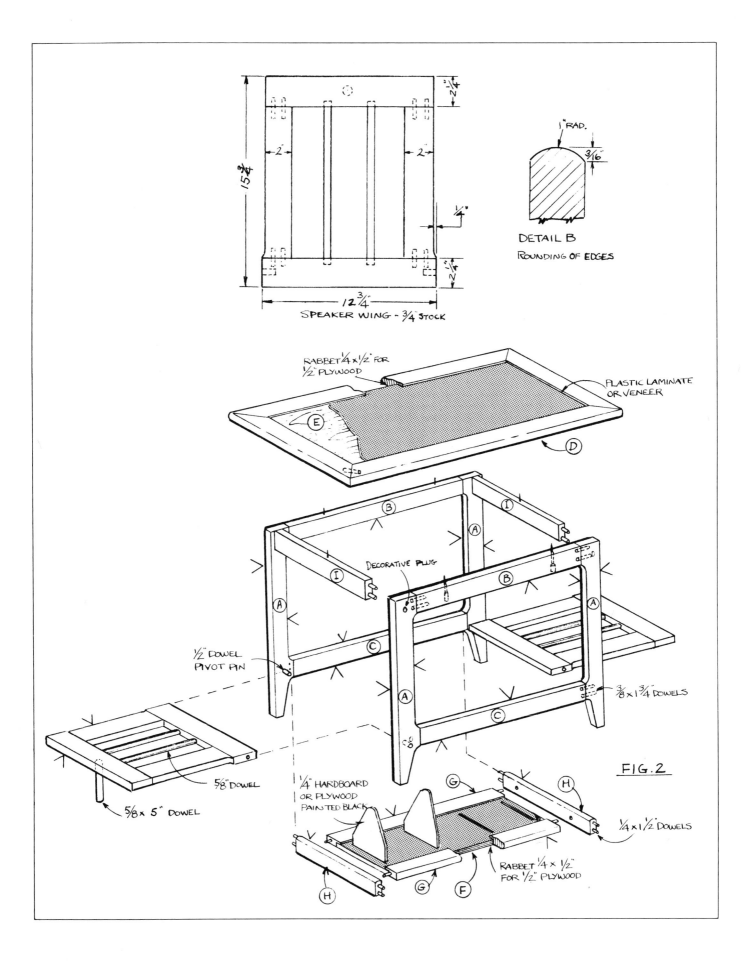

$15\frac{3}{4}$

$2\frac{1}{4}$

2

2

$\frac{1}{4}$"

$2\frac{1}{4}$

$12\frac{3}{4}$"

SPEAKER WING - $\frac{3}{4}$ STOCK

1" RAD.

$\frac{3}{16}$"

DETAIL B
ROUNDING OF EDGES

RABBET $\frac{1}{4}$ x $\frac{1}{2}$ FOR
$\frac{1}{2}$" PLYWOOD

PLASTIC LAMINATE
OR VENEER

E

D

B

I

A

I

DECORATIVE PLUG

B

A

A

C

$\frac{1}{2}$" DOWEL
PIVOT PIN

C

A

$\frac{3}{8}$ x $1\frac{3}{4}$ DOWELS

FIG. 2

$\frac{5}{8}$" DOWEL

$\frac{5}{8}$ x 5" DOWEL

$\frac{1}{4}$" HARDBOARD
OR PLYWOOD
PAINTED BLACK

G

H

H

$\frac{1}{4}$ x $1\frac{1}{2}$ DOWELS

RABBET $\frac{1}{4}$ x $\frac{1}{2}$"
FOR $\frac{1}{2}$" PLYWOOD

H

G

F

the plywood as shown. A router makes an easy job of this, but a bit of patience and a sharp chisel will also yield good results.

Apply the veneer or laminate. Use a sharp knife to score and trim away the excess along the edges and covering the grooves. Make the rabbeted front and back frame rails G and the two lower end frame rails H.

Referring to Figure 1, dowel and glue the lower end frame rails H to the front and back rails G. After this frame has been clamped and allowed to dry, set the panel in place and fasten it from the bottom as you did with the tabletop.

Cut the record dividers to size as shown in Figure 1 and glue them into place. The left and right upper end rails I can now be cut; set them aside until you begin final assembly.

The folding stereo-speaker wings should now be built (unless the piece is to be used as an end table). Refer to Figures 2 and 3 for all details and dimensions. Use ⅜″ x 1¾″ dowels to strengthen all joints.

Before assembly apply a generous radius (see Detail B) to the rounding of all edges marked with a check (√) in Figure 2. This radius helps to give the table its clean lines, so use care here.

After careful sanding, the table is ready for assembly. Referring to Figure 2, drill dowel holes in parts A, H, and I as shown. Glue the four ½″ pivot pins into the frames, but do not glue the ends that insert into the speaker wings. The wings must be free to pivot so that, if desired, they can be folded up and out of the way.

Perhaps the easiest way to assemble the table is to lay the back frame assembly on its side, then fit up and glue one end of each upper end rail I. Then add the record-shelf assembly. Next, slip one end of each speaker wing onto the pivot pins. Take the front frame assembly and lower it onto the mating parts. Use a pipe clamp at each joint and allow to dry overnight.

The top can be joined by centering it on the upper rails and fastening from underneath with six 2″ #8 round-headed wood screws, as shown in Figure 2. The bottom of the rails must be counterbored with a ⅜″ drill.

Finish sand all surfaces, paying particular attention to the radius between the legs and rails. Thoroughly dust all parts with a tack rag, or go over the table with a vacuum cleaner dusting attachment.

An oil finish such as Watco Danish Oil is both appropriate and easy to apply. This is a deep penetrating oil and resin sealer-finish available in natural or dark shades. The natural oil contains no pigments and will not color the wood. Apply according to the directions on the label.

Tung oil is another penetrating oil finish that can be applied with a brush or rubbed on with a cloth. It's available in both clear and colored finishes. As always, apply according to the manufacturer's directions.

BILL OF MATERIALS

Key	Part	Pcs. Req'd	T	W	L
A	leg	4	1″	3″	22″
B	top rail	2	1″	2¼″	18″
C	bottom rail	2	1″	2″	18″
D	mitered frame assembly	1			
E	plywood top	1	½″	13½″	24″
F	plywood bottom	1	½″	7¼″	18⅞″
G	frame rail	2	1″	1½″	18⅞″
H	end frame rail	2	1″	1⅜″	13″
I	upper end rail	2	1″	2¼″	13″

Cranberry Scoop Magazine Rack

For generations cranberry pickers have used scoops for collecting the floating berries from bogs. With slight modification of an original scoop, a most attractive magazine rack reminiscent of an authentic bit of early Americana can be added to the den or living room. It's a good weekend project.

Pine is the proper choice of wood as the originals were invariably made of white pine. A #2 common grade with some small tight knots will be fine.

The back of the rack is glued up from two or more pieces, and the grain should run vertically and parallel to the tines. Lay out and cut the tines, rounding off the tips and beveling the back edges so that the tips are reduced to about ¼" in thickness. A rasp does a quick job.

The sides are cut after laying out a full-size pattern and transferring it to the ½" pine. The handle, which is of ¾" pine, also requires a full-size pattern. The curves of the handle are best finished off with a small-diameter drum sander.

Cut the front panel to length and shape the top edge with a jigsaw or drawknife as shown. The bottom panel is cut to fit between the front, back, and sides. Lay out the location of the feet on the bottom and drill for the four screws. Feet are shaped from ¾" pine as shown.

Sand all components very carefully, and round off the edges to simulate years of wear. This piece looks particularly good when distressed with a tire chain and awl.

Thirty years ago, a light honey or orange-tone stain was popular for Early American projects. However, a dark stain now seems to be in fashion. A good choice is either Minwax Early American or the darker Special Walnut.

After staining, fasten the handle to the front panel with two screws countersunk on the inner face, then join the sides to the back with 1½" brads or common nails for a more rustic effect. Screw the feet to the bottom and secure the bottom to the back and sides, again using nails. The front member with the handle is then attached.

Finish the rack with three coats of thinned orange shellac, rubbed down between coats with fine steel wool.

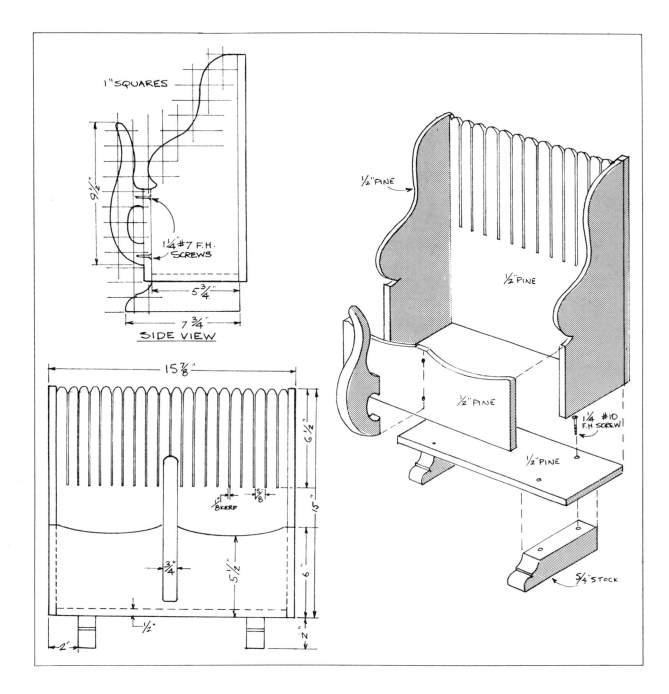

1" SQUARES

$9\frac{1}{2}$"

$1\frac{1}{4}$ #7 F.H.
SCREWS

$5\frac{3}{4}$"

$7\frac{3}{4}$"

SIDE VIEW

$15\frac{7}{8}$"

$6\frac{1}{2}$"

15"

$5\frac{1}{2}$"

6"

$\frac{3}{4}$"

$\frac{5}{8}$"

$\frac{1}{8}$ KERF

$\frac{1}{2}$"

2"

2"

$\frac{1}{2}$" PINE

$\frac{1}{2}$" PINE

$\frac{1}{2}$" PINE

$\frac{1}{2}$" PINE

$\frac{1}{2}$" PINE

$1\frac{1}{4}$ #10
F.H SCREW

$\frac{5}{4}$" STOCK

Three Gift Projects

Kangaroo Puzzle

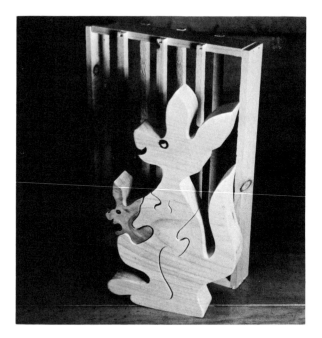

This is a jigsaw puzzle that young children are certainly going to enjoy taking apart and putting together.

Trace the pattern on a 7″-wide x 11″-long block of 1¼″-thick pine (actual). Using a jigsaw, carefully cut along all lines as shown.

Build the cage from ¼″ stock according to the dimensions shown. Use glue to fasten all joints. A narrow strip of leather tacked in place serves as the bottom hinge. Another narrow strip of leather fastened to a peg is used to "latch" the cage shut.

Reassemble the kangaroo in order to give the outside flat surfaces a good sanding. Use paint or a felt-tip pen to create the eyes.

We didn't apply any finish to our happy marsupials, choosing to leave them in their natural state.

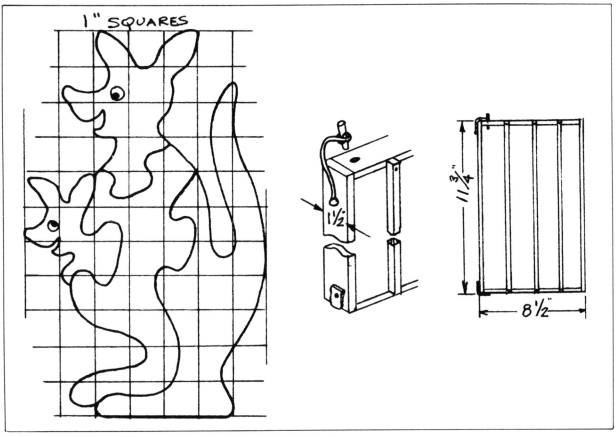

1″ SQUARES

Turtle Pull Toy

Start making the shell by gluing and clamping a piece of 1 x 6 x 10″ pine to the top of a piece ¾ x 6 x 10″. Set aside and allow to dry.

Referring to the pattern provided, cut out the front feet and head, and the back feet and tail from 1″ stock. Cut out and glue a 1 x 2½ x 3″ piece to the top of the head. Allow to dry and then cut to the same shape as the lower half of the head. Use a rasp, file, and sandpaper to shape the head and shell. Drill the head and insert ⅜″ rounded dowel "eyes."

Use a 1¼″ hole cutter to cut out two wheels from 1″ stock. Cut the axle block from ¾ x 1½ x 2¼″ material. Drill a 5⁄16″ axle hole and glue the block to the shell underside. Assemble and glue the ¼″-diameter axle to the wheels. Attach the front and back feet to the shell with pivot screws as shown. Use a piece of heavy wire to link the wheels to the front and back feet. Add a wide smile and bright pair of eyes with some paint or a felt-tip pen.

Here's a delightful pull toy that's guaranteed to light up the face of any preschooler. Even Mom and Dad feel compelled to "show Junior how to use it."

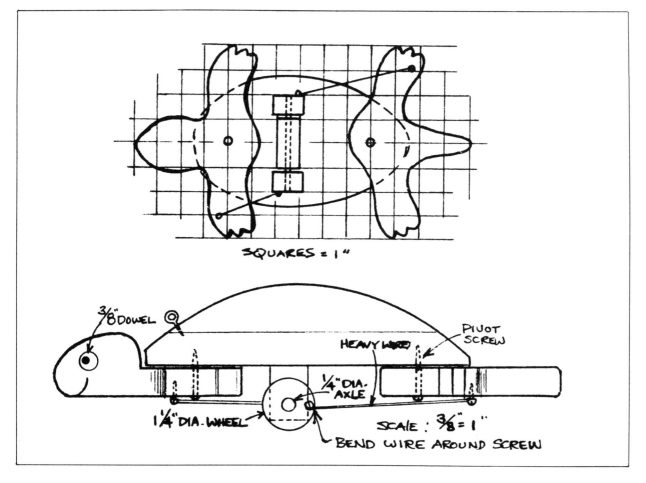

SQUARES = 1″

⅜″ DOWEL

PIVOT SCREW

HEAVY WIRE

¼″ DIA. AXLE

¼″ DIA. WHEEL

SCALE: ⅜″ = 1″

BEND WIRE AROUND SCREW

175

Pulley Planter

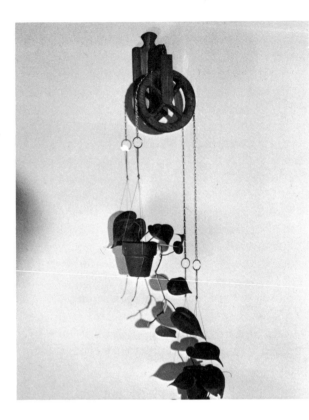

This plant bracket can be used to display almost any small potted houseplant. It's made entirely of pine and can be built in just a few hours' time.

Refer to the drawing and cut both bracket parts from ½" stock. If ½" pine is difficult to purchase in your area, you'll have to plane down a ¾" board. Smooth all rough edges with a file and sandpaper. Now attach the arm to the bracket back with two ⅞" #5 flat-headed wood screws. The dotted line on the back shows the location of the arm.

Cut the pulley to a diameter of 5", mount the disc in a lathe and cut a ⅜" groove (as shown) with a parting chisel. Lay out and cut all four spokes, then sand all surfaces thoroughly.

From ⅛" stock cut the 1"-wide x 4"-long yoke strips. Now cut the ¾ x ¾" support block. Glue and clamp the yoke strips to the pulley wheel and support block and allow to dry overnight. Attach a screw eye to the support-block top and a hook to the end of the bracket arm. Sand all surfaces and finish to suit.

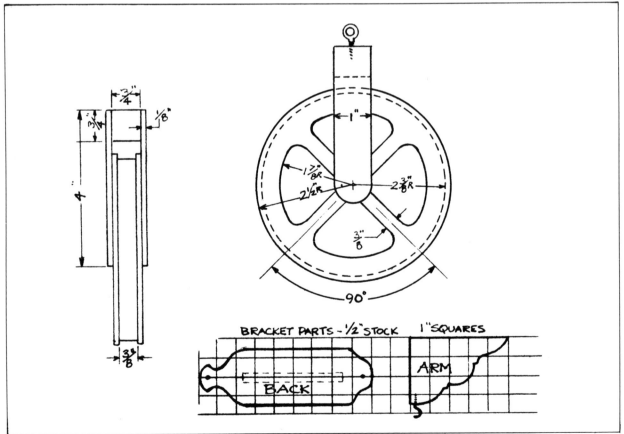

Four Wood Weather Vanes

Weather vanes are always fascinating, particularly the fanciful designs of the eighteenth century. Several of the examples shown here can be found in an excellent book, *The Pine Furniture of Early New England,* by Russell H. Kettell. If you're not concerned with wind direction, these vanes make striking wall decorations, either painted and antiqued or stained and varnished.

Many vane plans call for mounting and pivoting devices that require metalworking skills. We have tried to keep things simple and within the capacity of woodworkers. All of these vanes pivot on a stationary brass rod, except for the horse, which is epoxied to a rod that revolves on a ball bearing. Note that all the vanes have an off-center pivot point which enables them to swing into the wind. They will swing freely enough to work in a moderate breeze, but sensitivity can be increased by balancing them. Lay the completed vane across a dowel placed along the pivot point. Add lead weights until the vane is balanced. Then drill holes in the edges of the vane and insert the weights.

Horse

The horse is cut from glued-up 1″ pine or ¾″ exterior plywood. With solid stock be sure to edge join with ⅜″ dowel pins located after the pattern has been transferred. Drill the horse for a ⅜″ brass rod and fasten it to a 2 x 2 x 44″ beam also drilled for the rod. The rod is epoxied to the horse and beam, and rotates on a steel ball within a plugged tube partly filled with oil. The tube is set into a 2″-square wood post. A washer soldered to the brass rod holds the vane and a copper rain hood keeps the ball-bearing assembly dry. Stain the horse and finish with spar varnish, or finish with primer and oil paint.

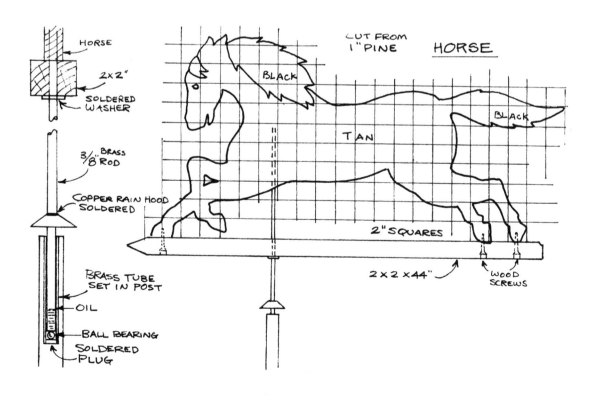

Arrow

An arrow is perhaps the most logical design for pointing the direction of the wind, and this one is adapted from an old and rather ornate vane.

Jigsaw addicts will have a good time shaping this design from ¾ x 6 x 42″ pine. The original vane pivoted on a ⅜″ rod sunk into a 3′-long flat pole which was ¾″ thick, tapered from 2″ at the bottom to ⅞″ at the top, and beveled at the top to drain rainwater. A washer was soldered to the rod as shown.

Stain the arrow and give it three coats of spar varnish; or seal the wood and paint it a dark red, black, or some other dark color.

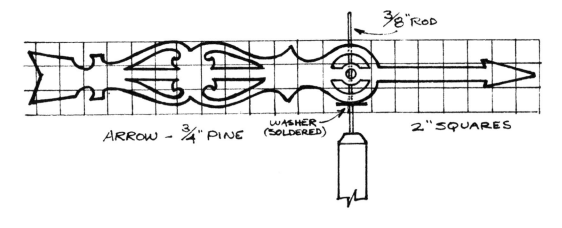

Snake

Ever since the Garden of Eden, snakes have been cast as villains in mythology; and though some people are repelled by these reptiles, we decided to include this eighteenth-century design because it's probably the most striking and original weather vane we've ever seen.

Temporarily butt two jointed 1 x 6 x 36″ pine boards together and transfer the pattern. Lay out ⅜″ dowel locations so they will reinforce the body of the snake. Drill for the dowels and edge join the boards with water-resistant glue.

Lay out and bore a ⁷⁄₁₆″ hole for the mounting rod, drilling through from both edges if necessary. Jigsaw the snake and finish sand. The snake may be stained and spar varnished or painted whatever color suits your fancy. Dark colors will stand out better against the sky.

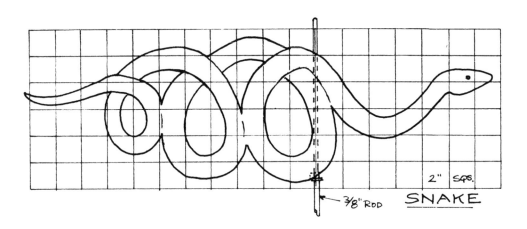

Codfish

Two hundred years ago when the codfish played a major role in the economy of coastal New England, its effigy graced many roof ridges, steeples, and tavern signs. Its importance has lessened considerably, but the codfish still makes a fine weather vane or wall decoration.

The body, including the tail, can be jigsawed from a 1 x 8 x 30″ piece of pine, after boring a ⁷⁄₁₆″ shaft hole for a loose fit over the rod. Shape the fins separately from ½″ pine and join them to the body with dowels and water-resistant glue. No self-respecting cod would appear in public without its chin barbel (a fleshy appendage on the lower jaw). This is duplicated with a nail forced through a predrilled hole and bent.

Apply primer and paint the codfish with oil paints. The underside is cream, within the limits of the dotted line shown. As a wall plaque, the cod can be painted or stained after sanding. Distress it slightly and use a dark stain such as Minwax Special Walnut. Seal with several coats of satin varnish.

A large washer is soldered to the brass rod. If the rod is inserted into a wooden pole, bevel the top edge of the pole to drain rainwater.

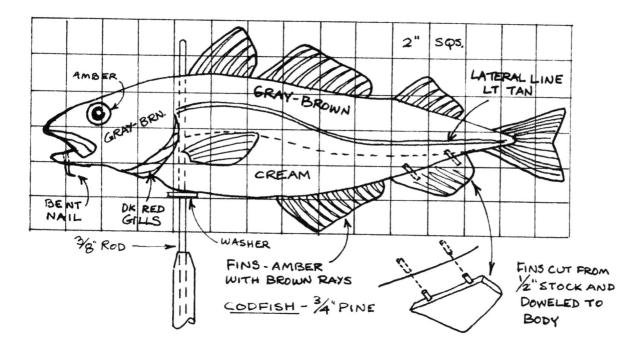

179

Blanket Chest

The blanket chest, a typical Early American piece, has always been a popular item for reproduction in the home workshop. Sitting at the foot of the bed, it is very useful for storage of blankets, sheets, and pillowcases. This particular design will also make a very nice toy chest. We've also seen blanket chests used for coffee tables.

' Most chests of this type were homebuilt of pine, usually from six very wide boards. Modern craftsmen will usually have to edge glue narrower stock to obtain the necessary width, but this extra work will help do away with the problem of cupping, which is encountered with very wide boards. In any case, avoid the use of plywood for the box itself; it's just not appropriate.

Start by gluing up sufficient ¾" #2 pine for the six boards of the chest. Allow extra length and width for final trimming. Lay out stopped rabbets on the back edges of both ends. If stopped rabbets are a problem for you, then run the rabbets all the way down and later glue in a filler block.

Lay out and cut dadoes for the bottom and the drawer frame, then cut the ⅜" notches for the rabbeted front board. Also cut the semicircular foot design.

The drawer frame can be of white pine, but hardwood is preferable. The frame rails are all ¾ x 1½" and are joined with two ¼ x 1½" dowel pins at each corner. Make sure that the frame is clamped so that it dries perfectly flat. Fasten the frame to the chest ends with counterbored wood screws.

Note that the bottom board is cut narrow enough to allow the front board to seat fully in the end notches. Slide the bottom board into its dadoes. Do not use glue on these dado joints.

Add the chest back and front, and fasten with finishing nails or decoratively headed nails. Angle the nails a bit, and set finishing nails slightly below the surface. Changes in the width of the sides and front due to humidity may cause cracking if these joints are glued.

Shape the drawer guide from a length of ¾ x ¾" hardwood and glue it to the drawer frame. The drawer construction, while not elegant, is in keeping with the general level of construction of the chest.

Referring to the sectional and exploded views of the drawer, you will see that the sides, front, and back are grooved to receive the plywood bottom. The sides and back are of ½" stock, while the front, which is rabbeted to receive the sides, must be ¾" thick.

Glue the sides to the front and reinforce the joint with ⅛" dowel pegs. This achieves a neat and strong joint without the fussiness of dovetails or combination joints.

The U-shaped runner should be routed from hardwood and glued to the drawer bottom in line with the notch in the drawer back. Leave the drawer front slightly oversize so it can later be trimmed to a neat fit in its opening. Note that the drawer guide also serves as a stop for the flush drawer front.

The lid is fitted on the front and ends with a ¾ x ⅝" strip, glued and nailed along the front edge of the lid and just nailed at the ends. This strip may be mitered or butt-joined at the corners. Mortise the backboard for solid-brass 1½ x 4½" offset chest hinges.

Apply a pigmented oil stain to all exterior surfaces. The interior of the chest and drawer may be sealed or painted. Pale blue and green were popular colors for the interior of old chests.

Finish the chest with three coats of low-luster urethane varnish. The final coat should be uniformly rubbed down with 4/0 steel wool, then waxed and buffed. Finally, fit the drawer with two turned wooden pull knobs.

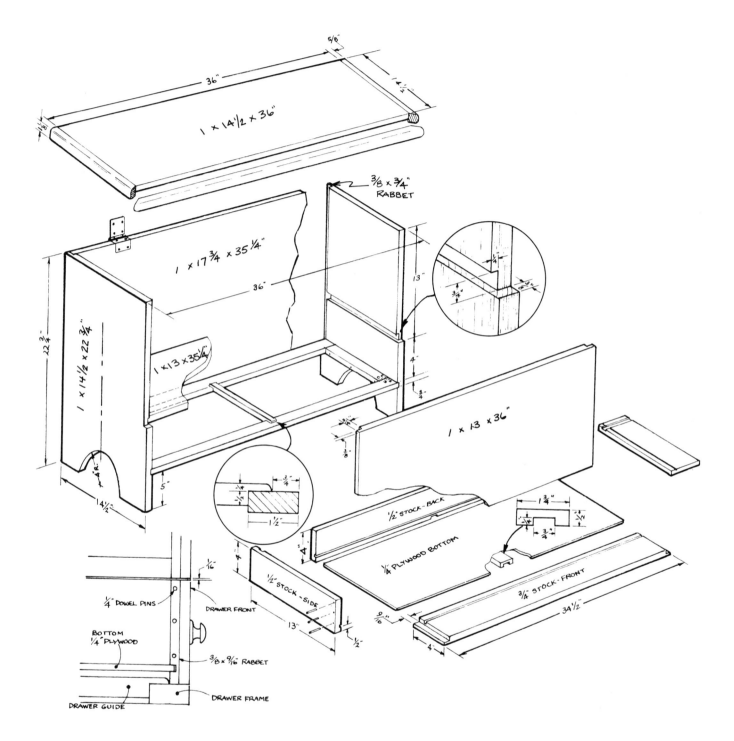

5/8"

1 x 14½ x 36"

36"

¼
2

⅛"

3/8 x 7/4"
RABBET

1 x 17¾ x 35¼"

36"

13"

¼
4

¾"
5/4"

4"

1 x 14½ x 22¾"

1 x 13 x 35¼"

¾"

4½"
5"

4½"

1 x 13 x 36"

½"
4

½"
3/8

1 3/4"

1½"

¾"

½" STOCK - BACK

¼ PLYWOOD BOTTOM

¾" STOCK - FRONT

34½"

¼
½

¾"

1½"

1/16"

¼" DOWEL PINS

DRAWER FRONT

BOTTOM
¼" PLYWOOD

3/8 x 9/16 RABBET

DRAWER FRAME

DRAWER GUIDE

½" STOCK - SIDE

13"

4"

9/16"

½"

4"

Cherry Dressing Mirror

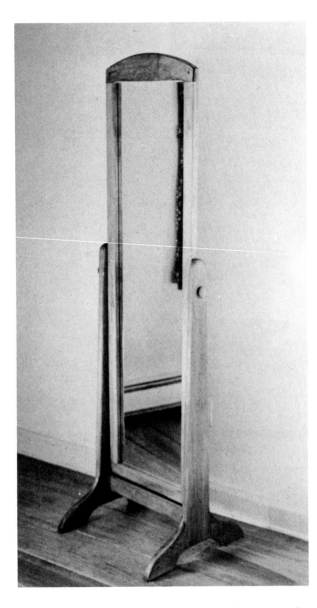

This slim and elegant free-standing dressing mirror is a very rewarding piece to build. We used 10½ board feet of ¾″ cherry. The 14 x 54″ mirror was purchased at a discount store and stripped of its cheap plastic frame.

Start construction with the base. Enlarge the pattern squares on template stock and transfer the shape of the feet. Lay out the wide dadoes and cut with repeated passes of a dado cutter. Next, the feet can be bandsawed to shape. Cut them slightly oversize to allow for slight irregularities and final shaping.

The tenon at the lower end of the upright supports is the widest point on the supports. Cut this for a snug fit in the foot dado and leave the tenon at least ½″ long to be trimmed flush with the foot bottom after the joint is secured.

Locate the ⁵⁄₁₆″-diameter holes in the uprights through which the ¼″ bolts will pass. Use a drill press or doweling jig to bore these holes as it is very important that they be bored true. Sand the uprights and feet, then glue and clamp them together. When the assembly is dry, use a rasp or cabinet file to shape a smooth curve from the feet to the uprights, and give a generous radius to all sharp edges.

The base crossmember is cut from ¾″ stock, and both the crossmember and the feet are bored for four ⅜ x 1½″ dowel pins. The top edge of the crossmember is exactly flush with the top edge of the feet. Glue and clamp the crossmember between the feet and keep the assembly square by clamping a piece of scrap, exactly the same length as the crossmember, between the upper ends of the uprights. Use a try square and framing square to make certain that all parts are squarely joined.

The four parts of the mirror frame are cut to length and notched for a half-lap joint at the corners. Join the frame with glue and wood screws driven from the back as shown, or drive the screws in from the front, counterboring them for the insertion of decorative plugs. The mirror rabbet on the back of the frame is easily cut with a router and ⅜″ rabbet bit and pilot. The rounded corners are then squared off with a chisel.

In keeping with the clean, contemporary lines of the base, the front inner edge of the frame is not molded but rather simply rounded off (as shown in the frame section detail). This process can be done by hand or with a router.

To locate the holes in the frame for the adjusting bolts, place a piece of ¼″-thick scrap along the top of the crossmember and rest the mirror on it. Use a pencil through the upright holes to mark the frame sides for drilling. Again, use a drill press or doweling jig to insure that the holes are bored true.

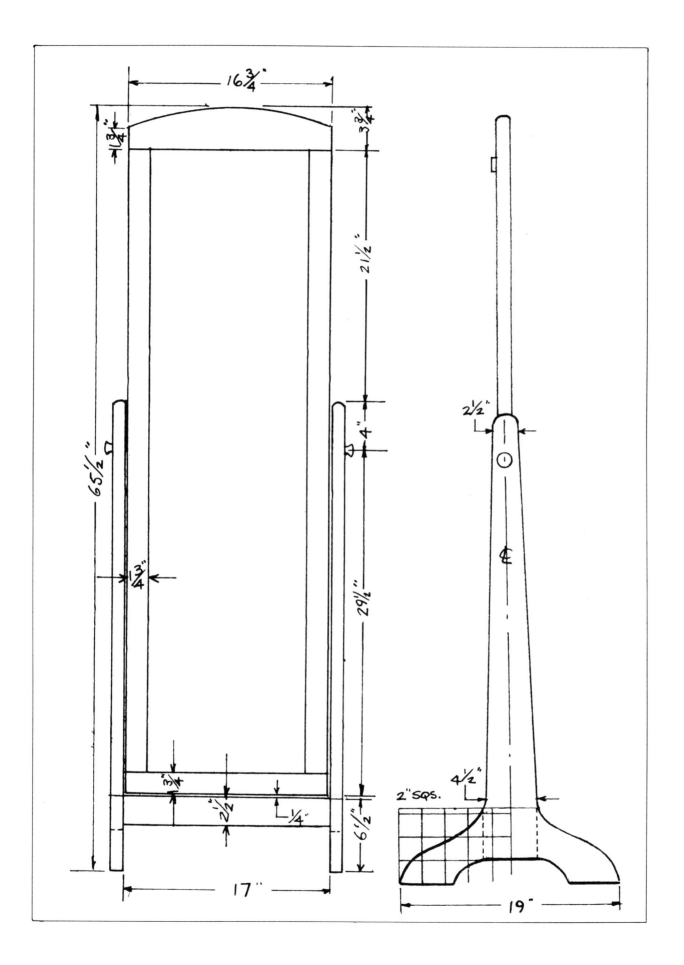

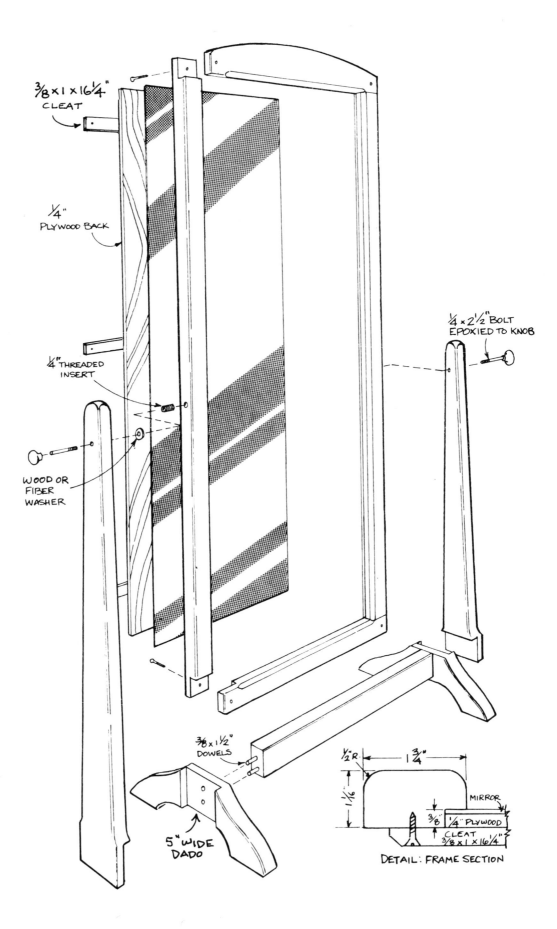

$\frac{3}{8} \times 1 \times 16\frac{1}{4}"$
CLEAT

$\frac{1}{4}"$
PLYWOOD BACK

$\frac{1}{4}"$ THREADED
INSERT

WOOD OR
FIBER
WASHER

$\frac{1}{4} \times 2\frac{1}{2}"$ BOLT
EPOXIED TO KNOB

$\frac{3}{8} \times 1\frac{1}{2}"$
DOWELS

5" WIDE
DADO

$\frac{1}{2}"$R

$1\frac{3}{4}"$

$1\frac{1}{16}"$

$\frac{3}{8}"$

MIRROR

$\frac{1}{4}"$ PLYWOOD

CLEAT
$\frac{3}{8} \times 1 \times 16\frac{1}{4}"$

DETAIL: FRAME SECTION

Drill ⅜″ holes deep enough to take ¼″ threaded inserts. These inserts have an inside thread for a ¼″ bolt, and sharp outside threads to cut into the wood. A screwdriver slot in one end provides the means of inserting them. They can be purchased in some hardware stores or by mail from Brookstone Co., 127 Vose Farm Rd., Peterborough, NH 03458.

The adjusting screws are made from 2½″ carriage bolts with their heads cut off and inserted into 1½″-diameter wood drawer pulls. Drill the pulls for a tight fit on the end of the bolts and dab a bit of epoxy on the bolt before twisting into the pull.

There will be about ⅛″ of space between the frame sides and uprights. This is taken up with a thin hardwood washer cut by hand or with a hole saw and electric drill. Fiber washers can also be used.

The mirror may have a cardboard backing glued to it. Do not try to remove it, as you'll surely scratch the silvering and spoil the mirror. Strip the commercial frame from the mirror and insert the mirror into the frame rabbet. It should fit easily.

If it's tight, ease the rabbet a bit. Cut a ¼″ plywood back for the mirror. This piece is held in place with three thin cleats screwed at each end to the frame.

Finishing is a matter of preference. We gave our mirror a very light coat of walnut stain to accentuate the grain, and finished up with three coats of Watco Danish Oil, a penetrating sealer that leaves a soft hand-rubbed glow.

Utility Table

This small utility table can be put to use in an endless number of ways. It makes an ideal stand for plants, books, an aquarium, or even a small portable television.

To make this a fairly simple project for beginners, we designed it with simple butt joints. More advanced woodworkers may want to incorporate the use of dadoes and rabbets for added strength. No matter what the level of ability, though, we think everyone can find this an enjoyable and rewarding weekend project.

Begin construction by cutting the sides from ¾″ stock to the dimension shown. If you can't get

12″ (nominal)-wide boards, you'll have to edge join two or three to get the width. Lay out the 3¾″ radius, then cut out with a jigsaw.

The bottom shelf is also made from ¾″ stock. After cutting to 10⅝″ wide x 18″ long, lay out and cut the front cutaway section.

Make the back from ¾″ stock that's cut 13½″ wide x 18″ long. Here again you'll probably have to edge glue stock to get enough width. The top is also made from glued-up ¾″ stock. To cover the end grain, add 1″ wide breadboard ends. It's best to cut these ends a little longer than necessary so that after fastening they can be cut perfectly flush.

The drawer assembly can be made next. Note that the front is of ¾″ stock, the back and sides are of ½″ stock, and the bottom is ¼″ plywood. Cut all parts to size, noting the ⅜ x ⅝″ rabbet in the drawer front. Cut a groove in the front and sides to accept the plywood bottom.

Assemble all parts as shown on the drawing. Use finishing nails or 1¼″ #8 flat-headed screws, drilled and counterbored for all joints. Use wood plugs to fill all counterbored holes.

Finish sand all surfaces thoroughly, and stain to suit. Finish with two coats of polyurethane varnish and rub to a final luster with 4/0 steel wool.

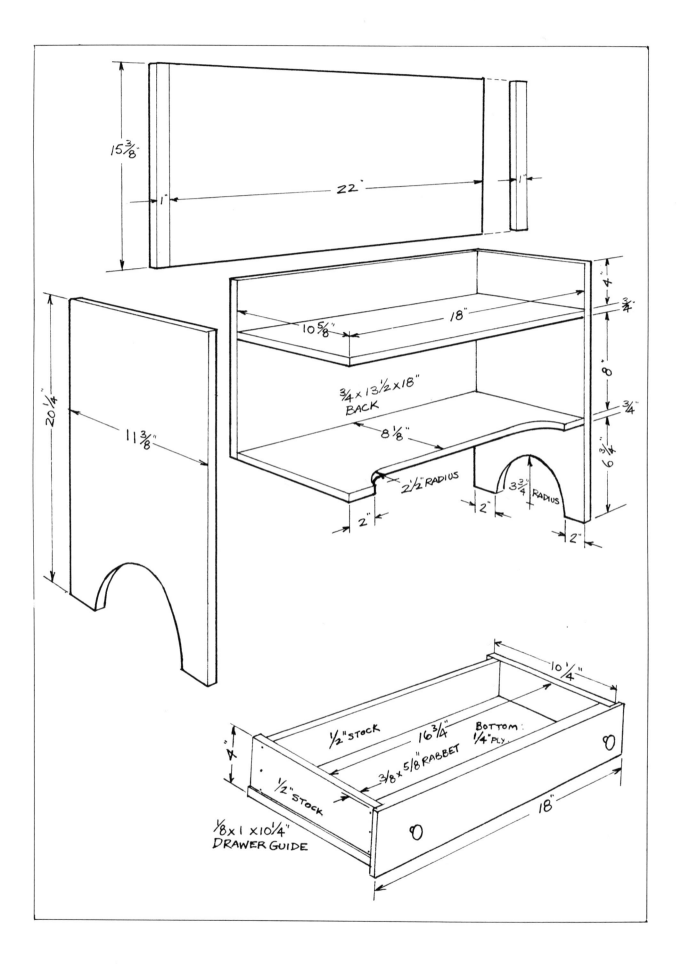

15 3/8"

1"

22"

1"

20 1/4"

11 3/8"

4"

3/4"

18"

10 5/8"

8"

3/4"

6 3/4"

3/4 x 13 1/2 x 18"
BACK

8 1/8"

2 1/2" RADIUS

3 3/4" RADIUS

2"

2"

2"

10 1/4"

1/2" STOCK

16 3/4"

BOTTOM
1/4" PLY.

4"

4"

3/8 x 5/8" RABBET

1/2" STOCK

18"

1/8 x 1 x 10 1/4"
DRAWER GUIDE

Early American Dry Sink

The dry sink is truly a classic piece of Early American furniture. Its charm and simplicity are timeless. We think the project shown here is a fine example of the basic dry sink design of the eighteenth century.

The uses for a dry sink in today's home are almost limitless. We use ours for a favorite reading light and to display a variety of potted plants. The lower cabinet collects almost anything you can think of.

Except for the back panel, which is ¼" plywood, this project is made entirely of 1" (¾" actual thickness) pine.

Begin construction by making the two sides A. You'll notice that they are 15¼" wide, and since pine boards of that width are pretty rare, it will be necessary to edge join at least two narrower boards. For construction of this size, it's advisable to reinforce the edge joints with dowels or

splines. Allow the glue to dry overnight, then cut the sides to length and width. Next, cut the ¼ x ⅜" rabbet (see the detail) that runs along the back of each side. Referring to the drawing, lay out and cut the ¼"-deep dadoes for the shelves. Using the grid pattern provided, lay out and cut the bottom curve.

The upper and lower shelves B can be made next. Like the sides, the shelves are rather wide, so narrower boards must be edge joined. After gluing and drying, cut the shelves to the dimensions specified.

The back C is made of ¼" plywood. The plywood grain should run vertically, and care must be taken to make sure that all cuts are square.

Tackle the front frame next. It's important that this frame be flat, so try to select boards that are free from warp. The frame must also be square, so make all measurements and cuts accurately. Cut the legs and rails to size, then lay out and drill dowel holes as shown. Glue and clamp the frame assembly and allow to dry overnight. Finally, lay out and cut the scrollwork.

The door assembly is next. Start with the center panel I, gluing up stock if you don't have a 12½"-wide board. After cutting the panel board to the proper length (20½") and width (12½"), use the table saw, radial-arm saw, or shaper to make the panel raising cut.

Cut the two door rails G and the two door stiles H to size as shown in the bill of materials. Refer to the tenon detail on the drawing for all dimensions. Next cut the ¼ x ⅜" groove (see the raised panel detail) on the inside edge of the four panel parts. Before gluing, assemble the frame to check for proper fit and squareness. Also, at this time, drill holes for the ¼" tenon pins.

Now, glue and clamp the two rails and two stiles around the center panel. Do not glue the panel in the grooves. Complete the assembly of the door panel and frame by cutting and gluing in the ¼" tenon pins.

The components for the tray can be cut next. Start with the tray bottom J, cutting to the length and width shown in the bill of materials. Next cut the two tray sides L, then lay out and

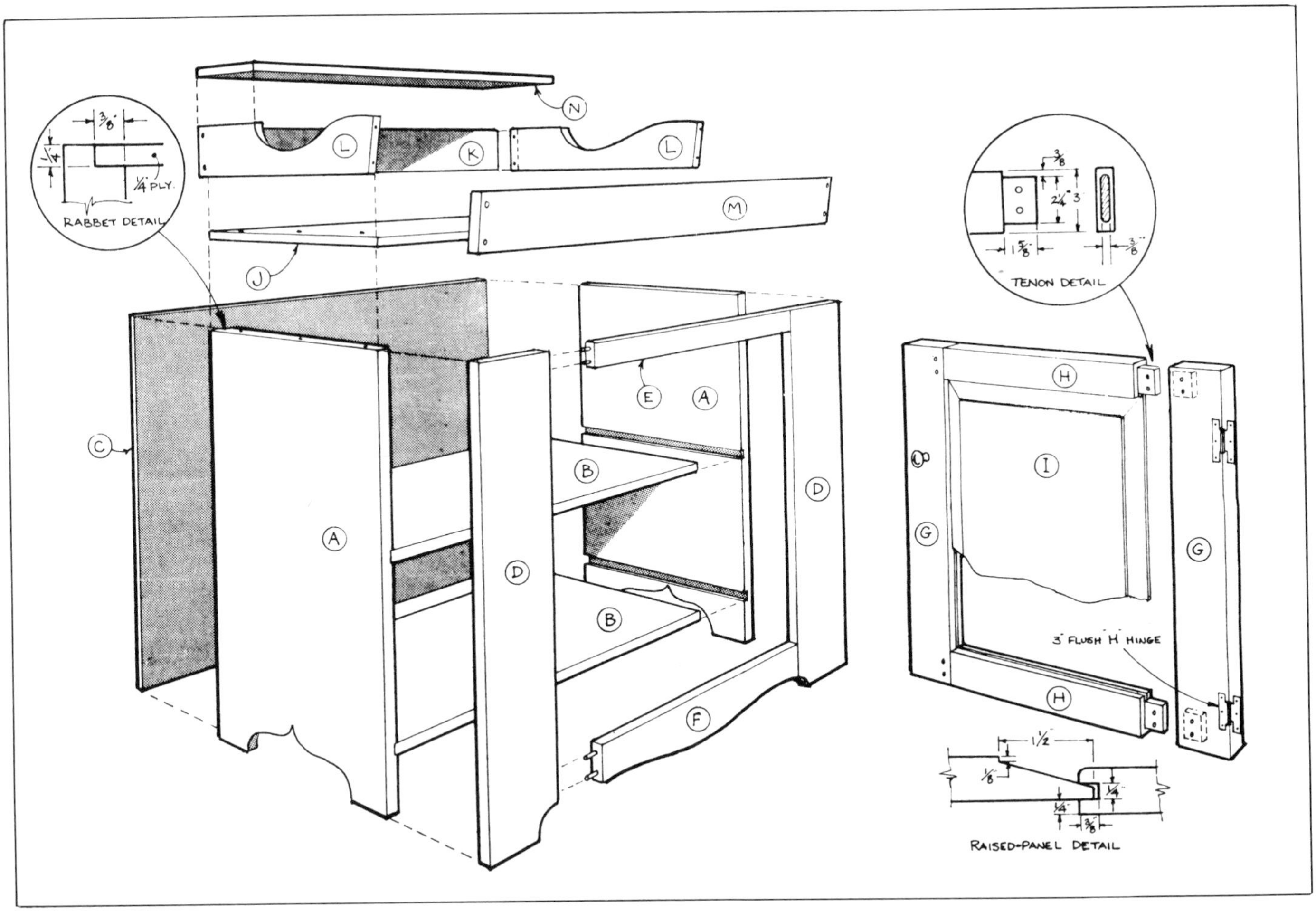
RABBET DETAIL
¼ PLY.
TENON DETAIL
3" FLUSH H HINGE
RAISED-PANEL DETAIL

cut the curves as detailed on the grid pattern. The tray back K, front M, and top N are then made.

Begin assembly of the base by joining the left and right sides to the front frame. Drill and countersink holes for 1½″ #8 flat-headed wood screws.

Slide the top and bottom shelves B into the dadoes. If this is a very snug fit, do this before joining the sides to the front frame. Now attach the plywood back with 2-penny nails.

Begin assembly of the tray by beveling the front end of part J to match the front angled cut of parts L. Also bevel the top and bottom edge of part M to match the angles as shown.

The tray bottom can now be attached to the base. Attach part J by drilling and counterboring for 1½″ #8 flat-headed screws. Use wood plugs to fill the holes. Employ the same method to attach all other parts of the tray.

Fit the door and attach it with two 3″ H hinges as shown. A ½ x ½ x 1½″ turnbutton is carved and

BILL OF MATERIALS

Key	Part	Pcs. Req'd	T	W	L
Base					
A	side	2	1″	15¼″	32″
B	shelf	2	1″	15″	33″
C	back (plywood)	1	¼	33¼″	31¾″
D	leg	2	1″	7″	32″
E	top rail	1	1″	2″	20″
F	bottom rail	1	1″	4″	20″
Door					
G	door rail	2	1″	4″	26″
H	door stile	2	1″	3″	15¼″
I	door panel	1	1″	12½″	20½″
Tray					
J	bottom	1	1″	15½″	34½″
K	back	1	1″	5¼″	34½″
L	sides	2	1″	5¼″	17¼″
M	front	1	1″	5″	36″
N	top	1	1″	6″	36″

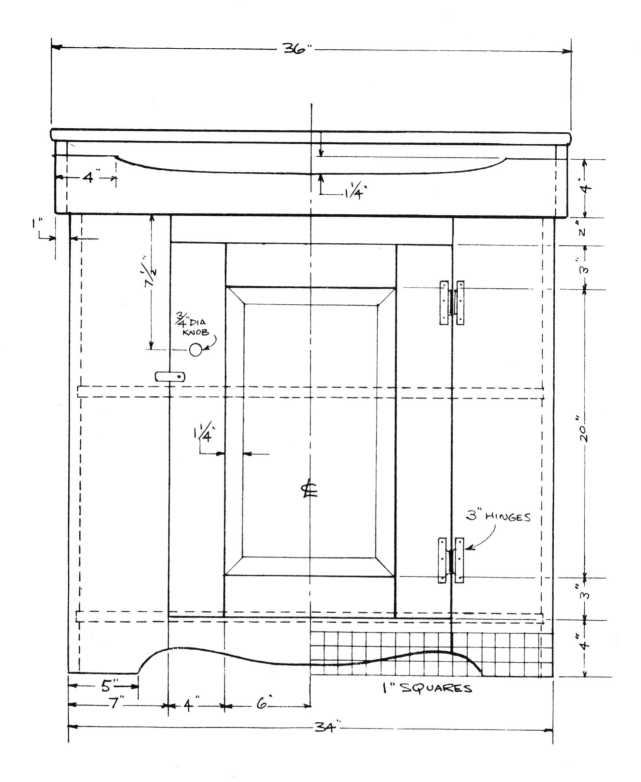

36"

4"

1¼"

4"

1"

2"

3"

7½"

¾"DIA
KNOB

1¼"

20"

℄

3" HINGES

3"

4"

5"

7"

4"

6"

1" SQUARES

34"

attached by drilling and counterboring a ¾″ #6 flat-headed screw. The screw is then covered with a wood plug.

Attach a ¾″-diameter wood knob to the door frame and plug all counterbored holes with wood plugs before finish sanding all surfaces.

We stained our sink with two coats of Minwax Special Walnut. After 48 hours, we applied two coats of Minwax Antique Oil finish, allowing 24 hours between coats. A soft cloth was used to hand rub the finish to a soft luster.

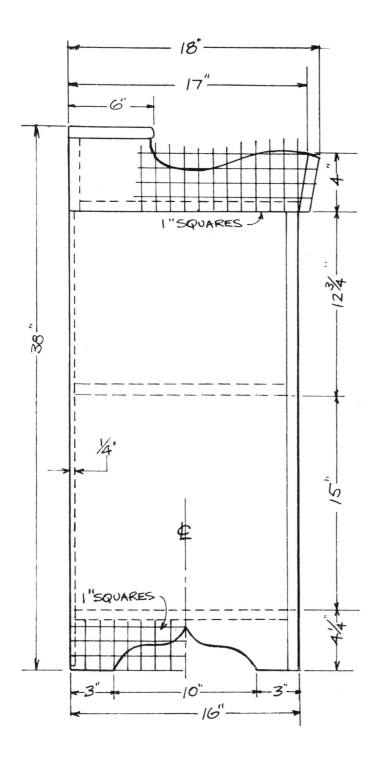

18"

17"

6"

4"

1"SQUARES

12¾"

38"

15"

¼"

₵

1"SQUARES

4¼"

3"   10"   3"

16"

Balancing Sawyer

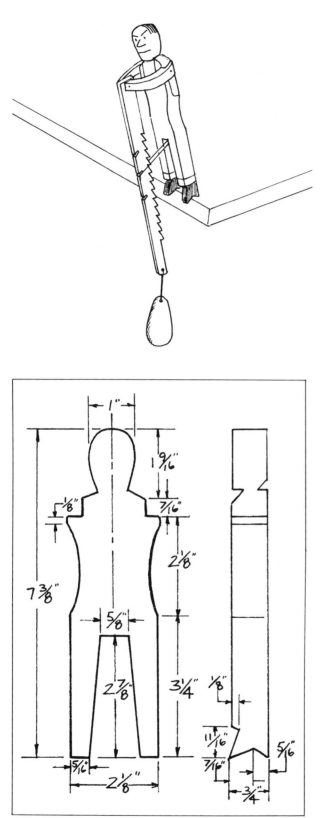

This old-time toy has amazed generations of children. They love to watch the little sawyer rocking back and forth while leaning out over the table edge in a most impossible way. Following the dimensions given in the drawings, cut the sawyer's body from ¾″ pine. Rip a strip ³⁄₁₆″ thick x 1″ wide x 15″ long and use it for the two arms and the long saw blade. Fasten the arms to the body with glue and brads, and brad the hands to the upper, or wide, end of the saw. Round off the edges of the arms and body, and sand. Seal with shellac or give the sawyer blue overalls and a red shirt as befits a rugged woodsman. Felt-tip pens can be used to color the pine to avoid having to clean brushes.

Rig a loop of thread around the sawyer's neck, down his back, and between his legs. Hook it around one of the three notches in the saw blade. There are several notches so that adjustments can be made. Tie another thread through the hole in the lower end of the saw and fasten it to a weight of about 12 ounces. The weight can be a smooth stone with a hole drilled through using a carbide bit, or a heavy fishing sinker. In a pinch, a small bag of sand will also serve.

Test the toy by placing the sawyer on the edge of a table and setting him in motion. You may have to adjust the amount of the weight and shift the thread harness to a higher or lower notch.

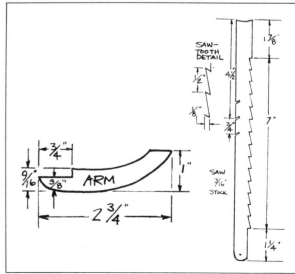

Spanish Chest

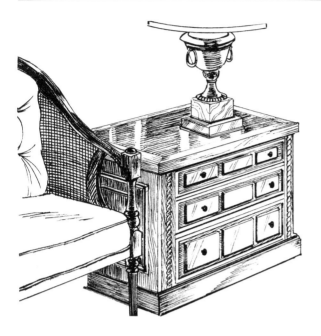

A hallmark of Spanish furniture is the use of boldly molded and carved panels. Although at first glance this small table/chest may appear to be a formidable project, it's really fairly simple to build.

Basically, it consists of a case made up of three plain panels and drawers embellished with applied moldings and trim. Since the chest is finished on all sides, it can be used to advantage as an end table alongside an easy chair, or a pair could be used to flank a sofa.

Unless you intend matching the chest to other furniture, red oak is probably the best choice of wood for all parts if a stained or natural finish is desired. An antiqued enamel finish is very striking and will hide grain irregularities and other defects. Another visually exciting method of finishing is to combine stain and enamel. In this case the panels and drawer fronts can be stained, while the trim is enameled in dark red, green, or any color that harmonizes with other furnishings.

Begin construction by jointing and edge gluing sufficient ¾″ stock to form the two end panels C and rear panel D. To achieve flat, stable panels, it's best to use fairly narrow boards of no more than 4″ width. The chest is not subjected to heavy use, so it's not necessary to reinforce the edge joints with dowel pins or splines, though

many particular woodworkers may prefer to do so. If the edges of the boards are jointed properly in full contact, and care is taken not to over-tighten clamps, thus squeezing out most of the glue, a bond stronger than the wood itself can be achieved.

Glue up all three panels slightly oversize, later trimming to final size. It's probably more convenient to add the molding trim to the well-sanded panels at this stage. The nose and cove molding O, shown in Detail A, is a standard type found in most lumberyards. Experienced woodworkers may prefer to cut their own from matching oak. If you use pine molding, sand it carefully and stain a sample length. Commercial pine molding varies widely in its ability to take a stain evenly. Some of it is so filled with pitch streaks or of such wild grain that staining is unsatisfactory. If you plan to paint the molding as a contrast with the stained panels, there will be no problem as long as the molding is well sanded and sealed.

A table-saw miter jig will prove invaluable for achieving perfect mitered corners. All vertical sections of the molding can be held with glue and brads. Horizontal moldings, which cross the grain of the panels, should be fastened only with brads. The panels will shrink and expand slightly in their width so it's best not to restrain this movement.

The two trim strips E are cut to length, and stopped dadoes are laid out for the two front drawer dividers as shown in Figure 4. Cut these dadoes by hand with a chisel or use a router. Upper and lower rails F and G are joined to the trim strips with glue and dowel pins as shown in Figure 5. When clamping this frame assembly be sure to keep it flat and square.

Apply glue to the front and back edges of the end panels, then add the back panel D and the front frame assembly. Apply pipe clamps and brace the case with strips of scrap to maintain squareness while the glue dries.

The drawer dividers J and the side and rear drawer supports I and K are cut to size and assembled as units with glue and dowel pins. Note that the front dividers are notched for a good fit

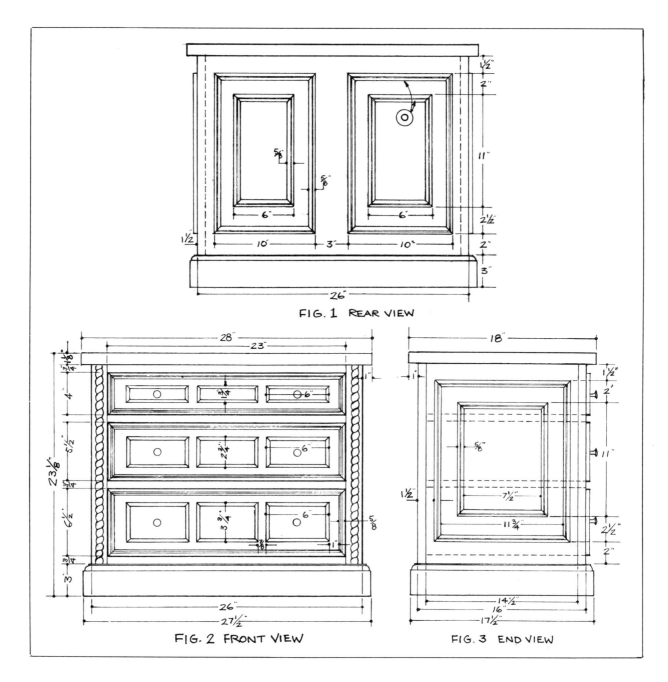

FIG. 1 REAR VIEW

FIG. 2 FRONT VIEW

FIG. 3 END VIEW

in the dadoes cut in the trim strips. Counterbore the side supports to a depth of ½″ and screw them to the end panels with 1½″ round-headed screws. Do not glue the supports to the end panels.

Finishing nails can be driven through the rear panel and into the rear drawer supports, or the rear supports can be counterbored and screwed in the same manner as the side supports. If finishing nails are used, set them so the holes can be filled later.

Six ¾ x ¾″ drawer guides L are cut to length and fastened to the drawer supports with glue. Do not glue the guides to the end panels. The

three cleats around the top edge of the case (M and N) are screwed to the panels flush with the top edges. Before fastening, drill slightly oversize holes for 1½″ round-headed screws to fasten the top.

Base trim H is shaped from ¾″ x 3″ x 8′ oak, which can be cut with a router and beading bit. The trim is mitered and fastened to the chest front and back with glue and screws driven from the inside. The end trim strips are just screwed in place.

The top is glued up from four or five lengths of 1⅛″ oak, trimmed to finish size and edged with

194

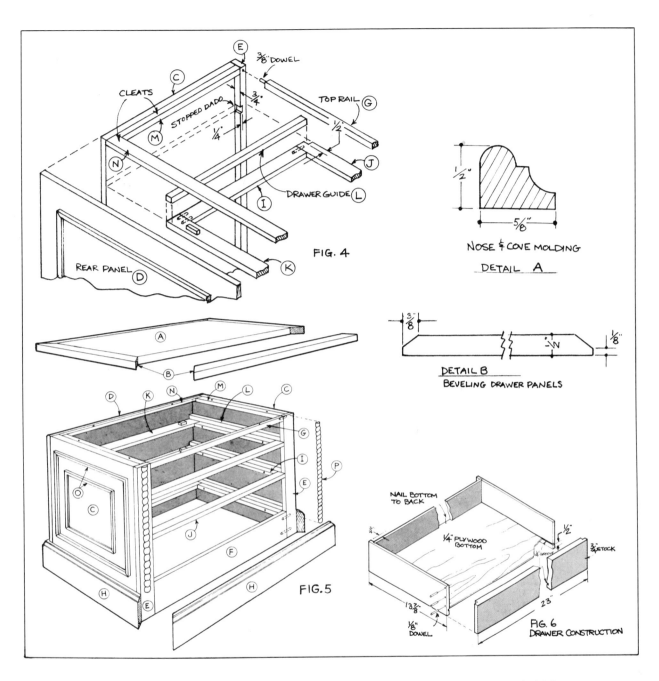

CLEATS

STOPPED DADO

E

C

M

N

3/8" DOWEL

3/4"

1/4"

TOP RAIL G

1/2"

J

DRAWER GUIDE L

I

K

FIG. 4

REAR PANEL D

A

B

D K N M L C

G

I

P

E

O

C

J

F

H H

E

FIG. 5

1/2"

5/8"

NOSE & COVE MOLDING

DETAIL A

3/8"

1/8"

N

DETAIL B

BEVELING DRAWER PANELS

NAIL BOTTOM TO BACK

1/4" PLYWOOD BOTTOM

1/2"

3/4"

3/4" STOCK

13 3/8"

1/8" DOWEL

23

FIG. 6

DRAWER CONSTRUCTION

1⅛ x 1″ oak strips mitered at the corners. Fasten long strips with glue and finishing nails. Short edging is fastened with nails only.

Drawers are constructed of oak, using ⅜″ or ½″ stock for the sides and back, ¾″ stock for the drawer fronts and ¼″ plywood for the bottoms. All drawers are flush-fitted in the openings, so it's best to cut the fronts a bit oversize and later trim them for an exact fit.

A dovetailed joint between the front and sides of the drawers is the preferred method of joining; however, the rabbeted and doweled joint shown in Figure 6 is both strong and good-looking. Note

that the drawer bottoms are held in grooves cut in the front and sides and are nailed to the bottom edges of the backs.

Cut the beveled trim panels from ½″ oak as shown in Detail B and fasten them to the drawer fronts with small brads. Then add the nose and cove molding around the drawer front, flush with the edges and with the coved portion of the molding facing in.

Two small ½ x ½ x 2″ hardwood stop blocks are glued to each rear drawer support to prevent the drawers from butting against the rear panel. They are glued to the supports about ½″ from the rear panel and 2″ in from each guide. Fit the finished drawers in place and then determine the exact location of the stop blocks.

The carved rope molding can be obtained from Craftsman Wood Service Company (see p. 243 for the address). This molding is trimmed to fit between the top and the base trim and is glued in place.

Finish sand the piece, breaking all sharp corners. If oak is used, the open grain should be filled. There's some disagreement as to whether stain or filler is applied first. Many different effects can be achieved with the use of natural and tinted fillers. As always, it's best to experiment first on a piece of matching scrap.

In this case, it's recommended that stain be applied first, and when the piece is dry, a filler tinted to match the stain is brushed on. Work one panel at a time so the filler doesn't harden before you can remove the excess. Rub the filler into the grain with a burlap pad, working first against the grain and then with it.

Allow the filler to dry and then apply thinned sealer. After drying overnight, sand with very fine grit paper, working with the grain. Dust carefully and apply two coats of a low-luster sealer. Seal inside the case and the bottom side of the top before screwing the top in place. Finally, add black hammered-finish drawer pulls.

BILL OF MATERIALS

Key	Part	Pcs. Req'd	T	W	L
A	top	1	1⅛″	16″	26″
B	top edging	1	1⅛″	1″	8′
C	end panel	2	¾″	14½″	22″
D	rear panel	1	¾″	22″	26″
E	front trim	2	¾″	1½″	22″
F	front lower rail	1	¾″	3¾″	23″
G	front upper rail	1	¾″	¾″	23″
H	base trim	1	¾″	3″	8′
I	side drawer support	6	¾″	1½″	12¼″
J	front divider	2	¾″	1½″	24½″
K	rear drawer support	3	¾″	1½″	24½″
L	drawer guide	6	¾″	¾″	14½″
M	side top cleat	2	¾″	¾″	13¾″
N	rear top cleat	1	¾″	¾″	24½″
O	nose and cove molding	1	½″	⅝″	40′
P	rope molding	1	⅜″	¾″	4′

Wall Clock

Considering the small amount of time and expense required to build it, this traditionally styled wall clock is an excellent project. The sturdy, long pendulum movement is powered by a single D-type flashlight battery, though other types of pendulum movements can be substituted.

We built the prototype of pine and it looks so good we'll probably make another of walnut. Oak and cherry are also good choices. You won't need much, but be sure that your stock is well seasoned and flat.

It's a good idea to have the movement on hand before starting. One suitable movement is Klockit's model 204-32, with brass pendulum and 99-0 hands. See p. 243 for the address.

The dial size is determined by the length of the hands. The hands supplied with this particular movement required a dial diameter of 5½″. You can make your own paper dial, as we did, or purchase one from the suppliers listed on page 243.

Let's start with the ½″-thick (actual) case sides A, which are cut to length and width. The curve on the bottom ends can be duplicated by using an

enlarged template of the pattern given, or it can simply be drawn freehand.

Locate the lower ¼ x ½″ dado that holds the case bottom B. As seen in Figure 1, the case bottom is concealed by the lower part of the door. A ⁵⁄₁₆ x ¼″ stopped rabbet is marked along the back edge of each side from the top down to the bottom dado. The top ends are also marked for a ¼ x ½″ rabbet to hold the case top C.

Rout the dado and rabbets in both sides, then clamp the sides together to cut the bottom curve. Cut parts B and C, rabbeting the back edges as shown in Figure 2.

The case back can be either ¼″ hardboard or plywood, covered on both sides with a suitable veneer. The brass pendulum bob looks especially good against a black-walnut-veneered panel.

If the case is to be stained, it's best to do this after careful sanding but before assembly, to prevent residue from the glue causing uneven staining. After the stain has dried, glue and clamp the case together. Brad the back panel in place to hold the case square. The battery is replaced by removing four screws holding the movement-dial assembly in the case. Make certain the case is perfectly square or you will have trouble fitting the door and mitered top molding.

The door is cut from ¾″ stock (actual). Cut upper and lower frame parts I and J to full width and join them to stiles H with two ¼ x 1″ hidden dowel pins at each corner. Be sure to locate the pins on parts H and J so you won't cut into them when shaping the bottom of the frame and glass rabbet.

Glue and clamp the rough frame, taking care to keep it flat and square. After the glue sets, lay out the curves at top and bottom. The inside curve on the frame pattern is used for both parts I and J. Jigsaw these curves, then use a router and ¾″ rabbet bit with pilot to cut the rabbet around the inner frame edge as shown in Figure 2 and the detail.

Mark the location of the stopped chamfers on the door frame and use a router or chisel to cut them. Next, prepare the muntin, part K, which is glued up from two pieces as shown in the detail

197

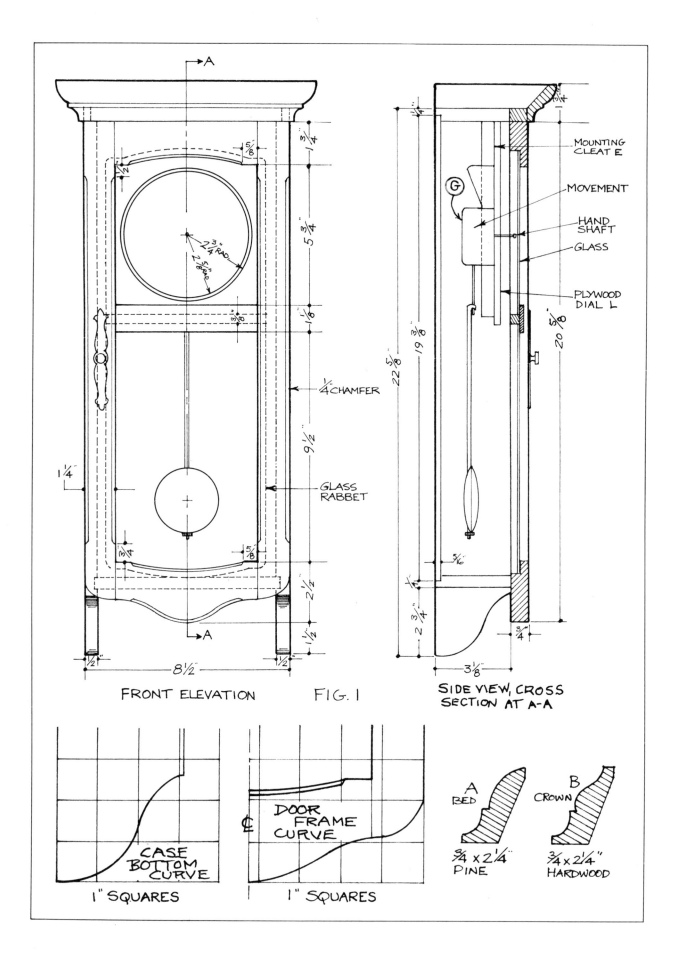

FRONT ELEVATION   FIG. 1

SIDE VIEW, CROSS
SECTION AT A-A

A

5/8
3/4
1/2
2 3/4" RAD.
2 5/8" RAD.
5 3/4
3/8
1 1/8
1/4 CHAMFER
9 1/2
1 1/4
GLASS RABBET
3/4
5/8
A
2 1/2
1/2
1/2
8 1/2
1/2

MOUNTING CLEAT E
MOVEMENT
HAND SHAFT
GLASS
PLYWOOD DIAL L
G
1/4
3/4
3/4
22 5/8"
19 3/8
20 5/8
5/16
2 3/4
3/4
3 1/8

CASE BOTTOM CURVE
1" SQUARES

DOOR FRAME CURVE
1" SQUARES

A
BED
3/4 x 2 1/4"
PINE

B
CROWN
3/4 x 2 1/4"
HARDWOOD

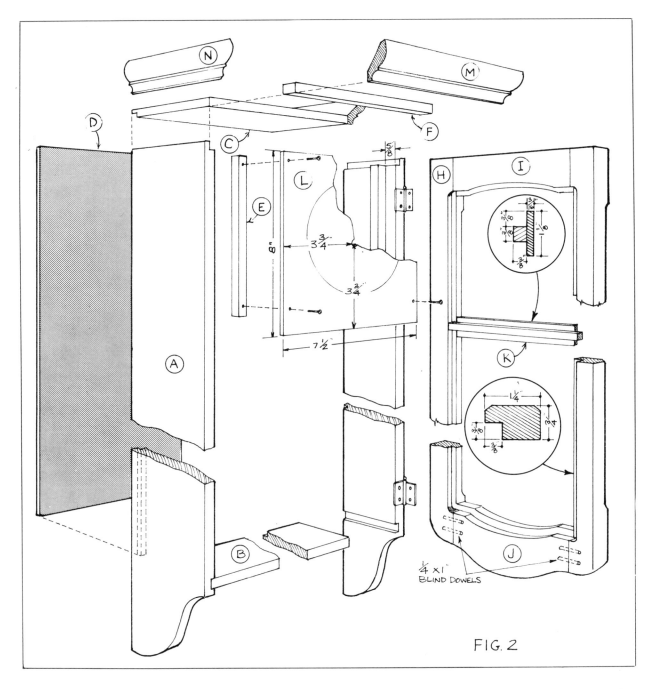

FIG. 2

of Figure 2. Glue the muntin in place between the frame sides. Add decorative ½″ dowel plugs at the corners, allowing them to protrude slightly.

Sand the completed frame carefully before staining. Cutting the glass to correspond with the curved rabbets is a nice touch, but not necessary, as a square-edge glass will be hidden. The two glass panes are held by four ¼″-square pine strips bradded to parts H; these are not shown in Figure 2.

Cut the ¼″ hardboard dial panel L and two mounting cleats E. Over panel L is glued heavy

white paper with a 5½″-diameter dial and 5¼″-diameter inner circle. The center of these concentric circles is located as shown in Figure 2 and is below the actual center of panel L.

If you prefer to make your own paper dial, the dial circles can be inked in with a drafting compass. The numerals, either roman or arabic, can be inked by hand, or transfer-type numerals can be purchased at art and drafting supply shops.

When you've completed the dial panel, drill a ⅜″ hole through the dial center. The movement is placed against the back of the panel with the hand shaft extending through the hole. A brass-threaded bushing screwed on the shaft from the front locks the movement in place. Our movement had a plastic mounting flange at the bottom, which we screwed to a ⅜ x ⅜ x 4″ pine strip glued to the back of the dial panel to provide additional anchoring of the movement. The hands are a friction fit on the shaft, which is capped with a small knurled nut.

The panel-movement assembly rests on and is screwed to cleats E, which are glued to the case sides. These cleats are located about ⅝″ in from the case front. The end of the hand shaft should just clear the door glass.

Now add the molding. We show two styles, bed and crown. If you build your case from pine, you can probably pick up a short length of bed molding at the lumberyard. If a fine hardwood is used, special crown moldings in cherry, oak, and walnut can be ordered from the Craftsman Wood Service Company (see page 243 for the address).

Before adding the molding, glue a stained filler strip F flush with the top front of the case. The molding is then finished and mitered to fit around the case.

A door pull, a small magnetic door catch, and loose-pin butt hinges are added. Mortise the door frame to a depth equal to the thickness of the hinge barrel. The hinge leaf on the case side is surface mounted. Use a couple of small brass mirror hangers to mount the clock level on the wall. Instructions packed with the movement will help you get your movement started and regulated.

BILL OF MATERIALS

Key	Part	Pcs. Req'd	T	W	L
A	side	2	½″	3⅛″	22⅝″
B	bottom	1	½″	3⅛″	8″
C	top	1	½″	3⅛″	8″
D	back	1	¼″	8″	19⅜″
E	cleats	2	½″	½″	8″
F	filler strip	1	¾″	½″	8½″
G	movement	1			
H	stiles	2	¾″	1¼″	20⅝″
I	upper frame rail	1	¾″	1¾″	6″
J	lower frame rail	1	¾″	2½″	6″
K	muntin	1	see detail		
L	dial panel	1	¼″	7½″	8″
M	front molding	1	as required		
N	side molding	2	as required		

Klockit model 204-32

Candle Box

The candle was an important source of light for homes in colonial America. The candle was portable and generated additional light where needed for such popular evening pastimes as reading, quiltmaking, and, no doubt, furniture making. It is generally believed that boxes of this style were hung on the wall and used to store a supply of those valued candles.

Today these quaint boxes are still useful in countless ways. We like to use ours to collect a variety of odds and ends that need to be kept handy. No matter how you choose to use it, though, it's sure to be a most interesting, attractive, and functional wall piece.

Except for the ⅛" plywood back and drawer bottom, the candle box is made entirely of ⅜" (actual thickness) pine. To begin construction, refer to the drawing and cut the sides to the dimensions shown, keeping in mind that a ⅛ x ⅛" rabbet runs the full length of each inside back corner. Next, cut the shelf and the bottom to size (⅜ x 4½ x 12"), then the ⅛" plywood back to 12¼" wide x 12⅛" high. Cut out the top, front piece, and lid as shown. Note that each of these three parts has a beveled edge, so use care and a sharp plane to make the joint well fitted. The drawer components can now be cut to size and assembled.

Thoroughly sand all surfaces, taking care to remove excess glue squeezed from joints. Use an antique pine stain followed by an antique oil finish, or several coats of a low-luster varnish. Attach the lid with decorative brass hinges as shown. Lastly, fasten the brass drawer pull.

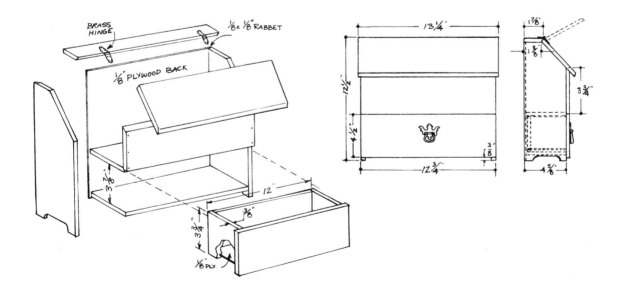

Louis XV Table

How does one go about dimensioning a Louis XV table for craftsmen to duplicate? The compound curves and carvings on legs and rails are, in some instances, so subtle as to defy accurate description in the usual kind of working drawing. There is much hand-tool work in such a piece as the little table shown, and no two tables will ever turn out exactly the same.

Whether or not you like the eighteenth-century French style of furniture, you just can't help but admire the workmanship. It's almost as if cabinetmakers of the period constantly tried to outdo each other, and themselves, by working out increasingly difficult design problems—sometimes almost to the point of impossibility.

The table shown in the photograph is in the private collection of Mr. and Mrs. B. Calick of Washington, Connecticut, and the owners kindly consented to our examination and measurement of it. As tables go, it is almost a miniature, but nevertheless an exquisite gem of the cabinet-maker's art.

We offer the table as an introductory project for those woodworkers who feel capable of handling the finely detailed work involved. The suc-

cessful joining and shaping of legs and rails should provide the confidence needed to attempt larger projects in a similar style, while the small size of the table will make mistakes less costly—no small concern when working with walnut, the wood used for the original.

The legs are shaped from 2¼ x 2¼ x 19½″ walnut after the dovetail rail slots have been laid out and cut. (See the Queen Anne Stool project, p. 7, for instructions on cutting cabriole legs.) Don't radius the front corners until the rails are shaped from ¹³⁄₁₆″ stock. Cut the rails to length, and prepare the dovetail ends. The serpentine-shaped fronts are cut with the band saw, but can also be rasped and filed. Allow about ³⁄₁₆″ extra wood at the lower edge of the rails for the small ridge and carving. Note that the rails are also curved in a vertical direction; this is most pronounced at the center, and the rails flatten out to fair with the upper legs.

The small but beautifully effective carving on each rail is done in shallow relief, so not too much background material has to be removed. Fit the rails to the legs temporarily, and use a template to scribe the curves from legs to rails, and along the bottom edges of the rails.

The legs are shaped on three corners as shown; each corner is given a gentle ridge rather than a sharply defined bead. The portion of the leg between these ridges is gouged slightly concave, tapering off at the ankle. The lower edges of the rails are carved in the same way, the ridge continuing from the legs.

The tabletop is glued up from ⅝″ solid stock, and may be covered, as is the original, with a fancy matched veneer; or it may be left plain. If the top is veneered, the underside should also be covered with a lower grade of veneer to equalize stresses on the "core."

A mitered molded edge is added to the panel, both for decoration and to conceal the end grain. On the original, both the veneered panel and the molded edges have a gentle serpentine shape. A good fit between molding and panel can be achieved by mitering and joining a frame from which the molding can be cut; this is clamped to

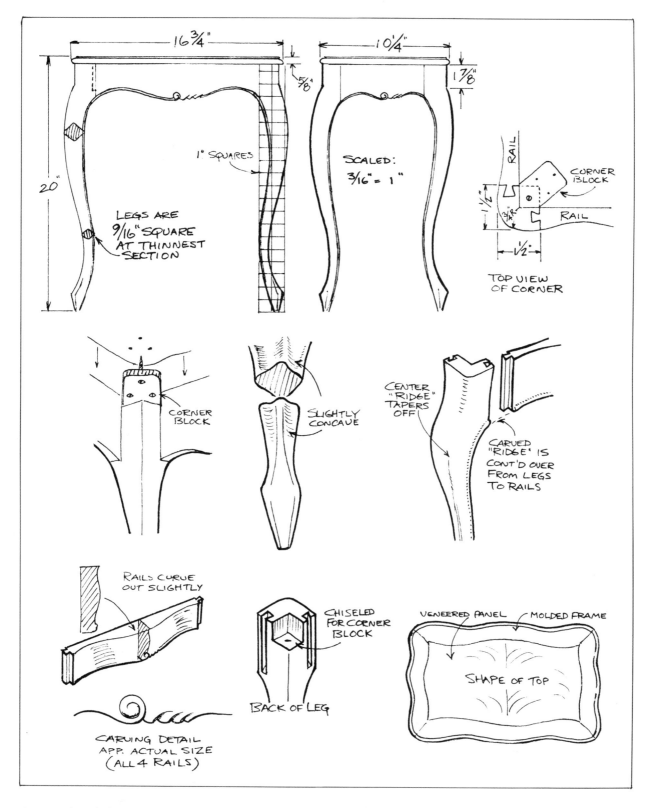

16 3/4"

10 1/4"

5/8"

1 7/8"

20"

1" SQUARES

SCALED: 3/16" = 1"

LEGS ARE 9/16" SQUARE AT THINNEST SECTION

RAIL

CORNER BLOCK

RAIL

1/2"

3/4" R

1/2"

TOP VIEW OF CORNER

CORNER BLOCK

SLIGHTLY CONCAVE

CENTER "RIDGE" TAPERS OFF

CARVED "RIDGE" IS CONT'D OVER FROM LEGS TO RAILS

RAILS CURVE OUT SLIGHTLY

CHISELED FOR CORNER BLOCK

VENEERED PANEL

MOLDED FRAME

SHAPE OF TOP

BACK OF LEG

CARVING DETAIL APP. ACTUAL SIZE (ALL 4 RAILS)

the panel and the two are cut together. Later, the outer edge of the molding can be shaped. The top is fastened by screwing up through the corner blocks, which are screwed to the tops of the legs.

Much of the success of this piece depends on scrupulous sanding of the curved and carved parts. The piece may be given a penetrating-oil-type finish or light antique stain followed by three coats of thinned white shellac rubbed down with 4/0 steel wool.

203

Inlaid Spool Chest

This chest is made of walnut with drawer sides of yellow pine. An inlaid veneer adds a special accent to the top. Four sides of the chest are of framed-panel construction, and the panels are of ¼″ birch plywood with walnut veneer applied to the face sides. Fir plywood is not a good choice as it has such a coarse grain that it tends to "telegraph" through the veneer in time.

Start by making the top, which is 13¾″ wide x 10½″ deep. The rails and stiles of all frames are made of ¾ x 1½″ strips, with the exception of the two stiles G on the rear panel, which are ¾ x ¾″. Stiles and rails are grooved to receive the veneered panel; be sure to stop the grooves on parts B as shown in the detail.

Ready-to-use inlaid veneers are sold by several mail-order firms; see the list of suppliers, p. 243. Our inlaid veneer, in a rose pattern, was glued to ¼ x 8 x 11¼″ plywood. The result was a handsome walnut-inlaid panel without the necessity of routing a recess for the inlay.

The width of the grooves depends on the thickness of the plywood you use plus one layer of veneer. As in most cases of fine cabinetwork, it's best to make test cuts in a piece of scrap first. The panels should have an easy slip fit in the grooves.

All stiles and rails were butt joined with glue and two ¼ x 1½″ dowel pins at the end joint. Care should be taken to avoid placing the dowels too close to the edge, or the dowels will be exposed

when the edges are molded. It's much easier to sand all panels and the inside edges of the frames before they are assembled.

The bottom is the same size as the top except that it is of solid stock rather than framed construction. A decorative edge on both bottom and top was cut with a router and ogee cutter, though a beading cutter will also do a good job.

Construction of the end framed panels is basically the same as for the top and bottom; the outside faces of the panels are covered with walnut veneer. After the end panels are assembled, two ⅜″ grooves ¼″ deep are cut across the inside faces to hold the drawer dividers. These dadoes are spaced 2¼″ apart.

If the dadoes are run across the back stiles E of the end panels, a small opening will be visible when the back is fitted between the ends. This opening can be filled with small pieces of walnut glued in place, but the better method is to stop the dadoes ¾″ from the back edges of the stiles, which is easily done with a router. One-quarter-inch-thick pine filler strips are glued to the inside of the end panels as shown to keep the center drawer from binding.

The back panel is a bit different from the preceding ones in that, as mentioned earlier, the stiles are narrower. Also, holes are drilled for dowels completely through parts G. Parts G are then glued to the back edge of each end panel. After clamping in position, place the drill bit

204

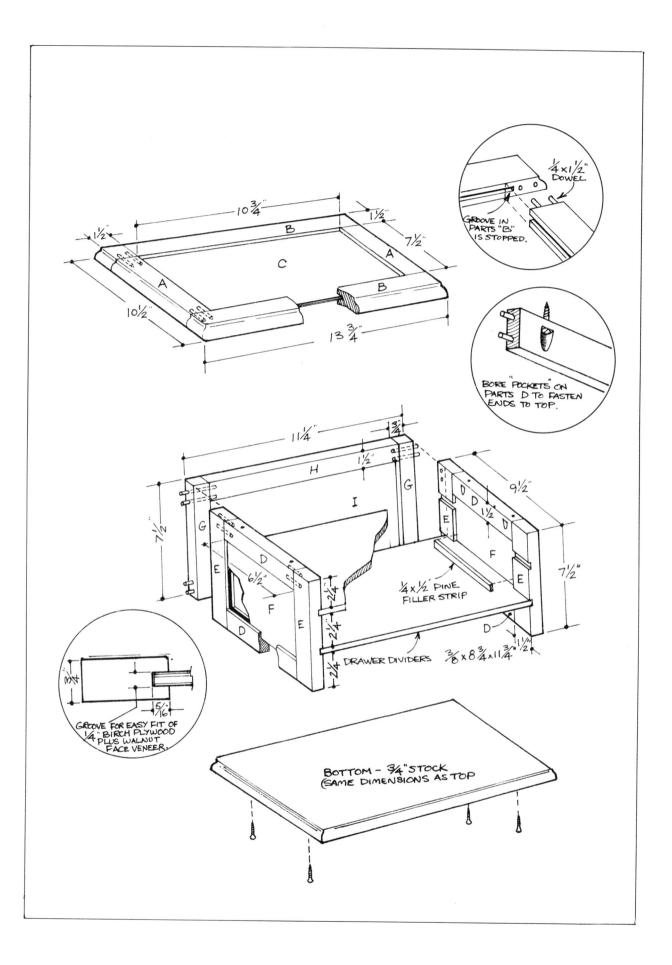

10¾"

1½"

B

A

C

A

B

1½"

7½"

10½"

13¾"

¼ x 1½" DOWEL

GROOVE IN PARTS "B" IS STOPPED.

BORE "POCKETS" ON PARTS D TO FASTEN ENDS TO TOP.

11¼"

¾"

H

1½"

G

9½"

7½"

I

G

D

1½"

D

E

E

E

F

E

¼ x ½" PINE FILLER STRIP

7½"

6½"

D

F

2¼"

E

2¼"

D

D

2¼"

DRAWER DIVIDERS   ⅜ x 8¾ x 11¼

1½"

3¾"

3/16"

¾"

GROOVE FOR EASY FIT OF ¼" BIRCH PLYWOOD PLUS WALNUT FACE VENEER.

BOTTOM - ¾" STOCK (SAME DIMENSIONS AS TOP)

through the holes in G and drill ½″ deep into each end panel stile E. Then the back panel is doweled and glued together so the three framed panels are assembled in one unit.

Fasten the top to the end panels with 1″ flat-headed screws driven up through "pockets" bored in rails D. The bottom is fastened by screwing into the lower end rails D. The drawer dividers are of ⅜″-thick walnut glued into the end-panel dadoes.

The drawer fronts, which fit flush, are cut from ¾″ stock. The sides and back are of ½″ yellow pine. The sides and front are grooved ¼″ up from the bottom edges to take a ¼″ plywood bottom. The drawer back butts against the bottom and is

fastened with small nails up through the bottom. We used dovetails for the front-side joints, but alternate methods can be used.

Before assembly, grooves need to be cut in the drawer front and back for ¼″-thick dividers. The spacing and number of these depend upon the size of spools used. We cut a decorative cove molding around the front edge of all the drawers; these can also be beveled.

The chest was given four coats of Deft clear finish, with sanding after the second and fourth coat. Then a final coat was applied with a spray can of Deft, which left a fine brush-free finish. Two ¾″ porcelain knobs per drawer completed the project.

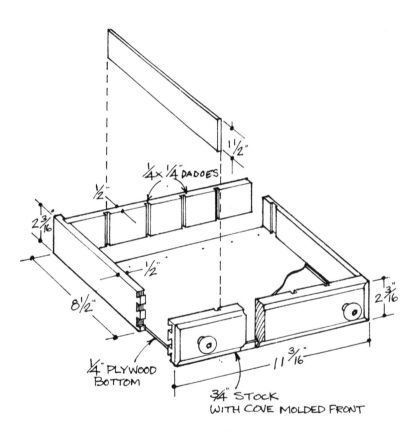

¼ x ¼ DADOES

1½″

2 3/16

½″

½″

8½″

¼″ PLYWOOD BOTTOM

2 3/16

11 3/16″

¾″ STOCK
WITH COVE MOLDED FRONT

206

Crocodile Pull Toy

Maybe this fellow doesn't cry crocodile tears, but he does act remarkably lifelike, rolling along snapping his great front jaw and wiggling that long tail. No matter how fierce his cousins may be, his big smile assures everyone that he's strictly warm and friendly.

Start with the body. Enlarge the grid pattern on cardboard, then transfer the profile to a piece of ¾″ maple or pine and cut to shape. Also cut out the upper jaw along the dotted line shown. Later this cutout will be sandwiched between two pieces of ⅛″ plywood to form the upper-jaw assembly.

Next, the table saw is used to split the tail lengthwise. Set the saw blade to a depth of about 2½″ and adjust the fence so that it cuts the tail exactly down the middle. Feed the tail into the blade and stop the cut at the point where the tail ends and the body begins. Now, draw vertical lines to divide the tail into about nine equal parts (each about 1¼″ long) and cut to length. Bevel the outside corners of each segment.

Trace the tail pattern on a piece of heavy cloth or, as we did, use an old pair of blue jeans. Be sure to leave a piece long enough to fit into the section cut from the body. Since the cloth should not show, retrace the entire pattern freehand, but make it about ⅛″ smaller in size. Cut out the smaller profile with a pair of sharp scissors.

Lay out the tail pieces in sequence, then apply a thin coat of glue to the inside surfaces and clamp firmly to the cloth. Allow to dry.

The upper-jaw cutout is glued between two pieces of ⅛″ plywood, which are cut to the profile shown as a solid line on the grid pattern. The jaw hinges at the eye on a ¼″ dowel. A ⁵⁄₁₆″ hole in the body allows room for smooth hinge action.

Trim the excess cloth on the tail to fit the saw cut in the body. Apply plenty of glue to the cloth, then assemble the clamp overnight. Use a 2″ hole saw to cut four wheels from ½″ stock. Cut two ellipses from ¼″ plywood and glue them to the inside of the two front wheels. Now drill ¼″-diameter holes at the center of all four wheels. After drilling ⁵⁄₁₆″ holes in the front and back of the body, glue and assemble the wheels to axles made from ¼″-diameter dowel stock. Make sure the ovals are in alignment so they make contact with the jaw at the same time.

Give the entire toy a thorough sanding and finish with two coats of penetrating oil finish. The pull string is glued into a small hole in the front jaw.

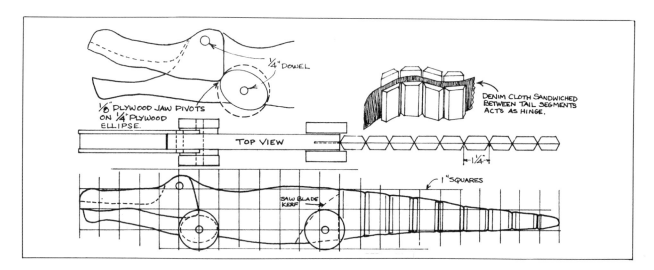

Record and Tape Cabinet

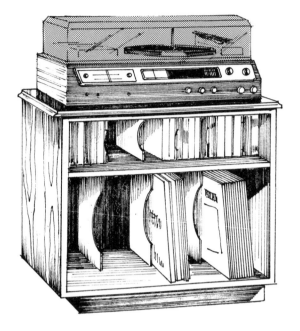

Here's a useful cabinet that provides a convenient place to store both record albums and tapes. The spacious storage area will hold almost 100 albums, while the tape rack neatly accepts either eight-track or cassette tapes. There's also plenty of room on top, so it accommodates almost any size or style stereo system.

A variety of woods can be used for this project: maple, birch, walnut, oak, even pine, are all appropriate choices. Select the one that best appeals to your needs, interest, and, of course, your pocketbook. You'll note that the dividers and back are hardboard.

Begin construction by making the two sides A. In order to get the 13″ width, it will be necessary to edge glue two or more boards. Glue and clamp the joint, then allow to dry overnight. After drying, cut the sides to final length and width. Referring to the drawing, lay out and cut the ¾ x ⅜″ rabbets for the top and bottom shelf, the ¾ x ⅜″ dado for the center shelf, and the ¼ x ⅜″ rabbet for the back.

Next, make the three shelves B. Stock will again have to be edge glued to get sufficient width. Cut to length and width after drying. In order to accept the record and tape dividers, ⅛″-wide x ¼″-deep stopped dadoes are cut into the shelves as shown. This is best done with a router using a ⅛″ straight bit. Lay out the dadoes carefully and make the cuts from the back so they don't show in front.

The top C can be done next. Edge glue stock as required, then cut to size. Use a router with a ⅜″ cove bit to cut the decorative molding on three edges.

Cut the tape compartment back D, the glue blocks E, and the back F to size. Take care to make sure the back is cut square. The tape dividers G and the record dividers H are cut from ⅛″ hardboard. Referring to the drawing, lay out and cut the radius for each part. Now cut out the base back and front I and the base sides J.

Before starting assembly, give all surfaces a thorough sanding. This step will make it much easier to final sand after assembly is complete.

Assemble the three shelves B to the sides A, using adequate glue to insure a good bond. Drill

BILL OF MATERIALS

Key	Part	Pcs. Req'd	T	W	L
A	side	2	¾″	13″	20″
B	shelf	3	¾″	12¾″	25⅝″
C	top	1	¾″	13¾″	27⅝″
D	tape compartment back (plywood)	1	½″	4¾″	24⅝″
E	glue blocks	2	¾″	¾″	24⅝″
F	back (hardboard)	1	¼″	25⅝″	20″
G	tape dividers (hardboard)	5	⅛″	4″	5¼″
H	record dividers (hardboard)	3	⅛″	6″	13½″
I	front and back base	2	¾″	2″	23⅛″
J	base end	2	¾″	2″	9½″

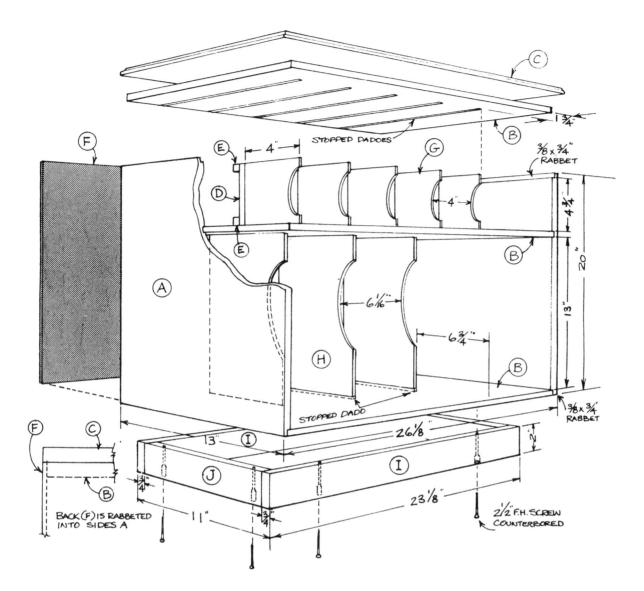

STOPPED DADOES

3⁄8 x 3⁄4"
RABBET

4"

E

D

F

A

H

STOPPED DADO

G

4"

4¼"

20"

13"

B

B

B

3⁄8 x 3⁄4"
RABBET

6 1⁄16"

6 3⁄4"

26 1⁄8"

13"

I

J

I

2"

23 1⁄8"

2½" F.H. SCREW
COUNTERBORED

F

C

B

BACK (F) IS RABBETED
INTO SIDES A

11"

3⁄4"

3⁄4"

and countersink holes for 1½″ #8 flat-headed wood screws. The holes will be plugged later.

Apply a thin coat of glue to the tape and record dividers G and H. Slide them in place from the back. You may need to sand the edges a little so they slide easily in the dadoes. Apply glue to the back of the tape dividers, then slide the tape compartment back D in place. Fit the glue blocks E in place and fasten with small nails. (Drive the nails by holding the hammer sideways.) Next the back F is attached with 2-penny nails.

Assemble the base frame (parts I and J) and attach it to the cabinet bottom with 2″ #10 round-headed wood screws counterbored to a depth of ½″. Finally, attach the top with countersunk 1½″ #8 flat-headed wood screws.

Now plugs can be glued into all countersunk holes and sanded smooth. Give the entire project one more going-over with fine sandpaper.

The final finishing method will depend upon the type of wood used, and, to a large extent, personal taste. Our walnut cabinet was finished with two coats of polyurethane satin finish followed by a thorough rubdown with 4/0 steel wool.

Shaker-style Table

A small table is always useful, and this Shaker-style design will harmonize with most furniture. Taken from a design originating in the early nineteenth century, this piece will prove to be a fair challenge for the woodworker of moderate skill.

Shakers often mixed woods in tables of this type. A common combination was a pine top with cherry or maple legs and rails. Whatever woods you choose, it's best to use a good-turning hardwood for the legs.

The top A is edge joined from several ¾″ boards with the grains alternated. Glued edge joints can be reinforced with ⅜″ dowel pins, but it's not absolutely necessary as long as care is taken when jointing and gluing.

While the top is clamped, cut rails C, D, E, and F, allowing for a ⅞″ tenon at each end. On parts C and D, tenons can be ⅜ x ⅞ x 4″. As shown in the detail, the tenon ends should be mitered to clear each other.

The tenon for drawer rail E runs to the top of the leg, while the tenon for rail F is blind. If the top-mounting method shown is used, run ⅜ x ⅜″ grooves along rails C and D, ½″ down from the top edges.

Having tenoned the rails, rip stock for the four turned legs. The turning blanks are 1¼ x 1¼ x

28″, allowing a bit of extra length at the top end so mortises can be chiseled out without danger of splitting. Locate the mortises using completed tenons to scribe their outlines and chisel out.

Turn the legs as shown in the detail. Use a gouge to cut the transition from square to cylinder. Note that the legs flare out a bit from the square to a point 2½″ down, then gradually taper to the ⅞″-diameter feet. Use a piece of wire to score the two rings near the top. Sand the legs to finish, running the lathe at slow speed, then burnish with a handful of hardwood shavings.

You can now dry-fit the rails and legs, and if all is well, assemble with glue and use four pipe clamps to square the assembly.

Drill 1″-deep holes through the legs and tenons for ¼ x 1″ pegs. These pegs are glue coated and driven almost, but not quite, in; allow about 1/16″ to protrude.

Next, cut ⅜ x 2 x 5″ filler blocks G, and glue and clamp to the rails about at their midpoints. Drawer guides H, which are preferably of oak, are cut to ½ x ½ x 18⅜″ and screwed to the filler blocks and legs. The guides should be inset ¼″ from the faces of the front legs to allow for the drawer front I, which is lipped.

Drawer sides, front, and back are grooved to receive a ¼″ plywood bottom L. Shakers invariably dovetailed drawer joints and, generally, the earlier pieces had larger dovetails. The oak strips M are cut to 7/16 x 7/16″ and fastened with glue and countersunk ¾″ flat-headed screws.

Cut top fasteners from hardwood to fit the rail grooves. Note that the ⅜″ tongues of the fasteners fit into grooves that are ½″ down from the rail tops. When the fasteners are screwed to the top, a wedging force is exerted to pull the top flat and tight. Use 1¼″ flat-headed screws to secure the top. A nicely turned drawer knob completes the woodworking.

Finish the piece with a light honey-toned stain and a couple of coats of a penetrating oil finish such as Watco Danish Oil or Minwax Antique Oil. These are easy to apply and will provide the soft luster seen on naturally finished Shaker originals.

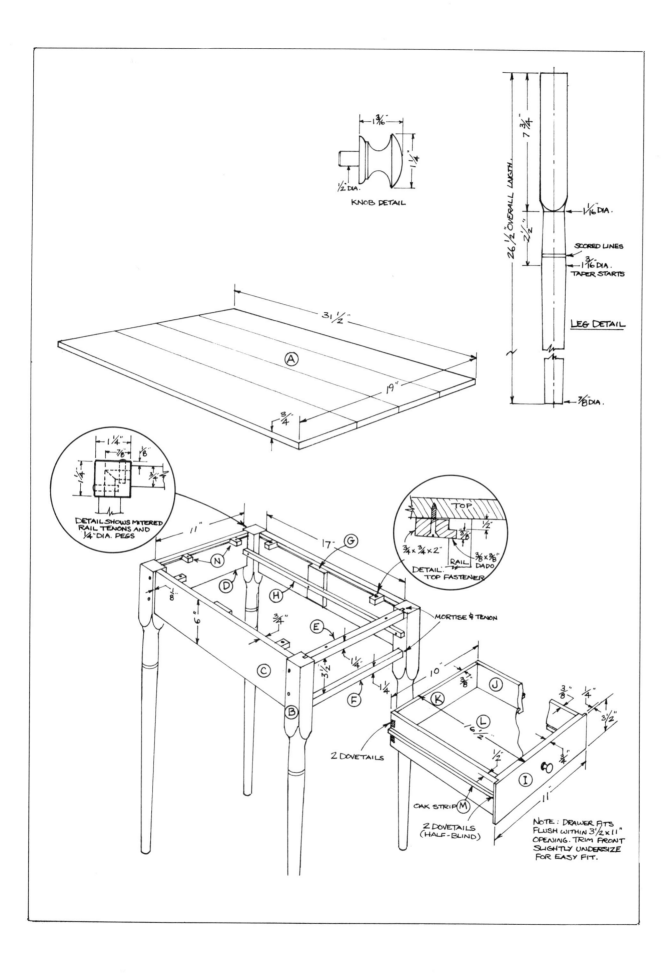

KNOB DETAIL

1³⁄₁₆"

1¼"

½" DIA.

LEG DETAIL

7¾"

26½" OVERALL LENGTH

2½"

1¹⁄₁₆ DIA.

SCORED LINES

1³⁄₁₆ DIA.
TAPER STARTS

⅜ DIA.

31½"

Ⓐ

19"

¾

DETAIL SHOWS MITERED
RAIL TENONS AND
¼" DIA. PEGS

1¼"

⅞"

⅛"

¼"

¾"

11"

Ⓝ

Ⓓ

17"

Ⓖ

Ⓗ

Ⓔ

⅛"

6"

¾"

Ⓒ

3½"

1¼"

1¼"

Ⓕ

Ⓑ

TOP

½"

¾ × ¾ × 2"

⅜
RAIL

⅜ × ⅜"
DADO

DETAIL:
TOP FASTENER

MORTISE & TENON

10"

⅜

Ⓙ

Ⓚ

Ⓛ

6½"

½"

¾

Ⓘ

Ⓖ

11"

3½"

¼"

⅜"

2 DOVETAILS

OAK STRIP Ⓜ

2 DOVETAILS
(HALF-BLIND)

NOTE: DRAWER FITS
FLUSH WITHIN 3½ × 11"
OPENING. TRIM FRONT
SLIGHTLY UNDERSIZE
FOR EASY FIT.

Swedish Door Harp

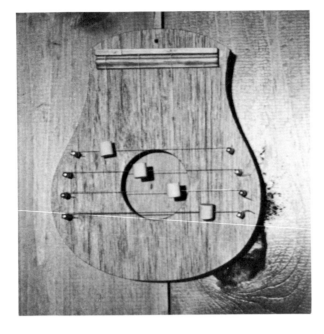

Hang this door harp on the inside of your front door and each time the door is opened you'll be rewarded with warm, melodious sound. The door movement sets the four wooden clappers in motion, causing each one to repeatedly strike the horizontal steel strings. Of Scandinavian origin, the door harp is a project that makes an ideal gift—one that's interesting, enjoyable, and easy to make.

The Autoharp pins are under a fair amount of strain when the guitar strings are tightened, so use maple for the frame. Begin by cutting two pieces ¾ x 2¼ x 9½" for the frame sides, and two pieces ¾ x 1¼ x 3⅝" for the top and bottom. Referring to the drawing, note that the dotted lines represent the dimensions of the frame parts be-fore the harp is cut to shape. Using this as a guide, glue and assemble the frame parts, then allow to dry thoroughly.

The front and back are made from ⅛" Honduras mahogany. Cut two pieces 8" wide x 9½" long to fit over the frame. Cut a 2½"-diameter hole in the front piece, then glue and clamp the front and back to the frame. After it is dry, transfer the outside profile of the harp to the glued-up stock and cut to shape.

Eight Autoharp pins are used to tighten the steel guitar strings. They are available from Fretted Industries, 1415 Waukegan Road, Northbrook, IL 60062. Locate and drill ³⁄₁₆ x ¾"-deep holes. Use a hammer to drive about ¼" of the threaded portion into the hole, then use a wrench to thread the pin so that the string hole is about ¾" above the surface. Cut steel B guitar strings (available at any musical instrument dealer) to length and tighten between each pin.

The bridge is made from ½ x ⅝" pine. To form its curved profile, use the table saw to run a lengthwise groove about ⅛" wide x ⁵⁄₁₆" deep. Use sandpaper to round off and shape the edges as shown in the drawing. Drill four ¹⁄₁₆"-diameter string holes in the bridge and glue it to the front.

The four clappers are made from ½" dowel stock cut to ½" length. Also, if available, ½"-diameter wooden balls can be used. Insert and glue the end of a piece of string into a small hole drilled in each clapper. Run the strings up through the bridge holes, adjust to length, and secure with a knot.

Sand thoroughly and stain to suit. Finish with two coats of polyurethane varnish.

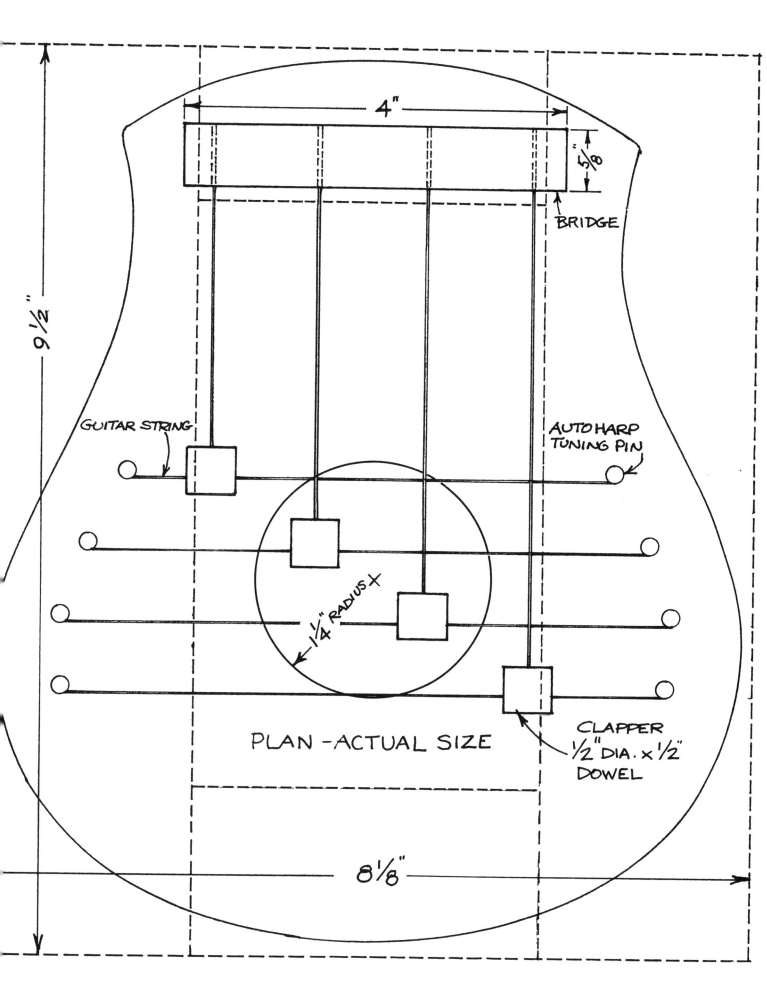

4"

5/8"

BRIDGE

GUITAR STRING

AUTO HARP
TUNING PIN

9 1/2"

1/4" RADIUS

PLAN - ACTUAL SIZE

CLAPPER
1/2" DIA. x 1/2"
DOWEL

8 1/8"

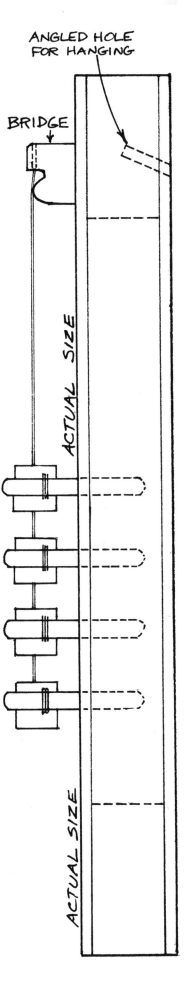

ANGLED HOLE
FOR HANGING

BRIDGE

ACTUAL SIZE

ACTUAL SIZE

214

Early American Harvest Table

For those who take pleasure in reproducing and living with Early American furniture, this striking example of an eighteenth-century harvest table will surely prove to be an irresistible project. With both leaves raised, it provides a generous 45 x 72″ dining surface; yet with the leaves down it takes up relatively little space. Most armless dining chairs will tuck in under the leaves for more efficient storage.

Although the table looks undeniably elegant with lathe-turned legs, you'll note that an alternate square-tapered leg is discussed. Figure 4 shows standard mortise-and-tenon joinery, which will withstand generations of use, while Figure 5 offers a simplified version that is appropriate for a utility table.

The first step in construction is to edge join ¾″ pine stock for the top and leaves. The top and leaves should be glued up about 1″ oversize in both length and width. Use four or five boards for the top and join with glue and ⅜ x 1½″ grooved dowel pins spaced about a foot apart. Join two boards for each leaf, again reinforcing the joint with ⅜″ dowel pins.

Trim the top and leaves to finish length but do not trim to finish width until the rule joint is routed. If you goof, or the router slips, you'll still have enough width for another try. If you choose to build the simplified utility-table version, or if you lack a router, you may want to leave the mating top and leaf edges square, fastening them with long decorative black strap hinges.

The side edges of the top are shaped using a router and ⅜″ bead cutter, while the leaves are routed with a ⅜″ cove cutter as shown in Detail B. Three 1½ x 3⅛″ table hinges are used for each joint. If you've never hinged a rule joint before, we suggest you rout a joint on scrap stock and practice mounting the hinges. The hinge barrel pin must be exactly centered below the top-leaf joint and recessed into a groove in the underside.

The stock for the legs, turned or square tapered, can be either solid or glued up from two pieces of ¾″ stock. Maple, birch, or cherry are preferred for turned legs, but clear pine will do if the narrower portions are left slightly larger in section. If you're an experienced turner, the legs will present no problem other than keeping them identical. For the square-tapered legs, use a tapering jig with your table saw to do the job quickly and cleanly.

Lay out mortises in the legs, allowing for a ⅛″ setback of the aprons as shown in Figure 4, and use a ⅜″ drill bit to clear out waste, finishing up with a chisel.

The aprons are next cut from ¾″ stock, and you'll note that their lengths differ according to what type joinery you use. Shape tenons on the apron ends and cut grooves as shown in Detail C for the tabletop fasteners. These are sold in many hardware stores or can be ordered from mail-order firms specializing in cabinetmaking supplies. It's best to have the fasteners on hand before cutting the grooves so that a perfect fit can be obtained.

Cut two long notches in both the front and back aprons for the swing-out supports. Note that one end of the notch is cut at about 45 degrees to serve as a stop, while the other end is cut square to the apron. Cut four wings to fit these notches and drill the wings and aprons for a ¼″ steel pivot pin. Use a doweling jig or drill press to drill for these pins, as they must be perfectly vertical. A small washer provides slight clearance

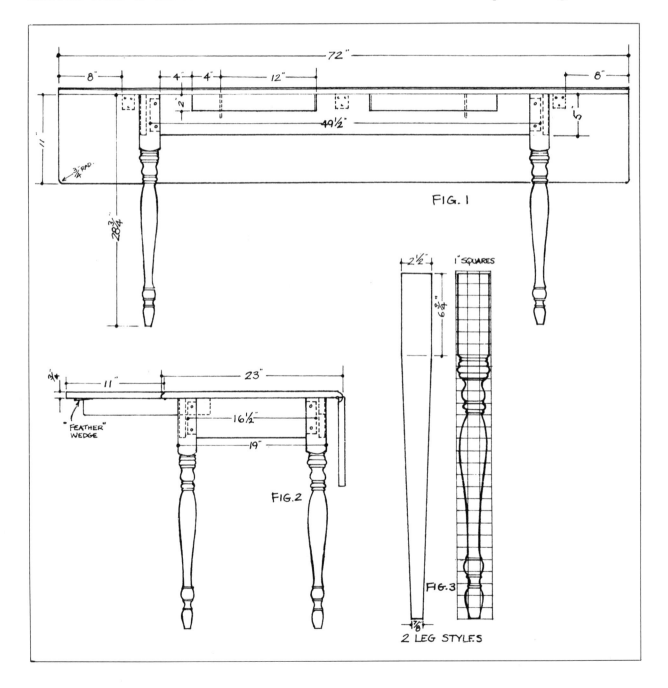

FIG. 1

FIG. 2

"FEATHER" WEDGE

FIG. 3

2 LEG STYLES

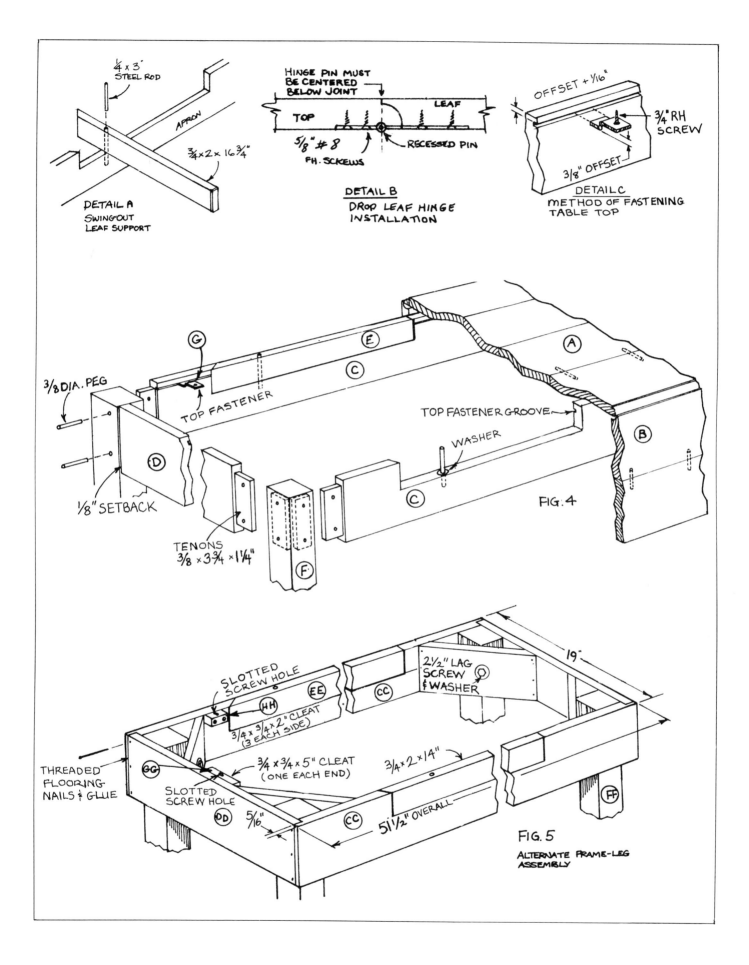

¼ x 3"
STEEL ROD

APRON

¾ x 2 x 16¾"

DETAIL A
SWING-OUT
LEAF SUPPORT

HINGE PIN MUST
BE CENTERED
BELOW JOINT

TOP   LEAF

5/8" #8
F.H. SCREWS

RECESSED PIN

DETAIL B
DROP LEAF HINGE
INSTALLATION

OFFSET + 1/16"

¾" RH
SCREW

3/8" OFFSET

DETAIL C
METHOD OF FASTENING
TABLE TOP

3/8 DIA. PEG

TOP FASTENER

TOP FASTENER GROOVE

WASHER

1/8" SETBACK

TENONS
3/8 x 3¾ x 1¼"

FIG. 4

A B C D E F G

SLOTTED
SCREW HOLE

2½" LAG
SCREW
¢ WASHER

19"

¾ x ¾ x 2" CLEAT
(3 EACH SIDE)

THREADED
FLOORING
NAILS ¢ GLUE

¾ x ¾ x 5" CLEAT
(ONE EACH END)

¾ x 2 x 14"

SLOTTED
SCREW HOLE

5/16"

51½" OVERALL

FIG. 5

ALTERNATE FRAME-LEG
ASSEMBLY

CC DD EE FF GG HH

between the wing bottom and the apron. However, the wings must be exactly flush with the top edges of the aprons or the leaves will sag.

After sanding, the legs and aprons can be assembled with glue and clamped overnight. For the version in Figure 5, glue and clamp the legs to the frame corners and secure with corner braces lag-screwed into the legs as shown.

The top and leaves can now be turned upside down and mortised for the six hinges. After the hinges are fitted, remove them and finish sand and stain the top, leaves, and frame to suit.

When applying a finish, be sure to cover the underside of the top and leaves and the inside faces of the aprons. A clear finish impervious to water and alcohol is best for tables. Three coats of a satin-luster varnish, rubbed down between coats with 4/0 steel wool is well worth the effort. Take extra care to remove all dust between coats of varnish. Rub the final coat down until all surfaces have an even sheen, then dust and apply a thin coat of furniture paste wax, followed by polishing with a soft cloth.

Finally, fasten the top to the frame using two offset fasteners at each end apron and three fasteners along each side. Fasten the leaves to the top and check the swing-out wings to make sure they support the leaves properly. If there is a slight amount of sag, glue thin hardwood "feather" wedges to the leaves as shown in Figure 2.

BILL OF MATERIALS

Key	Part	Pcs. Req'd	T	W	L
A	top	1	¾″	23″	72″
B	leaf	2	¾″	11″	72″
C	front and back apron	2	¾″	5″	49½″
CC	front and back apron	2	¾″	5″	51½″
D	end apron	2	¾″	5″	16½″
DD	end apron	2	¾″	5″	18⅜″
E	leaf support	4	¾″	2″	16¾″
EE	leaf support	4	¾″	2″	14″
F	leg	4	2½″	2½″	28¾″
FF	leg	4	2½″	2½″	28¾″
Detail B	hinge	6	1½ x 3⅛″		
G	top fastener	10			
GG	cleat	2	¾″	¾″	5″
HH	cleat	6	¾″	¾″	2″

Washstand

Before the introduction of indoor plumbing, washstands were necessary furnishings in most households. Besides providing a stand for the usual pitcher and bowl, some of the more elaborate versions had shaving mirrors and towel bars.

The antique example shown here is one of the more popular designs and lends itself well to a variety of modern uses as a lamp or end table, nightstand, or hall table, teamed with a mirror.

The fastenings, joinery, and tool marks on this piece date it probably to the early nineteenth century. The nicely turned legs are cherry; all other parts are clear pine. We would guess that it was built by a skilled country cabinetmaker. The unpinned mortise and tenon joints are still perfectly tight and the dovetail joints are carefully fitted, though the glue has failed on the rear corners of the drawer.

The plans offered here follow the original in all

details except for slightly thicker aprons, a plywood drawer bottom, and a different method of top fastening. The original one-piece top was glued to twelve blocks which were glued to the aprons. This procedure prevented shifts in the wood due to changes in humidity, and resulted in a crack in half the length of the top.

Start construction with the legs, which are ripped from solid cherry to 1¾″ square x 26¾″ long. Lay out and mark the location and length of each square section and use a parting tool to start the transition from squares to turned portions; then use the gouge to bring the turned portion down to a uniform 1½″ diameter. The various elements of the turning are then located and shaped with a gouge and skew chisel.

Finish sand the legs while they are still lathe-mounted, then remove them and plane the square sections down to 1⅝″ square. Lay out mortises for the aprons, lower rails, and lower drawer rail G, using the tenon dimensions given in Figure 3. Note that the mortises are located so that the aprons and rails are set in ⅛″. Drill out the mortises to a depth of 1″, using a ⅜″ drill bit, then trim the mortises with a sharp chisel.

The aprons and rails are next cut from ¾″ stock, either cherry or clear pine. Sand the outer surfaces of the aprons and rails, and test-fit the joints, making adjustments where needed. Identify the mating parts of each joint with a pencil mark on the inside faces.

The bottom shelf is glued up from ½″ stock and notched at each corner for a snug fit around the legs. The upper drawer rail F is cut and glued flush with the front edge of the shelf. The rear rail D is nailed to the rear edge of the shelf, ⅛″ in from the back edge. Use 4-penny finishing nails set below the surface of the shelf.

At this point, it's a good idea to sand and stain all parts. Staining before assembly helps prevent the often nagging problem of uneven stain at the joints. This problem usually results from glue that oozes from the joint on assembly. The glue dries clear and becomes difficult to see, and thus may not be completely removed when the project is sanded. When stain is applied, the glue won't

219

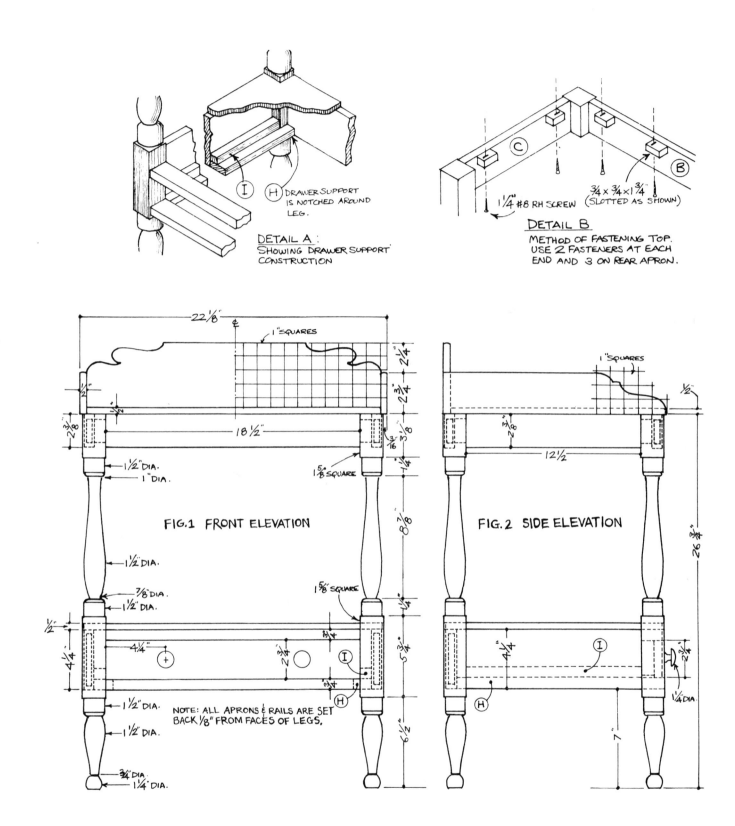

DETAIL A:
SHOWING DRAWER SUPPORT
CONSTRUCTION

DRAWER SUPPORT
IS NOTCHED AROUND
LEG.

DETAIL B
METHOD OF FASTENING TOP.
USE 2 FASTENERS AT EACH
END AND 3 ON REAR APRON.

1¼" #8 RH SCREW

¾ x ¾ x 1¾"
(SLOTTED AS SHOWN)

FIG.1 FRONT ELEVATION

22⅛"
1" SQUARES
18½"
1½" DIA.
1" DIA.
1½" DIA.
⅞" DIA.
1½" DIA.
4¼"
1½" DIA.
1½" DIA.
¾" DIA.
1¼" DIA.

NOTE: ALL APRONS & RAILS ARE SET
BACK ⅛" FROM FACES OF LEGS.

1⅝" SQUARE
1⅝" SQUARE

FIG.2 SIDE ELEVATION

1" SQUARES
12½"
26¾"
4¼"
1¼" DIA.
7"

220

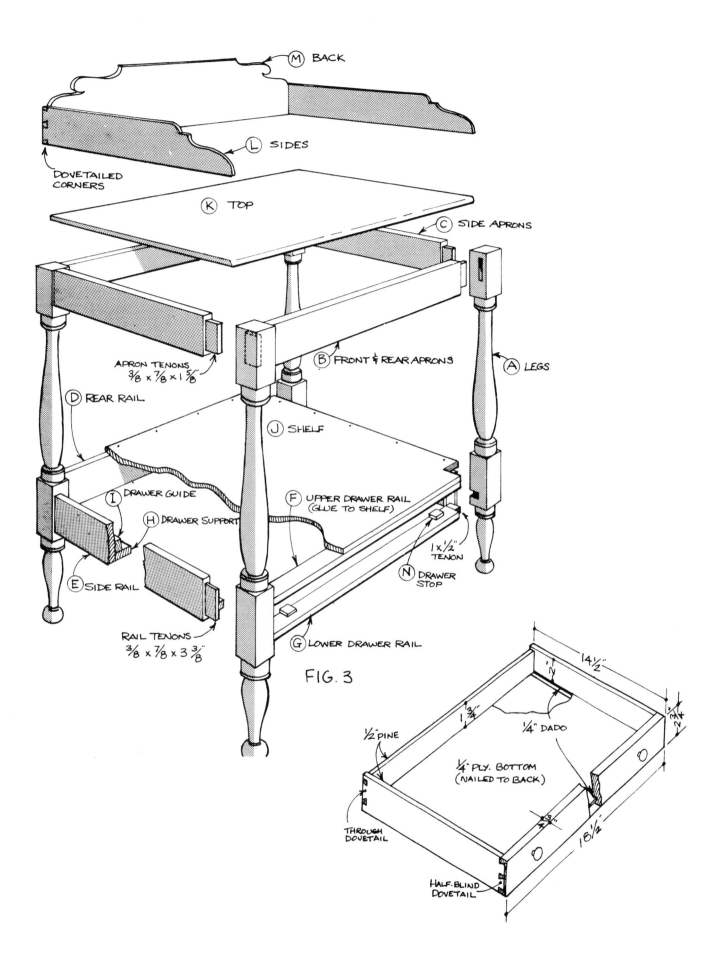

(M) BACK

(L) SIDES

DOVETAILED
CORNERS

(K) TOP

(C) SIDE APRONS

APRON TENONS
3/8 x 7/8 x 1 5/8"

(B) FRONT & REAR APRONS

(A) LEGS

(D) REAR RAIL

(J) SHELF

(I) DRAWER GUIDE

(F) UPPER DRAWER RAIL
(GLUE TO SHELF)

(H) DRAWER SUPPORT

1 x 1/2"
TENON

(E) SIDE RAIL

(N) DRAWER
STOP

RAIL TENONS
3/8 x 7/8 x 3 3/8"

(G) LOWER DRAWER RAIL

FIG. 3

14 1/2"

1 3/4"

3/4"
2 1/4"

1/2" PINE

1/4" DADO

1/4" PLY. BOTTOM
(NAILED TO BACK)

THROUGH
DOVETAIL

3/8"
1/4"

18 1/2"

HALF-BLIND
DOVETAIL

absorb as much stain as the wood, resulting in an area with an uneven and sloppy-looking stain.

Choose a stain that results in an "antique" look. Woodworkers tend to disagree as to exactly what an antique stain should look like, so it pretty much becomes a matter of individual taste. With pine, one method that has proved popular is the application of one coat of Minwax Special Walnut wood finish.

Glue a side apron and rail into the front and back legs. Use clamp pads to protect the legs and center pipe clamps on each joint. Repeat the process with the remaining side rail, apron, and legs.

After these dry, lay a leg-rail unit on a flat surface and add the lower drawer rail G and shelf-rail assembly. Next add the front and rear aprons and the other leg-rail unit. Turn the entire assembly upright and fasten four pipe clamps lengthwise, again using pads and centering clamps on each joint. Check the frame for squareness and tack diagonal braces in place as necessary to hold the frame square while the glue cures.

The top, unlike the original's 15½"-wide board, should be made by edge joining and gluing three or four ½"-thick boards. Use light clamp pressure to prevent buckling. The sides L and back M are cut from ½" stock, allowing enough length for the through dovetail joint at each corner. Enlarge the patterns in Figures 1 and 2 on thin cardboard; cut templates and transfer the outlines to the stock. Use a jig- or coping saw to cut the graceful curves.

The front edge of the top is rounded off and the top is fastened to the frame with screws and glue blocks as shown in Detail B. The sides and back are added to the top with 5-penny finishing nails set slightly below the surface. Do not glue the sides to the top.

Referring to Figure 3 and Detail A, cut the drawer supports H to length and notch them around the back legs. Glue and clamp these flush with the bottom edges of the side rails. The drawer guides I are then added.

Figure 3 shows drawer construction using authentic dovetailed joints. Note that the drawer back is narrower than the sides and is not grooved for the bottom, but rather rests upon it. Fasten the bottom to the back with a few thin box nails. Do not glue the bottom into its grooves; it should have a slightly loose fit. The addition of small drawer stops N, glued in place, and wooden drawer pulls completes construction.

Finish with several coats of either a low-luster varnish or one of the new penetrating oil finishes which are more satisfactory than the old boiled linseed oil finish.

BILL OF MATERIALS

Key	Part	Pcs. Req'd	T	W	L
A	legs	4	1⅝"	1⅝"	26¾"
B	front and rear aprons	2	¾"	2⅜"	20¼" (includes tenons)
C	side aprons	2	¾"	2⅜"	14¼" (includes tenons)
D	rear rail	1	¾"	4¼"	20¼" (includes tenons)
E	side rail	2	¾"	4¼"	14¼" (includes tenons)
F	upper drawer rail	1	¾"	1½"	18½"
G	lower drawer rail	1	¾"	1⅝"	19½" (includes tenons)
H	drawer support	2	¾"	1¼"	13¼"
I	drawer guide	2	¾"	¾"	12½"
J	shelf	1	½"	15½"	21½"
K	top	1	½"	15½"	21⅛"
L	sides	2	½"	2¾"	16"
M	back	1	½"	5"	22⅛"
N	drawer stop	2	¼"	¾"	1¼"

Pine Mirror Frame

The simple, straightforward design of this small wall mirror lends itself well to a wide variety of decorating styles.

Start with a 6′ length of ¾ x 1⅝″ pine and bevel both sides as shown by inclining the saw blade to 35 degrees. Then cut the ⅜ x ⅜″ rabbet to hold the glass, before cutting the stock to length and mitering the ends.

The mitered corners can be joined with glue and nails, ¼″ blind dowels, or ¼″-thick hardwood splines, depending on the amount of equipment you have on hand and how energetic you feel.

The glass is backed with hardboard, corrugated cardboard, or plywood held in the rabbet with about eight small brads pushed into place with long-nose pliers.

Although it's not necessary, a kraft-paper dust cover makes a nice finishing touch and can be easily applied.

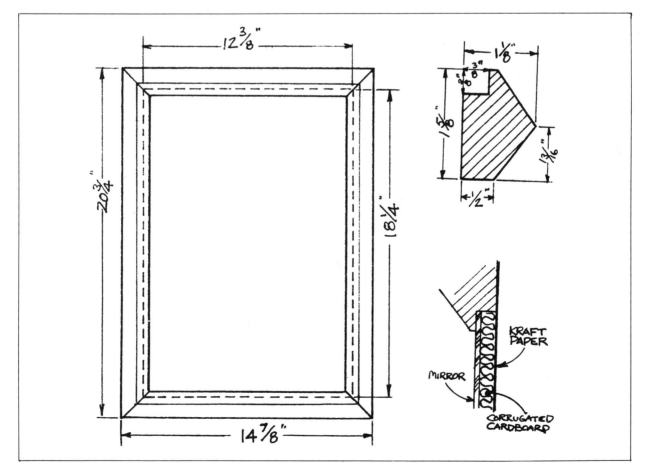

Paper-Towel Holder

An attractive pine paper-towel holder like this will be a welcome gift in any home. In fact, most homes can put several to use—in the bathroom, garage, laundry room, or workshop, it's a very handy accessory.

Make the back bracket first, cutting it from 1″ stock to the dimensions shown. Give a generous chamfer to the outside edge before sanding all surfaces smooth.

Cut out two ¾″ x 6″-diameter hubs and bore a 1¼″ center hole. File all rough edges and sand smooth.

Turn the 1⅛″-diameter center shaft to the profile shown.

Use four flat-headed wood screws to attach the two hubs to the back bracket at the location shown. Drill mounting holes to suit.

Final sand all surfaces, stain, and apply two coats of polyurethane satin varnish. Rub down the final coat with 4/0 steel wool.

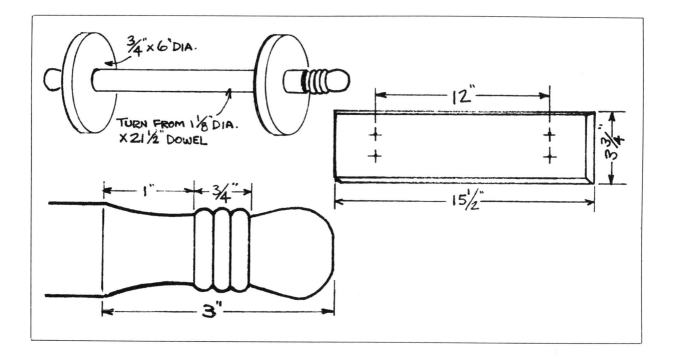

Porch Swing

As a holiday gift, a marketable project, or an addition to your own porch, this swing can be built with only a day's worth of labor for as little as fifty dollars in materials. For durability and an antique look, oak was chosen, but whatever wood is selected the porch swing will generate a lifetime of comfort and interest, reminiscent of days that need not remain bygone.

The project is begun by cutting to size parts A, B, and C, which comprise the seat frame. Care should be taken in sawing out the three pieces labeled C, since they will determine the shape or contour of the seat. Butt rails A and B to rails C and join them with pairs of 1½″ #8 flat-headed screws. Counterbore ⅜″ holes, plug them, and sand flush. Be sure to leave 3″ on either side of A to allow for the arm stumps.

The seat slats can be nailed to the frame using 1″ wire brads hammered into predrilled holes

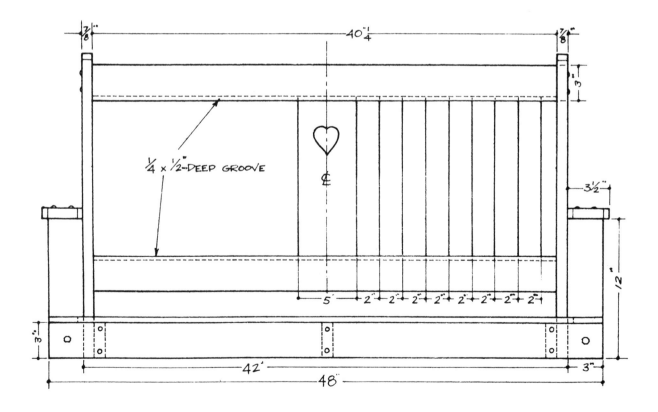

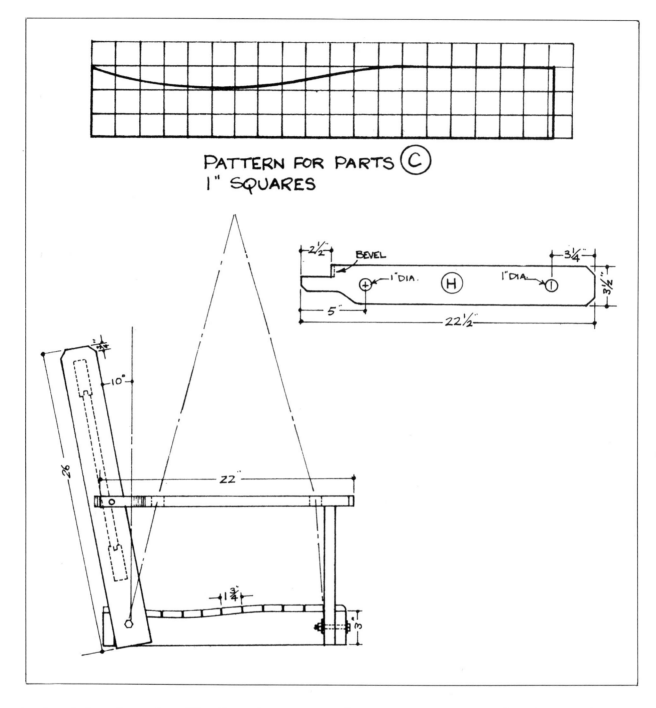

PATTERN FOR PARTS Ⓒ
1" SQUARES

and set below the surface. The dimensions given for parts J will allow about a ¹⁄₁₆″ gap between each slat to take care of swelling and water run-off. Note that the slats will overhang parts C by ½″.

Continue by making the back. Cut a ¼ x ½″-deep groove the length of the rails E. Then cut the corresponding tenons on slats F and G. Don't forget to cut out the heart design, or perhaps another of your own choosing. Assemble the back-rest with water-resistant glue, taking care that it

does not run onto exposed surfaces, and clamp the assembly. While it is clamped, if time is not to be wasted, the assembly can be joined to the upright supports D using wood screws in counter-bored holes that are plugged and sanded flush. The upper rail should be positioned 1″ from the top of the uprights.

Join the uprights to the seat frame with ½ x 3″ bolts and hex nuts, the nuts being on the outside. Drill ½″ holes 1½″ from the back of side rails C and 1½″ from the bottoms of uprights D.

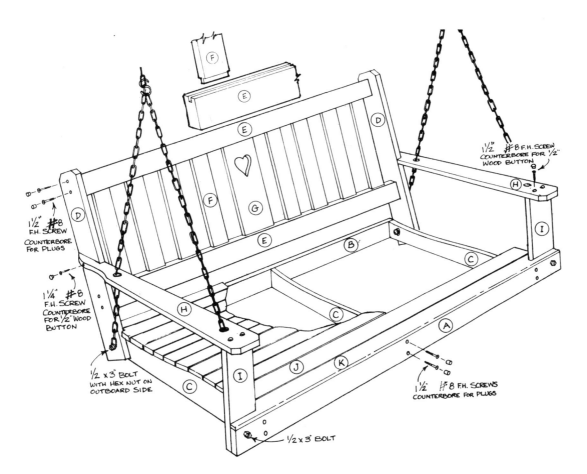

Labels in figure:
1/2" #8 F.H. SCREW COUNTERBORE FOR PLUGS

1/4" #8 F.H. SCREW COUNTERBORE FOR 1/2" WOOD BUTTON

1/2 x 3" BOLT WITH HEX NUT ON OUTBOARD SIDE

1/2 x 3" BOLT

1/2" #8 F.H. SCREWS COUNTERBORE FOR PLUGS

1/2" #8 F.H. SCREW COUNTERBORE FOR 1/2" WOOD BUTTON

Cut the armrests and arm stumps to size (parts H and I). If done according to the plan, they will allow the back to tilt approximately 10 degrees from the perpendicular. These two pieces are butted together and held with wood screws covered with wood buttons. The end of the arm should extend 1½″ beyond the edge of the stump. The other end is screwed to the uprights. The arm stumps are held to the frame with ½ x 3″ bolts.

Twenty feet of double-looped chain will suffice, with the shorter pieces that attach to the arm-stump/seat-frame bolts about three feet in length. S hooks will hold the two lengths together. To remove any stress on the roof of the porch, springs should be used there. Automobile hood springs are excellent for the purpose and can be obtained from an auto wrecking yard at a reasonable price.

The swing was finished with a mixture of a wood preservative such as McCloskey's Rot Fyter and a brown enamel. Mixing will take some experimentation, but if done properly, this treatment will seal the wood, stain it, and give it a gloss in one operation.

BILL OF MATERIALS

Key	Part	Pcs. Req'd	T	W	L
A	seat rail (front)	1	⅞″	3″	48″
B	seat rail (rear)	1	⅞″	3″	42″
C	seat rails (side, center)	3	⅞″	3″	19¼″
D	upright supports	2	⅞″	3″	26″
E	backrest rails (top and bottom)	2	⅞″	3″	40¼″
F	backrest slats	8	½″	2″	14″ (includes tenons)
G	center slat	1	½″	5″	14″ (includes tenons)
H	armrests	2	⅞″	3½″	22½″
I	arm stumps	2	⅞″	3″	12″
J	seat slats	10	½″	1¾″	43″
K	seat slat	1	½″	1¾″	48″

Toy Whale

This little whale provides plenty of amusing action as his mouth opens and closes and his body pivots up and down when he is pulled. Make a few for gifts, or set up for production and market them to toy and gift shops.

Enlarge the grid pattern on cardboard and transfer the shapes of the tail and body to ¾" pine or maple. Jigsaw the two separate body sections, terminating in a semicircle with a 1" radius.

The half-lap cuts are started with a 2" hole saw chucked into an electric drill. Locate the pivot point or center of the circle on each part, and start the center bit of the saw into the mark. Cut ⅜" deep, then remove the saw and cut away waste with a chisel.

Test the joint for a loose action by holding the parts together and moving them up and down. Shave a bit from each part until the joint pivots freely. Clean up the joint with sandpaper and secure the pieces with a brass 1" #8 flat-headed screw. Drive the screw into a countersunk hole and back off until the joint is free. Then file the protruding tip of screw flush.

The lower jaw is made of ¾" pine sandwiched between two pieces of ⅛" hardwood. The center piece should be cut to provide a recess for the upper jaw when the mouth is closed. Drill the pin hole through the main body, making it slightly oversize for a loose fit of a ¼" pin. The lower jaw should be drilled for a tight fit over the pin.

Drill the body for a loose fit of the wheel axle. Use a hole saw to cut 2" discs from ¾" stock. Drill off-center holes part way into each disc, run the axle through the body, and glue the wheels to it. The center hole in the wheels can be plugged.

Give the toy a very thorough sanding and finish with two coats of penetrating-oil finish. The pull cord is inserted into a hole in the top of the head and secured with a small peg glued into the hole.

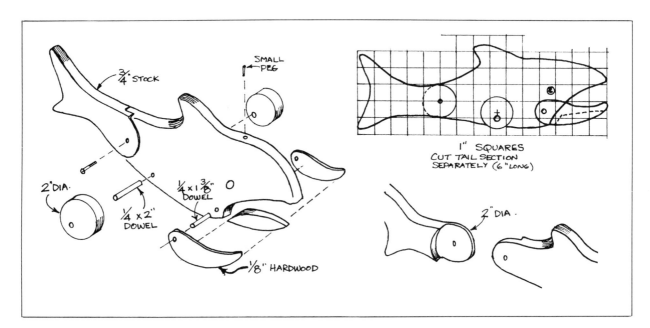

Tot's Tricycle

This walker tricycle, built of hardwood, will provide many hours of fun and exercise for the tot who has recently started walking.

Start by cutting the seat to shape from ¾″ stock and bore for an easy fit of the 1″-diameter steering-post tenon. Cut the ¾ x 5 x 8″ subseat

and attach it to the underside of the seat as shown using glue and four 1½″ countersunk flatheaded screws.

Cut rear axle supports from ¾″ stock, miter the ends to fit flush against the underside of the seat, and bore for an easy sliding fit of a ¾″-diameter wooden axle. Attach supports to the sides of the subseat with glue and 1½″ flatheaded screws.

Wheels are cut from hardwood or ¾″ plywood and bored for a snug fit over the axles. Both front and rear axles are prevented from shifting sideways by ⅛″ dowel pegs inserted through the axles.

The steering post is in two parts, both of which are 1¾″ square and center-bored for a 1″-diameter tenon. Chamfer the upper post as shown and drill for the handlebars and tenon. Glue the tenon into the upper post only. Notch the lower post to provide slight clearance for the wheel. The short axle is glued to the wheel and revolves in slightly oversize holes in the post. Drill through the front of the lower post and tenon for a 2″ carriage bolt.

Sand all parts carefully and round off all sharp corners to prevent splintering.

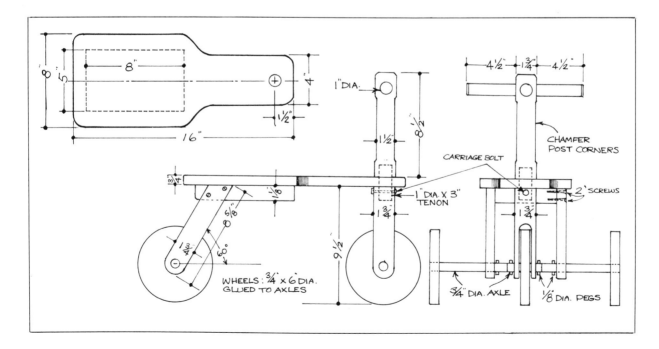

Skyhook

Simple wooden toys seem to have as much appeal for adults as they have for children. Some designs have been around in one form or another for centuries, which is proof enough of their intrinsic amusement value.

You've got to see this toy in action to appreciate it. The balancing act it performs on the end of your finger or the edge of a table is almost unbelievable. If ever there was an ideal first project for the young woodworker, this is it. Hardwood is best for this toy, as considerable force is applied to the sharp end of the Skyhook when balancing a leather belt and the edge will quickly round off if soft pine is used, causing the toy to sway from side to side.

The illustration is actual size, so it can be cut out or transferred to tracing paper and marked directly on the wood. Close adherence to the dimensions given will insure a surprising performance. Be sure to make the point of the hook straight across. To use, simply insert a leather belt in the slot and balance the end on your finger. If the buckle is very heavy, you will have to adjust the belt in the slot to its approximate center of balance. One last point: Only a leather belt will work; cloth belts lack the necessary weight and stiffness.

If you are inclined to make handcrafted wooden toys for sale, the Skyhook in particular is a money-maker, as it can be stack-sawed from layers of wood and many dozens can be produced in a short time.

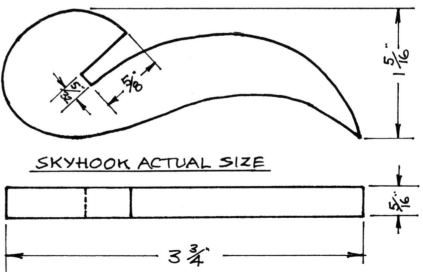

SKYHOOK ACTUAL SIZE

Rolltop Desk

Part I—The Base

This classic rolltop desk is an ambitious under-taking for the advanced woodworker, but well worth the effort, as the end result is an impressive and useful piece of furniture that should last for generations. With its paneled sides and back, we believe it represents one of the finest examples of its type to be found and can be displayed with pride anywhere.

The desk shown was made from black walnut salvaged from old buildings and accumulated over a long period of time. Most of these desks were made of oak, however, and this would be an appropriate and far more economical wood to use.

The drawer sides are best made of ½″ stock, while the drawer bottoms are of ¼″ plywood. Drawer frames can be made of any clear, well-seasoned hardwood, but those front rails that can be seen should be of wood that matches the exterior of the desk.

For the base, start with the end-panel assemblies. All of the lumber in the basic framework of the desk is of ¾″ thickness (actual), with the exception of the raised panels, which are of ½″ stock.

The raised panels are cut using a shaper with a Rockwell panel-raising cutter. The outer edges of each raised panel are cut to ¼″ thickness to fit into a corresponding groove in the stiles and rails (Detail A, p. 234).

The stiles and rails are joined with ⅜ x 2″ dowels, two used in each joint. The grooves cut to hold the raised panels and center stiles B should be ¼″ wide and ⅜″ deep for an easy fit of the panels and to allow for movement due to changes in humidity. Do not glue the panels in place. The center stiles B have tenons ¼″ thick by ¼″ long on each end. These tenons fit into the rail grooves and can be glued in place; the 22½″ length includes the tenons.

The kneehole-panel assemblies are constructed exactly like the ends with the exception of the rear stiles, labeled A2 in Figure 1. These stiles are 2¼″ wide rather than 3″. The back-panel assembly (Figure 2) is constructed in the same manner as the end and kneehole panels.

The drawer dividers are detailed in Figure 3. It's advisable to make them slightly wider than the 12″ shown. Note that guides are not required on the two uppermost drawer-divider assemblies G. After they are joined and glued, run one side through the jointer to be assured of straightness. Then trim the opposite side with the table saw to an exact finished width of 12″. The sides will be

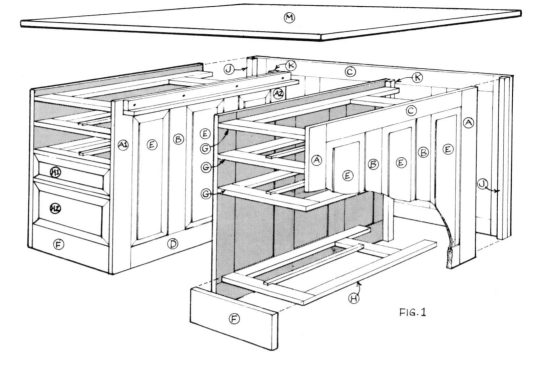

FIG. 1

both straight and parallel, an important point since this is the framework that holds the end and kneehole panels together. The drawer dividers are held in place with counterbored screws into each stile.

When all dividers are installed, you will have two drawer units, or pedestals, which are then attached to the back panel assembly. Two ¾"-square cleats K are glued along the rear inner edges of the kneehole panels. Screws are then driven through these and into the back panel. The ends of the back panel also have cleats J of the same thickness so that they too can be screwed into the end panels (see Figure 1).

The kneehole-drawer guides I1 and I2 are also used to hold the top slab. These guides are each glued up from two pieces, then screwed flush with the top inside edges of the kneehole panels. Holes are bored up through the guides for counterbored 3" screws driven into the top (Figure 8).

The kneehole drawer, unlike the rest of the drawers, is not dovetailed at the front corners. Instead, the back side of the front is dadoed to receive the sides. A pencil-trough insert can be made by using the table saw to make a cove cut in a piece of suitable stock, which is then glued in place against the rear of the drawer front.

Figure 7 shows the construction of all other drawers using half-blind dovetails at the front corners. These joints can be cut with a router and dovetail jig. For those who lack the time and equipment, rabbet joints can be substituted for the dovetails but this will necessitate cutting the drawer fronts from 1⅛"-thick stock to allow the rabbets to hold the sides. This substitution will affect the overall length of the drawer sides and the location of the drawer guides.

Before assembly, you may want to run small grooves in some of the drawer sides so that partitions can be added as needed for such things as canceled checks and card files. The drawer fronts should fit in their respective openings with a slight clearance at the top and both ends.

The drawer pulls (Figure 9) can be individually shaped from quarter-round stock or by using the lathe-turning technique in which a turning square is glued up with a ⅝" piece in the middle. A 2½"-diameter cylinder is turned and cut to produce four or more pulls when cut into quarters. The pulls are 6" long and have finger grooves hollowed out with a router or dado head and table saw. After splitting the turning into two parts, position the pieces over the dado head and clamp them to the table, then slowly raise the spinning blades.

As can be seen in Figure 6, the pull-out writing boards consist of a piece of ⅝" particle board ve-

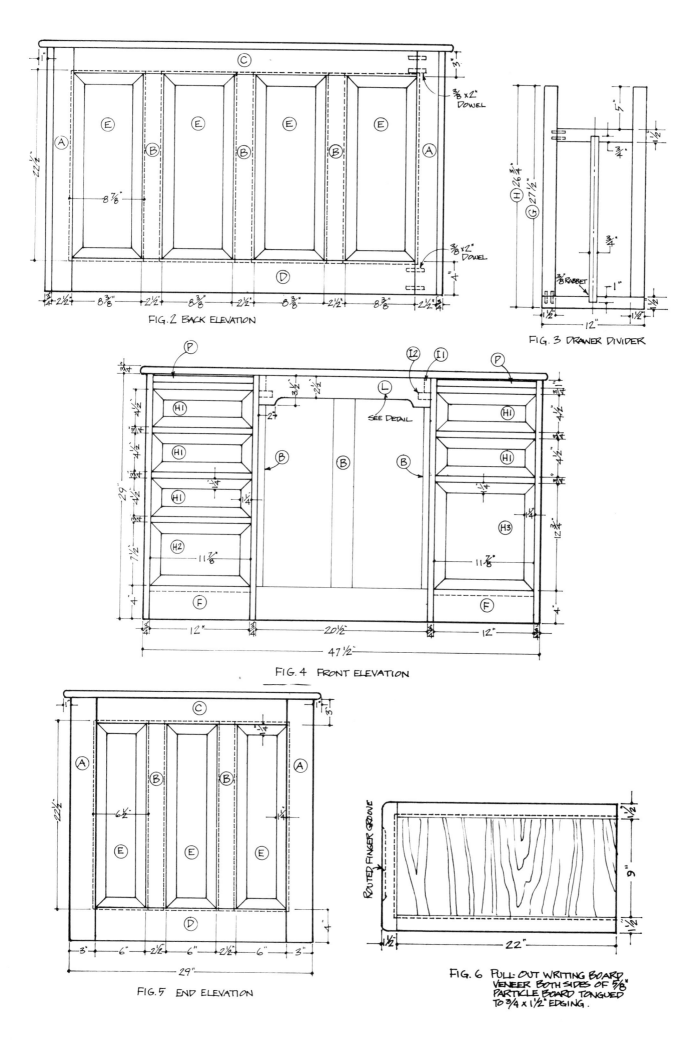

FIG. 2 BACK ELEVATION

FIG. 3 DRAWER DIVIDER

FIG. 4 FRONT ELEVATION

FIG. 5 END ELEVATION

FIG. 6 PULL-OUT WRITING BOARD, VENEER BOTH SIDES OF 5/8" PARTICLE BOARD TONGUED TO 3/4 x 1 1/2" EDGING.

ROUTED FINGER GROOVE

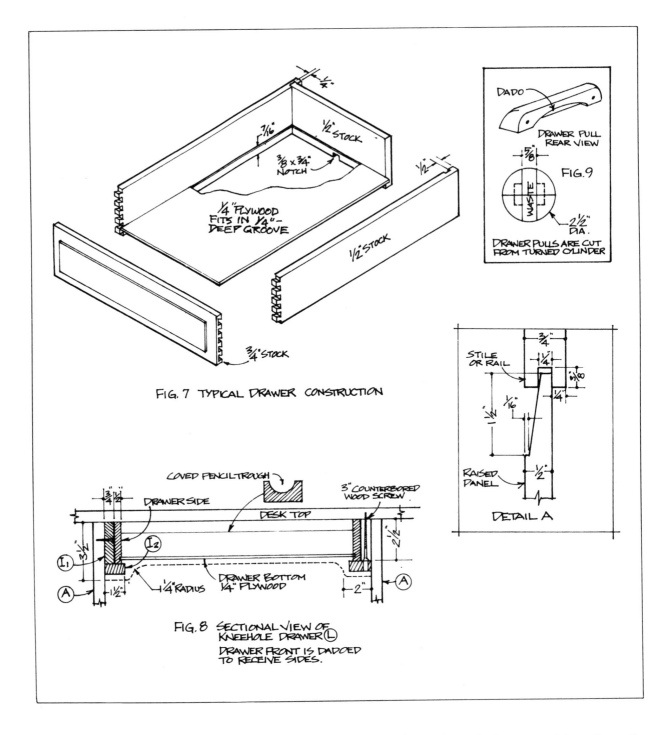

FIG. 7 TYPICAL DRAWER CONSTRUCTION

DRAWER PULL REAR VIEW

FIG. 9

DRAWER PULLS ARE CUT FROM TURNED CYLINDER

DETAIL A

FIG. 8 SECTIONAL VIEW OF KNEEHOLE DRAWER (L) DRAWER FRONT IS DADOED TO RECEIVE SIDES.

neered on both sides. This veneered panel is edged along both sides and front with ¾ x 1½″ strips. The whole unit is joined with tongues and grooves or with ⅜″ dowel pins.

The desk top is glued up from ¾″ stock, edge joined, and reinforced with ⅜″ dowel pins or ¼″ plywood splines.

It's a good idea to seal the underside of the top with several coats of varnish before installing it. On the outer edges, the top is held with screws that go down through the top and into the rails of the base unit, and also into the top rail across the back. These screws are countersunk flush with the top since they will be covered when the rolltop unit is installed. If you wish to use the desk alone, without the rolltop unit, counterbore the screws and plug the holes with plugs cut from the face grain of scrap stock. The rolltop unit can be built at a later date as time and finances permit (see Part II, following).

BILL OF MATERIALS—DESK BASE

Key	Part	Pcs. Req'd	T	W	L
Panel Assemblies					
Base Ends (Fig. 5; 2 req'd)					
A	stile	4	¾"	3"	29"
B	stile	4	¾"	2½"	22½"
C	rail	2	¾"	3"	23"
D	rail	2	¾"	4"	23"
E	panel	6	½"	6½"	22½"
Kneehole Sides (Fig. 1; 2 req'd)					
A1	stile	2	¾"	3"	29"
A2	stile	2	¾"	2¼"	29"
B	same as Base Ends				
C	same as Base Ends				
D	same as Base Ends				
E	same as Base Ends				
Back (Fig. 2; 1 req'd)					
A	stile	2	¾"	2½"	29"
B	stile	3	¾"	2½"	22½"
C	rail	1	¾"	3"	41"
D	rail	1	¾"	4"	41"
E	panel	4	½"	8⅞"	22½"
Front Base Trim (Fig. 4; 2 req'd)					
F		2	¾"	4"	12"
Drawer Divider Assemblies (Fig. 3; 7 req'd)					
G	front rails	7	¾"	1½"	12"
	rear rails	7	¾"	1½"	9"
	side rails	14	¾"	1½"	26"
	guides	7	¾"	¾"	21"
Bottom Drawer Divider Assemblies (Fig. 3; 2 req'd)					
H	front rails	2	¾"	1½"	12"
	rear rails	2	¾"	1½"	9"
	side rails	4	¾"	1½"	25¼"
	guides	2	¾"	¾"	20¼"
Drawers (Figs. 4 and 7; 5 req'd)					
Drawer Assemblies					
H1	front	5	¾"	4½"	12"
	sides	10	½"	4½"	22¼"
	back	5	½"	4½"	11½"
	bottom	5	¼"	11½"	21⅜"
Drawer (Figs. 4 and 7; 1 req'd)					
H2	front	1	¾"	7½"	12"
	sides	2	½"	4½"	22¼"
	back	1	½"	4½"	11½"
	bottom	1	¼"	11½"	21⅜"
Drawer (Figs. 4 and 7; 1 req'd)					
H3	front	1	¾"	12¾"	12"
	sides	2	½"	12¾"	22¼"
	back	1	½"	12¾"	11½"
	bottom	1	¼"	11½"	21⅜"
Kneehole Drawer Guides (Fig. 8)					
I1		2	¾"	2½"	27½"
I2		2	¾"	1½"	27½"
Cleat (Fig. 1)					
J		2	¾"	¾"	29"
Cleat (Fig. 1)					
K		2	¾"	¾"	29"
Kneehole Drawer (Fig. 8; 1 req'd)					
L	front	1	¾"	3½"	20½"
	sides	2	½"	2½"	20"
	back	1	½"	2½"	18½"
	bottom	1	¼"	as req'd	as req'd
Desk Top					
M		1	¾"	31"	49"
Writing Board (Fig. 6; 2 req'd)					
P	veneered part. board	1	⅝"	9½" (includes tenons)	22¼" (includes tenons)
	front edging	1	1"	1½"	12"
	side edging	2	1"	1½"	22"
	stops	2	⅜"	¾"	¾"

Rolltop Desk

Part II—The Top

Now that the lower desk has been completed, we turn our attention to the rolltop section. The construction of the end panels with tambour grooves is the most difficult part of the entire project, but any woodworker with moderate skill should be able to do a creditable job if care is used in laying out, cutting, and squaring up the rolltop unit.

A method has been worked out that will enable the builder to perform all operations with a table saw, router, and hand tools. Certain operations can be done on the shaper and those who have access to this machine will, no doubt, put it to good use.

The framed end panels are tackled first. Referring to Figure 1, you will see that the end panels consist of four frame parts, A, B, C, and E, surrounding a raised panel D. First cut stiles A and rails C and B. Enlarge the grid pattern of Figure 2 and prepare a template for cutting the double curve of rails E from ¾″ stock.

All four frame parts must be grooved to hold the beveled edges of the raised panel D. The straight pieces will present no problem, but the curved rail is somewhat of a challenge because the tight radius of the inside curves precludes the use of a router. The grooving can be done with a shaper or with a centuries-old hand tool called a scratch stock.

The scratch stock shown in Figure 3 can be quickly made from scrap hardwood. A blade is ground from an old scraper or saw blade. File the cutting edge square and burnish a burr on the edge. The blade does the grooving by scraping rather than by cutting.

Insert the blade to take a light cut and clamp it. Push forward, repeating strokes until the blade no longer removes material, then set the blade for a deeper cut. Continue until a depth of ⅜″ has been achieved (Figure 4).

When the end-panel rails and stiles have been grooved, lay out ⅜″ dowel-pin locations for joining them. At the top joint, between B and E, care should be exercised so that positioning of the dowels does not interfere with the tambour groove.

Assemble the frames temporarily with slightly loose dowels and check for squareness and well-fitted joints. Lay the frames over a glued-up panel that is to be beveled, and use a sharp pencil to scribe a line around the inside edges of the frame.

Cut panel D ¼″ larger all around than the pencil line to allow for fit in the frame grooves. Use a compass and straightedge to mark this cutting line, then jigsaw the panel to shape and sand the edges to remove any bumps or slight irregularities.

Beveling of the three straight edges to form a raised center panel is a routine table-saw operation. The curved portion can be beveled by hand once you've cut a clean lip to start the bevel. One way to do this is by cutting a template from hardboard or plywood. This template, which is shown as B on Figure 2, is clamped to the panel. A router with a ⅝″ O.D. pilot-bushing attachment and a ¼″ straight bit is run along the edge of the template and cuts the lip to a depth of 1/16″ (Figures 5 and 6). Don't forget that panels D are mirror images of each other, and not identical.

After running this groove, use a plane to remove most of the waste down to a 3/16″ feathered edge. Finish off the curved bevel with a chisel, file, and sandpaper.

The entire end panel can now be finish sanded and glued together with short dowel pins. Follow the same procedures for building the other end

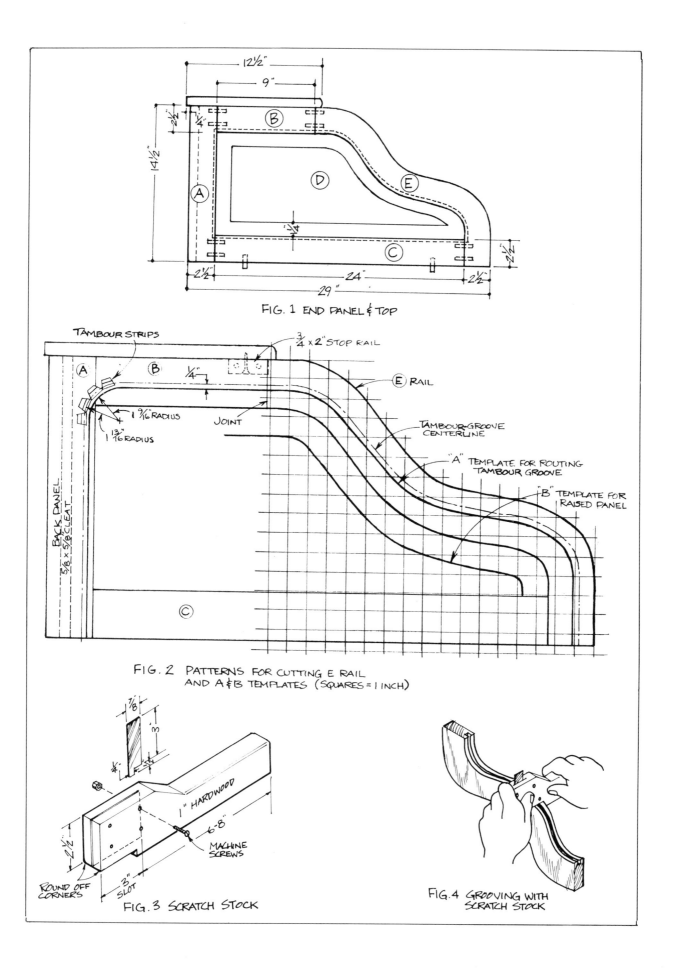

FIG. 1 END PANEL & TOP

12½"

9"

14½"

2½"
¼"

Ⓑ

Ⓐ

Ⓓ

Ⓔ

¼"

Ⓒ

2½"

2½" 24" 2½"

29"

FIG. 2 PATTERNS FOR CUTTING E RAIL
AND A & B TEMPLATES (SQUARES = 1 INCH)

TAMBOUR STRIPS

Ⓐ Ⓑ ¼"

¾ x 2" STOP RAIL

Ⓔ RAIL

1 9/16" RADIUS

JOINT

1 13/16" RADIUS

TAMBOUR-GROOVE
CENTERLINE

"A" TEMPLATE FOR ROUTING
TAMBOUR GROOVE

"B" TEMPLATE FOR
RAISED PANEL

BACK PANEL

5/8 x 5/8 CLEAT

Ⓒ

FIG. 3 SCRATCH STOCK

7/8

3

¼"

1" HARDWOOD

6-8"

2½"

3"
SLOT

MACHINE
SCREWS

ROUND OFF
CORNERS

FIG. 4 GROOVING WITH
SCRATCH STOCK

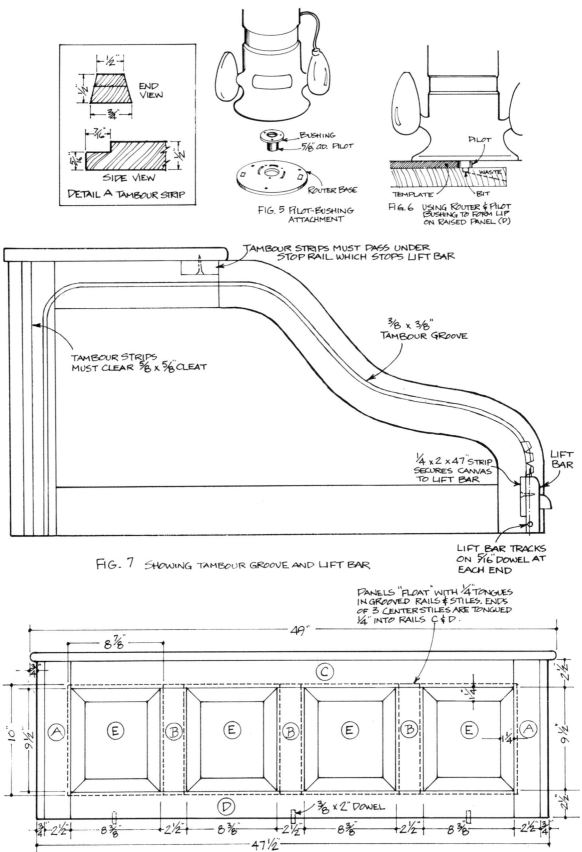

END VIEW

SIDE VIEW

DETAIL A TAMBOUR STRIP

BUSHING
5/8" O.D. PILOT

ROUTER BASE

FIG. 5 PILOT-BUSHING ATTACHMENT

PILOT

WASTE

TEMPLATE
BIT

FIG. 6 USING ROUTER & PILOT BUSHING TO FORM LIP ON RAISED PANEL (D)

TAMBOUR STRIPS MUST PASS UNDER STOP RAIL WHICH STOPS LIFT BAR

3/8 x 3/8" TAMBOUR GROOVE

TAMBOUR STRIPS MUST CLEAR 5/8 x 5/8 CLEAT

1/4 x 2 x 47" STRIP SECURES CANVAS TO LIFT BAR

LIFT BAR

LIFT BAR TRACKS ON 5/16" DOWEL AT EACH END

FIG. 7 SHOWING TAMBOUR GROOVE AND LIFT BAR

PANELS "FLOAT" WITH 1/4" TONGUES IN GROOVED RAILS & STILES. ENDS OF 3 CENTER STILES ARE TONGUED 1/4" INTO RAILS C & D.

49"

8 7/8"

C

2 1/2

A   E   B   E   B   E   B   E   A

10"   9 1/4   9 1/4   2 1/2

1/4

D   3/8 x 2" DOWEL

3/4 2 1/2   8 3/8   2 1/2   8 3/8   2 1/2   8 3/8   2 1/2   8 3/8   2 1/2 3/4

47 1/2"

FIG. 8 BACK PANEL

238

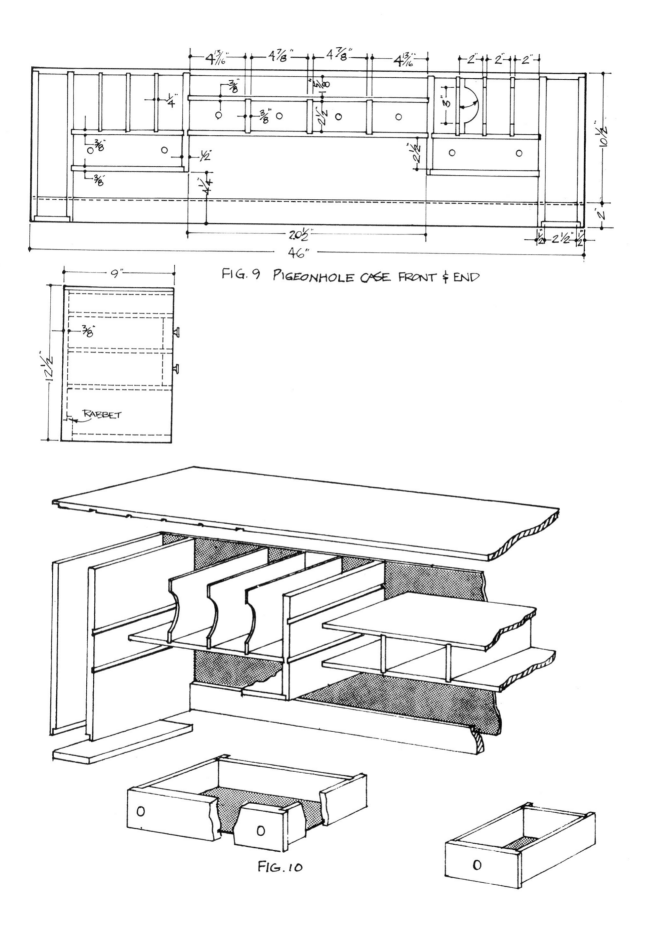

FIG. 9 PIGEONHOLE CASE FRONT & END

RABBET

FIG. 10

239

panel, but don't forget that the panels are left and right mirror images.

The tambour-tracking groove, which is ⅜″ wide x ⅜″ deep, is routed into each end panel, again using a template and a router with ⅜″ pilot bushing. A single template is used and reversed for the alternate end panel. Thus slight irregularities in one groove will be transferred and will correspond on the opposite groove.

Again referring to Figure 2, enlarge the grid pattern and cut template A, cutting as accurately as possible and sanding until all curves are smooth and continuous, without bumps or depressions. Make reference marks on the template so it can be positioned identically on each end panel.

It's best to screw the template to the workpiece. This saves a lot of fussing with clamps, and the screw holes can be filled later. Consider fastening the template to a piece of scrap and making a trial run or two to get the feel of running the router around the curves.

When fastening the template to the end panel, note that the groove you are going to rout does not exactly parallel the outside edge of the curved rail E, but veers away so that the tambour will clear the stop rail across the front of the rolltop case (Figures 2 and 7).

After routing the first groove, remove the template and, using the reference marks, locate it on the other end panel for the other groove. When the grooves have been routed to a depth of ⅜″, sand them smooth with a small sanding block, then seal them with a thinned shellac and a thin coat of wax.

Having completed the end panels, we can proceed to the construction of the framed back panel shown in Figure 8. Follow the same general procedures as used for the framed panels that make up the base of the desk (see Part I of the project). The back is fastened between and flush with the ends using ⅜″-square cleats and screws. Square up the assembly and tack a strip across the bottom near the front edges to hold it square.

The top piece, which is ¾ x 12½ x 49″, is attached to the end back panels with 1¼″ #10 flatheaded screws, counterbored and covered with flush wood plugs.

The pigeonhole case (Figures 9 and 10) is constructed separately and inserted as a unit. It should be a good sliding fit between the end panels. Use dadoes and rabbets to attach the various partitions and shelves. The upright dividers at each end are cut from ¼″ plywood and shaped with a jigsaw. All drawers are constructed with ⁵⁄₁₆″ stock. The drawer fronts are of ½″ stock and fitted flush. Drawer bottoms are ⅛″ or ¼″ plywood.

The back of the pigeonhole case conceals the tambour when it is in the up or open position. Cut the case back from ⅜″ plywood and apply a veneer that matches the rest of the desk to the side facing front. The back is rabbeted into a ¾ x 2 x 44½″ rail fitted into notches in the case uprights.

When the case is completed, place the rolltop assembly on a flat surface and insert the pigeonhole unit. Later, this can be fastened with small finishing nails driven into the end panels.

Thirty tambour strips are required, but you may have to rip fifty to get enough good ones. The strips are dimensioned as shown in Detail A. A saw-blade angle of 12 to 14 degrees will provide the relief angles on each strip so they can travel through the S curve. Rip the strips to a rough length of about 47½″. They will be trimmed later to finish length as determined by your measurements from one groove bottom to the other.

Because of intrinsic tensions in the ripping stock, you may find that many strips will warp immediately, or after a couple of days. A small degree of lateral warp is acceptable as this will be removed in a jig that holds the strips flat and square while the canvas is glued in place.

Figure 11 shows such a jig. Use a half sheet of ¾″ particle board for the base, which should be cut to 31″ high x 51″ long. Fasten two rabbeted strips to the base, then add a back stop strip as shown. Slide the sanded tambour strips into the jig face side down. Then slide in a stop strip and fasten another strip 4″ further down. Cut wedges and tap them into place between the last two strips. Make wedges just tight enough to close the gaps between the tambour strips. Tap all the strips until they are flat against the base.

The canvas backing can be secured at art supply shops. For the original desk denim was used, but artist's canvas of about 10 ounces in weight is good. The canvas is cut to a height of 24½″ and a length of 44⅞″. The finished tambour strips should measure 46¾″ in overall length, and when the shoulders are cut the distance between shoul-

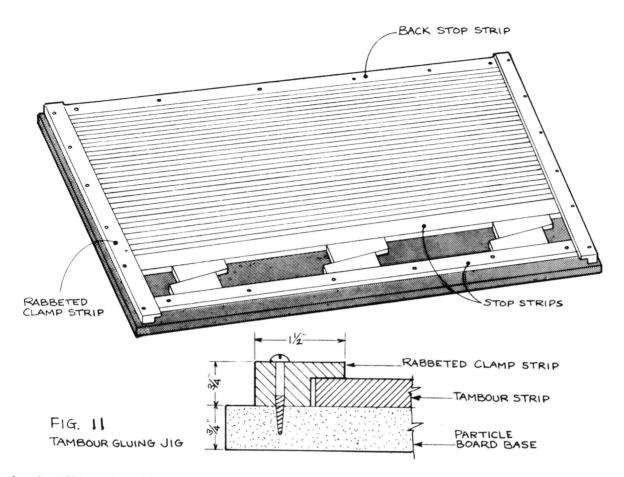

BACK STOP STRIP

RABBETED
CLAMP STRIP

STOP STRIPS

1½"

¾"

¾"

RABBETED CLAMP STRIP

TAMBOUR STRIP

PARTICLE
BOARD BASE

FIG. 11
TAMBOUR GLUING JIG

ders is 45⅞". If the width of your rolltop assembly is slightly off, you will have to adjust tambour length accordingly after attaching the canvas.

The canvas is fastened ½" in from the points where shoulders will be cut on the strips. Allow a 2" overhang beyond the first tambour strip, which will be fastened to the lifting bar (Figure 7).

Working a section of about four strips at a time, apply Titebond glue and lay the canvas along guidelines penciled on the tambour strips. Do not allow the glue to drip between the strips. Use a roller or veneer hammer to smooth the canvas and spread the glue.

Allow the tambour to dry for 24 hours before removing it from the jig. The tambour can now be trimmed at each end to a finish length of 46¾". The shoulders on the strip ends can be cut with a router and a clamped guide strip (as shown in Detail A).

Make the lift bar according to the specifications given in the Bill of Materials. Cut a strip of ¼" stock to fasten the 2" tail of canvas to the lift bar using countersunk flat-headed screws

screwed through the strip and canvas and into the bar (Figure 7). Note that the bar is fitted with ⁵⁄₁₆"-diameter dowel pins at each end to enable it to track in the grooves.

The tambour can now be fitted into its grooves. A bit of sanding at the ends of the tongues may be necessary. The strip shoulders should not rub along the end rails because that will eventually cause unsightly marks that are visible when the desk is open. When the tambour tracks easily, remove it and apply a finish, taking care to keep it off the canvas.

The rolltop section is joined to the desk with ⅜"-diameter x 2½"-long dowel pins. These pins are permanently glued to parts C (Figure 1) and D (Figure 8) of the rolltop and fit into (but are not glued into) corresponding holes in the desk top. This method makes for easy removal and replacement of the rolltop unit. Seven dowel pins are required to join the desk and rolltop. Dowel-pin holes in both units are drilled to ⅜"-diameter x 1¼" deep.

The rolltop lock model #L31 was obtained from the Wise Company (see p. 244 for the address). It is of brass and iron construction, furnished with two keys and a trap-door catch. Screw holes are bored and countersunk for #4 screws. The matching escutcheon, model #E22, is made of gauge brass. Drill and mortise the desk top and lift bar as required for installation. Also select an appropriate lock and escutcheon for the kneehole drawer.

Choosing a final finish will depend upon the type of wood used for the desk as well as individual taste; however, it should be done with patience and care. Sand thoroughly, making sure to remove all tool marks.

The original walnut desk was finished with four coats of Deft clear wood finish, with light sanding after the second and fourth coats. For the final coat, a can of Deft spray was used, leaving a fine finish free from brush marks.

BILL OF MATERIALS—DESK TOP

Key	Pcs. Req'd	T	W	L
Back (Figure 8; 1 req'd)				
A	2	¾″	2½″	14½″
B	3	¾″	2½″	10″
C	1	¾″	2½″	41″
D	1	¾″	2½″	41″
E	4	½″	8⅞″	10″
End Panels (Figure 1; 2 req'd)				
A	2	¾″	2½″	14½″
B	2	¾″	2½″	9″
C	2	¾″	2½″	24″
D	2	½″	10″	24½″
E	2	¾″	6½″	24″
Top (Figures 1 and 8)				
	1	¾″	12½″	49″
Tambours				
	30	½″	¾″	47½″
Lift Bar				
	1	¾″	2⅞″	45⅞″

Sources of Supply

North America

The following is a list of companies that specialize in mail-order sales of woodworking supplies. Write to them for the cost of their current catalog.

General Line Suppliers

(Hardwood, veneer, hand tools, hardware, clock and lamp parts, finishing supplies, etc.)

Albert Constantine & Sons, Inc.
2050 Eastchester Road
Bronx, NY 10461

Barap Specialties
835 Bellows Ave.
Frankfort, MI 49635
(does not carry hardwood)

Craftsman Wood Service Co.
1735 West Cortland Ct.
Addison, IL 60101

The Woodworker's Store
21801 Industrial Blvd.
Rogers, MN 55374

Brookstone Co.
127 Vose Farm Rd.
Peterborough, NH 03458

Hand Tools

The Fine Tool Shops
20-28 Backus Avenue
Danbury, CT 06810

Frog Tool Co., Ltd.
700 West Jackson Blvd.
Chicago, IL 60606

Garrett Wade Co.
302 Fifth Avenue
New York, NY 10001

Lee Valley Tools, Ltd.
857 Boyd Avenue
Ottawa, Ontario, Canada K2A 2C9

Leichtung, Inc.
4944 Commerce Parkway
Cleveland, OH 44128

Woodcraft Supply Corp.
313 Montvale Avenue
Woburn, MA 01888

Hardwoods

American Woodcrafters
1025 S. Roosevelt Ave.
Piqua, OH 45356

D. A. Buckley
Rt 1
West Valley, NY 14171

Croy-Marietta Hardwoods, Inc.
121 Pike Street
Marietta, OH 45750

Educational Lumber Co., Inc.
21 Meadow Road
Asheville, NC 28803
(Minimum of 50 board feet for each thickness of
any one species)

John Harra Wood & Supply Co.
511 West 25th Street
New York, NY 10001
(Also carries hand and power tools)

Sterling Hardwoods, Inc.
412 Pine Street
Burlington, VT 05401

Hardware

Allen Specialty Hardware
P.O. Box 10833
Pittsburgh, PA 15236

Ball and Ball
463 West Lincoln Highway
Exton, PA 19341

The Decorative Hardware Studio
160 King Street
Chappaqua, NY 10514

Horton Brasses
Nooks Hill Rd.
Cromwell, CT 06416

Paxton Hardware Co.
Upper Falls, MD 21156

Period Furniture Hardware Co., Inc.
123 Charles Street
Boston, MA 02114

Ritter & Son Hardware
Gualala, CA 95445

The Wise Co.
6503 St. Claude Ave.
Arabi, LA 70032

Veneer

A Cut Above
P.O. Box 139
Greensburg, OH 44232

Artistry In Veneers, Inc.
633 Montauk Avenue
Brooklyn, NY 11208

Bob Morgan Wood
1123 Bardstown Rd.
Louisville, KY 40204

Wood Shed
1807 Elmwood Ave.
Buffalo, NY 14207

Clock Parts

Armor Products
P.O. Box 290
Deer Park, NY 11729

Craft Products Co.
2200 Dean St.
St. Charles, IL 60174

Klockit, Inc.
P.O. Box 629
Lake Geneva, WI 53147

Newport Enterprises, Inc.
2313 West Burbank Blvd.
Burbank, CA 91506

Mason and Sullivan Co.
39 Blossom Ave.
Osterville, MA 02655

Westwood Clock'N Kits
3210 Airport Way
Long Beach, CA 90806

Great Britain

General Line Suppliers

(Hardwood, veneer, hand tools, hardware, clock and lamp parts, finishing supplies, etc.)

General Woodwork Supplies
80 Stoke Newington High Street
London N.16

J. Simble & Sons
76 Queens Road
Watford
Herts.

Stobart and Son Ltd.
Woodwork Book Specialists
67-73 Worship Street
London EC2A 2EL

Woodmen
43 Crwys Road
Cardiff
Glamorgan

Hand Tools

Rogers
47 Walsworth Road
Hitchin
Herts. SG4 9SU

Parry's Tools
Old Street
London E2

Cecil Tyzack Ltd
79/81 Kingsland Road
London E2 8AG

Sargents Tools
62/64 Fleet Street
Swindon, Wilts.

Alec Tiranti Ltd
21 Goodge Place
London W1

Buckingham Tool Co.
Landsdowne Warehouse
Landsdowne Road
Aldershot
Hants.

Hardwoods

Berrycroft Products
P.O. Box 2
Lydney
Glos.

R. E. & R. Duffield & Sons Ltd.
The Boat House
River View Road
Ripon
N. Yorks

Mailwood
26 Swinnow Avenue
Bramely
Leeds
LS13 4NL

Woodley Timber Co. Ltd.
Norton Works
Norton Road
Woodley
Berks.

Seasoned Hardwood Timber Co.
Unit 2
156 High Street
Arlesey
Beds.
SG15 6RP

Hardware

Woodcraft Supply (UK) Ltd.
St. Peters Hill
Brixham
Devon

Classic Brass
1 West Road
Westcliffe
Essex

Builders Direct Mail
Poynings
Sussex

Woodfit Ltd.
115 Whittle Low Mill
Chorley
Lancs. PR6 7HB

Cabinetware
Leas End
Underbarrow
Nr. Kendal, Cumbria

V. H. Willis & Co.
190–192 West Street
Bedminster
Bristol

Veneer

Art Veneers Ltd
Industrial Estate
Mildenhall
Suffolk IP28 7AY

Elliott Bros.
Four Winds
Moorwoods Lane
Dore
Derbys.

S. Gould (Veneers)
342 Uxbridge Road
London W12

R. Aaronson (Veneers) Ltd.
45 Redchurch Street
London E2

Clock Parts

Charles Greville & Co. Ltd.
Unit 5
Rear Airport House
Purley Way
Croydon
Surrey

Runchmans
4 Walfords Close
Harlow
Essex

Classic Clocks
33–35 St. John's Square
London EC1M 4DM

Timecraft
10 Edinburgh Road
Formby
Liverpool

G. K. Hadfield
Blackbrook Hill House
Tickow Lane
Shepshed
Leics, LE12 9EY

Emperor Clock Co.
The Parade
Trumps Green Road
Virginia Water
Surrey GU25 4EH

Imperial to Metric Conversion Table

Measures of Length—Basic S.I. Unit—
Metre = 100 Centimetres = 39.37 Inches

Fractional Equivalents

in.–cms.	in.–cms.
1/16 = 0.15875	1/8 = 0.31700
3/16 = 0.47625	1/4 = 0.63500
5/16 = 0.79375	3/8 = 0.95250
7/16 = 1.11125	1/2 = 1.27040
9/16 = 1.42875	5/8 = 1.58730
11/16 = 1.74625	3/4 = 1.90500
13/16 = 2.06375	7/8 = 2.22250
15/16 = 2.38125	1 = 2.54000

Feet	Centi-metres	1	2	3	4	5	6	7	8	9	10	11
Inches (cms)		2.54	5.08	7.62	10.16	12.70	15.24	17.78	20.32	22.86	25.40	27.94
1	30.48	33.02	35.56	38.10	40.64	43.18	45.72	48.26	50.80	53.34	55.88	58.42
2	60.96	63.50	66.04	68.58	71.12	73.66	76.20	78.74	81.28	83.82	86.36	88.90
3	91.44	93.98	96.52	99.06	101.60	104.14	106.68	109.22	111.76	114.30	116.84	119.38
4	121.92	124.46	127.00	129.54	132.08	134.62	137.16	139.70	142.24	144.78	147.32	149.86
5	152.40	154.94	157.48	160.02	162.56	165.10	167.64	170.18	172.72	175.26	177.80	180.34
6	182.88	185.42	187.96	190.50	193.04	195.58	198.12	200.66	203.20	205.74	208.28	210.82
7	213.36	215.90	218.44	220.98	223.52	226.06	228.60	231.14	233.68	236.22	238.76	241.30
8	243.84	246.38	248.92	251.46	254.00	256.54	259.08	261.62	264.16	266.70	269.24	271.78
9	274.32	276.86	279.40	281.94	284.48	287.02	289.56	292.10	294.64	297.18	299.72	302.26
10	304.80	307.34	309.88	312.42	314.96	317.50	320.04	322.58	325.12	327.66	330.20	332.74
11	335.28	337.82	340.36	342.90	345.44	347.98	350.52	353.06	355.60	358.14	360.68	363.22
12	365.76	368.30	370.84	373.38	375.92	378.46	381.00	383.54	386.08	388.62	391.16	393.70
13	396.24	398.78	401.32	403.86	406.40	408.94	411.48	414.02	416.56	419.10	421.64	424.18
14	426.72	429.26	431.80	434.34	436.88	439.42	441.96	444.50	447.04	449.58	452.12	454.66
15	457.20	459.74	462.28	464.82	467.36	469.90	472.44	474.98	477.52	480.06	482.60	485.14
16	487.68	490.22	492.76	495.30	498.84	500.38	502.92	505.46	508.00	510.54	513.08	515.62
17	518.16	520.70	523.24	525.78	528.32	530.86	533.40	535.94	538.48	541.02	543.56	546.10
18	548.64	551.18	553.72	556.26	558.80	561.34	563.88	566.42	568.96	571.50	574.04	576.58
19	579.12	581.66	584.20	586.74	589.28	591.82	594.36	596.90	599.44	601.98	605.52	607.06
20	609.60	612.14	614.68	617.22	619.76	622.30	624.84	627.38	629.92	632.46	635.50	637.54

Example:

(1) To convert 13 feet 6 inches to centimetres, read along line 13 under feet and under column 6 inches read 411.48 cms. To reduce to metres move decimal point two spaces to left; thus, 4.1148 metres is the answer.